Behavioural Economics

Han Bleichrodt

Behavioural Economics

Advanced Economic Policy and Theory

palgrave
macmillan

Han Bleichrodt
University of Alicante
Alicante, Spain

ISBN 978-3-031-69165-2 ISBN 978-3-031-69166-9 (eBook)
https://doi.org/10.1007/978-3-031-69166-9

This Palgrave Macmillan imprint is published by the registered company Springer Nature Switzerland AG
The registered company address is: Gewerbestrasse 11, 6330 Cham, Switzerland

To my loved ones

Contents

List of Figures

List of Tables

Preface

1

When I told I was writing a textbook, people often asked me "what is your intended audience?" I answered that I hope there is something in it for students at all levels. The basis of the book is an introductory course that I taught at the Erasmus University College. For this course I used Chapter 2, a quick version of Chapters 3–6, and (parts of) Chapters 7, 8, 9, 11, and 12. For upper undergraduate courses I treat Chapters 3–6 in detail and add Chapter 10 on ambiguity. For masters and PhD courses I add the material in the extension blocks. For behavioral health economics, I center on the health applications. A course on behavioral finance may find Chapters 8–11 particularly useful. Throughout the book I added references that deepen the topics. I hope that this way the book is indeed useful for all students of behavioral economics.

To write clearly, I used George Orwell's six rules:

1. Never use a metaphor, simile or other figure of speech which you are used to seeing in print.
2. Never use a long word where a short one will do.
3. If it is possible to cut a word out, always cut it out.
4. Never use the passive where you can use the active.
5. Never use a foreign phrase, a scientific word or a jargon word if you can think of an everyday English equivalent.
6. Break any of these rules sooner than say anything outright barbarious.

To these I added Mario Vargas Llosa's suggestion to minimize adjectives. I tried to avoid the **Frank Zappa trap**. For me, Zappa is a great songwriter, but he never had a real hit single. I believe he was unable to write something simple (although his lyrics did not help either, see Bio 1.1). He had to include complexity. I tried to avoid complexity although some Zappa may have appeared in the extensions.

H. Bleichrodt, *Behavioural Economics*,
https://doi.org/10.1007/978-3-031-69166-9_1

Fabio Maccheroni and Anna Petruchenya encouraged me to write this book. Olivier L'Haridon read the whole manuscript and gave many comments. Karel Bleichrodt, Carlos Cueva, Victor Gonzalez Jimenez, David Jimenez-Gómez, and Adam Sanjurjo read parts of the book. Peter Wakker shared his experiences with writing a book. I also benefited from talking to the many speakers that Adam Sanjurjo invited for the Alicante micro seminar. Thank you all.

Thanks to the people at Palgrave MacMillan and Springer (Ellie Duncan, Ruth Jenner, Karthika Sundar, and Aishwarya Balachandar) for their help and patience. And finally thanks to all the students I have had in class. I enjoy teaching and see it as a privilege to help young people find their way in life. I hope this book reflects my passion.

Bio 1.1: Frank Zappa Meets the Mothers of Prevention

Frank Zappa, an American musician and composer of rock, jazz, and classical music, was known for his nonconformity, virtuosity, and satire of American culture. In 1985 he appeared before a US Senate committee to argue against the Parents Music Resource Center (PMRC). This group of wives of powerful men in Washington was led by Tipper Gore, the wife of then senator and later vice president, presidential candidate, and Nobel laureate Al Gore.

The PMRC aimed to end the immorality of modern rock music. Among others, they proposed labels depending on whether a record's songs were blasphemic or sexually explicit (*X*), violent (*V*), invited to use drugs or alcohol (*D/A*) or had occult content (*O*). The music industry wanted to follow these "Tipper stickers", because they hoped that by doing so the Senate would impose restrictions on home taping. Zappa, who dubbed the PMRC the "Mothers of Prevention," a paraphrasis of his first band the Mothers of Invention, was strongly against.

The Senate committee was thought to be a shoe-in for the PMRC as it consisted of five of their husbands, including Al Gore. It turned out differently. In front of 35 television channels and hundreds of journalists Zappa explained the arbitrariness, practical problems, and undesired side-effects of the PMRC's proposals and concluded "people who write bad laws are in my opinion more dangerous than songwriters who celebrate sexuality."

After Zappa's testimony, the ideas of the PMRC disappeared from the political agenda. Only the Tipper stickers survived, but these became a badge of honor for rap and rock artists in the 1990s. One of Zappa's records *Jazz from Hell* also received a sticker warning for explicit texts. The album is fully instrumental.

The PMRC hearing had an aftermath. Although blacklisted by the censors, Zappa's music was popular in communist Europe and a symbol of resistance against the regimes. In Vilnius, Lithuania's capital, there is a bust of Zappa to mark the end of communism. In 1990 Czech president Vaclav Havel, a lifelong fan, appointed Zappa as Czechia's Special Ambassador to the West on Trade,

Culture, and Tourism. This disgruntled US secretary of state James Baker, whose wife was in the PMRC. He warned Havel that "you can do business with the United States or with Frank Zappa." After this, Zappa's ambassadorship was changed into an unofficial cultural attaché.

The Art of Behavioural Economics

2

2.1 What Is Behavioural Economics?

In an interview with the Ten Percent Happier podcast, Nobel laureate Richard Thaler describes behavioural economics as "economics that has been enriched by the understanding of behavioral science, which means psychology and related sciences". Thaler's definition shows how economists can learn from psychology. However, psychologists can also learn something from economists. This makes behavioural economics more than just an applied branch of psychology.

This something is to take theories seriously. The psychological literature is rife with framing and contextual effects. Most of these are hard to model and have not made it into behavioural economics. They cannot be put into a theory that makes predictions and serves as a basis for policy. Behavioural economists should cherish this theoretical rigour and this book reflects this.

Definition 2.1: Behavioural Economics

Behavioural economics is economics that has been enriched by the understanding of behavioural science, which means psychology and related sciences, while taking theories seriously.

Taking theories seriously means not trying to explain violations of rationality by introducing even higher degrees of rationality. Ariel Rubinstein (2006) gives an example of deviations from the rational model of time preference (see Chapter 11), where people perfectly foresee their deviations. Other examples are models where

H. Bleichrodt, *Behavioural Economics*,
https://doi.org/10.1007/978-3-031-69166-9_2

agents solve complex optimization problems to choose their reference point or their deliberately biased beliefs.[1]

Taking theories seriously further means using inputs that can be observed, and not derived concepts like utility. That does not mean using only choices, the traditional input of economic models. Behavioural economics has led to the use of new type of data, like neuroimaging and genetic information (see Chapter 6). Behavioural economics stands for an open-minded approach to economics, open to insights and methods from other sciences but subject to the rigour of economic models.

An example is Daniel Kahneman and Amos Tversky's prospect theory, which marks the starting point of behavioural economics. As we will see in Chapters 9 and 10, prospect theory explains deviations from expected utility, the rational theory of decision under risk. It does so using concepts that were known since the 1950s. Economists thought these concepts could not be modelled satisfactorily. Prospect theory put them into a coherent theory, a rational theory of irrational behaviour so to speak. It not only introduced insights from psychology into economics, but did so in a consistent theoretical framework, which allowed to derive predictions that could be tested.[2] Moreover, it can be derived from a set of axioms, conditions on preferences, which makes it possible to assess the appeal of the model.

2.2 A Short History

As said, behavioural economics started in 1979 with Kahneman and Tversky's prospect theory. Some argued that the origins of behavioural economics are in Adam Smith's "The Theory of Moral Sentiments", and Smith indeed alludes to the behavioural concept of overconfidence (see Chapter 8). However, calling Smith, the father of modern economics, the first behavioural economist seems far-fetched and an attempt to sell behavioural economics to mainstream economists.

The 1980s were a period of hubris. In addition to Kahneman and Tversky scholars like Thaler, Graham Loomes, Jack Knetsch, Robert Sugden, George Loewenstein, and Drazen Prelec challenged the traditional theories of risk, intertemporal choice, and social choice. Behavioural economists were like children in a candy store with the candy the intriguing findings from psychology that contradicted economic theory. Ever more anomalies were uncovered and the *Journal of Economic Perspectives*

[1] Someone described these belief formation models as "Baron von Munchhausen models" after the eighteenth-century fictional German nobleman, known for his tall stories, who claimed to have pulled himself and his horse out of a swamp by his own hair.

[2] Prospect theory was not entirely satisfactory in this respect as we will see in Chapter 9. To exclude implausible predictions, Kahneman and Tversky introduced an editing phase which complicates testing the theory. In 1992 Kahneman and Tversky published a new version of prospect theory, which no longer had an editing phase and which could be fully derived from axioms on individual choice behaviour.

even dedicated a special series to it. The main tool of behavioural economists were classroom experiments, using pencil and paper, and mostly hypothetical questions.

The 1990s were more sobering. Amos Tversky passed away in 1996 at the age of 59, a blow to behavioural economics. Moreover, behavioural economists started to reconsider earlier findings. Experiments became more sophisticated, increasingly using computers in specialized labs and real choices. Behavioural economists like Colin Camerer, John Hey, and Loomes and Sugden, realizing that people make mistakes, explored whether error theories could explain the deviations from rational models. The 1990s also saw breakthroughs in applying behavioural economics to economic decisions. An example is David Laibson's (1997) work on saving.

In the 2000s, Daniel Kahneman received the first Nobel prize for behavioural economics.[3] Thaler and Cass Sunstein developed the idea of **nudging**, influencing people's choices based on behavioural economic insights to help them make better decisions. Nudging quickly became popular in policy. I discuss it in Chapter 12. The 2000s also saw a move from experiments to field data inspired by researchers like John List, Ulrike Malmendier, and Esther Duflo. Finally, there was a shift to complement choice data with new types of data. Camerer, Loewenstein, and Prelec, joint with among others Ernst Fehr, Craig Fox, and Russell Poldrack started neuroeconomics, which used neuroimaging to see what was going on in people's brains when they make choices. The hope was that these data would lead to better economic theories. I discuss neuroeconomics in Chapter 6.

The 2010s saw another Nobel prize in behavioural economics, this time for Richard Thaler (2017). In addition to neuroeconomics, scholars like Magnus Johannesson, Dan Benjamin, Niels Rietveld, and Roy Thurik studied whether people's genes could explain their choices and economic outcomes. The 2010s were also another period of sobering. The initial enthusiasm about nudges cooled off following doubts about their long-term effects and the departure from office of proponents like Nicolas Sarkozy, David Cameron, and Barack Obama. Behavioural economists like Anna Dreber became interested in the reproducibility of earlier findings. Some refer to this as the "replicability crisis", although that seems too strong given that most results could be replicated. Finally, there were some suspected cases of data manipulation by behavioural economists, damaging the credibility of the field.

This more critical view reflects that behavioural economics is now part of mainstream economics. Most economics departments give courses and programmes in behavioural economics and have a lab to run experiments. Early contributions emphasized how behavioural economics differed from traditional economics. Terms like "the behaviouralist revolution" and "homo sapiens instead of homo economicus", reflected this wave of excitement. Once behavioural economics became more established, it drew more criticism and its limitations became clearer. In this, behavioural economics resembles prospect theory. Initially, scholars mostly demonstrated how

[3] It was shared with Vernon Smith who got it for his contributions to experimental economics. It shows the interplay between behavioural and experimental economics and how experiments had evolved since the late 1970s.

prospect theory improved expected utility. When prospect theory became dominant, at least as a descriptive theory, it turned into the theory to challenge. As a result, its limitations became clear and the early-days enthusiasm was replaced with the sobering but more mature view that prospect theory cannot explain all patterns of behaviour. This also holds for behavioural economics. Behavioural economics has enriched economics, but it does not replace all of mainstream economics.

2.3 Is Behavioural Economics Descriptive or Normative?

I emphasized the importance of rigorous theories, ideally based on axioms. Axioms are conditions on agents' preferences. I give examples throughout the book. Axioms allow testing a theory's predictions and assessing their appeal as a recommendation for rational behaviour. In other words, they make it possible to evaluate both a theory's **descriptive validity**, whether it describes how people do behave, and its **normative validity**, whether it prescribes how people should behave.

Most scholars see behavioural economics as descriptive, but not normative. Behavioural economics develops models of how people behave. Traditional economic models use plausible assumptions for rational behaviour and remain the cornerstone of normative economics. Behavioural economics identifies and models the deviations from rationality and uses these models to correct biases and make recommendations that are in line with the normative models.

The approach is summarized by Leonard Savage's reaction when confronted with his choices in a paradox proposed by the French economist Maurice Allais that violated his sure-thing principle.[4]

Table 2.1 gives an example. You face an urn with 100 balls of which 10 are red, 89 blue, and 1 yellow.[5] One ball is drawn at random from the urn. In the first choice, bet S (S for safe) gives €1 million regardless of the colour of the ball that is drawn. Bet R (risky) pays €5 million if the ball is red, €1 million if the ball is blue, but nothing if the ball is yellow. Which bet would you choose?

The bets S and R give the same payoff (€1 million) if a blue ball is drawn. The bets S' and R' in the second choice are obtained from S and R by replacing the common outcome if a blue ball is drawn into receiving nothing. Which bet would you now choose?

Savage's sure-thing principle, which is widely seen as a principle of rationality, says that if two bets give the same outcome under some state of nature then changing this common outcome into some other value will not affect preferences. So what happens under blue should not affect your choice, because the bets always give the same outcome for blue (€1 million in the first choice and €0 in the second choice).

[4] I will discuss Allais' paradox in Chapter 9 and Savage's sure-thing principle in Chapter 10.

[5] The argument also holds if we leave the number of balls unspecified. Allais' paradox holds both for decision under risk (probabilities known) and uncertainty (probabilities unknown).

Table 2.1 Savage's choices

		Color		
		Red	Blue	Yellow
Choice 1	Bet S	€1M	€1M	€1M
	Bet R	€5M	€1M	€0
Choice 2	Bet S'	€1M	€0	€1M
	Bet R'	€5M	€0	€0

Thus, if you choose S in the first choice you should choose S' in the second and if you choose R in the first choice you should choose R' in the second. However, most people (including Savage) choose S in the first choice and R' in the second. These choices are highlighted in green. Why? Because S gives €1 million with certainty while R has the risk of winning nothing. On the other hand, changing the outcome under blue into €0 makes that both S' and R' are risky. The difference between an 11% and a 10% chance of winning feels small so most people go for the larger amount.

Savage acknowledged that he had violated the sure-thing principle, but now that he saw that, he would like to change his choices to satisfy it. Savage changed the second choice to S'. Savage's behaviour reflects the dominant view in behavioural economics. Behavioural economics identifies the deviations from rationality and suggests ways to correct these. This is also the idea of nudging, which aims to help people correct errors and to steer their behaviour in a direction that they themselves see as better (see Chapter 12).

Not everyone agrees. Back in 1974, Paul Slovic and Amos Tversky tried to repeat Savage's reasoning in two experiments. In their first experiment, subjects started with the choices in Table 2.1. A majority (59%) chose S and R' and violated the sure-thing principle. They then saw two (written) arguments. One by Dr. A (for Allais), who argued for S and R' by the certainty argument given above and one by Dr. S. (Savage), who explained the logic of the sure-thing principle and argued for either S and S' or for R and R'. The arguments did not help much. After seeing them, only 4 out of 29 subjects changed their choices and 3 of them found Dr. A. more convincing.

In the second experiment, subjects first saw the arguments of Dr. A. and Dr. S. They then rated on a scale from 0 to 10 how convinced they were by these arguments. Finally, they made the choices in Table 2.1. A small majority found Dr. A. more convincing and the average rating for Dr. A was 6.9 against 6.2 for Dr. S. However, only 35% chose S and R'. Even though they found Dr. A more compelling, his recommendation appeared too conservative for some subjects.

Follow-up experiments confirmed the results of Slovic and Tversky. Kirby Nielsen and John Rehbeck (2022) found that only one-third of the subjects who violated the sure-thing principle changed their choices when the violation was pointed out to them. Steve Humphrey and Nadia-Yasmine Kruse (2024) confirmed Slovic and Tversky's findings in a study with more subjects and real choices (Slovic and Tversky used hypothetical choices). Presenting the arguments of Allais and Savage led to more violations of the sure-thing principle.

These results challenge the plausibility of the sure-thing principle as a condition for rational choice. Maybe some rational models are not as rational as we thought. Some behavioural economists have argued that if emotions or feelings are strong, they have a role in prescriptive analyses. Take loss aversion, the finding that people frame outcomes as gains and losses from a reference point and are more sensitive to losses than to gains. Loss aversion is one of the main findings from behavioural economics and part of prospect theory. If losses hurt more than gains shouldn't that be part of a normative theory?

Tversky and Kahneman (1981) argue that rational choice has focused too much on whether preferences satisfy a set of axioms. It ignored the question whether the set of values that represent the decision maker's preferences makes sense. For example, Savage's axioms (of which the sure-thing principle is one) ensure that agents behave as if they assign beliefs (subjective probabilities) to uncertain events. Examples of uncertain events are "what is the probability that the stock market goes up tomorrow" or "what is the probability that a patient displaying symptoms X has disease Y". That agents behave in line with Savage's axioms does not mean that their beliefs make sense. Some beliefs, even when satisfying Savage's axioms, are implausible and thus irrational because they conflict with available evidence. Examples are beliefs in supernatural phenomena or superstitions (see also Gilboa et al. 2008).

Tversky and Kahneman (1981) argue that coherence with a set of axioms is only one aspect of rationality. Rationality also requires that preferences predict how we experience outcomes when they occur. So, if losses hurt more than gains then rational choice should take account of this. Rational choice should be about "what will I feel then?" rather than about "what do I want now?"

Extension 2.1: What Is Knowledge?

The debate about what is rational resembles the question "when do we know that a proposition is true?" Plato suggested that subject S knows proposition P if and only if the following three conditions hold:

1. P is true.
2. S believes that P is true.
3. S is justified in believing P.

I know that the earth is round if it indeed is round, if I believe that it is round, and if my belief is justified. If I believe that it is round because a magician in the thirteenth century turned it from flat into round then my belief is not justified. This is similar to Gilboa et al.'s argument about implausible beliefs.

American philosopher Edmund Gettier argued that even having a justified belief in something that is true is not enough to say that an agent knows a proposition. He gives the following example, that I slightly adjusted. Suppose that I compete for a grant with a male colleague from another university. I know that my colleague has €5 in his pocket, because I just borrowed it to him and he said "thanks I really had no money on me". The president of the jury has told me that it will award the grant to my colleague. So I have strong evidence for proposition P:

> The academic who will get the grant has €5 in his pocket.

However, unknown to myself, the jury overturns the president and gives the grant to me. And, again unknown to myself, I have another note of €5 in my pocket. Then P is true, I believe that P is true, and my belief is justified given the information that I have. However, I do not know that P is true. It is true by the €5 note in my pocket which I do not know to be there. I base my belief on the €5 note in my colleague's pocket, who I falsely believe will get the grant.

Gettier's example shows that when we predict correctly, our beliefs, even when based on solid grounds, may be wrong and we really may have no idea what we are talking about. It is something to keep in mind when assessing predictions.

2.4 Transitivity and Completeness

The above suggests that the normative status of behavioural economics models is open for debate and that "rational" conditions like the sure-thing principle may be less appealing than often claimed. This begs the question whether there are conditions that are normative beyond doubt.

Two candidates are **transitivity** and **completeness**. Let $\succcurlyeq$ denote an agent's preference relation over a set of outcomes $\mathcal{C}$. Outcomes can be many things. Examples are money or consumption goods, but they can also be multi-attribute. For example, in health economics outcomes are combinations of quantity of life and quality of life.

By $x \succcurlyeq y$ we mean that outcome x is at least as preferred as outcome y. If $x \succcurlyeq y$ but not $y \succcurlyeq x$ then x is **strictly preferred** to y: $x \succ y$. If both $x \succcurlyeq y$ and $y \succcurlyeq x$ hold then x and y are **indifferent**: $x \sim y$.

A common assumption in (behavioural) economics is that $\succcurlyeq$ is transitive and complete.

Definition 2.2: Transitivity

The preference relation $\succcurlyeq$ is **transitive** if for all outcomes $x, y, z \in \mathcal{C}$ if $x \succcurlyeq y$, and $y \succcurlyeq z$ then also $x \succcurlyeq z$.

If patients prefer living for 30 years with back pain (followed by death) to living for 15 years in full health (followed by death) and also prefer living for 15 years in full health to living for 20 years with migraine then transitivity requires that they will also prefer living for 30 years with back pain to living for 20 years with migraine.

Definition 2.3: Completeness

The preference relation $\succcurlyeq$ is *complete* if for all outcomes $x, y \in C$ either $x \succcurlyeq y$, or $y \succcurlyeq x$ or both.

Completeness says that for any two outcomes x and y, the agent always has a preference between them. It rules out the possibility that the agent cannot choose between two outcomes.

Transitivity and completeness allow defining a utility function over the set of outcomes C. A function U **represents** a preference relation $\succcurlyeq$ if $x \succcurlyeq y$ implies that $U(x) \geq U(y)$ and if $U(x) \geq U(y)$ then $x \succcurlyeq y$.

Theorem 2.1: The Existence of Utility

If the set C contains a finite number of elements[a] and the preference relation $\succcurlyeq$ is transitive and complete then there exists a utility function U that represents $\succcurlyeq$.

[a] This means that we can give each element of C a number. For example, if a set has 100 elements we can give each element a number between 1 and 100.

I will give the proof of Theorem 2.1 here. It shows how utility representations, which we will meet throughout the book, are constructed and the role that preference conditions play in their construction.

Proof of Theorem 2.1

Because C is finite we can write the elements of C as $(x_1, \ldots, x_n)$. Because $\succcurlyeq$ is complete and transitive we can order the elements of C, for example from least to most preferred. Defining $U(x_i) = i$ then gives the desired representation.

Exercise 2.1: Utility

Show that the utility function constructed in the above proof represents $\succcurlyeq$. That is, show that if $x_i \succcurlyeq x_j$ then $U(x_i) \geq U(x_j)$ and that if $U(x_i) \geq U(x_j)$ then $x_i \succcurlyeq x_j$.

The proof of Theorem 2.1 shows that the utility function is not unique. For example, we might as well have defined it as $U(x_i) = i^2 - 4$ and it would still represent $\succcurlyeq$ over C (see Exercise 2.2).

Exercise 2.2: Uniqueness

Show that the utility function $U(x_i) = i^2 - 4$ represents $\succcurlyeq$

In fact, any transformation $\phi(i)$ such that $\phi(i+1) > \phi(i)$ would work. Formally, we say that the utility function is **ordinal**: it is unique up to positive monotonic transformations. Later we will see other forms of uniqueness of utility.

Extension 2.2: Infinite Outcome Sets

In Theorem 2.1 the set $\mathcal{C}$ is finite. The gist of the theorem, that transitivity and completeness ensure the existence of a utility function does not change if we allow $\mathcal{C}$ to be infinite. We just need to add some structure to $\mathcal{C}$. The utility function maps the elements of $\mathcal{C}$ to the real numbers. A property of the real numbers is that between any real numbers a, c there is a rational number b such that $a \geq b \geq c$. Formally, the rational numbers are **dense** in the real numbers. Moreover, the set of rational numbers is **countable**: There is a one-to-one relation between the set of rational numbers and the set of natural numbers. To ensure that we can represent $\succcurlyeq$ by a utility function, we impose a similar structure on $\mathcal{C}$. We assume that $\mathcal{C}$ contains a countable dense subset $\mathcal{D}$: for any elements $\alpha, \gamma \in \mathcal{C}$ there exists a $\beta \in \mathcal{D}$ such that $\alpha \succcurlyeq \beta \succcurlyeq \gamma$. This can be achieved by assuming that $\mathcal{C}$ is a separable topological space (for definitions see Dugundji 1966).

Economics usually assumes that the utility function U is **continuous**. Debreu (1954, Theorem II) showed that this holds if the sets $\{x \in \mathcal{C} : x \succcurlyeq y\}$ and $\{x \in \mathcal{C} : y \succcurlyeq x\}$ are closed for all $y \in \mathcal{C}$. Preference characterizations for another common assumption, that U is differentiable (which means, for example, that indifference curves are smooth), are scarce. Nielsen (1999) gives preference conditions that ensure that the utility function in expected utility (see Chapter 9) is differentiable. This is the only characterization I know.

2.4.1 Transitivity

Theorem 2.1 shows that transitivity is necessary for a utility function over outcomes. Transitivity seems obvious, but do people satisfy it? And is it normative?

Amos Tversky (1969) challenged transitivity based on the concept of **just noticeable differences**. If a difference in score between alternatives falls below a threshold, agents will ignore it. A difference has to be sufficiently large to be noticeable and affect preference.

According to Tversky, when comparing multidimensional alternatives agents first focus on the most important dimension. They choose an alternative if it is sufficiently better on that dimension than the other alternatives. If the difference on that dimension

Table 2.2 A problem set of Tversky (1969)

Profiles	Dimensions		
	I	E	S
a	69	84	75
b	72	78	65
c	75	72	55
d	78	66	45
e	81	60	35

is less than noticeable, they compare alternatives on the second most important dimension, and so forth. Such an ordering is called **lexicographic**, because it orders outcomes like the lexicon orders words alphabetically. Duncan Luce (1956) gave a formal theory of lexicographic orderings.

For example, Tversky asked his subjects to choose between college applicants based on intellectual ability (I), emotional stability (E), and social facility (S), all expressed on a scale from 0 to 100. Subjects knew that dimension I was most important, but that the other dimensions also mattered.

Table 2.2 shows one set of stimuli. In a preliminary session Tversky estimated that the just noticeable difference on dimension I was equal to 9. The dominant pattern that Tversky observed was $a \succ b, b \succ c, c \succ d, d \succ e$, but $e \succ a$.

Exercise 2.3: Just Noticeable Differences

Explain that this pattern violates transitivity, but is consistent with the theory of just noticeable differences.

When presented with their intransitivity, subjects were surprised and indicated that they must have made a mistake. Tversky is adamant that even though transitivity is not (always) descriptive, it is valid as a normative principle of choice.

The Experiment of Starmer (1999)

Tversky preselected subjects who were prone to intransitive choices.[6] Chris Starmer (1999) presented a violation of transitivity, which was not subject to this criticism.

[6] Another problem is that Tversky did not have a valid statistical test of intransitivity. Geoffrey Iverson and Jean-Claude Falmagne (1985) developed a conservative test, which showed that transitivity could not be rejected based on Tversky's data. This was also the conclusion of Regenwetter et al. (2011). They show that Tversky's data (and those of other studies claiming to find intransitivity) can be explained by a model in which agents have a set of transitive preference relations and for each choice problem choose one of these with some probability. Because agents use different preference relations for different problems, preferences may appear intransitive.

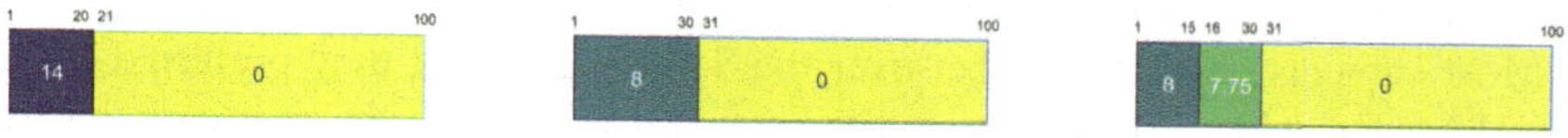

(a) gamble A (b) gamble B (c) gamble C

Fig. 2.1 The three gambles in Starmer (1999)

Starmer gave his subjects the three gambles shown in Fig. 2.1.

A ticket was drawn from a box with 100 tickets numbered $1 - 100$. Bet A paid £14.00 if a ticket with number $1 - 20$ was drawn and nothing otherwise. Bet B paid £8.00 if a ticket numbered $1 - 30$ was drawn and nothing otherwise. Finally, bet C paid £8.00 if a ticket with number $1 - 15$ was drawn, £7.75 if a ticket numbered $16 - 30$ was drawn and nothing otherwise.

25% of Starmer's subjects preferred A to B and C to A. However, B is better than C, because it gives at least as good an outcome as C for each lottery ticket (technically we say that B **first order stochastically dominates** C). Indeed, 98% of the subjects who chose A over B and C over A chose B over C. These subjects violated transitivity: $A \succ B$, $B \succ C$, but $C \succ A$.

An explanation is the following. Bets A and B only have one positive amount (£14 respectively £8) and subjects find the extra 10% chance of winning too low to compensate the extra £6 in A. C has two positive amounts and this makes C appear more attractive than A. However, when they compare B with C subjects realize that B is better than C and go for B.

Psychologists have indeed shown that splitting an event (in this case drawing a ticket with number between 1 and 30) into two makes a bet seem more attractive. The psychologist Michael Birnbaum (2008) built a theory (**configural weighting**) that can explain such **event splitting effects**. Economist have not adopted this theory. Event-splitting effects depend on the context in which decisions are made. Economists like their models to have more general applicability than just within a given context. This is an example where behavioural economics differs from cognitive psychology. I will discuss other examples of event splitting effects in Chapter 8 where we will see that the probability of an event increases when it is split into subevents.

The Preference Reversal Phenomenon

The best known violation of transitivity is the **preference reversal phenomenon** (PR). This challenges economics, because it indicates that choices, the main data of economics (see Chapter 3), can be inconsistent.

The PR was discovered by two psychologists Sarah Lichtenstein and Paul Slovic (1971). They gave their subjects two bets of approximately equal expected value: a P-bet that gave a high probability to win amount x and a \$-bet that gave a smaller probability to win a larger amount y. For example, in one of their experiments the P-bet was a $\frac{28}{36}$ chance to win \$10 and the \$-bet a $\frac{3}{36}$ chance to win \$100.

Most subjects chose the P-bet over the \$-bet suggesting they preferred the P-bet. However, when asked to price the bets, that is, to state the cash amount they saw as equally attractive as the bet, they priced the \$-bet higher than the P-bet. Pricing suggests subjects preferred the \$-bet. Both choice and pricing are valid ways to elicit preferences, but they gave different results. And it is unclear which one is better. Lichtenstein and Slovic found the PR in several studies, including one with experienced gamblers playing for real money in a Las Vegas casino (Lichtenstein and Slovic 1973).[7]

Economists were not so easily convinced that choices were flawed. David Grether and Charles Plott (1979) gave 13 reasons why Lichtenstein and Slovic's results might not be robust and designed a series of experiments to control for these. Among the explanations they controlled for were:

1. **Hypothetical bias**. In Lichtenstein and Slovic's studies choices were either hypothetical or for points with unknown value.[8] This may have led their subjects to pay insufficient attention. If subjects were asked to answer the questions for real money, they would answer more seriously and the PR might disappear.
2. **Income effects**. Lichtenstein and Slovic (1973) played out bets as soon as subjects stated their preferences. As subjects faced various tasks, their wealth changed during the experiment. Economic theory permits that agents have different risk preferences at different wealth levels (the common finding is that risk aversion decreases with wealth) and this could have led to the PR.
3. **Strategic responding**. Prices are usually determined by asking subjects for how much they would sell the bets. This may have led to bargaining strategies. As the value of the \$-bet was more ambiguous, overstating selling prices (a common bargaining strategy) will affect the price of the \$-bet more. Letting subjects choose between a money amount for sure and the bet (without telling them they owned the bet) removes this bias.
4. **Unsophisticated subjects**. Many of the experiments were performed in a classroom setting with psychology undergraduates participating as subjects. It is hard to generalize from such a special pool of subjects.
5. **Psychology bias**. The funniest explanation Grether and Plott examined was that Lichtenstein and Slovic are psychologists. Subjects speculate about the purpose of the experiment. Psychologists tend to deceive their subjects and this can lead to odd responses that do not reflect true preferences.

[7] The PR is mostly studied for risk. However, it has also been found in other domains. For example, Tversky et al. (1990) found an even higher rate of reversals for time preferences. People chose a smaller amount to be paid sooner over a larger amount to be paid later, but priced the larger later option higher than the smaller sooner option. See also Li and Loomes (2022).

[8] Lichtenstein and Slovic (1973) and Slovic (1975) also found the PR for real rewards.

None of the explanations could explain the PR. It appeared again and again. Later studies, testing further explanations, confirmed Grether and Plott's conclusion. The PR is robust and cannot be explained by peculiarities in the experimental procedures.

Extension 2.3: Explaining the PR by Intransitivity

Intransitive preferences can explain the PR. The mathematician Peter Fishburn (1982) developed a general model of intransitive choice. Examples of intransitive models in behavioural economics are regret theory (Loomes and Sugden 1982) and salience theory (Bordalo et al. 2012).

In an intransitive model, we cannot define a utility function over single outcomes as in Theorem 2.1. Instead, we define the utility function over pairs of outcomes. Formally, $x \succcurlyeq y \iff \phi(x, y) \geq 0$. If $\phi(x, y) = u(x) - u(y)$ we are back at the utility representation of Theorem 2.1.

For decisions under risk, the case of the PR, the objects of choice are probability distributions $x = (p_1 : x_1, \ldots, p_n : x_n)$ where $p_i : x_i$ stands for getting x_i with probability p_i. In Fishburn's model:

$$x \succcurlyeq y \iff \sum_{i=1}^{n} p_i \phi(x_i, y_i) \geq 0. \tag{2.1}$$

The function ϕ is **skew-symmetric**: $\phi(x_i, y_i) = -\phi(y_i, x_i)$.

Exercise 2.4: Skew-symmetry

Show that skew-symmetry implies that $\phi(x_i, x_i) = 0$. Thus, an outcome cannot be preferred to itself.

To show that Eq. 2.1 can explain the PR, assume that the agent reframes the choice between the P-bet and the \$-bet as a $\frac{3}{36}$ chance to get \$10 in the P-bet and \$100 in the \$-bet, a $\frac{25}{36}$ chance to get \$10 in the P-bet and \$0 in the \$-bet, and a $\frac{8}{36}$ chance to get \$0 in both bets.

Because the agent chooses the P-bet over the \$-bet:

$$\frac{3}{36}\phi(10, 100) + \frac{25}{36}\phi(10, 0) > 0. \tag{2.2}$$

Because the agent prices the \$-bet higher than the P-bet, there must be some amount c that lies between the cash equivalent of the \$-bet, $ce(\$)$, and that of the P-bet, $ce(P)$: $ce(\$) > c > ce(P)$. By Eq. 2.1, $\phi(ce(\$), c) > 0$ and $\phi(c, ce(P)) > 0$. Because the \$-bet is indifferent to $ce(\$)$ and the P-bet is indifferent to $ce(P)$ we get:

$$\frac{3}{36}\phi(100, c) + \frac{33}{36}\phi(0, c) > 0 \tag{2.3}$$

and

$$\frac{28}{36}\phi(c, 10) + \frac{8}{36}\phi(c, 0) > 0. \tag{2.4}$$

Summing the inequalities Eqs. 2.2, 2.3, and 2.4 gives:

$$\begin{aligned}&\frac{3}{36}\,[\phi(10, 100) + \phi(100, c) + \phi(c, 10)] +\\ &\frac{25}{36}\,[\phi(10, 0) + \phi(0, c) + \phi(c, 10)] +\\ &\frac{8}{36}\,[\phi(0, 0) + \phi(0, c) + \phi(c, 0)] > 0.\end{aligned} \tag{2.5}$$

The third expression in Eq. 2.5 is 0, by skew-symmetry. To explain the PR, the sum of the first two expressions in Eq. 2.5 must be positive, which holds if for all outcomes a, b, c with $a \succ b \succ c$, $\phi(a, c) > \phi(a, b) + \phi(b, c)$. Loomes et al. (1991) call this **regret-aversion**.

Exercise 2.5: Regret Aversion

Show that regret-aversion and skew-symmetry make the expression in Eq. 2.5 positive.

Loomes et al. (1991) found that intransitive choice patterns accounted for between 14 and 29% of their observations. Cycles consistent with regret-aversion were significantly more common than cycles in the opposite direction. They conclude that their results challenge the descriptive validity of transitivity.

Is Transitivity Normative?

As we saw above, transitivity is not (always) descriptive. But is it normative? The dominant view is yes. Tversky is clear on this. Nielsen and Rehbeck (2022) also find support for it: A majority of their subjects wanted to satisfy it and when faced with their violations they decided to change their choices.

The normative defence for transitivity is that it avoids **money pumping**. Suppose agents choose between three alternatives A, B, and C and they prefer A to B, B to C, and C to A. So they are intransitive. The agents initially have option A. As they prefer C to A, they are willing to pay some amount ϵ_1 to trade C for A. Having C

Table 2.3 Violation of equivalence

	Probabilities		
	$\frac{1}{3}$	$\frac{1}{3}$	$\frac{1}{3}$
Prospect 1	A	B	C
Prospect 2	B	C	A

we now offer them to trade C for B and, as they prefer B to C, they are willing to pay ϵ_2 to make this trade. Finally, having B, the agents will be willing to pay ϵ_3 to trade B for the preferred A. As a result, the agents end up with the same alternative A that they started with having lost $\epsilon_1 + \epsilon_2 + \epsilon_3$. A skilful bookmaker could repeat these trades and drive the agents to bankruptcy.

Defenders of intransitivity as a normative principle argue that rational agents will not be money pumped (e.g. Fishburn 1991). After one round of trades, having lost $\epsilon_1 + \epsilon_2 + \epsilon_3$, the agent sees what is going on and commits to an option. Loomes and Sugden (1982) call the money pump process a fallacy. If A, B, and C are all available then propositions about pairwise choices (about how choices are made when there are only two options) are irrelevant.

Another normative argument against intransitivity is that it leads to strict preferences between equivalent options. See Table 2.3. Assume, that the agent is intransitive and that $A \succ B$, $B \succ C$, and $C \succ A$. There are three states of nature each with the same probability $\frac{1}{3}$. Because $A \succ B$, $B \succ C$, and $C \succ A$, prospect 1 gives in each state a better outcome than prospect 2 and should be preferred.

However, if we look at the prospects in isolation then they both give a $\frac{1}{3}$ probability of A, a $\frac{1}{3}$ probability of B, and a $\frac{1}{3}$ probability of C. They lead to the same probability distribution over outcomes and are equivalent. How can we have a preference between equivalent options? Defenders of the normative status of intransitivity, like Fishburn and Loomes and Sugden, point out that the independent evaluation of acts removes an essential element: state-by-state comparisons invoke feelings of regret and rejoice. If such feelings have normative relevance then they should play a role and prospects 1 and 2 in Table 2.3 are not equivalent. The choice is between "choosing act 1 and rejecting act 2" and "choosing act 2 and rejecting act 1" and these are not the same.

The normative status of transitivity depends on whether we can evaluate options in isolation or whether we should evaluate them jointly and allow that feelings like regret and rejoice play a role in normative evaluations. Most behavioural economists believe these feelings should play no role and that intransitivity cannot be normative. But, some disagree and there is no consensus.

2.4.2 Completeness

The other requirement for a utility function is completeness. Completeness is almost always assumed in economic analyses (for example, the well-known indifference curve analysis is based on it), but it is not so plausible. In 1962, Nobel laureate Robert Aumann wrote that "of all the axioms of utility theory, the completeness axiom is perhaps the most questionable. Like others of the axioms, it is inaccurate as a description of real life; but unlike them, we find it hard to accept even from the normative viewpoint" (Aumann 1962, p. 446).

According to Aumann, there are situations in which agents do not have a preference. For example, when asked to choose between hypothetical situations they will never face or between complex situations, in which they have no intuition what to do. Think of pension plans or complex medical interventions like the choice between dialysis and kidney transplant in the case of renal failure. Agents may prefer to defer these decisions to specialists.

On the other hand, as Peter Wakker (2010) points out, in these decisions agents also have to make a choice ("doing nothing" is also a choice). He argues that completeness is reasonable as an approximation.

What can be saved of utility theory if we give up completeness? We can still define a utility function U for which $x \succ y$ implies that $U(x) > U(y)$. However, the opposite, that $U(x) > U(y)$ implies that $x \succ y$ is not necessarily true. It is possible that for two alternatives x, y, $U(x) > U(y)$, but not $x \succ y$ because $\succcurlyeq$ is incomplete and the agent is unable to express preference between x and y.[9]

Efe Ok (2002) gave a solution. Before giving Ok's result we need two more definitions.

Definition 2.4: Reflexive

The preference relation $\succcurlyeq$ is *reflexive* if for all outcomes $x \in \mathcal{C}$: $x \sim x$.

Reflexivity says that every outcome is indifferent to itself. This is an innocent assumption.

Definition 2.5: Preorder

The preference relation $\succcurlyeq$ is a *preorder* if it is transitive and reflexive.

Theorem 2.2: Ok (2002): Representation of Incomplete Preferences

If the set $\mathcal{C}$ is finite and the preference relation $\succcurlyeq$ is a preorder then there exists a set of utility functions $\mathcal{U}$ such that for all $x, y \in \mathcal{C} : x \succcurlyeq y$ iff $U(x) \geq U(y)$ for all $U \in \mathcal{U}$.

---

[9] Formally, the problem is that the range of U is a set of real numbers, which are completely ordered by the greater than relation. However, the domain of U, the set of outcomes is not completely ordered because preferences can be incomplete.

Theorem 2.2 may reflect cautious agents. They are unsure about their preferences and only choose x over y if x is better than y according to every utility function that they consider realistic (see Cerreia-Vioglio et al. 2015 for more on this). If for some realistic utility functions x is preferred and for others y, the agents are undecided and prefer not to make a choice or leave it to an expert.

Extension 2.4: Infinite Sets

Like in Theorem 2.1, we need to add assumptions when $\mathcal{C}$ is infinite. Let $x \bowtie y$ mean that x and y are incomparable, i.e. neither $x \succcurlyeq y$ nor $y \succcurlyeq x$. Ok (2002) extends Theorem 2.2 to infinite sets $\mathcal{C}$ by requiring that $\succcurlyeq$ is not "too incomplete", which he defines as: any subset $\mathcal{A}$ of $\mathcal{C}$ with $x \bowtie y$ for all distinct $x, y \in \mathcal{A}$ must be finite. There can be infinitely x, y for which $x \bowtie y$ but they cannot all be mutually incomparable. So, there must be a $z \in \mathcal{A}$ such that $x \bowtie y$, and $y \bowtie z$, but not $x \bowtie z$.

In Extension 2.2 we assumed that $\mathcal{C}$ contains a countable dense subset $\mathcal{D}$. We make the same assumption here when $x \succ y$, but need to add something for the case $x \bowtie y$. We say that the set $\mathcal{D}$ is upper $\succcurlyeq$ dense in $\mathcal{C}$ if for any incomparable x, y ($x, y \in \mathcal{C}$ with $x \bowtie y$), there is a $z \in \mathcal{D}$ such that x is strictly preferred to z ($x \succ z$), but z is incomparable to y ($z \bowtie y$). Upper-denseness limits the richness of the sets of indifferent and incomparable outcomes. Ok defines $\succcurlyeq$ as upper separable if there exists a countable set $\mathcal{D}$ in $\mathcal{C}$, which is both dense and upper $\succcurlyeq$-dense.

By adding the assumptions of "not too incomplete" and upper separability, Ok extends Theorem 2.2 to infinite $\mathcal{C}$.[a]

[a] Strictly speaking, $\mathcal{C}$ must also be a topological space. That is, there exists a collection τ of subsets of $\mathcal{C}$ such that (i) $\varnothing$ and $\mathcal{C}$ belong to τ; (ii) Any union of elements of τ also belongs to τ; and (iii) any finite intersection of elements of τ also belongs to τ.

Empirical Evidence

There is little empirical evidence on incompleteness, because it is hard to detect. An exception is the study of Elena Cettolin and Arno Riedl (2019) who found that about 25% of their subjects had incomplete preferences (see Experiment 2.1).

Experiment 2.1: Testing Incompleteness

Subjects chose between two urns, both with 100 balls which are either black or red. In the **known urn** subjects know the number of black and red balls. In the **unknown urn** they do not. Subjects can choose their winning colour and receive €15 if a ball of their winning colour is drawn. Cettolin and Riedl (2019) varied the proportion of winning balls in the known urn from 0 (no chance of winning) to 100 (sure win). For each proportion, subjects said whether they wanted to draw a ball from the known urn, the unknown urn (which composition was held constant throughout) or whether they preferred chance to determine from which urn the ball would be drawn. If subjects choose chance for more than one composition of the known urn then their preferences are either incomplete (they cannot choose and prefer chance to resolve their choice) or they like randomization. This happened for 50% of the subjects. If subjects like randomization they would be willing to pay (WTP) a positive price to let chance decide, but when their preferences are incomplete their WTP is zero. About half of the subjects who chose chance for more than one composition of the known urn had WTP zero. So, 25% of the subjects had incomplete preferences.

Miguel Costa-Gomes and co-authors (2022) compared a treatment in which subjects were forced to choose with a treatment in which they could defer choice to a later moment at a cost. Around one-third of their subjects deferred at least once. Their choices were more consistent than those in the forced choice group. The model that best described the subjects who preferred deferral, had transitive but incomplete preferences.

Valuing Health and Safety More evidence on incompleteness (or imprecision as they call it) of preferences comes from the work of Michael Jones-Lee and Graham Loomes on the money value of health and safety. The use of a money value of preventing deaths is common in countries like the US and the UK. It makes government policy more transparent. For example, the construction of a new highway will lead to benefits in the form of reduced travel time, but has a cost in terms of health. It causes more pollution, which has negative health effects. By putting a money value on these health effects, cost-benefit analyses can account for them and improve the allocation of resources. Many countries are reluctant to put a money value on health, arguing that health is priceless. There are two problems with this argument.

1. In our private decisions we trade off money or comfort against a higher risk of death or injury. We accept a risky job for more salary and (at least in the Netherlands) do not wear a bike helmet even though this increases our injury risk. If health were priceless, we would never make these trade-offs. But if we personally do not consider our health infinitely valuable, why should governments do?
2. Not putting a money value on health means that they get a value zero and are ignored in cost-benefit analyses. Refusing to put a money value on health has adverse consequences.

But valuing health is difficult. Many biases affect these violations (see for example Loomes 2006 and Cropper et al. 2011), several of which we discuss in later chapters.

The common way to determine the money value of health is to ask how much people are willing to pay for a given reduction in a health risk. To illustrate, Table 2.4 shows two health states that Richard Dubourg, Jones-Lee, and Loomes (1994) valued,

Table 2.4 Health states in Dubourg et al. (1994)

(a) health state S	(b) health state X
In hospital • 1-4 weeks • Moderate to severe pain **After hospital** • Some pain gradually reducing, but may recur when you take part in some activities • Some restrictions to leisure and possibly some work activities for the rest of your life	**In hospital** • 1-4 weeks • Slight to moderate pain **After hospital** • Some pain/discomfort, gradually reducing • Some restrictions to work and leisure activities, gradually reducing • After 1-3 years, return to normal health with no permanent disability

as part of a large study commissioned by the UK Department of Transport. The annual incidence of these injuries at the time of the study was 24 in 100,000 for injury S and 36 in 100,000 for injury X.

Subjects said how much they were willing to pay (WTP) for a safety feature in their car that would reduce the annual risk of these injuries by half. That is, the risk of S reduced from 24 in 100,000 to 12 in 100,000 and the risk of X from 36 in 100,000 to 18 in 100,000. The median annual WTP to reduce the risk of S by 12 in 100,000 was £80. So, the amount 100,000 members of the general population would be willing to pay each year for this safety device was £8 million. As this would prevent 12 cases of injury S (the risk reduction of injury S was 12 in 100,000), the money value of preventing injury S was £$\frac{8M}{12}$ = £750,000.

Exercise 2.6: Road Safety

The median amount respondents were willing to pay to reduce the risk of X was £72.50. Compute the implied money value of preventing injury X.

Dubourg et al. (1994) thought that their subjects would have difficulty trading off risk, health, and money, as they are not part of our day-to-day considerations. They showed a list of money values for which subjects could say that they "would definitely pay", "would definitely not pay", or "were not sure". The not sure category allowed for incomplete (or imprecise) preferences. 20 to 25% of the responses used the not sure category. This percentage is similar to the proportion of incomplete preferences found by Cettolin and Riedl (2019) and Costa-Gomes et al. (2022).

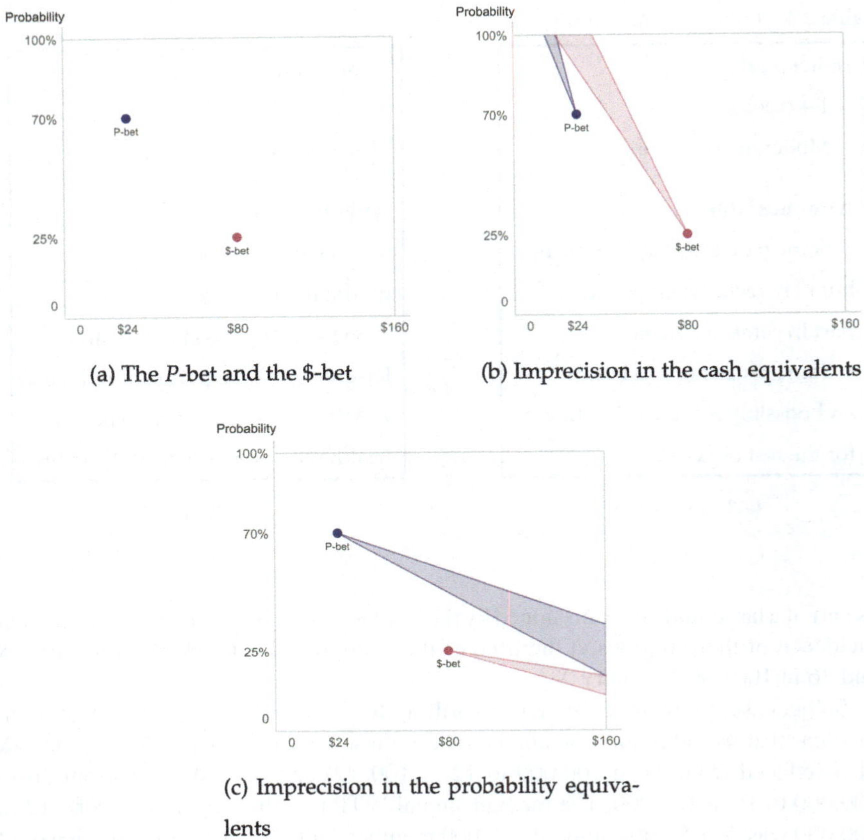

Fig. 2.2 How imprecision can explain the PR

Can the Preference Reversal Be Explained by Incomplete Preferences?
In Sect. 2.4.1 we discussed the preference reversal (PR) phenomenon. I explained that intransitivity can partly explain it. What about incompleteness? Can this cause the PR? Some evidence that it indeed can come from a study by David Butler and Loomes (2007).

Panel A of Fig. 2.2 shows a *P*-bet and a $-bet. In the PR task subjects are asked two things. First, to choose between the *P*-bet and the $-bet and, second, to state the amounts for sure, the cash equivalents, that are equally valuable as these bets.

Stating a cash equivalent means mapping the bets to a point on the 100% probability line (see Panel B of Fig. 2.2). In doing so, people can be unsure about their preferences. In pricing the *P*-bet they are, for example, sure that they prefer the bet to $8 and that they prefer $14 to the *P*-bet, but for amounts in between they are unsure. So $8 – $14 is the "imprecision interval" of the *P*-bet.

Because the $-bet lies further away from the 100% line and is less similar to a sure outcome, its imprecision interval is wider. There are more values for which subjects are unsure about their preferences. Moreover, there is more room for imprecision above the upper bound of the *P*-bet's imprecision interval (the agent can be unsure for any amount between \$14 and \$80) than below its lower bound (the agent can be unsure between \$0 and \$8). As a result, the imprecision interval of the \$-bet will be asymmetric and hardly overlap with that of the *P*-bet. See Panel B of Fig. 2.2.

Butler and Loomes (2007) do not explain how subjects choose their reported cash equivalent from their imprecision intervals. However, given that the imprecision interval of the \$-bet is wider and more asymmetric than that of the *P*-bet, the cash equivalent of the \$-bet likely exceeds that of the *P*-bet. Panel B of Fig. 2.2 shows the data from one of the experiments. The imprecision interval of the \$-bet lies almost entirely above that of the *P*-bet even though more than 70% of their subjects chose the *P*-bet over the \$-bet.

Butler and Loomes (2007) also found a reverse PR predicted by imprecision. They asked for both the *P*-bet and the \$-bet their **probability equivalent**: the probability *p* for which they were indifferent between a *p* chance of \$160 and the bet. Subjects indicated the values of *p* for which they definitely preferred the bet, those for which they definitely preferred \$160 with probability *p*, and those for which they were unsure.

Panel C of Fig. 2.2 shows that in this new task subjects mapped the *P*-bet and the \$-bet on the \$160 line. The *P*-bet is now more dissimilar. So, by the same argument as above, the imprecision interval of the *P*-bet will be wider and more asymmetric than that of the \$-bet and its **probability equivalent** will be higher. Panel C shows that the data from Butler and Loomes (2007) confirmed this prediction.

Unfortunately, it is unclear whether this really leads to a new preference reversal as most subjects chose the *P*-bet over the \$-bet. To get a new PR the *P*- and \$-bet should be slightly adjusted (for example, by increasing the amount subjects could win in the \$-bet) so that most subjects now prefer the \$-bet in a direct choice. It can then be tested whether the imprecision interval of the *P*-bet is still wider and asymmetric relative to that of the new \$-bet.

2.5 Scale Compatibility

I end this chapter with one more explanation for the PR, proposed by Amos Tversky, Paul Slovic, and Daniel Kahneman (1990) (TSK). They argue that the PR is caused by a violation of **procedure invariance**, the assumption that theoretically equivalent methods to measure preferences (like pricing and choice) give the same preference order. According to TSK, in choice people focus on the most important dimension. They call this the **prominence effect**. For decision under risk, probability is prominent. As the *P*-bet offers a higher probability of winning (and the bets are equal in expected value), people choose the *P*-bet over the \$-bet.

TSK explain the higher price of the \$-bet by **scale compatibility**: A dimension that is more compatible with the response scale gets more weight. In pricing the response scale is money. So, scale compatibility predicts that subjects will pay more attention to the payoffs of the bets. As the \$-bet has a higher potential payoff, its price will be higher. TSK present evidence that the cause of the PR is overpricing the \$-bet (see Experiment 2.2).

Experiment 2.2: Experiment TSK

TSK asked their subjects to perform 5 tasks:

1. choose between the P-bet and the \$-bet.
2. choose between the P-bet and a sure amount X with the same expected value.
3. choose between the \$-bet and X.
4. price the P-bet.
5. price the \$-bet.

The intransitivity explanation assumes procedural invariance and predicts $\$ \succ X \succ P \succ \$$ (see Extension 2.3). TSK assume transitivity within choice. They focused on the subjects who chose P over \$, but gave a higher price to the \$-bet than to the P-bet: $ce(\$) > X > ce(P)$ (ce stands for "cash equivalent"). They distinguished three possibilities:

1. overpricing of the \$-bet. Then $X \succ P \succ \$$ and $ce(\$) > X$.
2. underpricing of the P-bet.
3. both overpricing of the \$-bet and underpricing of the P-bet.

Exercise 2.7: Predictions TSK

1. Show that underpricing of the P-bet implies $P \succ \$ \succ X$ and $X > ce(P)$.
2. Show that both overpricing of the \$-bet and underpricing of the P-bet implies $P \succ X \succ \$$ and $ce(\$) > X > ce(P)$.

Two thirds of the subjects displaying a PR overpriced the \$-bet and only 10% were intransitive. So the PR was mainly due to overpricing of the \$-bet.

Exercise 2.8: Scale Compatibility

Explain that when we ask for probability equivalents (as in the experiment of Butler and Loomes), scale compatibility predicts that the probability equivalent of the P-bet will be higher than that of the \$-bet.

Exercise 2.8 shows that scale compatibility and imprecision make similar predictions. The asymmetry of the imprecision intervals in Butler and Loomes's argument also predicts that the $-bet will be overvalued. The two explanations differ in the reason why an attribute gets overweighted. Butler and Loomes argue that it is due to imprecision and dissimilarity. TSK claim that it is due to scale compatibility.

References

Aumann, R. J. 1962. Utility theory without the completeness axiom. *Econometrica* 30:445–462.

Birnbaum, M. H. 2008. New paradoxes of risky decision making. *Psychological Review* 115: 463–501.

Bordalo, P., N. Gennaioli, and A. Shleifer. 2012. Salience theory of choice under risk. *Quarterly Journal of Economics* 127: 1243–1285.

Butler, D. J., and G. C. Loomes. 2007. Imprecision as an account of the preference reversal phenomenon. *American Economic Review* 97: 277–297.

Cerreia-Vioglio, S., D. Dillenberger, and P. Ortoleva. 2015. Cautious expected utility and the certainty effect. *Econometrica* 83: 693–728.

Cettolin, E., and A. Riedl. 2019. Revealed preferences under uncertainty: Incomplete preferences and preferences for randomization. *Journal of Economic Theory* 181: 547–585.

Costa-Gomes, M. A., C. Cueva, G. Gerasimou, and M. Tejiščák. 2022. Choice, deferral, and consistency. *Quantitative Economics* 13: 1297–1318.

Cropper, M., J. K. Hammitt, and L. A. Robinson. 2011. Valuing mortality risk reductions: Progress and challenges. *Annual Review of Resource Economics* 3: 313–336.

Debreu, G. 1954. Representation of a preference ordering by a numerical function. In *Decision processes*, ed. R. M. Thrall, C. H. Coombs, and R. L. Davis, 159–165. New York: Wiley.

Dubourg, W.R., M.W. Jones-Lee, and G.C. Loomes. 1994. Imprecise preferences and the WTP-WTA disparity. *Journal of Risk and Uncertainty* 9: 115–133.

Dugundji, J. 1966. *Topology*. Boston: Allyn and Bacon.

Fishburn, P. C. 1982. Nontransitive measurable utility. *Journal of Mathematical Psychology* 26: 31–67.

Fishburn, P. C. 1991. Nontransitive preferences in decision theory. *Journal of Risk and Uncertainty* 4: 113–134.

Gilboa, I., A. W. Postlewaite, and D. Schmeidler. 2008. Probability and uncertainty in economic modeling. *Journal of Economic Perspectives* 22: 173–88.

Grether, D. M., and C. R. Plott. 1979. Economic theory of choice and the preference reversal phenomenon. *American Economic Review* 69: 623–638.

Humphrey, S. J., and N.-Y. Kruse. 2024. Who accepts Savage's axiom now? *Theory and Decision* 96: 1–17.

Iverson, G., and J.-C. Falmagne. 1985. Statistical issues in measurement. *Mathematical Social Sciences* 10: 131–153.

Laibson, D. 1997. Golden eggs and hyperbolic discounting. *Quarterly Journal of Economics* 112: 443–478.

Li, Z., and G. Loomes. 2022. Revisiting the diagnosis of intertemporal preference reversals. *Journal of Risk and Uncertainty* 64: 1–23.

Lichtenstein, S., and P. Slovic. 1971. Reversals of preference between bids and choices in gambling decisions. *Journal of Experimental Psychology* 89: 46–55.

Lichtenstein, S., and P. Slovic. 1973. Response-induced reversals of preference in gambling: An extended replication in Las Vegas. *Journal of Experimental Psychology* 101: 16–20.

Loomes, G. 2006. (How) Can we value health, safety and the environment? *Journal of Economic Psychology* 27: 713–736.

Loomes, G., and R. Sugden. 1982. Regret theory: An alternative theory of rational choice under uncertainty. *Economic Journal* 92: 805–824.

Loomes, G., C. Starmer, and R. Sugden. 1991. Observing violations of transitivity by experimental methods. *Econometrica* 59:425–439.

Luce, R. D. 1956. Semiorders and a theory of utility discrimination. *Econometrica* 24:178–191.

Nielsen, L. T. 1999. Differentiable von Neumann-Morgenstern utility. *Economic Theory* 14: 285–296.

Nielsen, K., and J. Rehbeck. 2022. When choices are mistakes. *American Economic Review* 112: 2237–2268.

Ok, E. A. 2002. Utility representation of an incomplete preference relation. *Journal of Economic Theory* 104: 429–449.

Regenwetter, M., J. Dana, and C. P. Davis-Stober. 2011. Transitivity of preferences. *Psychological Review* 118: 42–56.

Rubinstein, A. 2006. Comments on behavioral economics. In *Advances in economic theory (2005 World Congress of the Econometric Society)*, 246–254. Cambridge: Cambridge University Press.

Slovic, P. 1975. Choice between equally valued alternatives. *Journal of Experimental Psychology: Human Perception and Performance* 1: 280.

Starmer, C. 1999. Cycling with rules of thumb: An experimental test for a new form of non-transitive behaviour. *Theory and Decision* 46: 139–157.

Tversky, A. 1969. Intransitivity of preferences. *Psychological Review* 76: 31–48.

Tversky, A., and D. Kahneman. 1981. The framing of decisions and the psychology of choice. *Science* 211: 453–458.

Tversky, A., P. Slovic, and D. Kahneman. 1990. The causes of preference reversal. *American Economic Review* 80:204–217.

Wakker, P.P. 2010. *Prospect theory: For risk and ambiguity*. Cambridge: Cambridge University Press.

A Short History of Utility

3

In Chapter 2 we saw how utility can be derived if the preference relation $\succcurlyeq$ satisfies completeness and transitivity (and what can still be done if these conditions are relaxed). This utility concept only orders alternatives and has no psychological meaning. However, economists have not always seen utility this way. In this chapter, I give a short overview of the evolution of the concept of utility from the classical economists to the now dominant neoclassical view.[1] It prepares for the next chapter where we will see that behavioural economics can be seen as a return to a more classical view of utility.

It is useful to distinguish three types of utility:

1. **Ordinal utility**. This is the utility we discussed in Chapter 2. It can only be used to rank alternatives and is unique up to positive monotonic transformations.
2. **Cardinal utility**. Utility differences can be ranked, i.e. statements like the utility difference between good A and good B is larger than the utility difference between good C and good D are meaningful. This means that we can freely choose the unit and scale of utility and that utility is unique up to positive linear transformations: if U represents preferences then $U' = \alpha U + \beta$ with $\alpha > 0$ and β any real number does so as well.
3. **Classical utility**. Utility has a unit, i.e. there is a natural zero. Statements like "the utility of good A is twice that of good B" make sense and ratios of utilities are meaningful. This means that we can choose the unit of utility and that it is unique up to multiplication by a positive constant: if U represents preferences then $U' = \alpha U$ with $\alpha > 0$ does so as well.

[1] For more detailed surveys see Stigler (1950), Lewin (1996), and the various papers by Ivan Moscati quoted throughout this chapter.

H. Bleichrodt, *Behavioural Economics*,
https://doi.org/10.1007/978-3-031-69166-9_3

3.1 The Classical Economists

3.1.1 Jeremy Bentham

The British philosopher and economist Jeremy Bentham put the notion of utility to the forefront in the early 1800s. For Bentham human behaviour was the result of two opposing forces: pain and pleasure. Pain and pleasure were single sensations. Bentham did not distinguish between different types of pain and pleasure.

Happiness was the result of these opposing forces and Bentham used utility to measure happiness. For Bentham utility was a psychological concept, which measured an agent's happiness. Bentham's utility measure was classical: It measured the intensity of happiness and could be compared across people.[2]

Bentham suggested that the unit of utility was "that pleasure which is the faintest of any that can be distinguished" (this resembles the psychological notion of just noticeable differences discussed in Chapter 2). Bentham also suggested that pleasure could be measured by the amount of money that the agent was willing to pay to obtain it. Hence, for Bentham utility was measurable like, for example, length. There is a natural unit and statements like "good A has twice the utility of good B" make sense.

Bentham's aim was a more rational system of civil and criminal law. For this he needed cardinal and interpersonally comparable utility. Bentham argued that society should maximize the total amount of happiness (as proxied by utility) and, as he realized that happiness increases in wealth but at a decreasing rate, he argued in favour of an equal distribution of wealth (although he ultimately rejected equality of wealth in favour of security of property).

After Bentham utility disappeared for a while from economics. This was due to the emergence of the Ricardian school, with its emphasis on explaining prices by objective factors like the amount of labour used and technological change. Ricardo avoided subjective notions like utility. Because of this focus on objective factors, Ricardo did not believe in the concept of decreasing marginal utility, for example.

3.1.2 The Marginal Revolution

Interest in utility revived in the 1870s by the work of William Stanley Jevons, Carl Menger, and Léon Walras.[3] They developed a theory of exchange value in terms of marginal utility, which for them was the key concept of economic analysis and still is.

Inspired by Bentham, Jevons defined economics as "the calculus of pleasure and pain". However, Jevons did not believe there was a unit in which pleasure and pain

---

[2] Bentham even thought that the comparison of pain and pleasure could be extended to animals. He thought the suffering of animals could be directly compared with human suffering.

[3] Many of their ideas were already present in the work of Gossen who Stigler (1950, p. 314) describes as "one of the most tragic figures in the history of economics....He displayed every trait of the crank, excepting only one: history has so far believed that he was right".

could be measured. Because measurability in his time meant that there was a unit of measurement, Jevons, unlike Bentham, thought that utility could not be measured. To defend his use of marginal calculus, which appeared to depend on the measurability of utility, Jevons kept open the possibility that in the future utility might be measurable, much like probability, heat, and electricity had for a long time been considered unmeasurable. Jevons believed that his theory was largely independent of the measurability of utility. Moreover, pleasure and pain could be observed indirectly through its effects on markets and by people's willingness to pay for additional units of a good.

Menger was less clear on the measurability of utility. He believed that utility could not be measured by money, that marginal utility was decreasing (which at least requires cardinal utility), that a zero point of marginal utility exists and he mentions that the ratios of marginal utilities have meaning. So Menger was closer to a classical concept of utility than Jevons.

Like Jevons, Walras believed that utility could not be measured. He thought there was no unit of measurement and ratios of utilities were without meaning. However, this put Walras in a conundrum because he believed that his economic analysis depended on the measurability of utility. To solve it, Walras argued that although utility is not directly measurable we can derive demand functions from it and carry out the analysis of demand, supply, and exchange by treating marginal utility as if it were measurable. Like Jevons, he argues that the measurement of utility is analogous to the measurement of gravity. Unlike Jevons, however, Walras did not believe that consumers' willingness to pay for a good could be used as a measure of their marginal utility.

Menger and Walras did not write about the interpersonal comparability of utility. It is likely that at least Walras thought this was impossible given his views on the nonexistence of classical utility. Jevons wrote that utility could not be interpersonally compared although at some places in his analysis he used it.

Both Jevons and Walras assumed that total utility was additive across goods: $U(x_1, x_2, \ldots, x_n) = U_1(x_1) + U_2(x_2) + \cdots + U_n(x_n)$ where x_i is the amount consumed of good i and U_i is the utility of good i. Additivity ensures that demand curves are always downward-sloping.

Francis Edgeworth introduced more general utility functions, which allow for interdependencies between goods. He also introduced the notion of indifference curves into economics. His utility concept was similar to Jevons': Utility was a real psychological concept, which made it possible to derive economics from one single law of human nature: the maximization of utility.

Nonadditive general utility implies problems for economic analysis that Edgeworth did not solve. Demand curves may be upward sloping and even decreasing marginal utility does not exclude the possibility of concave indifference curves. Consequently, the tangency conditions of micro economics (equality between the ratios of marginal utilities and prices) are no longer sufficient to find the optimal quantities of consumption and equilibria are unstable. Alfred Marshall therefore rejected Edgeworth's suggestion of a general utility function and returned to additive utility (although he was not always consistent in his writing, see Moscati (2007) for details).

Economic methodology in this period was based on two key ideas. The first key idea was **verificationism**. As John Neville Keynes (1890, p. 14), the father of John Maynard Keynes, emphasized, economics was a deductive science that derived its laws from "a few simple and indisputable facts of human nature". This made it impossible to test. If an economic law was violated, then this indicated that it did not apply to the situation at hand. The focus was on situations in which the laws held and not on situations where they could be falsified. Economics hardly used data and did not aspire to be a universal social science. Lewin (1996) calls it an "armchair approach".

The second key idea was **introspection**. Social scientists acknowledged that, unlike the physical sciences, they could not run controlled experiments. But, they had a source of data unavailable to physical scientists: introspection. Because social science studies human behaviour and we are humans, we can use our introspection to better understand the motives underlying human behaviour. The classical economists gave introspection a central role and focused on one particular motive of human behaviour: the fulfilment of goals.

This focus on goal achievement was criticized by other human scientists. In particular, psychologists like William James emphasized that behaviour is often impulsive rather than goal-oriented. Instinct theory was becoming dominant in psychology and emphasized the role of habits and other human instincts in guiding behaviour. Instinct theory posed a serious challenge to the idea that people always aimed for the hedonic optimum. Keynes and Marshall acknowledged that economics left out important human motives, but wrote that it was impossible to include all human motives in economic theory. However, over time they changed the tone of their writing: They moved away from Bentham's hedonic calculus and avoided words like pleasure and pain.

3.2 The Ordinal Revolution

Around 1900, the focus in human science shifted from subjective introspection to observed behaviour, a movement called **behaviouralism**. John Watson (1913) claimed that psychology had largely been unsuccessful due to the mistaken idea that introspection was the only method available. This led to the undesirable situation that if findings could not be reproduced this was "due to the fact that your introspection is untrained" (p. 163). Watson argued that psychology should be based on observed behaviour (and as a result animal psychology was as valid a field of study as human psychology). By becoming behaviourist, psychology could obtain the rigour of the physical sciences.

According to Watson, psychological concepts should have empirical meaning so that they could be tested. Moreover, the scientific approach shifted from verificationism (exploring under which conditions a theory held) to falsificationism (finding conditions under which a theory does not hold). Theories should have real-world implications and specify which observations would challenge their validity.

3.2.1 Fisher and Pareto

Behaviouralism also affected economics. Economists became reluctant to explain empirical phenomena by vague and unobservable psychological notions like (hedonic) utility and the concept of marginal utility came into discredit.

Pioneers to free economics from its psychological foundations were Irving Fisher and Vilfredo Pareto, Walras' successor at the University of Lausanne. A serious limitation of classical utility theory was the absence of a measure of utility. Fisher tried to find an empirical measure of utility based on the economic choices of agents, but realized that his method only worked for additive utility.

Pareto made two important contributions. First, retaining cardinal utility, he solved the problems of nonconvex indifference curves and upward sloping demand curves, that plagued Edgeworth's general utility function.[4]

Second, Pareto showed that the main results of consumer demand theory do not need cardinal utility. He explored two approaches:

1. a **choice-based** approach which does not use utility and bases consumer theory on observed market data.
2. a **preference-based** approach which uses utility, but only as an ordinal index that ranks options.

Pareto thought that classical notions like pleasure and pain could not be measured and hoped that by using choice data or ordinal utility instead, economics could be put on a par with the physical sciences. For Pareto, ordinal utility did not have any psychological interpretation. It only summarized the empirical regularities of choice behaviour. Pareto was not interested in the motives behind economic decisions, which he found irrelevant. He was interested only in the patterns he could derive from observed quantities like prices.

Pareto's choice-based and preference-based approach both had problems. Pareto did not seem to be aware that using ordinal utility implies that we can no longer use concepts that are not unique up to positive monotonic transformations. One example is decreasing marginal utility, to which Pareto repeatedly refers. Decreasing marginal utility has no meaning under ordinal utility as the sign of the second derivative is not well-defined under positive monotonic transformations. See Extension 3.1.

Extension 3.1: Decreasing Marginal Utility Is a Cardinal Property

Let $U = U(x_1, \ldots, x_n)$ be a utility function that satisfies decreasing marginal utility with respect to good i, i.e. for which the second derivative $U_{ii} = \frac{\partial^2 U}{\partial^2 x_i} < 0$. Let f be a positive monotonic transformation of U. Then $V = f \circ U$ also

[4] Even though his convexity conditions were too strong and the economic meaning of Pareto's formula for $\frac{\partial x_i}{\partial p_i}$, the change in the demand of good x_i in response to a change in its price p_i is unclear (Moscati 2007).

represents preferences. However, $V_{ii} = f'' \times U_i^2 + f' \times U_i$ can be positive if f'' is sufficiently positive. So decreasing marginal utility need not be preserved for an ordinal utility function.

Pareto also defined complementarity and substitutability of goods in terms of cross-partial derivatives, which, again, have no meaning for ordinal utility (see Extension 3.2).

Extension 3.2: Complementarity and Substitutability Are Cardinal Properties

Pareto (like Edgeworth) defined complementarity of goods as $U_{ij} = \frac{\partial^2 U}{\partial x_i \partial x_j} > 0$ and substitutability as $U_{ij} < 0$. Define a positive monotonic transformation $V = f \circ U$ of U. Then $\frac{\partial^2 V}{\partial x_i \partial x_j} = f'' \times U_i \times U_j + f' \times U_{ij}$ can be negative if $U_{ij} > 0$ when f'' is sufficiently negative and positive if $U_{ij} < 0$ when f'' is sufficiently positive. Pareto's complementarity and substitutability can change under positive monotonic transformations.

Further, in spite of his attempts to replace additive utility by general utility, Pareto keeps using an additive utility function. Additivity is also not preserved under positive monotonic transformations.

Exercise 3.1: Additivity Is Not ordinal

Show that the square of an additive utility function $U(x_1, \ldots x_n) = U_1(x_1) + \cdots U_n(x_n)$ is not additive.

Finally, Pareto did not verify whether the second-order conditions for a maximum and the formula for $\frac{\partial x_i}{\partial p_i}$ that he derived using cardinal utility remained valid under positive monotonic transformations, i.e. when utility is ordinal.

3.2.2 Johnson and Slutsky

Pareto's work inspired later writers like Johnson, Slutsky, Hicks, Allen, and Samuelson to make ordinalism the dominant approach in consumer theory. William E. Johnson and the Russian economist Eugen Slutsky perfected Pareto's analysis of consumer demand theory with a general (nonadditive) utility function. Johnson (1913), whose students included John Maynard Keynes and Frank Ramsey (see Chapter 10) derived the income-consumption and price-consumption curves and showed that Giffen goods (goods for which an increase in price leads to an increase in the quantify bought) must be inferior goods.

Johnson still used cardinal concepts. He used equality of marginal utility, gave meaning to the difference between indifference curves, and made assumptions about the sign and the magnitude of the second-order and cross-partial derivatives of the utility function. As we saw in Extensions 3.1 and 3.2, these concepts have no meaning for ordinal utility, because they can vary with positive monotonic transformations of the utility function.

Slutsky (1915) filled all the remaining holes in consumer demand theory with general utility.[5] Slutsky showed that it was possible with ordinal utility to determine the conditions for utility maximization, to derive the effects of prices (both of the good itself and of other goods) and income on demand, and to determine whether goods were complements or substitutes. Slutsky's approach is still used in modern-day microeconomics, which shows the importance of his contribution.

Unfortunately, Slutsky's work went unnoticed until the 1930s. Slutsky's article was written in Italian and published in an Italian journal and he was working in Kiev, far from Oxford and Cambridge the heart of economics at the time. Moreover, history was not on his side. The First World War and the Bolshevik Revolution in Russia complicated contact with the outside world. In the late 1920s, under the influence of Stalin's ever more extreme policies, Slutsky decided to stop working on economics, which he thought too dangerous and moved to safer areas like probability theory and meteorology. He was probably right. Nikolai Kondratiev, Slutsky's boss at the Moscow Conjuncture Institute and known for his theory of long cycles, was arrested in 1930 and executed in 1938.

Slutsky left the door open for future applications of psychological concepts in economics. However, the discrepancies within the hedonistic school and the attacks on it from outside, made it impossible to reach a consensus on a hedonic concept of utility. Therefore, he wanted to free economics from all psychological concepts. Slutsky formulated demand theory entirely in terms of prices, quantities, and the budget. He realized that it was impossible to derive the sign of the second-order derivative of utility from observed choice and that Pareto's definitions of complementarity and substitutability had no meaning for ordinal utility.

Slutsky suggested that decreasing marginal utility, complementarity, and substitutability can be "founded upon some sort of internal evidence". He called this "faith in the consciousness of economic conduct". It cannot be derived from choice, smells like introspection, and is essentially cardinal in nature. Moreover, Slutsky derived his results in terms of one selected utility function, but did not check whether they still held under positive monotonic transformations of utility. That is, he did not check whether they were indeed ordinal properties.

---

[5] He derived the second-order conditions for the constrained maximization of utility, the exact expressions for the demand effect of changes in own price ($\frac{\partial x_i}{\partial p_i}$), the prices of other goods ($\frac{\partial x_i}{\partial p_i}$), and income ($\frac{\partial x_i}{\partial I}$), the notion of compensating variation, the decomposition of the demand effect of price changes in a substitution effect and an income effect, the proof that the substitution effect is always negative (and hence that the law of demand holds for compensated demand), that the income effect can be positive or negative, and that Giffen goods are strongly inferior which implies that the positive income effect of a price increase outweighs the negative substitution effect.

Slutsky's conditions marked the transition from an economic science based on unobservable psychological concepts to a science based on observable quantities. He hoped that this would also make it easier to test economic theory. In particular, which is interesting for behavioural economics, Slutsky emphasized the need for experiments to test economic theory as the real world would never give sufficient information to do so.

3.2.3 Hicks and Allen

John Hicks and Roy Allen (Hicks and Allen 1934a, b) praise Pareto's *Manual* as "the most complete theory of value produced by economic science" (p. 52). However, they also note that Pareto had not fully examined what adjustments in the marginal theory of value were necessary when utility was only ordinal. In particular, as we saw above, Pareto still used assumptions about the signs of the second and cross-partial derivatives of the utility function.

Hicks and Allen belong to the choice-based school that aims to base consumer theory entirely on observed choice. They replace marginal utility, the foundation of classical economics, by the **marginal rate of substitution** and define equilibrium as the allocation where the marginal rate of substitution is equal to the price ratio. The marginal rate of substitution, the amount of good j that must be given up for an extra unit of good i to leave the consumer indifferent between the old and the new allocation, can be observed and quantified. It does not need utility.

The marginal rate of substitution makes it possible to define key concepts like the elasticity of substitution and the income elasticity of demand without using marginal utility. Hicks and Allen decompose the effect of a price change on demand into a substitution and an income effect and give new non-cardinal definitions of when goods are complements and substitutes.

3.2.4 Samuelson

The movement to free demand theory of utility and its relation to psychology and introspection reached its zenith with Paul Samuelson's (1938a) revealed preference. Samuelson's objection against Hicks and Allen was their assumption that the marginal rate of substitution is decreasing. Hicks and Allen needed this to get convex indifference curves. According to Samuelson, this assumption could only be defended using introspection. In other words, Hicks and Allen's criticism of utility turned back on itself. Just like we do not know by introspection the behaviour of utility, we cannot know the behaviour of the marginal rate of substitution. Seeing the marginal rate of substitution as an entity free from psychological introspection is an "artificial convention" (p. 62).

Samuelson showed that consumer theory can be defined in terms of income, prices, and observed purchases in the market. His **revealed preference theory** uses observable quantities and does not need the marginal rate of substitution. Samuelson only assumed the **weak axiom of revealed preference**. It says that if at prices P^a bundle X^a is bought while bundle X^b is also available then it cannot be that at prices P^b bundle X^b is bought while bundle X^a is also available. In other words, if at prices P^b bundle X^b is bought then buying bundle X^a at prices P^b would exceed the consumer's income. Samuelson showed that almost all the results of demand theory that could be obtained under ordinal utility can also be derived under the weak axiom of revealed preference. Utility is (largely) superfluous.[6]

Samuelson was not against the notion of utility or aiming to remove it from economics. He just showed that utility was unnecessary for demand theory. In the same year as he published his note on revealed preference, Samuelson published three papers that used utility and contributed to it. Moreover, in his *Foundations of Economic Analysis* (Samuelson 1947), Samuelson played down the importance of the revealed preference approach and formulated demand theory in terms of ordinal utility.

The Hicks-Allen approach to define economics in terms of the marginal rate of substitution never became successful. In the meantime Slutsky's paper was rediscovered showing that Hicks and Allen's results could also be derived using ordinal utility. As a result, economics moved from Pareto's choice-based approach to his preference-based approach.

Allen (1936) acknowledged that many of the results in Hicks and Allen (1934a, b) were already given by Slutsky. He addressed limitations in Slutsky's analysis. In particular, he showed that Slutsky's results did not depend on the utility function selected and were robust to ordinal transformations of utility.

Allen (1936) still preferred the choice-based approach. However, in *Value and Capital* Hicks (1939), adopted the preference-based approach and used the ratio of the marginal utilities of an ordinal utility function instead of the marginal rate of substitution as the key concept of demand theory. Hicks fine-tuned Slutsky's results and showed that his and Allen's results could be obtained simpler using ordinal utility. After *Value and Capital*, the preference-based approach became dominant in consumer theory. It got an axiomatic basis in the 1940s and 1950s by the French economist Gérard Debreu. In Debreu (1954), he identified the conditions under which a preference relation can be represented by a continuous utility function. In Debreu (1959), he showed when this function is quasi-concave. This is all the Slutsky-Hicks consumer theory needs as it ensures that the second-order conditions of the optimum hold.

Extension 3.3: The Integrability Problem

Because nearly all results of demand theory can be derived both by Samuelson's weak axiom of revealed preference (WARP) and by ordinal utility, we may wonder whether WARP makes it possible to describe the consumer's preferences by a utility function. This is known as the **integrability prob-**

[6] The only exception is the symmetry of the cross-price substitution effects, i.e. the symmetry of the substitution matrix.

lem. Finding such a utility function would reconcile the choice-based and the preference-based approach.

Let $X = \mathbb{R}^n_+$ be a set of commodity bundles and let Σ^n be the collection of budget sets $B = x \in \mathbb{R}^n_+ : p \cdot x \leq I$, where p is a price vector and I the consumer's income. Each budget set specifies which bundles the consumer can buy given prices p and income I. We can define the revealed preference relation xRy if there is a budget set B that contains both x and y and the consumer chooses x instead of y. Let D denote the demand function that assigns to each budget set B the bundle that the consumer chooses from it. We say that a preference relation $\succcurlyeq$ **rationalizes** D if for every budget B:

$$D(B) = x \in B : x \succcurlyeq y \text{ for all } y \text{ in } B.$$

The essence of the integrability problem is to study when the demand function can be rationalized by a weak order.

Let xPy if xRy and $x \neq y$. WARP excludes cycles of length 2. It cannot be that xPy and yPx both hold. However, it does not exclude longer cycles: the cycle xPy, yPz, and zPx is possible. The Dutch-American economist Hendrik Houthakker (1950) showed that if we strengthen WARP to the **strong axiom of revealed preference** (SARP) that excludes cycles of any length k then D can be rationalized by a weak order. According to Houthakker, integrability is a spurious problem as WARP and SARP are close.

Ken Arrow (1959) argued that Houthakker's proof did not fully settle the issue. It might still be possible that WARP implies SARP under the assumptions that economists usually make about utility (continuity, differentiability, and convexity). David Gale (1960) showed that for 3 goods this is not the case. Hans Peters and Peter Wakker (1994) showed that it is not true for any number of goods. Hence, we really need to strengthen WARP to SARP to be able to represent the consumer's choice problem as the maximization of a utility function subject to a budget constraint.

The distinction between WARP and SARP is not so important. Arrow (1959), Corollary to Theorem 3 showed that it only matters if we restrict attention to choices observed in the market. If we also permit agents to make choices outside the market (as behavioural economists do in experiments) then WARP implies transitivity and WARP and SARP are equivalent. Amartya Sen (1973) argues that there is no reason to restrict attention to market choices and to exclude all others.

3.3 The Limitations of Revealed Preference

Economists quickly realized that deriving preferences from observed market choices is complex. Indifference curves cannot be derived from consumer expenditures and to derive the preferences from single agents we must follow them over a long time during which, most likely, their preferences change confounding our measurements.

Moreover, not everyone agreed that economics should try to copy the methods of physics and dismiss all psychology. Frank Knight, one of the leaders of the Chicago school of economists in the 1940s, argued that it makes no sense to copy the approach of physics, because economics has a different focus. Introspection is necessary to derive preferences. They cannot be derived from observed behaviour alone.

Amartya Sen (1973) is particularly critical of revealed preference. According to Sen, even the claim that revealed preference freed economics from the concepts of preference and utility does not stand scrutiny. WARP can serve one of two aims:

1. As a hypothesis subject to empirical testing.
2. As a principle of consistency.

Because empirical testing of WARP is impossible given the infinite amount of price-income configurations that would have to be checked, Sen claims that the only defence of WARP is as a principle of consistency.[7] However, this leads to a paradox: How can we determine whether an axiom or principle is consistent without referring to preferences or introspection? In Sen's words: "What makes [violations of WARP] look inconsistent is precisely the peep into the head of the consumer, the avoidance of which is alleged to be the aim of the revealed preference approach" (p. 243). Sen raises several other objections against revealed preference, but the essence of his critique is that pure revealed preference is too limited to base economics on and that ridding economics of all introspection is a lost case.

One point Sen makes is particularly interesting for behavioural economics. This is the idea that the only data economics should use are observed (incentivized) choices. Sen believes this is "extremely questionable" and "extremely limiting for empirical work". Sen suggests using stated preferences and questionnaires in addition to observed choices. He believes that "we have been prone, on the one hand, to overstate the difficulties of introspection and communication, and on the other, to underestimate the problems of studying preferences revealed by observed behavior".

Example 3.1: Questionnaires

Questionnaires are often used to measure people's subjective well-being, their poverty or their health. For example, happiness research asks people where they stand on a so-called **Cantril ladder**, which ranges from 0, the "worst possible life for you", to 11, "the best possible life for you". Similarly, health

[7] I do not agree with Sen on the empirical testing of WARP. Testing any axiom requires in principle an infinite amount of data. However, we need axioms to develop theories. The best we can then hope for is not to observe systematic violations of these axioms and that they hold approximately. To me, this is a satisfactory empirical basis for an axiom. I agree with Sen that we need introspection to assess the validity of WARP.

economists measure quality of life by asking people to rate their health on a scale from 0, "death", to 1, "full health". Economists are sceptical about these data, because they are not based on choices and people have no incentives to respond truthfully. However, they are used a lot for policy decisions.

3.4 The Return of Cardinal Utility

3.4.1 Oskar Lange

The idea of cardinal utility never disappeared from economics (Moscati 2013). Even though Pareto argued that utility was not measurable, i.e. statements like the utility of bundle x is twice as large as the utility of bundle y are meaningless, he did not exclude the possibility that people could rank the size of changes in utility, i.e. whether the change from bundle x to bundle y was larger than the change from bundle s to bundle t. This is in line with decreasing marginal utility, which he, as we saw, used in his analysis.

The idea that people can rank differences in utility was kept alive in the 1920s by economists like Amoroso, Bowley, Rosenstein-Rodan, and Oskar Morgenstern. They did not refer, however, to the notion of cardinal utility and insisted that they did not assume that utility was measurable.

This changed in the 1930s. In 1934, the Polish economist Oskar Lange published an article in the *Review of Economic Studies* (Lange 1934). Lange pointed out that in his *Manual*, Pareto assumed that people can rank both bundles of goods (his postulate 1) and changes in bundles of goods (his postulate 2). Postulate 2 follows because Pareto uses the signs of the second derivatives of the utility function. According to Lange, these two assumptions imply that utility is measurable (see Extension 3.4). Although postulate 2 is not necessary for the definition of the consumer's equilibrium, it is necessary to give a welfare interpretation to that equilibrium. While postulate 1 can be expressed in terms of objective behaviour, postulate 2 which is about gains in utility (the input of welfare analysis) requires psychological introspection. Lange saw a role for psychology in economics.

Lange's analysis turned out to be wrong as was pointed out by Henry Phelps Brown (1934) and solved by Franz Alt (1936). However, it led to new interest in cardinal utility. In 1937, one year before his famous paper on revealed preference, Samuelson (1937) wrote a paper on intertemporal choice in which he introduced the discounted utility model (see Chapter 11). Within this model, the individual must trade off differences in utility against changes in timing and Pareto's postulate 2 was necessary for this. Independent from Alt, Samuelson also solved the problem raised by Phelps Brown (Samuelson, 1938b). Samuelson was the first to define cardinal utility as utility unique up to positive linear transformations.

Extension 3.4: Lange's "Proof" of Measurability of Utility

If people can only rank goods then many utility functions are possible: any positive monotonic transformation $\phi(U)$ of a utility function U is also a utility function. If people can also rank changes in utility then we could find bundles x, y, and z, with x better than y and y better than z, such that the change from x to y is exactly equal to the change from y to z. That is,

$$U(x) - U(y) = U(y) - U(z),$$

or

$$U(x) - U(z) = U(x) - U(y) + U(y) - U(z) = 2\big(U(y) - U(z)\big).$$

So statements that the move from z to x is twice as large as that from z to y make sense. Moreover, because we must also have that

$$\phi(U(x)) - \phi(U(z)) = 2\big(\phi(U(y)) - \phi(U(z))\big)$$

and ϕ must be a linear function. Hence, utility must be unique up to unit and scale.

Lange used the same utility function to rank both goods and differences between goods. To say that the difference between x and y is equal to the difference between y and z means that there is a function G, unique up to positive monotonic transformations, such that $G(x, y) = G(y, z)$. It is not necessarily true that $G(x, y) = U(x) - U(y)$. Moreover, there is no reason why we could sum different values of G, i.e. there is no reason why $G(x, z) = G(x, y) + G(y, z)$. These properties require additional assumptions as Alt (1936) showed. Alt was one of the first to apply topological analysis to economics. This became more common since the 1950s by the work of Debreu and others. Samuelson (1938b) solved the problem in Lange's analysis by directly assuming that $G(x, z) = G(x, y) + G(y, z)$.

3.4.2 Risk and Welfare

Six years after Samuelson's revealed preference paper, Von Neumann and Morgenstern (1944) (vNM) gave an axiomatization of expected utility, which became the dominant theory of decision under risk (see Chapter 9) and in which the utility function is cardinal. vNM were sceptical about Pareto's postulate 2, that people could rank differences in utility, and did not assume it. They derived cardinal utility from a set of axioms on the agent's preferences over risky lotteries.

In the next decades, economists became increasingly aware of the need for a cardinal concept of utility. This is particularly true for welfare economics, where, as Lange already mentioned, we need cardinal utility to make comparisons across people (see Harsanyi 1955; Sen 1970). Similarly, in applied economic analysis, a cardinal measure of utility is often necessary (see Example 3.2).

Example 3.2: Economic Evaluations of Health Care

A problem in health policy is that the costs of health care spiral out of control. Figure 3.1 shows the evolution of the amount spent per capita on health care adjusted for purchasing power parity in the US, the Netherlands, and Spain. In 1970 these countries spent approximately $300 per head on health care. By 2022, this amount had increased to $4000 in Spain, to $7000 in the Netherlands, and to $13,000 in the US. As a percentage of GDP, the amount spent on health care nearly doubled in the Netherlands (from 5.6% to 10.1%), more than doubled in the US (from 6.2% to 16.5%), and tripled in Spain (from 3.1% to 9.7%).

Such increases are unsustainable, especially because they accelerate due to ageing populations, increases in life-expectancy, continuing improvements in medical technology, and rising health expectations. European governments try to curb the rise in health care costs by applying cost-benefit analysis. For example, in the UK, the National Institute of Clinical Excellence (NICE) only admits new medicines and treatments to the National Health Service (NHS) when they cost less than £30,000 per year in good health gained.

How can we measure the benefits of health care? Simply counting life years gained does not work, because many medical interventions improve quality of life and not life duration. Examples are treatment for migraine or asthma. Health economists have solved this by using **quality-adjusted life years** (QALYs). QALYs are life years adjusted by weights that reflect the quality of life in which they are spent. Quality of life weights are measured on a scale ranging from 0 (death) to 1 (full health). For instance, by the rating scale of Example 3.1.

To use QALYs in health policy, the differences between them must be meaningful. Hence, QALYs are a cardinal measure of utility. What is more, health policy must trade off the QALYs gained by one patient group against those gained by another. So QALYs are not only cardinal, but also interpersonally comparable (see Bleichrodt 1997).

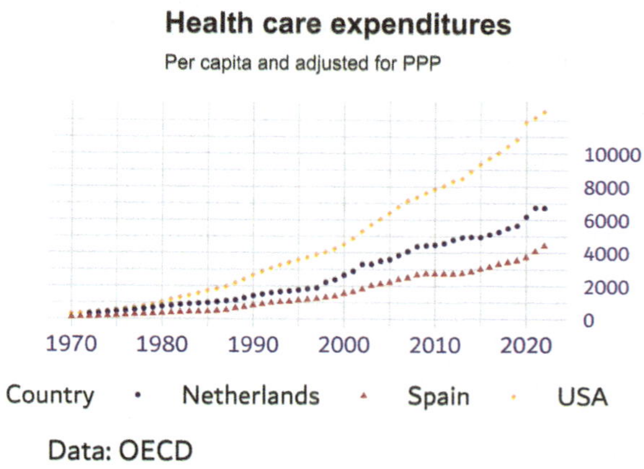

Fig. 3.1 Health care expenditures adjusted for purchasing power parity

3.5 Utility Theory After Revealed Preference

Von Neumann and Morgenstern's derivation of cardinal utility from risky choice led to a debate about what their utility stood for. Most economists agreed that it was a mathematical construct that had no relevance outside risk. Arrow (1951, p. 425) wrote about vNM utility that "the utilities assigned are not in any sense to be interpreted as some intrinsic amount of good in the outcome". Savage (1954) and Duncan Luce and Howard Raiffa (1957, p. 32), who refer to the idea that risky and riskless cardinal utility are the same as a "fallacy", thought the same. This has long been the dominant view in economics.

However, not everyone agrees. First, von Neumann and Morgenstern themselves consider a wider interpretation of utility (see Wakker 1994) and use risky utility as a unit of exchange in game theory. Second, Nobel laureates John Harsanyi and Maurice Allais argued that risky and riskless utility are the same. For example, Allais (1953) writes that the persistence of the "mistaken idea" that concave utility reflects decreasing marginal utility suggests that the idea is not entirely void of sense after all.

Finally, the emergence of alternative theories for expected utility (see Chapter 9) reopened the debate about the nature of the utility function. One of the key insights of Kahneman and Tversky's prospect theory is that people evaluate outcomes as deviations from a reference outcome. The reference outcome gets utility 0, which makes the utility function a ratio scale, unique only up to unit.

A central insight of behavioural economics is that people are loss averse: losses loom larger than gains. This is often expressed as the absolute value of the utility of a loss is larger than the utility of its commensurate gain. However, such statements only make sense if we can compare levels of utility and the ratio of utilities, by which loss aversion is often measured, must be meaningful. The often-cited loss aversion coefficient of 2.25 of Tversky and Kahneman (1992), which says that losses weight more than twice as heavy as corresponding gains, requires that utility ratios are meaningful. So, the utility concept in prospect theory is based on Pareto's postulate

3, which says that people are able to judge how much more preferable one change in outcomes is than another. Pareto rejected this postulate and it was not followed up in mainstream economics.

Under prospect theory, unlike under expected utility theory, attitudes towards risk are not determined by utility alone (see Chapter 9). This makes it possible that prospect theory's utility function has relevance outside risk and measures attitudes towards outcomes. Behavioural economists have indeed applied prospect theory's utility function outside risk. In Chapter 7 we will see that Kahneman and Tversky apply their utility function to explain consumption decisions under certainty. George Loewenstein and Drazen Prelec apply prospect theory's utility function to decisions over time (see Chapter 11).

The use of one utility function in different contexts is not restricted to prospect theory. Steffen Andersen and co-authors (2008) use the expected utility function measured under risk in a discounted utility model of choice over time. To Arrow and most leading economists of the twentieth century this made no sense.

The other theory of decision under risk that emerged in the early days of behavioural economics, Loomes and Sugden's (1982) regret theory, even more clearly deviates from the neoclassical concept of utility. Loomes and Sugden introduce a cardinal **choiceless utility** function, which assigns to each outcome its utility without having been chosen. They distinguish choiceless utility, because in regret theory choice involves a comparison between options and this comparison leads to feelings of regret and rejoice. These feelings are separate from the experience of the outcome itself. They write (p. 807), "what we understand by choiceless utility is essentially what Bernoulli and Marshall understood by utility—the psychological experience of pleasure that is associated with the satisfaction of desire". Loomes and Sugden believe in introspection and utility in regret theory is a return to a classical concept of utility.

3.6 Is There One Unifying Concept of Utility?

Several studies have tried to empirically answer the question whether there is one common concept of utility. Their findings are mixed. Ale Smidts (1997) measured the preferences of Dutch farmers about variations in the price of potatoes. This is a real-world problem with which the farmers were familiar and that strongly affected their income.

Smidts measured the farmers' utility under risk using the certainty equivalent method that I will discuss in Chapter 9. He measured their riskless utility by asking for each price interval $[A, B]$ the price C such that the price increase from A to C was equal in value to that from C to B. Riskless (V) and risky (U) utility were different, but there was an exponential relation $U = \frac{1-e^{-cV}}{1-e^{-c}}$ between them. The coefficient c reflects the farmers' **intrinsic risk attitude** (see Extension 3.5).

Extension 3.5: Dyer and Sarin's Theory

In the early 1980s Jim Dyer and Rakesh Sarin (1982) developed a theory of riskless and risky utility. In it agents' risk attitudes are determined by their **strength of preference** and their **intrinsic risk attitude**. In the spirit of Lange, Dyer and Sarin assume two preference relations:

1. A relation $\succcurlyeq$ over prospects, from which we can derive a preference relation over outcomes by focusing on prospects that give an outcome with certainty
2. A relation $\succcurlyeq^*$ over pairs of outcomes where $wx \succcurlyeq^* yz$ means that the strength of preference of w over x exceeds the strength of preference of y over z.

$\succcurlyeq$ satisfies the axioms of expected utility and is represented by a von Neumann Morgenstern utility function U. $\succcurlyeq^*$ is represented by a **measurable value function** V that satisfies $wx \succcurlyeq^* yz$ iff $V(w) - V(x) \leq V(y) - V(z)$. To get this representation we need the axioms of Alt (1936) or Krantz et al. (1971).

The two relations $\succcurlyeq$ and $\succcurlyeq^*$ are related by requiring $wx \succcurlyeq^* yx$ iff $w \succcurlyeq y$. Thus, V is an ordinal function on the set of outcomes. Dyer and Sarin note that V can only be measured through introspection. So they make a case for introspection in economics. $U = \phi(V)$ where ϕ measures agents' intrinsic risk attitude: their risk attitude corrected for their decreasing marginal value of goods. An agent is **intrinsically risk averse** if ϕ is concave, **intrinsically risk loving** if ϕ is convex, and **intrinsically risk neutral** if ϕ is linear. If ϕ is exponential, the case studied by Smidts, then intrinsic risk aversion is constant.

Another way of defining intrinsic risk aversion is the following. Let x_e be the outcome such that $yx_e \sim^* x_e z$, i.e. x_e is the outcome such that the strength of preference between y and x_e is exactly equal to the strength of preference between x_e and z. In other words, x_e is a **midpoint** (in terms of V) between y and z. Let x_c be the outcome for sure that is equivalent to a prospect that gives a 50% chance of y and a 50% chance of z. The agent is intrinsically risk averse if $x_c < x_e$, intrinsically risk loving if $x_c > x_e$ and intrinsically risk neutral if $x_c = x_e$

Smidts assumed expected utility for risk. Many studies show that people violate expected utility (see Chapter 9) and these violations may have biased Smidts' measurements. In a medical decision context, Peep Stalmeier and Thom Bezembinder (1999) showed that when risky choices are analysed under prospect theory then risky and riskless utility are the same.

They measured preferences over days with migraine. Let (z, M) denote the health state "living z days per week with migraine". In their riskless measurement, Stalmeier and Bezembinder (1999) asked their subjects, for example, "which difference is larger: the difference between $(0, M)$ and $(z_{.5}, M)$ or the difference between $(z_{.5}, M)$ and $(3, M)$". The duration $z_{.5}$ was varied between 0 and 3 until the subject said that the differences were equal. Setting $V(0, M) = 1$ and $V(3, M) = 0$, it then follows that $V(z_{.5}, M) = 0.5$.

Exercise 3.2:

Having found $z_{.5}$ such that $V(z_{.5}) = 0.5$, explain how we can find $z_{.75}$ such that $V(z_{.75}) = 0.75$ and $z_{.25}$ such that $V(z_{.25}) = 0.25$.

Mohammed Abdellaoui, Carolina Barrios, and Peter Wakker (2007) found that risky and riskless utility for money were also the same under prospect theory. They used two different methods to measure risky utility. Under both there was no difference between risky and riskless utility.

The results of Stalmeier and Bezembinder (1999) and Abdellaoui et al. (2007) support that there is one concept of utility that can be applied across domains. This is important because in real-world applications utilities measured in one context are used in other contexts. In economic evaluations of health care (see Example 3.2), for example, riskless and risky methods to measure quality of life are used interchangeably.

However, not all studies find that utility is the same across decision contexts. Mohammed Abdellaoui, Olivier l'Haridon, Corina Paraschiv, and I (Abdellaoui et al. 2013) measured utility under both risk and time. Several authors have emphasized the similarities between how people assess risk and time (see Chapter 11), and this seemed a domain where equality of utility is plausible. We used a method that takes account of the main empirical findings on decision under risk and over time. Nevertheless, we found that utility for time was more linear than risky utility.[8]

On the other hand, evidence from neuroscience (see Chapter 6) shows that preferences under risk and over time are governed by a similar biological system. So they seem to be related (Pine et al. 2010).

Hui-Kuan Chung et al. (2019) tested whether prospect theory's utility function for risk, which is concave for gains and convex for risk, could also be applied in a riskless context. If so indifference curves for gains will be convex (the marginal rate of substitution between goods x and y increases the more we have of good x), but for losses they will be concave.

Their experiments conflicted with this prediction. Under risk utility was concave for gains and convex for losses, but indifference curves were convex for both gains and losses. The problem with their analysis (see Wakker 2022) is that they measure riskless utility by choices between bundles of goods. As we saw, such choices can be represented by an ordinal utility function. To determine the curvature of indifference curves, we need information about the second and cross-partial derivatives of utility and these are not preserved under positive monotonic transformations of utility (see Extensions 3.1 and 3.2). If U is the risky and V the riskless utility function, then there is a positive monotonic function ϕ such that $U = \phi(V)$ that explains all

[8] James Andreoni and Charles Sprenger (2012) also found different utility under risk and over time. However, they assumed expected utility and constant discounting, two assumptions that are systematically violated, see Chapters 9 and 11.

the data of Chung et al. This resembles the problems in Pareto's analysis when combining decreasing marginal utility and ordinal utility. It highlights the importance of understanding the properties of utility, that we discussed in this chapter.

3.7 Conclusion

We have seen how the concept of utility has evolved over time. While the classical economists thought of utility as a broad concept close to psychology, over time it became narrower and economists tried to free itself from psychology. In the end, this approach turned out to be too limited, especially for welfare analysis and applied work. In the next chapter I explain how behavioural economics implies a (partial) return to a broader concept of utility. It challenged revealed preference by showing that choice can be inconsistent (the preference reversal phenomenon of Chapter 2) and has led to new notions of utility inspired by psychology.

References

Abdellaoui, M., C. Barrios, and P.P. Wakker. 2007. Reconciling introspective utility with revealed preference: Experimental arguments based on prospect theory. *Journal of Econometrics* 138: 356–378.

Abdellaoui, M., H. Bleichrodt, O. L'Haridon, and C. Paraschiv. 2013. Is there one unifying concept of utility? An experimental comparison of utility under risk and utility over time. *Management Science* 59: 2153–2169.

Allais, M. 1953. Le comportement de l'homme rationnel devant le risque: critique des postulats et axiomes de l'école américaine. *Econometrica* 21: 503–546.

Allen, R.G. 1936. Professor Slutsky's theory of consumers' choice. *Review of Economic Studies* 3: 120–129.

Alt, F. 1936. Über die messbarkeit des nutzens. *Zeitschrift für Nationalökonomie/Journal of Economics* 161–169.

Andersen, S., G.W. Harrison, M.I. Lau, and E.E. Rutström. 2008. Eliciting risk and time preferences. *Econometrica* 76: 583–618.

Andreoni, J., and C. Sprenger. 2012. Risk preferences are not time preferences. *American Economic Review* 102: 3357–3376.

Arrow, K.J. 1951. Alternative approaches to the theory of choice in risk-taking situations. *Econometrica* 19: 404–437.

Arrow, K.J. 1959. Rational choice functions and orderings. *Economica* 26: 121–127.

Bleichrodt, H. 1997. Health utility indices and equity considerations. *Journal of Health Economics* 16: 65–91.

Chung, H.-K., P. Glimcher, and A. Tymula. 2019. An experimental comparison of risky and riskless choice-limitations of prospect theory and expected utility theory. *American Economic Journal: Microeconomics* 11: 34–67.

Debreu, G. 1954. Representation of a preference ordering by a numerical function. In *Decision processes*, ed. R.M. Thrall, C.H. Coombs, and R.L. Davis, 159–165. New York: Wiley.

Debreu, G. 1959. *Theory of value: An axiomatic analysis of economic equilibrium*, vol. 17. Yale University Press.
Dyer, J.S., and R.K. Sarin. 1982. Relative risk aversion. *Management Science* 28: 875–886.
Gale, D. 1960. A note on revealed preference. *Economica* 27: 348–354.
Harsanyi, J.C. 1955. Cardinal welfare, individualistic ethics, and interpersonal comparisons of utility. *Journal of Political Economy* 63: 309–321.
Hicks, J.R. 1939. *Value and capital*. Oxford: Clarendon Press.
Hicks, J.R., and R.G. Allen. 1934a. A reconsideration of the theory of value. Part I. *Economica* 1: 52–76.
Hicks, J.R., and R.G. Allen. 1934b. A reconsideration of the theory of value. Part II. A mathematical theory of individual demand functions. *Economica* 1: 196–219.
Houthakker, H.S. 1950. Revealed preference and the utility function. *Economica* 17: 159–174.
Johnson, W.E. 1913. The pure theory of utility curves. *Economic Journal* 23: 483–513.
Keynes, J.N. 1890. *The scope and method of political economy*. London: MacMillan.
Krantz, D., R.D. Luce, P. Suppes, and A. Tversky. 1971. *Foundations of measurement, Vol. I: Additive and polynomial representations*. New York: Academic Press.
Lange, O. 1934. The determinateness of the utility function. *Review of Economic Studies* 1: 218–225.
Lewin, S.B. 1996. Economics and psychology: Lessons for our own day from the early twentieth century. *Journal of Economic Literature* 34: 1293–1323.
Loomes, G., and R. Sugden. 1982. Regret theory: An alternative theory of rational choice under uncertainty. *Economic Journal* 92: 805–824.
Luce, R.D., and H. Raiffa. 1957. *Games and decisions: Introduction and critical survey*. New York: Wiley.
Moscati, I. 2007. History of consumer demand theory 1871–1971: A Neo-Kantian rational reconstruction. *European Journal of the History of Economic Thought* 14: 119–156.
Moscati, I. 2013. How cardinal utility entered economic analysis: 1909–1944. *European Journal of the History of Economic Thought* 20: 906–939.
Peters, H., and P.P. Wakker. 1994. WARP does not imply SARP for more than two commodities. *Journal of Economic Theory* 62: 152–160.
Phelps Brown, E.H. 1934. Notes on the determinateness of the utility function: I. *Review of Economic Studies* 2: 66–69.
Pine, A., T. Shiner, B. Seymour, and R.J. Dolan. 2010. Dopamine, time, and impulsivity in humans. *Journal of Neuroscience* 30: 8888–8896.
Samuelson, P.A. 1937. A note on measurement of utility. *Review of Economic Studies* 4: 155–161.
Samuelson, P.A. 1938a. A note on the pure theory of consumer's behaviour. *Economica* 5: 61–71.
Samuelson, P.A. 1938b. The numerical representation of ordered classifications and the concept of utility. *Review of Economic Studies* 6: 65–70.
Samuelson, P.A. 1947. *Foundations of economic analysis*. Cambridge, MA: Harvard University Press.
Savage, L.J. 1954. *The Foundations of Statistics*. New York: Dover Publications.
Sen, A. 1970. *Collective Choice and Social Welfare*. San Francisco: Holden-Day.
Sen, A. 1973. Behaviour and the concept of preference. *Economica* 40: 241–259.
Slutsky, E. 1915. Sulla teoria del bilancio del consumatore (translated by Olga Ragusa). *Giornale degli economisti e rivista di statistica* 1–26.
Smidts, A. 1997. The relationship between risk attitude and strength of preference: A test of intrinsic risk attitude. *Management Science* 43: 357–370.
Stalmeier, P.F., and T.G. Bezembinder. 1999. The discrepancy between risky and riskless utilities: A matter of framing? *Medical Decision Making* 19: 435–447.
Stigler, G.J. 1950. The development of utility theory. I. *Journal of Political Economy* 58: 307–327.
Tversky, A., and D. Kahneman. 1992. Advances in prospect theory: Cumulative representation of uncertainty. *Journal of Risk and Uncertainty* 5: 297–323.

Von Neumann, J., and O. Morgenstern. 1944. *Theory of games and economic behavior*. Princeton University Press.

Wakker, P.P. 1994. Separating marginal utility and probabilistic risk aversion. *Theory and Decision* 36: 1–44.

Wakker, P.P. 2022. Transforming ordinal riskless utility into cardinal risky utility: A comment on Chung, Glimcher, and Tymula (2019). *American Economic Journal: Microeconomics* 14: 561–565.

Watson, J.B. 1913. Psychology as the behaviorist views it. *Psychological Review* 20: 158–177.

Utility in Behavioural Economics

4

4.1 Decision Utility and Experienced Utility

The deviations from rationality he and Tversky observed, made Kahneman reconsider the meaning of rational choice. Economics defines rationality as consistency with a set of axioms, but without any reference to the consequences of choices. Sen (1993) made a similar point. He argued that rationality of choice cannot be defined without reference to something external to an agent's choices, like objectives, values, or norms.

Kahneman (1994) distinguishes two types of utility:

1. **decision utility**, which we use to make decisions. It is the weight we give to an outcome when we choose. This is the utility that economists commonly use.
2. **experienced utility**, which measures the hedonic experience of the outcome of choice. This is what Bentham had in mind: The pleasure and pain the agents derive from the consequences of their choices. Kahneman et al. (1997, p. 380) write that this utility can be interpersonally comparable.

Traditional economics assumes that experienced and decision utility are the same. Kahneman argues that they can differ for two reasons: people do not remember past utility well and they are bad at predicting future utility. Let us look at both of these.

4.1.1 Past Utility

To remember how good or bad past experiences were, requires recalling the hedonic experiences of past episodes and to combine these into an overall evaluation. People have problems with both. When they consider past experiences, they focus on the peak experience and on the experience at the end of the episode, but ignore the episode's duration. Kahneman calls this the **peak-end rule**.

H. Bleichrodt, *Behavioural Economics*,
https://doi.org/10.1007/978-3-031-69166-9_4

Exercise 4.1: Peak-End Rule

Consider the following two profiles of experienced utilities where higher numbers mean "more pleasant":

- $A = (12, 10, 16, 14, 12, 4)$
- $B = (4, 4, 2, 17, 5, 5)$

Which profile will the agent remember as more pleasant according to the peak-end rule?

The peak-end rule can lead to normatively problematic behaviour. Consider two medical treatments A and B where B is obtained from A by adding an extra period of light pain. See Fig. 4.1. I guess you agree that A should be chosen over B. However, the peak-end rule predicts that people will remember B as less unpleasant than A because the pain added at the end is light. The peak pain is the same in both treatments, but the pain at the end of B is less than that of A. That the pain lasts longer in B is irrelevant according to the peak-end rule, because duration does not (or relatively little) affect remembered utility.

In a series of papers with medical doctor Donald Redelmeier, Kahneman found support for the peak-end rule. For example, Redelmeier et al. (2003) study the remembered utility of patients undergoing a colonoscopy to detect colorectal cancer. Colorectal cancer is a leading cause of death in developed countries and governments have introduced periodic screening for persons at risk (usually those above 50 years). The most effective screening method is colonoscopy, but it can be unpleasant and painful. If people have a less unpleasant memory of the screening, they are more

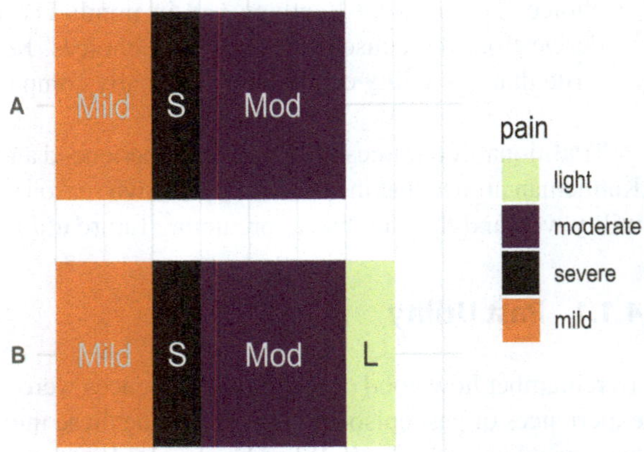

Fig. 4.1 An illustration of the peak-end rule

likely to show up for subsequent screening with the benefits of avoided morbidity and mortality.[1]

Redelmeier et al. (2003) studied two ways to perform colonoscopy: the common procedure in which the colonoscope was removed immediately after the procedure and a modified procedure in which the colonoscope rested in the rectum for an extra 3 minutes after the procedure. The pain in the modified procedure lasted longer, but it was relatively light at the end.[2] So the common and modified procedures are like profiles A and B in Fig. 4.1.

Exercise 4.2: Colorectal Cancer Screening

Explain that the peak-end rule predicts that patients will remember the modified procedure as less unpleasant than the common procedure.

Patients recorded both the pain at various moments during the procedure and after the procedure on a scale from 0 ("no discomfort") to 10 ("awful discomfort"). There were no differences in the pain experienced during the common stages of the procedures. This suggests that the two groups were similar except for the pain experienced at the end. In line with the peak-end rule, the patients who got the modified treatment reported that the screening procedure was less painful than the patients who received the common treatment: 4.4 versus 4.9, which was statistically significant at the 1% level. Patients in the modified procedure were 1.4 times (41%) more likely to return for follow-up screening than those who had received the common treatment. This shows how behavioural economics can be important for real-life decisions.

Exercise 4.3: Incompleteness

Suppose a patient has experienced the following three pain profiles where higher numbers mean "more pain":

- $A = (10, 2, 2, 7)$
- $B = (25, 14, 14, 14, 6)$
- $C = (9, 8, 8, 8, 8)$

The patient behaves according to the peak-end rule. The patient has to repeat one of the treatments and can choose which one. The patient decides to choose the treatment they remembered as least unpleasant. Explain that the patient will be unable to choose. This exercise shows that the peak-end rule can lead to incomplete preferences.

[1] Remembered pain predicts future treatment choices. For example, 20% of women who refuse breast cancer screening do so because of remembered pain. Similarly 10% of people who fail to visit a dentist and 40% of people who suffered a cardiac arrest cite earlier pain as the main reason not to show up at follow-up treatment.

[2] The most painful part of a colonoscopy is when the colonoscope moves or takes a suction.

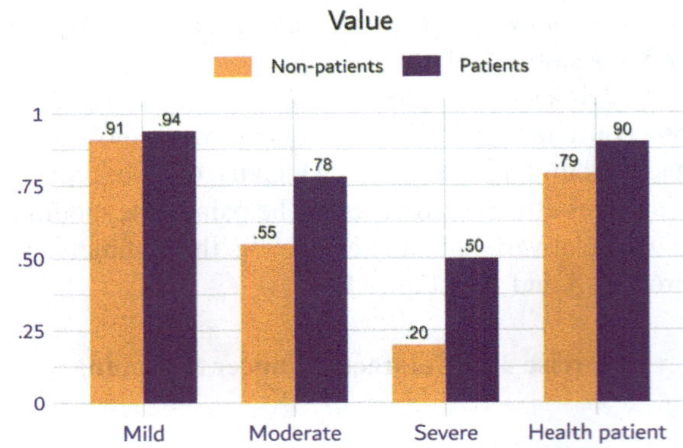

Fig. 4.2 Health state valuations for patients and non-patients. Data from de Wit et al. (2000)

4.1.2 Future Utility

People are bad at predicting future outcomes. They underestimate how quickly they adapt to substantial changes in circumstances. This is well-known in health valuation. Patients typically give a higher value to health states than non-patients. For example, Ardine de Wit et al. (2000) compared the values of dialysis patients and non-patients for four health states: a mild state, a moderate state, a severe state, and the health state of the dialysis patients. Figure 4.2 shows that the patients valued all health states higher. Because the valuation scale ranged from 0 to 1 and valuations for the mild state were close to 1 (a **ceiling effect**) the differences were small for the mild state. For the other states they were larger.

The difference raises a question for health policy: Whose values should we use? Those of the patients, because they know what it means to live in the health state, or those of the general population, because they pay for health care (most countries fund health care out of the public budget), they have a more disengaged view, and they may be future patients? The difference affects economic evaluations of health care. If we use patients' values then the benefit of treating a disease is lower than when we use non-patients' values. Most health economists recommend using the general population values. Do you agree?

Philip Brickman et al. (1978) found early evidence that people find it hard to predict future utility. They compared the reported happiness of 22 persons who had won large amounts in the Illinois State lottery (between $50,000 and $1 million in 1978 dollars which is between $240,000 and $4.8 million in 2025 dollars) with a control group and 29 accident victims who were either paraplegics (paralysed from the waist down) or quadraplegics (paralysed from the neck down).

Subjects reported their current and past[3] happiness on a scale from 0 ("not at all") to 5 ("very much"). Figure 4.3 shows that there was no difference in reported

[3] For the lottery winners past was before winning the lottery, for the accident victims it was before the accident, and for the controls it was 6 months ago.

Fig. 4.3 Reported happiness in Brickman et al. (1978)

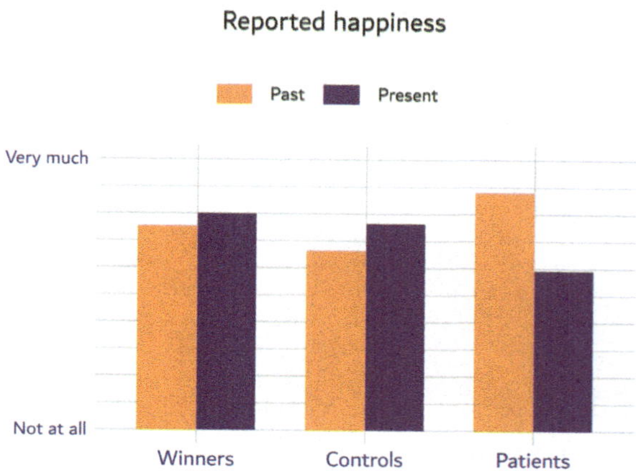

happiness[4] between lottery winners and controls. Moreover, lottery winners' past and current happiness did not differ. Winning the lottery had no effect on happiness.

The accident victims were less happy, but not much less than the lottery winners even though their health was seriously impaired. However, they rated their past happiness higher than the other groups (a "nostalgia effect").

Apparently, people adapt quickly even to life-changing events. Later research confirmed this using larger datasets and other events. Clark et al. (2008a) studied subjective well-being (SWB) over a period ranging from 4 years before until 5 years after an event in a German sample of 130,000 persons. Clark and Georgellis (2013) repeated their analysis using 120,000 persons in the British Household Panel Survey. Both studies showed adaptation to events like marriage, childbirth, divorce, and widowhood. See Fig. 4.4 for some examples. Figure 4.4a and b show that women adjusted to positive life-changing events like marriage and childbirth (the graphs for men are similar, but less pronounced). Figure 4.4c shows that they also adjusted to a negative event like the death of their partner.

Adaptation does not always occur. Figure 4.4d shows that men did not adapt to unemployment (for women the effect was less pronounced). People also do not adapt well to pain, disability, and poverty. Adaptation happens often, but not always.

Adaption is central in Scitovsky's (1976) *The Joyless Economy*. Scitovsky distinguishes between **comforts**, goods to which we adapt (consumption goods), and **pleasures**, goods to which we do not adapt (beautiful scenery or meeting friends). His advice is to spend your money on pleasures and avoid (as far as possible) comforts.

A reason why people are poor at predicting the future is that they exaggerate the degree to which their future and current tastes are the same. This is called **projection bias** (Loewenstein et al. 2003). People know that their future preferences will change, but they underestimate by how much.

---

[4] "No difference" means not statistically significant at the 5% level.

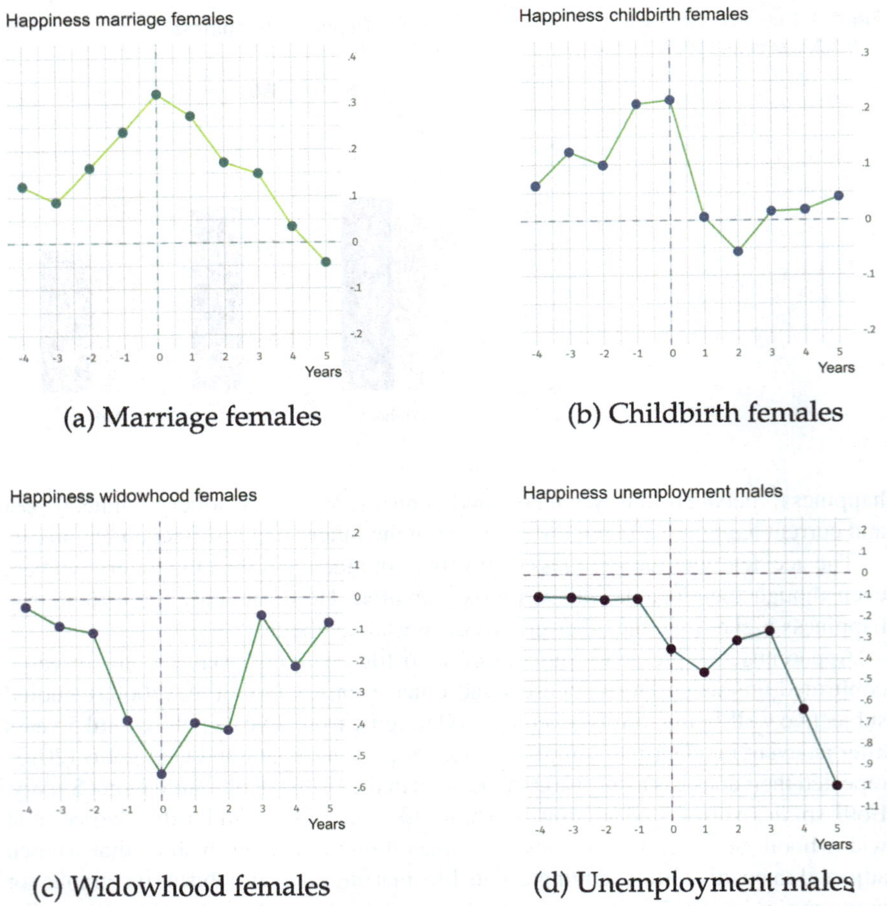

Fig. 4.4 Happiness over time in the data from Clark et al. (2008a)

An example is women giving childbirth. Jay Christensen-Szalanski (1984) studied the preferences of 18 pregnant women about getting anaesthesia during childbirth. One month before childbirth a majority of the women said they wanted no anaesthesia and they stuck to this preference during the early phases of delivery. However, during active labour they chose anaesthesia. One month after delivery, the women again said they would have preferred avoiding anaesthesia. Patients' values may not be representative of their long-term preferences and people make unreliable assessments of outcomes they never experienced. For more evidence of projection bias see Experiment 4.1.

Experiment 4.1: Projection Bias of Employees and Drug Users

Daniel Read and Barbara van Leeuwen (1998) studied the food choices of 200 employees. Their subjects chose between an unhealthy (chocolate bar or salty snack) and a healthy (apple or banana) snack one week before and at the moment of consumption. Read and van Leeuwen manipulated the hunger state of their participants by asking them to make the choices after lunch when they were satiated (state S) or late in the afternoon when they were hungry (state H).

Figure 4.5 shows their results. They support projection bias: 78% of the hungry subjects predicted that they would choose the unhealthy snack next week at the end of the afternoon. By contrast, only 56% of the satiated subjects predicted that they would choose the unhealthy snack next week at the end of the afternoon. Likewise, 42% of the hungry subjects predicted that they would choose the unhealthy snack next week after lunch, while 26% of the satiated subjects predicted that they would choose the unhealthy snack next week after lunch.

Subjects realized that their hunger state matters, but not enough. A difference remains between hungry subjects and satiated subjects. The figure also shows that all subjects actually chose the unhealthy snack more often than they predicted (like the women in Christen-Szalanski's study chose anaesthesia more often than expressed earlier). This discrepancy between plan and choice is called **dynamic consistency**. I return to it in Chapter 11.

Badger et al. (2007) found projection bias for 13 heroin addicts. The addicts chose between an extra shot of the heroin substitute Buprenorphine (BUP) and money. There were two treatments: now in which they got their chosen option immediately and delayed in which they got their chosen option in 5 days. The addicts chose both before (treatment deprived) and after (treatment satiated) having received a shot of BUP.[a]

When deprived, the addicts valued an extra shot of BUP at \$60, when satiated at \$35. As current craving is unrelated to craving in 5 days, this suggests that they underestimated their future craving. The addicts did not learn: the discrepancy remained when the choices were repeated.

[a] Although a single shot of BUP eliminates craving, a double shot produces a longer, more satisfying high.

Exercise 4.4: Cold-Weather Items

Michael Conlin et al. (2007) studied catalogue orders of cold-weather items. They found that a decline in the order date temperature of 30° Fahrenheit led to a 3.95% increase in the probability that an item would be returned at a later date. Explain that their data are consistent with projection bias.

Fig. 4.5 The results of Read and van Leeuwen (1998)

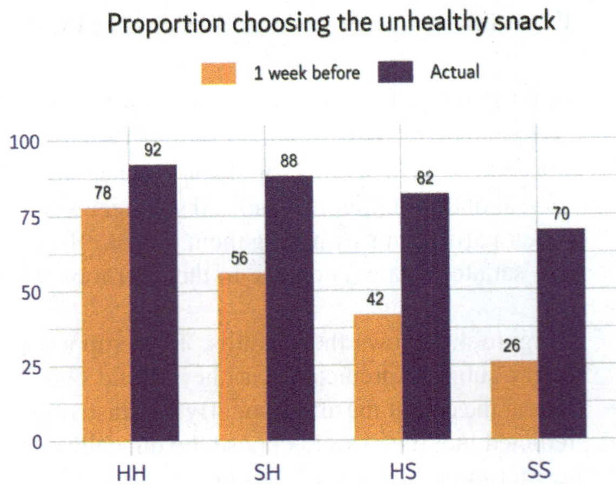

Exercise 4.5: Hungry Hikers

Leaf Van Boven and George Loewenstein (2003) asked their subjects to imagine a hiker who was lost in the forest without food and water. They asked them whether they thought the hiker would regret more not having carried food or water. Sixty-two per cent thought water. The subjects then had to run fast for 20 minutes on a treadmill. After that exercise they were asked again whether they thought the hiker would regret more not having carried food or water. Eighty-eight per cent now thought water. Explain that these findings are consistent with projection bias where we project our own preferences on those of others.

4.2 Happiness

Weighing the different notions of utility, Kahneman argues to use experienced utility in policy.[5] For example, Paul Dolan and Kahneman (2008) propose it for health policy, because it gives a more realistic measure of people's health. Existing methods such as the **standard gamble** and the **time trade-off** (see Example 4.1) reflect what people want at the time of the assessment, but not how they actually experience the

[5] Although in Kahneman and Sugden (2005) he seems more hesitant (p. 176) "The change [from using experienced instead of decision utility as the standard of policy evaluation] is so great that neither author is ready to advocate it unconditionally".

health states. Another advocate of using experienced utility in public policy is Raj Chetty (2015).

Example 4.1: Standard Gamble and Time Trade-Off

The standard gamble and time trade-off were proposed by the Canadian health economist George Torrance in the early 1970s (Torrance et al. 1972). They are widely used to measure quality of life. The standard gamble asks respondents to compare an impaired health state for sure, for example, living with migraine for the rest your life, with a treatment that gives a probability p of full health and a probability $1 - p$ of immediate death. The probability of full health is varied until a respondent is indifferent between the two options. The utility of the migraine is then set equal to the indifference probability p.

In the time trade-off respondents are asked to compare living for a given duration T in an impaired health state, like migraine, with living for $T_1 < T$ years in full health. The duration T_1 is varied until the respondent is indifferent and the utility of the impaired health state is then set equal to the ratio $^{T_1}/_{T}$

The standard gamble gives systematically higher utilities than the time trade-off when they are analysed under standard economic theories. This makes that policy recommendations depend on the method used. The solution (again) is to apply insights from behavioural economics, in particular prospect theory. See Bleichrodt (2002) and Stefan Lipman et al. (2019) for details.

In the 1970s, pioneers like Bernard van Praag and Richard Easterlin already used measures of experienced utility, like happiness and subjective well-being. Van Praag asked respondents to assign descriptions to income levels. For example, respondents said which income they found sufficient. The main determinant of sufficient income was current income, in line with adaptation.

Happiness data led to new insights and the study of questions that previously were thought to be beyond the realm of economics. An example is the Okun index, a crude measure of a country's economic health, that is used in macroeconomic policy. It is equal to the sum of unemployment and inflation and based on the Phillips curve which argues that there is a trade-off between inflation and unemployment. Happiness data challenge the Okun index (Di Tella et al. 2001; Blanchflower et al. 2014). Unemployment is twice as important for life satisfaction as inflation, calling for an adaptation of the Okun index.

Another example is inequality. Inequality is usually seen as bad and the more inequality the worse. Happiness research suggests that the relation between subjective well-being and income inequality is more complex (Clark and d'Ambrosio 2015). It depends on whether people had equal opportunities and whether it is due to own responsibility. Subjective well-being does not vary much with the Gini index, a common measure of income inequality.

The role of own responsibility is also important for inequalities in health. Marc Fleurbaey and Erik Schokkaert (2009) distinguish between legitimate and illegitimate inequalities. Legitimate inequalities are caused by factors that fall under the agent's own responsibility (like an unhealthy lifestyle). Illegitimate inequalities are caused by factors beyond the agent's responsibility (like genetic endowment). The view that legitimate inequalities are of no concern for policy is harsh. It deprives people of the right to make mistakes. Ethicists are reluctant to punish people for their past mistakes. For example, they resist proposals to let obese people pay more for their health insurance.

Exercise 4.6: BBQ-ers

What is your opinion about the role that legitimate inequalities should play a role in health policy? Should we let smokers or BBQ-ers pay more for their health insurance?

Finally, happiness data have been used to value goods that are not traded in markets. Examples are aircraft noise, green spaces, and informal care. To include these in cost-benefit analyses, we must put a money value on them. How can we do this if there is no market for these goods? We could ask people how much they are willing to pay, for example, to have a green space in their neighbourhood. Such measures are subject to biases, which make them unreliable. A solution is to use happiness measures. Using happiness to value non-market goods was already suggested by Bentham.

Take informal care (care given by family members or friends) as an illustration. Informal care is often ignored in economic evaluations although it is a substantial part of health care. Bernard van den Berg and Ada Ferrer-i-Carbonell (2007) tried to value informal care by estimating the trade-off between extra income and extra hours of informal care that would keep the subjective well-being (SWB) of caregivers constant (see Extension 4.1). Their analysis assumes that utility and subjective well-being are substitutes. Below, I will discuss whether this assumption is justified.

Extension 4.1: The Value of Informal Care

Assume that caregivers have a utility function U, which depends on income y, hours of informal care h, and other factors z:

$$U(y, h, z).$$

We are interested in the marginal rate of substitution $\frac{dy}{dh}$ between income and hours of informal care. Totally differentiating the utility function and setting the change in utility dU equal to 0 gives:

$$dU = \frac{\partial U}{\partial y}dy + \frac{\partial U}{\partial h}dh = 0.$$

From which it follows that

$$\frac{dy}{dh} = -\frac{\partial U/\partial h}{\partial U/\partial y}.$$

Because, U cannot be observed directly, Van den Berg and Ferrer-i Carbonell (2007) propose to use SWB (which can be measured) instead and regress SWB on income and hours of informal care. The regression coefficients of income and hours of informal care then estimate $\partial U/\partial y$ and $\partial U/\partial h$ and their ratio is an estimate of dy/dh.

4.3 Experienced Utility and Policy

Policy makers readily embraced happiness as an input for policy. Many countries collect data on happiness and some even set up ministries of happiness. An important stimulus was the **Easterlin paradox**, named after Richard Easterlin. The paradox is that while at a given point in time more income leads to more happiness, over time it does not. For example, income in Japan increased fivefold in the decades after the second world war, but reported happiness stayed the same.

Later research showed that more income gives some more happiness, but it confirmed that there is more to happiness than income alone. This made governments reconsider their focus on economic growth and increases in gross domestic product (GDP). Happiness research has highlighted the role of factors beyond the purely economical on subjective well-being. Immaterial concepts like trust, generosity, altruism, and social support especially promote well-being.

An explanation for Easterlin's paradox is that people care more about their relative income (their income compared to that of others) than about their absolute income. Bruno Frey and Alois Stutzer (2002) and Andrew Clark et al. (2008b) estimate that relative income contributes twice as much as absolute income to well-being. Relative evaluation is a key concept in behavioural economics. It underlies, for example, prospect theory (see Chapters 7 and 9).

Exercise 4.7: The Easterlin Paradox

Explain how a focus on relative income can explain the Easterlin paradox.

This raises a doubt. Many decision biases stem from the evaluation of outcomes as changes from a reference point. But if relative evaluations lead to inferior decisions and happiness data mainly reflect relative evaluations, should we use them as a basis for policy? In other words, is experienced utility not subject to the same biases as decision utility? There is evidence that mood affects experienced utility. People are happier on sunny days than on rainy days. Do we want such mood swings to be the basis of economic policy? There are 3 more problems with using experienced utility in policy.

1. Measuring experienced utility. Dolan and Kahneman (2008) argue to use the **day reconstruction method** in health state valuation. This method asks respondents to divide the previous day into a number of episodes and then to rate on a 0-6 scale the extent to which they experienced states like being happy, angry, worried, during those episodes. A limitation of this method is that people are bad at remembering the past.

It is also unclear how to construct a cardinal measure from this scale. Respondents rate several feelings, but we do not know how these should be traded off. Kahneman and Alan Krueger (2006) suggest to take either the average of the positive categories minus the average of the negative categories or the proportion of time in which the highest-rated feeling was a negative one. This proposal lacks a theoretical underpinning. We do not know whether it reflects people's preferences. Some attributes may be more important for well-being than others, but the measure does not reflect this.

Further, our day-to-day experiences are affected by emotions that, on hindsight, were not so important. Should policy be affected by such transitory emotions? The pregnant women in the study of Christensen-Szalanski (1984) probably would say no. Afterwards they preferred to have avoided anaesthesia. For them decision utility was the normative concept.

2. Adaptation. Another problem of using experienced utility is adaptation. Take the paralysed accident victims of Brickman et al. (1978). Their reported happiness was almost equal to that of the other subjects even though their health was seriously impaired. Basing health policy on their reported experienced utility would imply that treating them has little value: their well-being will hardly increase. However, if we asked paraplegics how serious their condition is, they would probably tell us "serious" and that treating them gives large benefits. Remember that they had a rosy view of their past happiness.

George Loewenstein and Peter Ubel (2008) found that colostomy patients, although reporting similar happiness as non-patients, would sacrifice up to 15% of their remaining life duration to live without colostomy. Using experienced utility in health policy would underestimate the seriousness of their disease and lead to a misallocation of resources.

Amartya Sen describes the case of Indian widows who are chronically malnourished and suffer from various illnesses, but report to be in good health. They are taught that they have no right to demand anything following the death of their husbands, so they believe their health problems are the normal way of affairs. Experienced utility says that alleviating their suffering gives no benefits.

Betsey Stevenson and Justin Wolfers (2009) found another conflict between objective and subjective data. Since the 1970s, the life of women in the US has objectively improved. The gender wage gap has decreased, educational attainment has improved, and women have more control over fertility. Nevertheless the subjective well-being of women has declined both absolutely and relative to men. In the 1970s women reported higher well-being than men. In the 2000s it was lower than that of men. This was true using various datasets and measures of well-being. Policy based on experienced utility would conclude that the objective advances of women were counterproductive. This seems wrong.

3. There is more to a good life than being happy. Proponents of experienced utility assume that people prefer what makes them most happy. In a triplet of papers, Dan Benjamin and co-authors (2012b, 2014a, 2014b) tested this. They gave their subjects the following two options: a (regular) job that pays $80,000 per year and allowed 7.5 hours of sleep on an average work night and a higher paid (irregular) job that pays $140,000 per year, but only allows 6 hours of sleep on an average work night: They then asked their subjects to choose between these options and to say which they thought would make them happier.

Money was more important for choice than for happiness. Happiness determined choice, but factors like purpose, the happiness of family members, health, security, and status also played a role. The more important decisions were, the less happiness played a role. This casts further doubt on experienced utility as the appropriate maximand. It also challenges the valuation of non-market goods using subjective well-being (see Extension 4.1) as utility and subjective well-being are imperfect substitutes.

Moreover, even if experienced utility were the appropriate maximand, we may question whether it is interpersonally comparable. Can we go all the way back to Bentham? When I was involved in a European project measuring inequalities in health (Van Doorslaer et al. 1997), we found that the Danes rated their health as worse than the Portuguese. By objective metrics, the health of Danes was at least as good as that of the Portuguese. Apparently, what people understand by good health varies, complicating interpersonal comparisons. Probably, a similar comparability problem holds for measures of SWB.

4.3.1 Nussbaum's Critique

There are also philosophical arguments against using experienced utility in policy. Although Kahneman et al. (1997) argue that they do not necessarily endorse "Bentham's view of pleasure and pain as the sovereign masters of human action", in later works (for example in Dolan and Kahneman 2008), Kahneman defends basing policy on measures of happiness. Martha Nussbaum, a leading philosopher, challenges this view (Nussbaum 2012).

The source of pleasure matters. Nussbaum raises three objections. First, she notes that Bentham's idea of pleasure as a single sensation that depends only on its intensity and duration is controversial.[6] For philosophers like Aristotle and John Stuart Mill pleasures cannot be defined independently of the activity that led to them. Mill, who writes about Bentham that he "failed in deriving light from other minds", distinguishes "higher" and "lower" pleasures. Examples of higher pleasures are music,

[6] According to Nussbaum (p. 336), Kahneman used an even simpler notion by ignoring duration in his focus on momentary experiences.

virtue, learning, and contemplation. For Mill, the source of pleasure matters, not only its intensity and duration.

Aristotle thought that activity was more important than pleasure. An action can be worthwhile, even if it does not lead to pleasure. This is called the **ethics of virtues**. It focuses on the kind of person we should be and less on the consequences of our actions, which is the focus of Bentham's utilitarianism. According to Aristotle, happiness is about flourishing as a human being. That is, living an active life that is full of intrinsically valuable activities. A necessary condition for a happy life is reflection. Without it happiness cannot exist. Hence, Mill's famous quote that it's better to be Socrates dissatisfied than a fool satisfied. According to the Roman stoic philosopher Seneca, born in Córdoba, there is nobody less fortunate than those about whom adversity forgets, because they do not have the opportunity to put themselves to the test.

Emotions are not just positive or negative. Nussbaum's second objection is that emotions are not simply positive or negative, as assumed in the day reconstruction method. Emotions depend on assessments of the world and they are only appropriate and valuable when these assessments are correct. Fear is a valuable emotion if my life is at stake, but not on a rollercoaster.

Correcting false assessments about the world is the essence of cognitive behavioural therapy, developed by Aaron Beck since the 1950s. Beck distinguished two types of thoughts: rational and automatic (an idea picked up later by Kahneman). Automatic thoughts often work well, for example, when I am driving my car and at the same time think about writing the next chapter of this book. But they also regularly go wrong, blocking more rational explanations. Then they lead to distorted thinking and emotions like anxiety and depression. Such emotions and distorted thoughts should be picked apart by asking questions in a Socratic manner. For example, to someone with vertigo he would ask "how likely is it that if you step on this high balcony, you will actually fall over the rail?" This way Beck managed to treat his own fear of blood. Simply pointing out the fact that he was still alive was sufficient. For Beck it was clear that emotions based on false assumptions about the world should be remedied. Experienced utility and the day reconstruction method do not distinguish between emotions based on correct or false assessments.

The distinction between positive and negative emotions is also problematic. Kahneman treats anger as a negative emotion (and it often is), but it can also be a force for social change. The anger caused by the death of George Floyd in 2020 due to police violence led to positive changes in racial attitudes.

There is no clear dichotomy between positive and negative emotions. Uncertainty brings both hope and fear and where there is love there will also be fear and anxiety. Caring about the world is impossible without the often painful feelings of compassion. In other words, separating emotions into positive and negative is too crude a distinction.

Maximizing pleasure may not be optimal. Nussbaum's third objection is that even if we could measure pleasure in Bentham's sense, maximizing it (and minimizing pain) may not be optimal. Again, it depends on the source of pleasure. Pleasures from "bad activities" should not be rewarded. Think about football hooligans enjoying acts of vandalism, racists enjoying their racism or sadists their sadism. Nobel laureate John Harsanyi, who supported utilitarianism, argued to restrict utilitarianism by excluding pleasures that result from actions that go against human dignity and equality. Harsanyi's restriction stems from Immanuel Kant's **ethics of duties**, universal principles and norms of conduct which our actions should satisfy.

In *The subjection of women*, an attack on the patriarchal society of his time, Mill makes a similar point. He notes that existing marriage laws, which allow men to subordinate their wives, undoubtedly bring great pleasure to many men. However, these pleasures, as they are unjust in nature, should play no role in the decision to abolish these laws and replace them by laws that ensure the equality between men and women. Mill lived by his word. When he married in 1851 Harriet Taylor, a philosopher herself who contributed to his *Principles of Political Economy* and *On Liberty*, the couple made an official statement that they would renounce from the abuse of power that the institute of marriage gave to the husband.

Similarly not all "pains" are necessarily bad. For example, developing compassion for others typically requires facing your own weaknesses and suffering. But a society without such compassion is hard and unforgiving against, for example, the poor.

Example 4.2: Beyond Utilitarianism in Health Policy

The common way to aggregate QALYs is by adding them. This is called **QALY utilitarianism**. QALY utilitarianism discriminates against those with poor health prospects (because they cannot gain many QALYs) and the elderly (whose remaining life duration is short). Health economists have sought to address this. The Norwegian health economist Erik Nord suggested to weight people by their health status so that those in worse health get more priority (Nord 1993). The British health economist Alan Williams advocated that everyone has a right to **fair innings** of health, for example, 70 years in good health, and that the weight given to people should depend on how far off they are from their fair innings (Williams 1997). Elly Stolk and co-authors (2004) suggest to give people different weights depending on the proportion of their remaining expected QALYs that they lose as a result of illness.

These proposals are a form of weighted utilitarianism. The Scottish health economist Gavin Mooney (1998) proposed a more drastic departure. He argues that the process patients go through during treatment is relevant. Aspects like being cared for and having one's dignity and autonomy respected should be taken into account in policy decisions. This reflects the distinction between a purely utilitarian ethics and Kant's ethics of duties.

Happiness data are useful. They have led to the insight that there is more to well-being than just income and growth and that happiness has economic consequences. Happier people are more productive and have higher future earnings and better health. Moreover, life satisfaction better predicts support for the incumbent government than economic factors like growth, unemployment, and inflation.

The choice between decision and experienced utility boils down to the question of whose values should count. Nobel laureate Thomas Schelling (1984) claims that the history of an individual can be seen as a succession of different selves (an idea adopted in many behavioural economic models). The question then is to which self should we give priority? Kahneman, especially in his later works, seemed to argue in favour of the current self.[7] Christensen-Szalansky in his study of pregnant women on the other hand seemed to consider the choice for anaesthesia at the moment of labour as an infringement of the women's long-term values. I believe Nussbaum is closer to Christensen-Szalansky than to Kahneman. What is beyond doubt is that Kahneman's work on happiness has led to a reconsideration of the concept of utility and to new insights on what utility is and how to interpret it.

4.4 Diagnostic Utility

I end the history of utility and how behavioural economics fits into it with diagnostic utility, a model that shows that choice may not reveal true preferences. Diagnostic utility combines insights from economics, psychology, and philosophy. It was developed by Drazen Prelec in a series of articles. Its motivation is an experiment by George Quattrone and Amos Tversky (1984) described in Experiment 4.2.

Experiment 4.2: Self-Signalling in Quattrone and Tversky (1984)

The experiment had several parts. First, subjects were asked to immerse their arm in a bucket with cold water as long as they could. The average was around 40 seconds. Subjects were then told that recent medical research had discovered an inborn heart condition. People with this condition are frequently ill, prone to heart disease, and have shorter than average life expectancy. Disposition to this heart condition could be diagnosed by the effect of exercise on the cold water test they just performed. Subjects were randomly divided into two groups. One group was told that people who are likely to develop the disease (the bad type) are more tolerant to cold water after exercise. The other group was told the opposite: cold water tolerance decreases after exercise for the bad type.

Subjects then rode an exercise bike for a minute and repeated the cold water test. The majority of subjects (27 out of 38) behaved in the direction of good news. Those who were told that exercise improved cold water endurance for the bad type withdrew their hand quicker than before (on average 8 seconds). Those who were told the opposite kept their hand longer in the water than before (on average 12 seconds). Subjects were willing to suffer more pain to

[7] Although he wrote "I am my remembering self, and the experiencing self, who does my living, is like a stranger to me".

receive a good signal. Only 9 subjects admitted that they had purposefully tried to alter the time they kept their hand in the water after exercise.

Quattrone and Tversky's subjects tried to derive information about themselves from their choices. This is called **self-signalling**. Agents are unsure about their type and by choosing a given action they reveal information about their type even when these actions give no direct benefits in outcomes. Examples are following a diet or a training regime and facing the temptation to eat a chocolate or skip a training session due to bad weather. Both are attractive and do not affect the likelihood of achieving the goal. The agents nevertheless resist the temptation. They are unsure about their type (their willpower to follow the diet or training) and by resisting the temptation they signal to themselves that they are disciplined.

Prelec (2013) gives the example of calvinism. According to seventeenth-century calvinism, people were predestined at birth whether or not they go to heaven. Their actual deeds on earth had no impact (see Bio 4.1). But if actual behaviour has no effect, calvinists might as well indulge in the pleasures of life. However, they were known for their sober style of living. An explanation is that by living soberly and working hard, they gave themselves a signal that they are probably predestined.

Bio 4.1: Gomarus and Arminius

In the Dutch Republic, there was a theological debate in the early seventeenth century between Franciscus Gomarus, who believed in predestination, and Jacobus Arminius, who did not. It led to a conflict between Maurits, the prince of Orange and stadtholder, who sided with Gomarus and the land's advocate Johan van Oldenbarnevelt, who supported Arminius. Maurits won and van Oldenbarnevelt was beheaded in The Hague on 13 May 1619.

Ronit Bodner and Prelec (2003) formalize these intuitions. In their model, self-signalling agents take account of:

1. their outcome utility $u(x, \theta)$, the utility derived from an outcome which may depend on the (unknown) type θ.
2. their probability distribution over types $f(\theta)$ that reflects how likely they think to be a specific type.
3. a utility function $V(\theta)$ over types, that reflects how attractive they find a type.

Let $C = \{x, y, z, ...\}$ be the agent's set of options. The utility from choosing action x from choice set C is the sum of **outcome utility**, and **diagnostic utility**, the utility of what choice reveals about their type:

$$U(x, C, \theta) = \underbrace{u(x, \theta)}_{\text{outcome utility}} + \underbrace{\sum_{\theta} f(\theta|x, C)V(\theta)}_{\text{diagnostic utility}}. \tag{4.1}$$

As an example, take Quattrone and Tversky's subjects. Let x be the time subjects hold their hand in the water. There are two types: bad and good. Subjects hope to be of the good type, but they are not sure. They have a probability distribution $f(\theta)$ over the two types, where $f(\theta^b)$ is the subjects' probability that they are of the bad type and $f(\theta^g)$ their probability that they are of a good type.

Suppose the subject is of the group who was told that exercise reduces cold water tolerance for the bad types. Let x^1 be the time they held their hand in the water in the first part. After this time, holding their hand longer in the water hurts and gives negative outcome utility. However, it also reduces the probability that the subject is of the bad type: $f(\theta^b \mid x)$ falls with x. So if subjects find the bad type sufficiently unattractive ($V(\theta^G)$ is sufficiently larger than $V(\theta^b)$) then choosing x^1 is not optimal. The subjects will immerse their hand longer than x^1.

Exercise 4.8: Ramadan Fasting

The length of daily fasting during the Ramadan depends on the interaction between the rotating Islamic calendar and a country's latitude. Felipe Campante and David Yanagizawa-Drott (2015) found that longer Ramadan fasting had a negative effect on output growth in Muslim countries, but increased subjective well-being among Muslims. Explain these findings using diagnostic utility.

Bodner and Prelec's diagnostic utility model is part of a string of models based on the idea that there are two selves that compete with each other. In diagnostic utility, the competition takes place at the same point in time between the self that focuses on outcome utility and the self that focuses on diagnostic utility. In the ego utility model of Köszegi (2006) and the model of motivated beliefs of Bénabou and Tirole (2016) (see Chapter 8) the selves deceive each other over time. The models vary in the form of the second term in Eq. 4.1. For example, Köszegi (2006) takes a general utility function $u\big(f(\theta)\big)$ over the distribution of types.

Diagnostic utility implies that choices may not reveal true preferences. Revealed preference may reveal less than we would like. It raises doubts about measures of preferences, especially for sensitive issues. Katherine Coffman et al. (2017) find underreporting of antigay sentiments and of the size of the lesbian, gay, bisexual, and transgender (LGBT) population. They asked people directly and in a veiled way about their attitudes regarding LGBT issues (see Experiment 4.3). When asked directly, 16% of the subjects said they would not be happy to have an openly LGBT manager at work. In the veiled method, 27% said so. Likewise, when asked directly 11% said they did not consider themselves heterosexual. With the veiled method this increased to 19%.

Experiment 4.3: The Item Count Technique

The **item count technique** aims to reduce socially desirable answers. There are two groups of subjects, the direct group and the veiled group, and a common set of N questions. These are usually not sensitive and are like "I remember where I was when Spain won the European championship football", "I spent a lot of time playing video games as a kid", "I support legalizing marijuana", and "I have voted for a right-wing party". The questions are negatively correlated so that subjects do not answer "yes" or "no" to all questions (for example, most people who support legalizing marijuana do not vote for right-wing parties).

The direct groups report the number Y^d of the N statements to which they answered "yes". Then they answer the sensitive question, for example, "Would you be happy to have an openly lesbian, gay, or bisexual manager at work?" Let d be the response to this question. It is 1 if the subject answers "yes" and 0 if the subject answers "no".

In the veiled group the sensitive question is added to the N statements. So subjects face $N + 1$ items and report to how many they answered "yes". Denote this by Y^v. Consequently, in the veiled group we cannot directly observe subjects' answers to the sensitive question.

Exercise 4.9: Item Count Technique

Argue that if subjects are reluctant to answer honestly to sensitive questions, the mean of $Y^d + d$ will exceed the mean of Y^v when the socially desirable answer is "yes" and it will be less than the mean of Y^v when the socially desirable answer is "no".

Because people are reluctant to report behaviour that violates social norms, Galesic et al. (2021) suggest to ask people what they think someone in their social circle would respond. This may reduce the diagnostic utility component in preference measurement. Psychological research has shown that asking people about others leads to better predictions than self-predictions. Wändi Bruine de Bruin and co-authors (2022) show that it improves election predictions. Sonja Radas and Prelec (2019) show that it can identify subjects who give reliable answers to survey questions.

Extension 4.2: Bayesian Truth Serum

Prelec's (2004) **Bayesian truth serum** (BTS), which incentivizes subjects to respond truthfully to questions which answer cannot be verified, used predictions about the answers of others. Suppose that there are 2 types of people. For example, those who are fine with an LGBT manager and those who are not. The BTS assumes that subjects have the same probability distribution about how likely these types are.

Consider subjects who are fine with an LGBT manager. They have one data point (their own opinion) and will update their prediction of the proportion of subjects that are fine with an LGBT manager to take this into account. So these subjects think that the proportion of subjects that are fine with an LGBT manager will be higher than others think. In other words, their answer is "surprisingly common". The BTS pays subjects if their answer is surprisingly common so it is in their best interest to answer truthfully.

Exercise 4.10: BTS

Explain that people who are not fine with an LGBT manager will also believe their answer is surprisingly common and, thus, also have an incentive to answer truthfully.

4.4.1 Self-Deception

Diagnostic utility is close to **self-deception**. Self-deception has been discussed widely and its origins date back to Aristotle and St. Augustine. It underlies much of our understanding of human character. It plays a central role in marxism, psychoanalysis, and atheism, which all aim to cure people from what they believe is self-deception.

Danica Mijović-Prelec and Prelec (2010) model self deception assuming that people have three beliefs:

1. **deep beliefs**. These are largely inaccessible. For example, my deep belief is that I lack self-discipline.
2. **stated beliefs**. These are the beliefs people express.
3. **experienced beliefs**. These determine the emotional state following the statement of beliefs.

Agents deceive themselves when their stated beliefs differ from their deep beliefs. Self-deception is successful when experienced beliefs match stated beliefs. In other words, when stated beliefs sound convincing.

Some authors claim that self-deception is a bias like any other. People rate themselves as superior on most desirable characteristics. However, we can explain this bias by ignoring evidence to the contrary. It need not reflect self-deception.

What makes self-deception distinct is that it evokes strong emotions when challenged. This may indicate that deep down, agents know that their stated beliefs are untrue. Moreover, if self-deception is a bias how can it sometimes fail? If it is just a bias wouldn't agents always be able to convince themselves? However, if their deep beliefs are strong enough, their stated belief will ring hollow and the discrepancy between experienced and stated belief will make that self-deception fails.

In Quattrone and Tversky's experiment, deep down their subjects knew that their water tolerance had not changed. They acted in the desired direction to deceive themselves that they do not have the heart condition. Whether they succeed depends on the extent to which they are convinced that their water tolerance has indeed changed. In the debriefing after the experiment, several students told Quattorne and Tversky that they had tried to manipulate the test and were pessimistic about their heart condition. For them, self-deception had not functioned. For another experiment where subjects deceived themselves see Experiment 4.4.

Experiment 4.4: Guessing the Gender of Korean Letters

Mijović-Prelec and Prelec (2010) asked subjects to guess the gender of 100 Korean characters (male or female). Korean characters do not have a gender, but subjects did not know this (they excluded subjects who knew Korean). The majority view in a group of previously tested subjects determined the correct answer for each character. Subjects were paid for their number of correct answers.

In the second part of the experiment, subjects faced the same set of characters (although their order was changed). They again classified them as male or female. In addition, they predicted what the sign of the next displayed character would be. They were paid for correct answers and predictions.

Suppose that a subject said in the first part that a character is male, but that in the second part before it shows up had predicted that the next character would be female. Self-deception occurs if the subject now states that it is female. Mijović and Prelec found that this occurred for 20–25% of the choices (depending on financial incentives) and for 27 to 75% of the subjects (depending on incentives and the level of statistical significance used).

Exercise 4.11: Exercise

Let MFF stand for "the subject said the character was male in the first part, predicted that it would be female in the second part and then stated that it was female". Explain that this reflects self-deception. How would you describe the pattern MMF? Explain that self-deception means that the patterns MFF and FMM are more common than the patterns MMF and FFM.

References

Badger, G.J., W.K. Bickel, L.A. Giordano, E.A. Jacobs, G. Loewenstein, and L. Marsch. 2007. Altered states: The impact of immediate craving on the valuation of current and future opioids. *Journal of Health Economics* 26: 865–876.

Bénabou and Tirole. 2016. Mindful economics: The production, consumption, and value of beliefs. *Journal of Economic Perspectives* 30: 141–164.

Benjamin, D.J., O. Heffetz, M.S. Kimball, and A. Rees-Jones. 2012. What do you think would make you happier? What do you think you would choose? *American Economic Review* 102: 2083–2110.

Benjamin, D.J., O. Heffetz, M.S. Kimball, and A. Rees-Jones. 2014a. Can marginal rates of substitution be inferred from happiness data? Evidence from residency choices. *American Economic Review* 104: 3498–3528.

Benjamin, D.J., O. Heffetz, M.S. Kimball, and N. Szembrot. 2014b. Beyond happiness and satisfaction: Toward well-being indices based on stated preference. *American Economic Review* 104: 2698–2735.

Blanchflower, D.G., D.N. Bell, A. Montagnoli, and M. Moro. 2014. The happiness trade-off between unemployment and inflation. *Journal of Money, Credit and Banking* 46: 117–141.

Bleichrodt,. 2002. A new explanation for the difference between time trade-off utilities and standard gamble utilities. *Health Economics* 11: 447–456.

Bodner, R., and D. Prelec. 2003. The diagnostic value of actions in a self-signaling model. In *The psychology of economic decisions*, ed. I. Brocas and J.D. Carrillo, 105–123. USA: Oxford University Press.

Brickman, P., D. Coates, and R. Janoff-Bulman. 1978. Lottery winners and accident victims: Is happiness relative? *Journal of Personality and Social Psychology* 36: 917–927.

Bruine de Bruin, W., M. Galesic, R. Bååth, J. De Bresser, L. Hall, P. Johansson, T. Strandberg, and A. Van Soest. 2022. Asking about social circles improves election predictions even with many political parties. *International Journal of Public Opinion Research* 34: 1–11.

Campante, F., and D. Yanagizawa-Drott. 2015. Does religion affect economic growth and happiness? Evidence from Ramadan. *Quarterly Journal of Economics* 130: 615–658.

Chetty, R. 2015. Behavioral economics and public policy: A pragmatic perspective. *American Economic Review* 105: 1–33.

Christensen-Szalanski, J.J. 1984. Discount functions and the measurement of patients' values: Women's decisions during childbirth. *Medical Decision Making* 4: 47–58.

Clark, A.E., and C. d'Ambrosio. 2015. Attitudes to income inequality: Experimental and survey evidence. In *Handbook of income distribution*, vol. 2, 1147–1208. Elsevier.

Clark, A.E., and Y. Georgellis. 2013. Back to baseline in Britain: Adaptation in the British household panel survey. *Economica* 80: 496–512.

Clark, A.E., E. Diener, Y. Georgellis, and R.E. Lucas. 2008a. Lags and leads in life satisfaction: A test of the baseline hypothesis. *Economic Journal* 118: F222–F243.

Clark, A.E., P. Frijters, and M.A. Shields. 2008b. Relative income, happiness, and utility: An explanation for the Easterlin paradox and other puzzles. *Journal of Economic Literature* 46: 95–144.

Coffman, K.B., L.C. Coffman, and K.M.M. Ericson. 2017. The size of the LGBT population and the magnitude of antigay sentiment are substantially underestimated. *Management Science* 63: 3168–3186.

Conlin, M., T. O'Donoghue, and T.J. Vogelsang. 2007. Projection bias in catalog orders. *American Economic Review* 97: 1217–1249.

De Wit, G.A., J.J. Busschbach, and F.T. De Charro. 2000. Sensitivity and perspective in the valuation of health status: Whose values count? *Health Economics* 9: 109–126.

Di Tella, R., R.J. MacCulloch, and A.J. Oswald. 2001. Preferences over inflation and unemployment: Evidence from surveys of happiness. *American Economic Review* 91: 335–341.

Dolan, P., and D. Kahneman. 2008. Interpretations of utility and their implications for the valuation of health. *Economic Journal* 118: 215–234.

Fleurbaey, M., and E. Schokkaert. 2009. Unfair inequalities in health and health care. *Journal of Health Economics* 28: 73–90.

Frey, B.S., and A. Stutzer. 2002. What can economists learn from happiness research? *Journal of Economic Literature* 40: 402–435.

Galesic, M., W. Bruine de Bruin, J. Dalege, S.L. Feld, F. Kreuter, H. Olsson, D. Prelec, D.L. Stein, and T. van Der Does. 2021. Human social sensing is an untapped resource for computational social science. *Nature* 595: 214–222.

Kahneman, D. 1994. New challenges to the rationality assumption. *Journal of Institutional and Theoretical Economics (JITE)/Zeitschrift für die gesamte Staatswissenschaft* 150: 18–36.

Kahneman, D., and A.B. Krueger. 2006. Developments in the measurement of subjective well-being. *Journal of Economic Perspectives* 20: 3–24.

Kahneman, D., and R. Sugden. 2005. Experienced utility as a standard of policy evaluation. *Environmental and Resource Economics* 32: 161–181.

Kahneman, D., P.P. Wakker, and R. Sarin. 1997. Back to Bentham? Explorations of experienced utility. *Quarterly Journal of Economics* 112: 375–406.

Köszegi, B. 2006. Ego utility, overconfidence, and task choice. *Journal of the European Economic Association* 4: 673–707.

Lipman, S.A., W.B. Brouwer, and A.E. Attema. 2019. QALYs without bias? Nonparametric correction of time trade-off and standard gamble weights based on prospect theory. *Health Economics* 28: 843–854.

Loewenstein, G., T. O'Donoghue, and M. Rabin. 2003. Projection bias in predicting future utility. *The Quarterly Journal of Economics* 118: 1209–1248.

Loewenstein, G., and P.A. Ubel. 2008. Hedonic adaptation and the role of decision and experience utility in public policy. *Journal of Public Economics* 92: 1795–1810.

Mijović-Prelec, D., and D. Prelec. 2010. Self-deception as self-signalling: A model and experimental evidence. *Philosophical Transactions of the Royal Society B: Biological Sciences* 365: 227–240.

Mooney, G. 1998. Beyond health outcomes: The benefits of health care. *Health Care Analysis* 6: 99–105.

Nord, E. 1993. The trade-off between severity of illness and treatment effect in cost-value analysis of health care. *Health Policy* 24: 227–238.

Nussbaum, M.C. 2012. Who is the happy warrior? Philosophy, happiness research, and public policy. *International Review of Economics* 59: 335–361.

Prelec, D. 2004. A Bayesian truth serum for subjective data. *Science* 306: 462–466.

Prelec, D. 2013. Decision Analysis from a Neo-Calvinist point of view. In *Behavioural public policy*, ed. by A. Oliver, 216–233. Cambridge University Press.

Quattrone, G.A., and A. Tversky. 1984. Causal versus diagnostic contingencies: On self-deception and on the voter's illusion. *Journal of Personality and Social Psychology* 46: 237–248.

Radas, S., and D. Prelec. 2019. Whose data can we trust: How meta-predictions can be used to uncover credible respondents in survey data. *PloS One* 14: e0225432.

Read, D., and B. Van Leeuwen. 1998. Predicting hunger: The effects of appetite and delay on choice. *Organizational Behavior and Human Decision Processes* 76: 189–205.

Redelmeier, D.A., J. Katz, and D. Kahneman. 2003. Memories of colonoscopy: A randomized trial. *Pain* 104: 187–194.

Schelling, Thomas. 1984. *Choice and consequence*. Cambridge: Harvard University Press.

Scitovsky, T. 1976. *The joyless economy: An inquiry into human satisfaction and consumer dissatisfaction.* Oxford: Oxford University Press.

Sen. 1993. Internal consistency of choice. *Econometrica* 61: 495–521.

Stevenson, B., and J. Wolfers. 2009. The paradox of declining female happiness. *American Economic Journal: Economic Policy* 1: 190–225.

Stolk, E.A., G. van Donselaar, W.B. Brouwer, and J.J. Busschbach. 2004. Reconciliation of economic concerns and health policy: Illustration of an equity adjustment procedure using proportional shortfall. *Pharmacoeconomics* 22: 1097–1107.

Torrance, G.W., W.H. Thomas, and D.L. Sackett. 1972. A utility maximization model for evaluation of health care programs. *Health Services Research* 7: 118–133.

Van Boven, L., and G. Loewenstein. 2003. Social projection of transient drive states. *Personality and Social Psychology Bulletin* 29: 1159–1168.

Van den Berg, B., and A. Ferrer-i Carbonell. 2007. Monetary valuation of informal care: The well-being valuation method. *Health Economics* 16: 1227–1244.

Van Doorslaer, E., A. Wagstaff, H. Bleichrodt, S. Calonge, U.-G. Gerdtham, M. Gerfin, J. Geurts, L. Gross, U. Häkkinen, R.E. Leu, et al. 1997. Income-related inequalities in health: Some international comparisons. *Journal of Health Economics* 16: 93–112.

Williams, A. 1997. Intergenerational equity: An exploration of the 'fair innings' argument. *Health Economics* 6: 117–132.

The Methods of Behavioural Economics Part 1

5

Experiments, Field Studies, and International Comparisons

In the previous chapters I discussed experiments as inspiration and testing ground for behavioural economic theories. Experiments are the main source of data for behavioural economics, but not the only one. Moreover, their design has evolved over the past decades. In this chapter and the next, I give an overview of the methods used by behavioural economists. They are a smorgasboard of topics related to the collection, analysis, and interpretation of data. Let's start with the main source, experiments.[1]

5.1 Experiments

In the early days of behavioural economics, experiments were typically performed during lectures and using hypothetical questions. How the data were collected was of little concern. The classical papers Kahneman and Tversky (1979) and Thaler (1981) do not even mention how the data were collected. There were exceptions like Grether and Plott (1979), discussed in Chapter 2, but the above fast and furious way of collecting data was common practice during the first ten years of behavioural economics.

That changed in the 1990s. Professional labs emerged in which experiments were run in a more controlled setting. The rise of the computer made it possible to move away from pen and paper experiments. This had several advantages:

[1] For an extensive outline of the use and design of experiments in economics see Nicolas Jacquemet and Olivier L'Haridon (2018).

H. Bleichrodt, *Behavioural Economics*,
https://doi.org/10.1007/978-3-031-69166-9_5

1. The computer could use earlier answers in later questions. This made it possible to elicit responses and measure model parameters more efficiently.
2. It became easier to check for data quality, for example, by repeating questions.
3. It became easier to randomize questions. The order in which questions are asked can affect people's preferences. With paper questionnaires it is more complex to randomize the question order and often only few different orders were used. The computer made randomization easier and more complete.

5.1.1 The Use of Incentives

Another change was the increased use of real incentives. Subjects got paid based on their choices. Many experimental economists believe that incentives are important and that we cannot trust subjects' responses to hypothetical questions. To defend this belief they often quote a study by Charles Holt and Susan Laury (2002).

Holt and Laury asked their subjects to choose between a safer and a riskier prospect where they varied the probability of winning.[2] Table 5.1 gives an example where the safe prospect (option A) gives a chance p of \$2.00 and a chance $1 - p$ of \$1.60 and the risky prospect (option B) gives a chance p of \$3.85 and a chance $1 - p$ of \$0.10. The probability p increases from 10% in steps of 10% until 100%. As p increases, B becomes more attractive compared with A. For low p, A is more attractive, but for $p = 100\%$ B gives \$3.85 for sure and A \$2.00. There will be a p for which subjects switch from A to B. This p is a measure of subjects' risk attitudes. The higher it is, the more risk averse is the subject.

Holt and Laury used different stake sizes. Table 5.1 is an example of their low stakes treatment. They also had treatments in which all money amounts were multiplied by 20, 50, and 90.[3] So in the 90 treatment, A was a p chance of \$180 and a $1 - p$ chance of \$144 and B a p chance of \$346.50 and a $1 - p$ chance of \$9. Agents usually become more risk averse if the stake sizes are multiplied. This is called **increasing relative risk aversion**. An early study that found it in a sample of Indian farmers with real payoffs exceeding their monthly income was by Hans Binswanger (1980).

Holt and Laury asked both hypothetical and real questions. In the real questions subjects played out one of their randomly selected choices for real. Suppose that in Table 5.1, the choice with $p = 50\%$ had been selected to be played out for real and a subject had chosen A. Then the prospect 50% chance of \$2 and 50% chance of \$1.60 was played out for real where the risk was resolved by throwing a ten-sided die.

Figure 5.1 shows the average number of times the safe lottery was chosen in the treatments. The figure suggests a difference between the hypothetical and the real treatment. In the real treatment risk aversion (the number of times the safe

[2] Their method is often called the Holt Laury method, even though it had been used before, for example, by Michele Cohen et al. (1987).

[3] Subjects faced only one of these higher stakes treatments. Most (175) faced the 20 treatment. 19 faced the 50 treatment and 18 the 90 treatment.

Table 5.1 A choice list used by Holt & Laury

Option A	Option B	Choice
1/10 of \$2.00, 9/10 of \$1.60	1/10 of \$3.85, 9/10 of \$0.10	
2/10 of \$2.00, 8/10 of \$1.60	2/10 of \$3.85, 8/10 of \$0.10	
3/10 of \$2.00, 7/10 of \$1.60	3/10 of \$3.85, 7/10 of \$0.10	
4/10 of \$2.00, 6/10 of \$1.60	4/10 of \$3.85, 6/10 of \$0.10	
5/10 of \$2.00, 5/10 of \$1.60	5/10 of \$3.85, 5/10 of \$0.10	
6/10 of \$2.00, 4/10 of \$1.60	6/10 of \$3.85, 4/10 of \$0.10	
7/10 of \$2.00, 3/10 of \$1.60	7/10 of \$3.85, 3/10 of \$0.10	
8/10 of \$2.00, 2/10 of \$1.60	8/10 of \$3.85, 2/10 of \$0.10	
9/10 of \$2.00, 1/10 of \$1.60	9/10 of \$3.85, 1/10 of \$0.10	
10/10 of \$2.00, 0/10 of \$1.60	10/10 of \$3.85, 0/10 of \$0.10	

Fig. 5.1 Holt and Laury's results

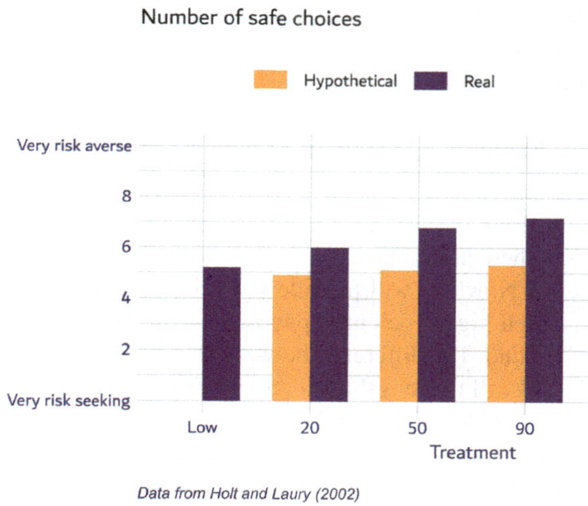

lottery was chosen), increased with stake size (consistent with increasing relative risk aversion), but in the hypothetical treatment it did not. For the 50 and 90 treatments the evidence is only tentative, because there were few subjects in these treatments. The most convincing evidence comes from comparing the low real treatment with the 20 hypothetical and 20 real treatments.[4]

A problem is that Holt and Laury asked the questions in a fixed order: first low real, then the three hypothetical treatments in the order 20-50-90, then the three real treatments in the order 20-50-90, and finally they repeated the low real treatment. This may have led to order effects. Psychologists emphasize **preference construction**: people's preferences are only rudimentary and they construct them during the

[4] Holt and Laury did not have a low hypothetical treatment.

experimental tasks (Slovic 1995). The order of the tasks may impact the construction process.

Glenn Harrison and co-authors (2005) found that Holt and Laury's results were indeed affected by an order effect. The stake effect halved when they controlled for the order effect. Harrison et al. (2005) did not test whether the difference between hypothetical and real questions was also reduced by controlling for the order effect. Holt and Laury (2005) did test this and found that it was robust: They still found a difference between real and hypothetical for high stakes, but not for low stakes.

Does this settle the issue? I do not think so. The main problem with Holt and Laury's study is their wording of the hypothetical questions. The hypothetical questions are part of a larger experiment in which some of the questions are for real. Holt and Laury go at great lengths to emphasize this in their instructions (see Example 5.1). They read like "do not worry too much about these questions as they will not be played out for real. The other ones are the ones that really count". It's no surprise that responses differ if the difference between the questions is stressed so much. A cleaner test would have compared a treatment with only hypothetical questions with a treatment with only real questions. I do not find Holt & Laury's findings convincing enough to discard hypothetical incentives.

Example 5.1: Holt and Laury's Instructions

Holt and Laury gave their subjects the following instruction before their hypothetical treatments:

"Now, we will provide you with the chance to make another choice, with much higher potential payoffs, as you can see from the sheet we are passing around. The difference between this part and all other decisions you have made and will make is that all payoffs from this round are hypothetical and will not be paid to you. Even though the earnings from this next choice larger, they are only hypothetical, and we would like for you to initial the statement at the top of the page indicating that you understand you will not be paid for the choice on that page. All other choices tonight will count towards your earnings. Let me reiterate that your choice in this part has no effect on your earnings and has no effect on what choices will be given to you subsequently; but we are interested in what you would do if you actually faced these choices, so please think about them carefully".

5.1.2 More Evidence on Incentives

Whether incentives matter in experiments had been studied before. Early reviews are by Vernon Smith and James Walker (1993) and by John Kagel and Alvin Roth (1995). These conclude that incentives have little effect and mainly reduce decision noise.

Jane Beattie and Graham Loomes (1997) compared three treatments: hypothetical, where subjects only received a show-up fee, real, in which subjects answered just one question for real, and a treatment, in which subjects answered several questions and one was randomly selected to be played out for real. This **random problem selection procedure** (RPSP) is often used to incentivize experiments and was also used by Holt and Laury. Beattie and Loomes (1997) found no difference between the three treatments. The only exception was in a more complex dynamic task.

Colin Camerer and Robin Hogarth (1999) reviewed 74 articles from four of the best economics journals. Incentives affected judgement tasks like memory or recall and socially desirable answers like the degree of altruism and cooperation. For other tasks they made little difference, except that they reduced noise. There was no study that rejected a rational economic theory at no or low stakes, but accepted it at higher stakes. The findings from behavioural economics are robust to using incentives.

Ralph Hertwig and Andreas Ortmann (2001) reviewed 10 psychological studies published in the Journal of Behavioral Decision Making. Most of these studies are about judgement tasks.[5] Like Camerer and Hogarth they find that incentives help in judgement tasks and reduce data variability. However, their sample of studies is small and the judgement tasks they study are rarely used in behavioural economics.

A key insight of behavioural economics is that people treat gains and losses differently. It is hard to incentivize losses. It is undesirable that subjects in an experiment really lose money. Often subjects receive an endowment from which they can cover any losses they make. However, this endowment can change subjects' preferences, because they do not see the "covered" losses as real. Richard Thaler and Eric Johnson (1990) found such a **house money effect**: giving subjects an initial endowment makes them more risk loving.

Nathalie Etchart and Olivier L'Haridon (2011) tested the effect of incentives for losses. They had three treatments: one purely hypothetical, one with an initial endowment that covered subjects' losses, and one with real losses in which subjects could lose up to €20.[6] Subjects participated in all three treatments, which were separated by 15 days to counter recall bias. The three treatments gave the same results. Incentives did not matter. That the endowment treatment did not differ from the hypothetical and real treatments contradicts the house money effect. Etchart and L'Haridon also compared hypothetical and real gains and found that they were similar.

Andreas Hackethal and co-authors (2023) studied the effect of incentives on four methods to elicit risk attitudes, one of which is the choice list method of Holt and Laury. They used three samples of subjects: students, private investors at a large German bank, and professional investors working at financial institutions across the EU. There was no effect of incentives in most of their tests and for all samples. There was only a small effect in the choice list method for students.[7] There was no

[5] Examples are the likelihood to play a gamble or the guilt of a suspect in a fictional crime.

[6] 17 out of their 46 subjects lost real money in this part.

[7] The small effect for professionals in the choice list method disappears after correction for multiple significance testing, the fact that we should use a lower significance level when we perform many statistical tests. (See Sect. 6.2)

difference either in response times, dropout, and inconsistency between hypothetical and real incentives. Their conclusion is clear: Incentives do not matter for risky choice.

The data of Hackethal et al. (2023) suggest that the choice list method should be used with caution. It led to more inconsistent data than the other methods to measure risk aversion. David Freeman et al. (2019) cast further doubt on the choice list method. They found that it leads to more risk loving behaviour than pairwise choices.

Many questions are hard to incentivize. Think about Kahneman's subjective well-being questions to define experienced utility, the Jones-Lee and Loomes' WTP questions to value road safety or the standard gamble (SG) and time trade-off (TTO) questions that are used to value health states. This is a problem for people who believe in incentives. If you believe incentives are necessary then (experimental) economics cannot give answers to societal problems like the allocation of the health care budget or protecting the environment. Economics becomes a social science that has no answer for many social problems. It returns to Marshall and John Neville Keynes who also saw a limited role for economics.

Fortunately, such a limited role for economics is unnecessary. Aurélien Baillon et al. (2022) incentivized subjective well-being and SG and TTO questions using Prelec's Bayesian truth serum (see Extension 4.2). Incentives had no effect. Incentivized and hypothetical questions gave the same results. This is good news for policy: Asking such hypothetical questions gives reliable input for policy decisions.

5.1.3 Is the RPSP Valid?

Using incentives, if possible, makes sense: It reduces noise. The above discussion shows that incentives are just less important than experimental economists suggest. If we can use incentives, the next question is how to do it. Two extremes are playing out all choices for real and asking just one question that is played out for real. Playing out all questions for real is problematic because it leads to income effects (previous earnings affect later choices) and it makes experiments expensive. Giving just one question that is played out for real is inefficient. It requires many subjects to test theories and it makes it impossible to run within-subject tests, which have more power to detect differences.

To address these problems most studies use the random problem selection procedure (RPSP). The RPSP randomly selects one choice to be played out for real at the end of the experiment. It assumes **isolation**. Subjects treat each choice as if it is the one to be played out for real.

Support for isolation comes from prospect theory. Kahneman and Tversky (1979) claim that before evaluating prospects, agents simplify them using **editing principles**. One of these principles is isolation. See Example 5.2.

Example 5.2: Isolation

Suppose you play a two-stage game. In the first stage there is a 75% chance that the game ends and you win nothing and a 25% chance that you go to the second stage. In the second stage you choose between a prospect that gives a 80% chance of €4000 (and nothing otherwise) and €3000 for sure. You must make your second-stage choice before the game starts (before the first stage).

Kahneman and Tversky (1979) found that 78% of their subjects chose the €3000.

Exercise 5.1: Isolation

Show that the two stages of the game together give a 20% chance of €4000 and a 25% chance of €3000.

In a direct choice between a 20% chance of €4000 and a 25% chance of €3000, 65% chose the 20% chance of €4000. Apparently, subjects isolated the second stage of the game and ignored the common first stage.

A drawback of the RPSP is that it dilutes incentives. It makes the cost of errors small. Consider the third choice in Table 5.1. Subjects choose between a $^3/_{10}$ chance of \$2.00 and a $^7/_{10}$ chance of \$1.60 versus a $^3/_{10}$ chance of \$3.85 and a $^7/_{10}$ chance of \$0.10. The difference in expected value is \$0.50. Holt and Laury's subjects made 50 choices in the real treatment, only 1 of which was played out for real. Consequently, the probability to select the above choice was $^1/_{50}$ and the expected cost of an error \$0.01. Even in the 90 treatments, the expected cost of error was only \$0.90.

In an earlier article, Holt (1986) himself argued against the RPSP. Holt wrote that subjects see an experiment using the RPSP as one large prospect. If they violate independence (see Chapter 9) then the experiment does not elicit their true preferences. Extension 5.1 explains Holt's argument.

Extension 5.1: Holt's Argument Against the RPSP

Suppose a subject performs two tasks, a choice between R_1 and S_1 and a choice between R_2 and S_2. One of these choices is played out for real and each has a probability of one half to be selected. According to Holt, subjects see a choice (R_1, R_2), R_1 in the first choice and R_2 in the second as a lottery $R_{1\,.5}R_2$ i.e. a 50% chance of getting R_1 and a 50% chance of getting R_2.

Assume that subjects reveal their true preferences if the choice is for real. Can we deduce from (R_1, R_2) that subjects truly prefer R_1 over S_1 and R_2 over S_2? Holt argues that this is only true if the independence axiom holds. The independence axiom says that for any three options x, y, z, $x \succcurlyeq y$ if and only if for all probabilities $\lambda : x_\lambda z \succcurlyeq x_\lambda z$.

Exercise 5.2: Holt's Argument

1. Show that if $R_1 \succcurlyeq S_1$ then by independence
$$R_{1.5}R_2 \succcurlyeq S_{1.5}R_2$$
2. Show that if $R_2 \succcurlyeq S_2$ then by independence
$$S_{1.5}R_2 \succcurlyeq S_{1.5}S_2$$
3. Show that transitivity implies that
$$R_{1.5}R_2 \succcurlyeq S_{1.5}S_2$$

Exercise 5.2 shows that under independence if $R_1 \succcurlyeq S_1$ and $R_2 \succcurlyeq S_2$ then we must have (R_1, R_2).

Exercise 5.3: The Reverse Implication also Holds

Show that the reverse implication also holds: if we observe (R_1, R_2) and independence holds then we must have $R_1 \succcurlyeq S_1$ and $R_2 \succcurlyeq S_2$. Hint: suppose this is not true and we have $S_1 \succ R_1$. Show that independence implies that $S_{1.5}R_2 \succ R_{1.5}R_2$, which contradicts the observed (R_1, R_2).

Exercises 5.2 and 5.3 show that if independence holds the RPSP truthfully reveals preferences. If not, then this may not be so.

Chris Starmer and Robert Sugden (1991) explored whether the RPSP gives the same result as a design in which subjects know which choice is played out for real. They divided their subjects into 4 groups. All groups answered first 20 hypothetical questions. Subjects in group A knew that question 22 would be played out for real, subjects in group D knew that question 21 would be played out for real, and subjects in groups B and C faced the RPSP and knew that question 21 and question 22 both had a 50% chance to be played out for real. The findings are inconclusive. χ^2-tests showed a marginal difference between RPSP and real ($p = 0.08$) in question 21 and no difference ($p = 0.31$) in question 22. Bayesian analyses (see Sect. 6.4) indicate that the data are inconclusive. The only conclusive evidence is support that the RPSP and hypothetical choice give the same results in question 21.

Robin Cubitt et al. (1998) ran a more extensive analysis with 550 subjects. Their first two experiments are inconclusive because subjects did not violate independence. As we saw in Extension 5.1, under independence, RPSP and real give the same results. In their third experiment, subjects violated independence and hypothetical, RPSP, and real gave the same results.

Several other studies compared RPSP and real. Beattie and Loomes (1997) found that real, RPSP, and hypothetical gave the same results. They also found violations of independence and thus their study presents evidence against Holt's conjecture. John Hey and co-authors (2005) found support for isolation and against Holt's hypothesis that subjects reduce the experiment to one prospect. James Cox et al. (2015) compared two versions of the RPSP and a treatment in which every choice is for real. In three tests they found support that RPSP and real give the same results, in one test they found evidence against isolation, and one of their tests was inconclusive.

Summarizing, RPSP and real usually give the same results and it seems fine to use the RPSP. Most studies found no difference between RPSP and hypothetical either, showing again that hypothetical choices give reliable results.

5.1.4 Do Incentives Harm?

In *The gift relationship*, Richard Titmuss (1970) argued that incentives might harm and undermine people's sense of civic duty. Titmuss considered blood donation. He claimed that paying blood donors might crowd out their intrinsic motivation to do good and result in lower levels of blood donation. One explanation for this comes from the diagnostic utility model discussed in Chapter 4. Giving blood signals that I am a socially responsible person. By accepting money for my donation this signal gets diluted.

Economists like Robert Solow and Ken Arrow (both Nobel laureates) were sceptical about Titmuss's claim. They believed that incentives could never decrease the quantity supplied. Around 2000 behavioural economists became interested in **crowding out**. Bruno Frey and Felix Oberholzer-Gee (1997) asked 305 inhabitants of two Swiss communities, designated as potential sites for the storage of radioactive waste, whether they supported the construction of these facilities in their communities. The interview took place one week before the actual referendum.[8]

Fifty per cent of their respondents supported the nuclear waste facility even though they knew the risks (one-third believed some local residents would die as a result of environmental harm) and saw the facility as a burden on the local community. This support was halved when financial compensation was offered. Crowding out of intrinsic motivation explains it.

Jose Luis Pinto Prades and I (2009) found something similar. We measured quality of life in a Spanish general population sample. We told our subjects that their answers would help to inform health policy (which was true). A few weeks after the experiment, we re-interviewed half of our sample. Because we interviewed subjects twice (for an hour), we wanted to pay them in the re-interview. Most subjects declined, because financial compensation removed their feeling to contribute to society.

Carl Mellström and Magnus Johannesson (2008) tested Titmuss's conjecture at the Gothenburg Regional Blood Center. Subjects were 262 undergraduate students (screened to exclude those who were already donors and those who could not be donors for medical reasons) who could chose to become a blood donor. They were

[8] Switzerland often uses referenda to make policy decisions.

randomly assigned to three treatment groups: a group that received no payment, a group that received 50 Swedish kronas (about €4.50) to become a donor, and a group that could choose between receiving 50 Swedish kronas and donating 50 Swedish kronas to the Swedish Children's cancer foundation. Figure 5.2 shows their results. Overall, the data are inconclusive. They do support crowding out for women. This disappears when the payment can be made to the charity. Several experiments suggest that women are more social than men. The common explanation is that women are more altruistic. The data of Mellström and Johannesson suggest another explanation: Women are more sensitive to social esteem.

During the Covid pandemic several countries gave financial incentives to encourage vaccination. These incentives were criticized for undermining intrinsic motivation and signalling that vaccines are risky. They might undermine people's trust in them.

Studies about the effect of financial incentives on Covid vaccinations are not fully informative about Titmuss's crowding out effects. Vaccination has both social and individual benefits. Moreover, the evidence is mixed. Katherine Milkman and co-authors (2022) found that "vaccine lotteries", in which vaccinated residents had a 50–100 times larger chance of winning than non-vaccinated residents, hardly affected vaccinations. They did not hurt, but did not help either.

By contrast, a Swedish study (Campos-Mercade et al. 2021) found that giving 200 Swedish kronas (about €18) increased first dose vaccinations by about 4%. It had no impact on the decision to take a second and third dose (Schneider et al. 2023). It did not affect other health behaviours like blood donation and flu shots either, nor moral values and the perceived safety and efficacy of vaccines. Financial incentives increased vaccinations more than nudges. Nudges are interventions based on behavioural economic insights that are popular in policy. I discuss them in Chapter 12. Nudges affected vaccine intentions, but not actual vaccinations.

Fig. 5.2 Mellström and Johannesson's results

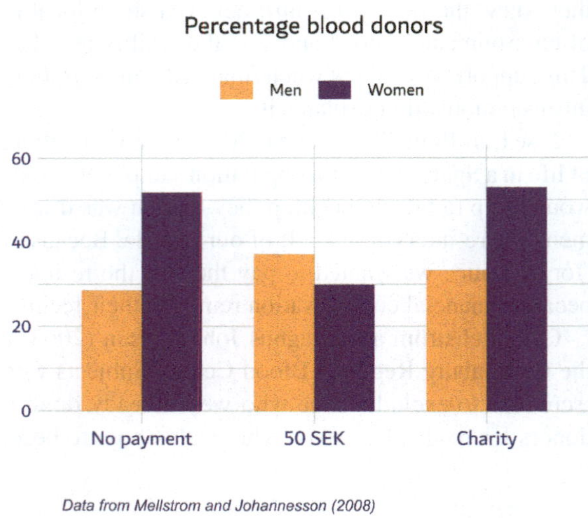

5.1.5 Wrapping Up

I believe that incentives in experiments are not so important. They may help when eliciting socially desirable responses like charity donations. However, if you cannot use incentives, as in policy questions about health and the environment, then that's fine. It is more important to avoid well-known biases, several of which I will discuss throughout the book.

The distinction between hypothetical and real is not black and white. It is not true that hypothetical and real always give the same result nor that hypothetical answers cannot be trusted. The truth lies somewhere in the middle, although I believe it is closer to hypothetical and real being similar than to the other extreme that hypothetical should never be used. Bardsley et al. (2020) reach a similar conclusion.

The meta-study by Johannes Abeler et al. (2019), with more than 44,000 subjects, gives further evidence that people generally report their preferences truthfully. They found that people are reluctant to misrepresent their preferences even if they would gain money by doing so. People want to be seen and want to see themselves as honest (see also Experiment 5.1). This is in line with diagnostic utility. Correctly reporting preferences is the norm and not the exception.

Experiment 5.1: Golden Balls

Martijn van den Assem et al. (2012) showed the importance of being seen as honest in the UK television show *Golden Balls*. At the end of the show, the two remaining contestants must split the jackpot they obtained together. They can choose "split" or "steal". If both "split" they share the jackpot, if one chooses "split" and the other "steal" the contestant who steals takes the whole jackpot, and if both "steal" they both go home empty-handed. Before the contestants make their decision they interact and make promises. In 53% of the negotiations, contestants made promises. Even though these promises were nonbinding and contestants could not be held accountable for them, they were the best predictor of choosing "split". For traditional economics, and many experimental economists, this does not make sense. These promises are "cheap talk" without consequences. In terms of diagnostic utility, however, they do make sense.

5.1.6 Experiments Run by Internet

Since the 2000s an increasing number of experiments are run online using platforms like Amazon's MTurk and Prolific. MTurk is an online labour market with a pool of over 500,000 participants. Requesters give a short description of the task, its expected duration, and the minimum payment. Although MTurk is not designed to run experiments, it can do so efficiently.

Online experiments have several advantages:

1. A more diverse subject pool.
2. The possibility to run large-scale studies.
3. As payment is low, the costs per participant are lower than in the lab.

Online experiments also have disadvantages. The low payments may dilute efforts. Empirical evidence suggests that this is not a problem, confirming, once again, that incentives are not so important. Another problem is the lack of control. In the lab, we can control who participates, we can avoid that people participate more than once, avoid communication between participants, answer questions, and control dropout. In the lab hardly anyone drops out. Online this happens more frequently. If this dropout is related to the experimental task and not random, it could bias the results.

Online studies give similar results as lab studies. Online subjects are risk averse for gains and risk loving for losses and overweight the present relative to the future. That said, the degree of the effects can differ. Paolacci et al. (2010) found that MTurkers are more risk averse. On the other hand, Jérôme Hergueux and Nicolas Jacquemet (2015) found that they are less risk averse and Benjamin Prissé and Diego Jorrat (2022) found no difference in risk aversion between online and lab studies. These last two studies used the choice list method. We saw above that this gives more risk loving.

Summing up, the results from online studies seem reliable, especially for identifying general patterns of behaviour. Because the size of the effects can differ, I prefer to avoid using online studies as the only data source. In particular, to estimate model parameters, where effect size is important, I prefer the control of the lab.

5.2 Field Studies

Experiments have many advantages, most importantly, they allow researchers to test exactly what they are interested in. Experimental questions can be tailor-made. A drawback is that experiments are abstractions from real-life decisions and often use convenience (student) samples. This limits their relevance for real-world behaviour. For that reason, behavioural economists became interested in using field experiments. This development was particularly pushed by Chicago economist John List.

Field experiments are not new to economics (Levitt and List 2009). The first field experiments took place in the 1920s and 1930s. These studies centred on agriculture and tested the effect of field uses (fertilization, sowing patterns) on yields. Scholars like Ronald Fisher and Jerzy Neyman developed statistical methods and showed the importance of randomization. The assignment of plots to treatments should be random to trust the results. Randomization is now routinely used in experiments where subjects (as far as possible) are randomly assigned to treatments.

The second wave of field experiments started in the 1960s and 1970s. These were large social experiments about the effects of electricity pricing, employment programmes, and negative income taxation.[9] Social experiments have explored public policies in among others health, housing, and welfare.

Social experiments resemble clinical trials, which are used to evaluate medical treatments. Consequently, they share similar limitations (Kramer and Shapiro 1984):

1. **Problems with randomization**. It can be complex to allocate subjects to experimental treatments. Consider a study of different employment programmes. If clients of an employment centre are randomly assigned to different programmes then they talk about these differences. This may confound the results. Consequently, it makes sense to randomize programmes by employment centre. However, this leads to **selection bias** if centres differ in the demographic or economic characteristics of their clients. Moreover, people are unwilling to participate in studies in which they are randomly assigned to a treatment group. This may lead to selective dropout which again would bias the results. An example is future mothers being randomly assigned to breast or formula feeding.
2. **Non-blinding**. Subjects know they take part in an experiment and this may affect their behaviour. Those in the treatment group may feel that they are special because they are among "the chosen". Those in the control group may compensate for not being chosen by changing their behaviour (a substitution effect).
3. **Effects of participation**. If subjects know that their behaviour is studied, like job search or electricity use, then they may change their behaviour to perform well. This is called the **Hawthorne effect**.

The third wave of field experiments aimed to avoid the randomization and awareness problems of the social experiments. As a result, their aims were more modest and their approach more opportunistic: They looked for possibilities to perform field experiments. Theoretically, they were more ambitious, as social experiments were interested in assessing new policy instruments and less in theory. By contrast, the field experiments of the third wave were often designed to test economic theories and estimate their key parameters.

Glenn Harrison and John List (2004) distinguish three types of field experiments. The first are the **artefactual field experiments**, which are lab experiments with a sample from the population of interest (and not a convenience sample). They are still run in a lab setting and use the tasks used in the lab.

Artefactual field experiments are often used in development economics. An example is the study by Maarten Voors and co-authors (2012). They ran a study in Burundi to test whether civil war violence affected people's preferences (measured using lab methods). If so, this would affect the possibility to recover from the civil

[9] Negative income taxation is an idea of Nobel laureate Milton Friedman. It means that the state guarantees each citizen a level of income. However, the federal contribution declines by some percentage with each euro earned. For example, if the negative tax is 50% then for each euro earned the federal contribution decreases by €0.50. If the guaranteed income is €10,000 and the agent earns €5000 the federal contribution is €10,000-0.50 × €5000 = €7500. A concern about negative taxation is that it dilutes work efforts.

war as preferences determine trust, saving, consumption, and investment decisions. Voors et al. found that more exposure to violence was associated with more altruism, more risk loving, and less weight for the future.

Framed field experiments use real-world tasks, but subjects still know that they participate in an experiment. Social experiments and randomized clinical trials are examples.

Finally, in **natural field experiments** subjects make real-world decisions and do not know that they participate in an experiment. An example is the study by Peter Schwardmann, Egon Tripodi, and Joël van der Weele (2022) of participants in a debating competition. They study self-persuasion: People's tendency to convince themselves that their views are correct. Self-persuasion limits the search for compromises and complicates negotiations. Even though the debaters were randomly assigned their viewpoint to defend, they were more likely to believe that a statement is true when it supports this viewpoint than if not. Moreover, during the debate they became more confident that their viewpoint would win.

Although they are not real field experiments, economists have also tested (behavioural) economic theories using televised **game shows**. The golden balls study of Experiment 5.1 is an example. Game shows offer higher stakes than lab studies. However, the setting is special, with pressure from the show host and the audience, which may affect behaviour.

Roel Beetsma and Peter Schotman (2001) found that prospect theory described the behaviour of participants in a word guessing show better than expected utility. Thierry Post and co-authors (2008) found that participants in the show *Deal or No Deal* behave according to reference-dependence. Reference points were sticky and did not change much to new information about the remaining prices in the game.

5.2.1 Drawbacks of Field Experiments

Field experiments have the advantage of realism: Decisions look more like those that people meet in real life than lab experiments. This increase in realism comes at the cost of a lack of control. In particular, field experiments have the following limitations.

1. They are **difficult to replicate**. Replication has become important in behavioural economics given concerns about the robustness of findings (see Chapter 6). Field experiments are harder to replicate than lab experiments. They are performed when the opportunity occurs, but the opportunity may not repeat itself. And even if they can be replicated, it is hard to follow the same experimental protocol.
2. It is **harder to test theories**. In the lab, we can ask the exact questions to test or measure a theory. In the field this is often impossible. For example, measuring the parameters of prospect theory in the field is hard without making simplifying assumptions.
3. **Limited collaboration**. Field experiments are often run in collaboration with governmental agencies or with companies. These have their own agenda and

impose constraints on the questions that can be asked or the results that can be published. Lab experiments do not have these problems.

4. **Ethical concerns**. Several ethical questions arise about field experiments. Should we ask subjects for their consent to participate in the study? If we do, they are aware that they participate in a study and this may lead to biases (see the discussion of social experiments). Related to that, what to do if one treatment gives better results than another? This is a common problem in clinical decision making. If a randomized clinical trial shows that one treatment gives better health outcomes, the trial is stopped. It is unethical to deny one patient group the benefits from treatment. Something similar can happen in economics. If one employment programme gives higher earnings and a higher probability of finding a job it is unethical to keep offering the inferior programme.
5. A final problem might be that responses are more **prone to errors**. In the experiments I ran outside the lab with more representative population samples this was typically the case. While average responses were similar, errors increased.

5.2.2 Does It Matter?

How important is it to perform field experiments? Are their results really different from what we observe in the lab? Some studies suggest they are. For example, Taisuke Imai et al. (2021) found less overweighting of the present compared with the future in the field than in the lab.

On the other hand, Matthias Benz and Stephan Meier (2008) found that social preferences in the lab and in the field are correlated. Students at the University of Zürich can donate each semester at inscription money to two social funds, one offering cheap loans for students with financial difficulties, the other helping foreign students studying in Zürich. A subset of the students also participated in two experiments. They could donate €12 to the same two social funds (in the first experiment) and to two unrelated charities (in the second experiment). Students who gave more in the field also gave more in the experiments. The correlations were around 0.25, which Benz and Meier see as surprisingly high given the difference in contexts and psychological evidence suggesting that the decision context affects decisions.

Jan Stoop (2014) studied whether people's behaviour in a dictator game differs between the lab and the field. In a dictator game a "dictator" receives an amount of money and decides how much to share with an anonymous "recipient". Economic theory predicts that dictators will not share anything. Lab experiments show that dictators share up to half of the money. This is usually explained by altruism or social norms.

Subjects received a transparent envelope with two notes of €5. The envelope was addressed to a volunteer of Tilburg University. It also contained a card to thank them.

In the lab study, student subjects received the envelope, read the instructions and then took the envelope home where they could decide to send it to the volunteer or not.

The artefactual field experiment was similar except that subjects were randomly selected from people who came to Tilburg city hall to renew their passports. This sample was more representative of Tilburg's population.

The framed field experiment differed from the artefactual field experiment in that subjects read the instructions at home. They knew however that they participated in an experiment.

Finally, in the natural field experiment subjects were unaware that they participated in an experiment. The card was "misdelivered" to them by the experimenter wearing the official uniform of the Dutch postal service. The postmark on the stamp was of the same day of the wrong delivery.

There were no differences between the four treatments: in all four around 50% of the subjects returned the envelopes to the addressed volunteer. There was no difference in prosocial behaviour between the lab and the different field studies.

Summing up, the conclusion is similar to that of the effect of incentives. Field experiments are an interesting addition to the behavioural economist's toolbox, but they have not led to fundamental new insights. The size of the effects has in some studies been smaller, but the insights from lab experiments are replicated.[10]

5.3 International Comparisons

In his book "The weirdest people in the world" Harvard professor Joseph Henrich argues that people in the Western world are the exception and differ substantially from human beings in other regions of the world. The reason is the extensive alphabetization in the Western world. While spoken language has played a major role in human evolution for hundreds of thousands of years, written language only exists for about 6000 years and our brains are not born with an organ to understand written language. Education creates this. Alphabetization changes our brain and affects our spatial reasoning, attention, memory, attitude towards risk, inductive reasoning and attitude towards equity. As a result, many findings in the social sciences that were thought to be robust did not replicate in other cultures.

This raises the question whether behavioural economics findings, mostly obtained using Western subjects, can be generalized to other cultures. Henrich's research suggests only to a limited extent. Empirical evidence, mainly obtained by German behavioural economists is more positive. The patterns found with Western subjects are robust, although the degree of the effects varies around the world.

Thorsten Hens et al. (2015) studied 7000 student subjects from 53 countries. They found that prospect theory's prediction that people are risk averse for gains and risk loving for losses holds throughout the world. However, people from richer countries were more risk averse for gains. This was also found by Ferdinand Vieder and co-authors (2015), who used a sample of 3000 students from 30 countries around the world, and by the group of Armin Falk (2018) who collected representative samples

[10] In Chapter 6, we will see that smaller effect sizes are common in replications, also when they are run in the lab.

from 76 counties involving 80,000 persons. People in Europe and South and East Asia are most risk averse, and people in Africa and the Middle East are most risk loving. All studies found at least as much variation in risk attitudes within countries as between countries. For example, all studies found that women are more risk averse than men for gains.

Ferdinand Vieider and Olivier L'Haridon found that other predictions of prospect theory, about probability weighting, attitudes towards ambiguity and loss aversion that I will discuss later, also hold across cultures even though, again, the degree varies (L'Haridon et al. 2018, L'Haridon and Vieider 2019). People from poorer countries are more tolerant to risk and ambiguity, but also more averse to losses and less sensitive to changes in probabilities. Taller people are more risk loving and more sensitive to changes in probability.

People discount the near future more than the far future (see Chapter 11). Northern Europeans and Americans are most patient and Latin Americans and Africans least. Patience is most closely associated with economic development (in particular GDP per capita). This could be because more patience leads to more schooling and higher savings.

5.4 Epilogue

The international comparisons also found that incentives do not affect risk attitudes. This highlights, once again, that they are not so important. The many refinements of behavioural economists' methods are valuable. However, they do not invalidate earlier results obtained using cruder methods. The results of pioneers like Tversky, Kahneman, and Thaler, whose methods probably would not withstand the scrutiny of modern-day behavioural economics, proved robust regardless of whether incentives were used, data were collected in the field or in non-Western countries. That is the comforting conclusion of this chapter.

References

Abeler, J., D. Nosenzo, and C. Raymond. 2019. Preferences for truth-telling. *Econometrica* 87: 1115–1153.

Baillon, A., H. Bleichrodt, and G.D. Granic. 2022. Incentives in surveys. *Journal of Economic Psychology* 93: 102552.

Bardsley, N., R. Cubitt, G. Loomes, P. Moffatt, C. Starmer, and R. Sugden. 2020. *Experimental economics*. Princeton University Press.

Beattie, J., and G. Loomes. 1997. The impact of incentives upon risky choice experiments. *Journal of Risk and Uncertainty* 14: 155–168.

Beetsma, R.M., and P.C. Schotman. 2001. Measuring risk attitudes in a natural experiment: Data from the television game show Lingo. *Economic Journal* 111: 821–848.

Benz, M., and S. Meier. 2008. Do people behave in experiments as in the field? Evidence from donations. *Experimental Economics* 11: 268–281.

Binswanger, H.P. 1980. Attitudes toward risk: Experimental measurement in rural India. *American Journal of Agricultural Economics* 62: 395–407.

Bleichrodt, H., and J.L. Pinto Prades. 2009. New evidence of preference reversals in health utility measurement. *Health Economics* 18: 713–726.

Camerer, C.F., and R.M. Hogarth. 1999. The effects of financial incentives in experiments: A review and capital-labor-production framework. *Journal of Risk and Uncertainty* 19: 7–42.

Campos-Mercade, P., A.N. Meier, F.H. Schneider, S. Meier, D. Pope, and E. Wengström. 2021. Monetary incentives increase COVID-19 vaccinations. *Science* 374: 879–882.

Cohen, M., J.-Y. Jaffray, and T. Said. 1987. Experimental comparison of individual behavior under risk and under uncertainty for gains and for losses. *Organizational Behavior and Human Decision Processes* 39: 1–22.

Cox, J.C., V. Sadiraj, and U. Schmidt. 2015. Paradoxes and mechanisms for choice under risk. *Experimental Economics* 18: 215–250.

Cubitt, R.P., C. Starmer, and R. Sugden. 1998. On the validity of the random lottery incentive system. *Experimental Economics* 1: 115–131.

Etchart-Vincent, N., and O. L'Haridon. 2011. Monetary incentives in the loss domain and behavior toward risk: An experimental comparison of three reward schemes including real losses. *Journal of Risk and Uncertainty* 42: 61–83.

Falk, A., A. Becker, T. Dohmen, B. Enke, D. Huffman, and U. Sunde. 2018. Global evidence on economic preferences. *Quarterly Journal of Economics* 133: 1645–1692.

Freeman, D.J., Y. Halevy, and T. Kneeland. 2019. Eliciting risk preferences using choice lists. *Quantitative Economics* 10: 217–237.

Frey, B.S., and F. Oberholzer-Gee. 1997. The cost of price incentives: An empirical analysis of motivation crowding-out. *American Economic Review* 87: 746–755.

Hackethal, A., M. Kirchler, C. Laudenbach, M. Razen, and A. Weber. 2023. On the role of monetary incentives in risk preference elicitation experiments. *Journal of Risk and Uncertainty* 66: 189–213.

Harrison, G.W., and J.A. List. 2004. Field experiments. *Journal of Economic Literature* 42: 1009–1055.

Harrison, G.W., E. Johnson, M.M. McInnes, and E.E. Rutström. 2005. Risk aversion and incentive effects: Comment. *American Economic Review* 95: 897–901.

Hergueux, J., and N. Jacquemet. 2015. Social preferences in the online laboratory: a randomized experiment. *Experimental Economics* 18: 251–283.

Hertwig, R., and A. Ortmann. 2001. Experimental practices in economics: A methodological challenge for psychologists? *Behavioral and Brain Sciences* 24: 383–403.

Hey, J.D., J. Lee, et al. 2005. Do subjects separate (or are they sophisticated)? *Experimental Economics* 8: 233–266.

Holt, C.A. 1986. Preference reversals and the independence axiom. *American Economic Review* 76: 508–515.

Holt, C.A., and S.K. Laury. 2002. Risk aversion and incentive effects. *American Economic Review* 92: 1644–1655.

Holt., and Laury. 2005. Risk aversion and incentive effects: New data without order effects. *American Economic Review* 95: 902–904.

Imai, T., T.A. Rutter, and C.F. Camerer. 2021. Meta-analysis of present-bias estimation using convex time budgets. *Economic Journal* 131: 1788–1814.

Jacquemet, N., and O. L'Haridon. 2018. *Experimental economics*. Cambridge: Cambridge University Press.

Kagel, J.H., and A.E. Roth. 1995. *The handbook of experimental economics*. Princeton: Princeton University Press.

Kahneman, D., and A. Tversky. 1979. Prospect theory: An analysis of decision under risk. *Econometrica* 47: 263–291.

Kramer, M.S., and S.H. Shapiro. 1984. Scientific challenges in the application of randomized trials. *Journal of the American Medical Association* 252: 2739–2745.

Levitt, S.D., and J.A. List. 2009. Field experiments in economics: The past, the present, and the future. *European Economic Review* 53: 1–18.

L'Haridon, O., and F.M. Vieider. 2019. All over the map: Heterogeneity of risk preferences across individuals, contexts, and countries. *Quantitative Economics* 10: 185–215.

L'Haridon, O., F. M. Vieider, D. Aycinena, A. Bandur, A. Belianin, L. Cingl, A. Kothiyal, and P. Martinsson,. 2018. Off the charts: Massive unexplained heterogeneity in a global study of ambiguity attitudes. *Review of Economics and Statistics* 100: 664–677.

Mellström, C., and M. Johannesson. 2008. Crowding out in blood donation: was Titmuss right? *Journal of the European Economic Association* 6: 845–863.

Milkman, K.L., L. Gandhi, S.F. Ellis, H.N. Graci, D.M. Gromet, R.S. Mobarak, A.M. Buttenheim, A.L. Duckworth, D. Pope, A. Stanford, et al. 2022. A citywide experiment testing the impact of geographically targeted, high-pay-off vaccine lotteries. *Nature Human Behaviour* 6: 1–10.

Paolacci, G., J. Chandler, and P.G. Ipeirotis. 2010. Running experiments on Amazon Mechanical Turk. *Judgment and Decision Making* 5: 411–419.

Post, T., M.J. Van den Assem, G. Baltussen, and R.H. Thaler. 2008. Deal or no deal? decision making under risk in a large-payoff game show. *American Economic Review* 98: 38–71.

Prissé, B., and D. Jorrat. 2022. Lab vs online experiments: No differences. *Journal of Behavioral and Experimental Economics* 100: 101910.

Rieger, M.O., M. Wang, and T. Hens. 2015. Risk preferences around the world. *Management Science* 61: 637–648.

Schneider, F.H., P. Campos-Mercade, S. Meier, D. Pope, E. Wengström, and A.N. Meier. 2023. Financial incentives for vaccination do not have negative unintended consequences. *Nature* 613: 1–8.

Schwardmann, P., E. Tripodi, and J.J. Van der Weele. 2022. Self-persuasion: Evidence from field experiments at international debating competitions. *American Economic Review* 112: 1118–1146.

Slovic,. 1995. The construction of preference. *American Psychologist* 50: 364–371.

Smith, V.L., and J.M. Walker. 1993. Monetary rewards and decision cost in experimental economics. *Economic Inquiry* 31: 245–261.

Starmer, C., and R. Sugden. 1991. Does the random-lottery incentive system elicit true preferences? An experimental investigation. *American Economic Review* 81: 971–978.

Stoop, J. 2014. From the lab to the field: envelopes, dictators and manners. *Experimental Economics* 17: 304–313.

Thaler, R. 1981. Some empirical evidence on dynamic inconsistency. *Economics Letters* 8: 201–207.

Thaler, R.H., and E.J. Johnson. 1990. Gambling with the house money and trying to break even: The effects of prior outcomes on risky choice. *Management Science* 36: 643–660.

Titmuss, R.M. 1970. *The gift relationship*. Crows Nest: Allen and Unwin.

Van den Assem, M.J., D. Van Dolder, and R.H. Thaler. 2012. Split or steal? Cooperative behavior when the stakes are large. *Management Science* 58: 2–20.

Vieider, F.M., M. Lefebvre, R. Bouchouicha, T. Chmura, R. Hakimov, M. Krawczyk, and P. Martinsson. 2015. Common components of risk and uncertainty attitudes across contexts and domains: Evidence from 30 countries. *Journal of the European Economic Association* 13: 421–452.

Voors, M.J., E.E.M. Nillesen, P. Verwimp, E.H. Bulte, R. Lensink, and D.P.V. Soest. 2012. Violent conflict and behavior: A field experiment in Burundi. *American Economic Review* 102: 941–964.

The Methods of Behavioural Economics Part 2

6

Neuroeconomics, Genoeconomics, and New Statistics

6.1 Neuroeconomics

As we saw in Chapter 3, choices are the basic data of economics. Behavioural economics allows for more data than choices alone. One of these is data about how the brain works. Since the early 2000s, pioneered by Colin Camerer, behavioural economists have been studying what happens in the brain when we make decisions. The hope was that these new data would enrich economic theory.[1]

The classical economists realized that economic decisions were driven by a complex interplay of emotions, impulses, and reflexes, but they believed that these could not be measured. Therefore, economics had to use choices.

Camerer and other neuroeconomists argue that new techniques to measure brain mechanisms have made these concerns obsolete. If we can measure feelings and thoughts thanks to science why not use these to improve economic theory? As we will see below, not every economist agrees with this stance, but let us first explore the methods of neuroscience and how the brain works.

6.1.1 The Methods of Neuroscience

Colin Camerer et al. (2004) distinguish 6 neuroscientific methods.

1. Studying the **brains of animals**. The human brain is essentially an animal brain covered by the prefrontal cortex, the "rational part" of our brain, which enables higher functions like language and planning. Studying animal brains therefore

[1] An overview of the methods neuroeconomics is Camerer et al. (2004).

H. Bleichrodt, *Behavioural Economics*,
https://doi.org/10.1007/978-3-031-69166-9_6

gives information about the human brain. Using animals, particularly rats, has the extra advantage that (parts of) the brain can be deliberately damaged or stimulated without (much) ethical concern. This is impossible with humans.

2. **Human physiological reactions**. These are often associated with emotions and can be measured. Examples are blood pressure, which tends to rise under stress, heart rate, sweating, or pupil dilation. Emotional states can be assessed by looking at facial expressions like frowning or smiling. Charles Noussair and co-authors (2024) use face reading software to measure the emotional content of facial expressions. Physiological reactions are, for example, used by Badger et al. (2007), discussed in Chapter 4, to measure the craving of their drug addicts.
3. **Brain imaging** involves taking images of the brain to assess which parts are active in different tasks. The oldest method is **electro-encephalogram** (EEG). This measures electrical activity outside of the brain by placing electrodes on subjects' heads. These measurements tend to be crude and do not record interior brain activity. **Positron emission topography** (PET) measures blood flow in the brain after a subject is injected with a weakly radioactive blood injection. The radioactive activity decays rapidly, so PET can only be used for short tasks. **Functional magnetic resonance imaging** (fMRI) measures changes in blood oxygenation, which indicates brain activity. It involves putting people in an (expensive) scanner. This means collaborating with a medical centre and makes replication by others harder. The signal from fMRI scans is weak, which means that studies must be repeated and that the truth is partly in the eye of the beholder. This makes interpretation of the study results subjective. To illustrate, Botvinik-Nezer et al. (2020) found that 70 independent research teams all reached different conclusions about which parts of the brain were active when analysing the same data.
4. While fMRIs measure the activity of thousands of neurons simultaneously, **single neuron measurement** isolates the functioning of single neurons. They do this by inserting tiny electrodes into the brain. Because these electrodes damage neurons these studies use animals. Consequently, single neuron studies only study basic emotional and motivational processes.
5. Chronic mental illnesses and degenerative brain diseases (**psychopathology**) also give insight into how the brain works. If a specific illness or the course of a disease can be traced to specific regions of the brain then this gives clues about the brain.
6. A final source of data is **brain damage in humans**. If for some reason, e.g. an accident or a disease, (part of) a person's brain is damaged then this may affect their behaviour. Studying such behaviour leads to a better understanding of the role of the brain in performing tasks. An example is the work of the Portuguese neuroscientist Antonio Demasio. Demasio emphasizes the role of emotions and feelings in decision making and in making us human.[2] His **somatic marker hypothesis** says that emotional defects impair decision making. He illustrates

[2] His book *Descartes' error* challenges René Descartes' ("I think, so I exist") idea that the body and the mind are separate. Demasio thought that the quote should be "I exist, so I think." Decision making arises as an interplay between body and mind and is influenced by both conscious and unconscious neural marker signals some of which express themselves in emotions and feelings.

this by studying humans with damage to the brain. Likewise, negative parenting (physical and verbal aggression, shouting, threatening, and humiliation) leads to changes in children's brains. This makes them less creative and more inclined to depression and anxiety. Their amygdala, the part of the brain that gives emotional signals in reaction to fear and anxiety, becomes more reactive to negative emotions and the prefrontal cortex, which regulates emotions, can deal less with anxiety and stress.

Nathalie Camille and co-authors (2004) studied the choices under risk of 5 subjects with damage to the medial orbifrontal cortex. They were less sensitive to the outcome that occurred under the prospect they did not choose (the **counterfactual outcome**) than a healthy control group. As counterfactual outcomes drive feelings of regret, they concluded that the orbifrontal cortex regulates feelings of regret. Benedetto de Martino, Camerer, and Ralph Adolphs (2010) studied the risk preferences of two patients suffering damage to the amygdala. They found that these patients were less loss averse than a control group.

6.1.2 Properties of the Brain

Three features of the brain are particularly interesting for behavioural economics:

1. **Automaticity**. Many brain activities are automatic, meaning that the prefrontal cortex is unaware of the reason why we take these activities. Examples are driving while simultaneously thinking about an upcoming talk and a way of reacting to a given situation. Reactions are often driven by habits that we are unaware of. Changing habits is hard. To do so we must use cognitive resources to counter automatic patterns. Cognitive therapy aims to become aware of and change automatic patterns. Automaticity also explains the importance of human capital. Experience makes tasks automatic and, consequently, replacing experienced employees is costly. Replacements have to build up experience and automaticity again.
2. **Modularity**. The brain is subdivided into different parts, which are responsible for different functions. In complex tasks these parts work together. The neuroeconomist's job is to find the connections that take place between the brain's modules. This can give useful information for economics. For example, if other modules are active when people are dealing with gains than when they are dealing with losses then this supports prospect theory's claim that people treat gains different from losses. Modularity also poses a challenge. As different modules usually work together, it is difficult to derive implications for economic theory from what is observed. Again, the truth is partly in the eye of the beholder.
3. **Sense-making**. The brain tries to make sense of our behaviour. It exaggerates this and sees patterns where there are none. Our expectations largely drive the patterns the brain "detects". So if I believe that I am bad at standing up for myself then my brain will interpret my behaviour that way and see evidence of it even if there is none.

It also means that the brain will miss evidence that is at odds with our expectations. However, sometimes this evidence is so strong that the brain changes its story. It typically does this so fast and efficiently that it seems that the new story was always correct. This is called **hindsight bias**. It explains why people see good decisions as wrong because they did not lead to the best outcome.
An example is the signing of Paul George by the Los Angeles Clippers in 2019. To sign George (who had finished third in MVP voting that year), the Clippers gave up rookie Shai Gilgeous Alexander and five draft picks. With hindsight this decision seems a mistake. George struggled with injuries after signing with the Clippers and left them in free agency in 2024. Gilgeous Alexander turned into an NBA all star and All-NBA 1st Team player at the age of 24. However, the signing of George convinced Kawhi Leonard, who won the 2019 NBA with the Toronto Raptors and was finals MVP, to also sign with the Clippers. That Leonard's time with the Clippers would also be plagued by injuries does not change that the decision was a good one.

Exercise 6.1: Hindsight Bias

In an interview with ESPN in February 2024, Doc Rivers, who was the Clippers head coach during the George trade, mentioned that he tried to convince Kawhi Leonard that Gilgeous Alexander would be a star: "I even brought it up to Kawhi: 'Are you sure? I think Shai's going to be an amazing player. It may take a year or two, but I think you're underestimating how good Shai's going to be'". Explain that this may be another example of hindsight bias.

6.1.3 The Contributions of Neuroeconomics

Addiction One application of neuroeconomics is the study of addiction. Addiction is hard for economists to model. Why on earth would a rational agent decide to get addicted? Nobel laureate Gary Becker and Kevin Murphy gave a rationalization of addictive behaviour (see Extension 6.1). In their model consumers are aware that they form an addictive habit and their decision to become addicted follows rational calculus. Their model predicts that the demand for addictive substances is sensitive to changes in prices. Empirical studies found some support for this prediction.

Extension 6.1: Rational Addiction

Becker and Murphy (1988) argue that addictive behaviour involves both **reinforcement**, greater past consumption increases the wish for current consumption, and **tolerance**, the utility from consumption is lower when past consumption is higher. The consumer's utility at time point t, U_t is equal to

$$U_t = U(c_t, S_t, y_t),$$

where c_t is consumption at time point t, S_t is the stock of "addictive capital" that depends on past consumption, and y_t is a non-addictive good. The idea of a stock of capital is similar to Michael Grossman's (1972) model of the demand for health, which is widely used in health economics.

Becker and Murphy model tolerance as $\frac{\partial U}{\partial S} = U_S < 0$, greater past consumption lowers current utility. Reinforcement requires that the marginal utility of current consumption increases with past use: $\frac{\partial U}{\partial c \partial S} = U_{cS} > 0$. The rate of addictive capital S decreases by a rate σ. The consumer discounts utility at a constant rate δ. We will see in Chapter 11 that constant discounting is controversial. Jonathan Gruber and Botond Köszegi (2001) show that with non-constant discounting addicts mispredict their future behaviour.

Reinforcement (which is crucial for addiction) increases with the discount rate (agents care less about the negative consequences of addiction when they care less about the future) and with the rate of depreciation of the addiction stock (the quicker the stock depreciates the fewer the negative effects of current consumption on future utility). The demand for addictive goods will be sensitive to changes in price. Because in the short run the stock of addictive goods is fixed, the long-run price elasticity will exceed the short-run elasticity. The model implies that legalizing drugs, which will decrease their price, will lead to more use. This holds particularly among the young and the poor who discount the future more.

Neuroeconomics gives another explanation. Every substance that is addictive for humans is also addictive for rats. This suggests that the addiction "decision" comes from the more primitive parts of our brain that we share with rats and not from the rational part (the prefrontal cortex). For policy it is important to know which story is true. If addiction is rational, there seems no role for policy. If not, there is a role for policy.

The rational addiction model cannot explain why addicts relapse even when prices have not changed. Badger et al. (2007) (Extension 4.1) found that even experienced drug users underestimate their future craving. This can explain why people start taking drugs (and other addictive habits like smoking or alcohol): They underappreciate future craving and are overconfident about their future ability to quit. It also suggests that drug laws may be too tough. If non-drug users underestimate craving they may wrongly believe that people with sufficient self-discipline will quit if given the proper motivation. So lawmakers (who, presumably, are no drug users) have too much faith in the deterrent effect of drug laws.

Risk attitudes Neuroeconomics suggests that people's reaction to risk is irrational. When people face risk, the amygdala is activated. As mentioned, the amygdala is associated with feelings of anxiety and fear and often acts against the rational part of the brain. Economists usually assume that risk aversion is rational and it is part of standard economic theory (see Chapter 9). The role of the amygdala in shaping our reaction to risk challenges this.

Time preference Samuel McClure and co-authors (2004) found that in decisions over time different parts of the brain were involved when one of the options was received immediately than when both options were received in the future. They saw this as evidence that immediate choices are impulsive and future choices rational and as support for the β - δ model that we will discuss in Chapter 11. In the β - δ model, people behave impatiently (impulsive) now and (more) patiently in the future. McClure et al. argue that their data support this struggle between irrationality (impatience) and rationality (patience).

Later studies challenged this interpretation. Paul Glimcher (2022) points out that future rewards are valued less (which can be rational as we will see in Chapter 11). Consequently, the subjective value signal may have been too weak to be detected by the fMRI scanner. Joseph Kable and Paul Glimcher (2007) found that as future amounts increased, the same areas of the brain were involved as in immediate choice.

Loss aversion Sabrina Tom and co-authors (2007) studied what happens in the brain when people face prospects with both gains and losses. They found that the brain regions that became more active as the size of the gains increased became less active as the size of the losses increased. They computed a measure of neural loss aversion by comparing the rate at which neural activity decreases with losses with the rate at which neural activity increases with gains. This neural measure correlates with a behavioural measure of loss aversion defined as the tendency to turn down prospects with losses.

This supports prospect theory. Unexpectedly people who were more behaviourally loss averse showed more neural sensitivity to both losses and gains. This suggests that loss aversion has to do with sensitivity to outcomes in general, not only to losses.

Gains and losses were coded by the same brain mechanisms. The amygdala did not become more active in the presence of losses. Apparently, loss aversion was not driven by feelings of fear or anxiety. On the other hand, De Martino et al. (2010) found that their two patients with damage to the amygdala were less loss averse than the control group.

6.1.4 Modern-Day Neuroeconomics

The early 2000s saw a bonanza of neuroeconomic studies. After this initial wave of enthusiasm a period of sobering set in. Economists realized that earlier contributions were perhaps overstated and that researchers had been carried away by their enthusiasm. They concluded that neuroscience had less to offer than initially hoped.

Neuroscience finds it hard to give the clear answers economists wished for. Most studies use **reverse inference**. They study a task, check which parts of the brain are active, and conclude that this part of the brain plays a central role in the task.

For example, Cary Frydman and Colin Camerer (2016) measured the brain activity when subjects see the price of a stock they just sold (a counterfactual outcome). The higher the price of this stock, the less activity there is in the vental striatum. Previous studies with counterfactual outcomes also found activity in the vental striatum. So, Frydman and Camerer argue that they found evidence of regret in the brain. Is this true and if so are feelings of regret indeed driving these decisions? In fMRI studies the brain usually lights up for all kinds of processes, not only for the cognitive process of interest. Consequently, it is hard to make the claim that a part of the brain is exclusively responsible for a cognitive process.

Even if we could claim exclusivity, it is unclear what this means for modelling decisions. Economists are interested in the consequences of decisions, not in the decision process (unlike psychologists and neuroscientists see Krajbich and Dean (2015)). They want to know how a set of background variables affects economic behaviour and are less interested in the actual process through which these variables lead to economic behaviour.

In the end, neuroeconomics had little effect on economics. On the other hand, economics had an impact on neuroscience. The standard of experiments in economics transformed the way neuroscientists perform experiments. The field is still very much alive even though its impact on economics has been less than its proponents hoped.

6.1.5 Random Utility

One contribution of neuroeconomics is a better understanding of why choices are **stochastic**. When presented the same choice repeatedly, subjects reverse up to 30% of their choices. Duncan Luce (1959) was a first to draw attention to the stochastic nature of choices. He suggested that agents choose between alternatives x and y according to the choice rule

$$P(x, y) = \frac{U(x)^{\epsilon}}{U(x)^{\epsilon} + U(y)^{\epsilon}}, \tag{6.1}$$

where $P(x, y)$ is the probability of choosing x over y, U denotes utility, and ϵ denotes how stochastic choices are. If $\epsilon = 0$, choices are random. The probability of choosing each alternative is ½ regardless of their utilities. The agent ignores utility and chooses randomly, e.g. by tossing a fair coin. The larger is ϵ the less random is choice and the more it is based on the difference in utility (attractiveness) between the options.

Exercise 6.2: Luce's Choice Rule

Show that if $\epsilon \to \infty$ choice is **deterministic** (fully determined by the difference in utility).

In the 1990s behavioural economists became increasingly interested in modelling stochastic choice and in the question whether the deviations from standard economic models were systematic or due to random errors. Three distinct models emerged.

1. David Harless and Camerer (1994) proposed the **trembling hand model**. Agents make a (constant error) ϵ of choosing the wrong (less preferred) alternative. Formally, $P(x, y)$ the probability to choose x over y is equal to:

$$P(x, y) = \begin{cases} \epsilon & \text{if } U(x) < U(y) \\ 1/2 & \text{if } U(x) = U(y) \\ 1-\epsilon & \text{if } U(x) > U(y) \end{cases} \tag{6.2}$$

   A limitation of the trembling hand model is that the error probability is constant and independent of the difference in attractiveness between the options. Intuitively, errors are more likely if the options are close in attractiveness than when one of the options is much more attractive than the other. Indeed, empirically the trembling hand model performs worse than the two models discussed next (Ballinger and Wilcox 1997; Carbone 1997; Loomes and Sugden 1995; Stott 2006).
2. The **Fechner model**, proposed by John Hey and Chris Orme (1994), solves the limitation of the trembling hand error by assuming that $P(x, y)$ depends on the utility difference between x and y. However, subjects make an error ϵ in computing this difference.

$$P(x, y) = F(U(x) - U(y) + \epsilon). \tag{6.3}$$

   A common specification is to assume that F is a logit or probit function. The logit function is defined as

$$P(x, y) = \frac{1}{1 + e^{-\epsilon\left(U(x)-U(y)\right)}}, \tag{6.4}$$

   where ϵ indicates the extent to which choice is random.[3]

[3] The probit function is defined as $P(x, y) = \Phi\big(U(x) - U(y), 0, \epsilon\big)$, where Φ is the cumulative normal distribution with mean 0 and standard deviation ϵ at point $U(x) - U(y)$. $P(x, y)$ increases with $U(x) - U(y)$.

Exercise 6.3: Fechner Model

Show that in Eq. 6.4:
(a) if $\epsilon = 0$ choice is random.
(b) the larger ϵ, the more choice is determined by the difference in utilities.
(c) if $\epsilon \to \infty$ choice is deterministic.

A limitation of the Fechner model is that it predicts implausible errors. Suppose x is a prospect that gives €10 with probability $^1/_2$ and nothing otherwise and y is a prospect that gives €9.75 with probability $^1/_2$ and nothing otherwise. Any agent will choose x over y, because x (first order stochastically) dominates y. However, because the utility difference between x and y is small, the Fechner model predicts that choice errors are common and agents will occasionally choose y. Indeed, Loomes and Sugden (1998) found less violations of dominance than the Fechner model predicted.

3. The **random preference model** of Loomes and Sugden assumes that agents have a set of preference relations from which they choose one randomly at the moment of choice. Random preference is similar to the idea of preference imprecision discussed in Chapter 2. The model of Mike Regenwetter and colleagues to explain violations of transitivity also belongs to this class.
   Suppose that agents only know that they want to satisfy dominance. Let Z be the set of preference relations that satisfy dominance and suppose agents consider each of these relations equally likely. Then $P(x, y)$ the probability of choosing x over y is equal to the proportion of preference relations in Z according to which x is preferred to y. Agents may wish to impose more restrictions (e.g. transitivity). This shrinks the set Z. They can also weight preference relations by their likelihood. The basic idea is that agents are unsure about their preferences, check according to which they prefer x to y, and weight them by how likely they are.

The question which error model fits best is still unresolved. Both the Fechner model and the random preference model have their pros and cons. Evidence suggests that at least the widely used logit and probit specifications of the Fechner model do not fit empirical data well.

Neuroeconomics suggests a different error story. A promising stochastic choice model is the **drift diffusion model**, developed by psychologist Roger Ratcliff and made popular by Jerome Busemeyer, who calls it **decision field theory**. The basic idea is that when they make a choice between x and y, agents compute the perceived value difference $V(x, y)$ between x and y. It starts at 0 and the agents adjust it by the formula

$$V_{t+1} = V_t + \tau \times \big(U(x) - U(y)\big) + \epsilon_t. \tag{6.5}$$

In Eq. 6.5, V_t is the value difference at time t, $U(x) - U(y)$ is the difference in utility between x and y, τ reflects the speed of adjustment, and ϵ_t is an error term, which reflects the mistake agents make in updating V. The larger the error term, the more stochastic are choices.

The brain keeps computing Eq. 6.5 until the perceived value difference exceeds a decision threshold. Then the agent chooses x if the perceived value difference is sufficiently positive and y if it is sufficiently negative. See Fig. 6.1. The agents keep computing the perceived value difference between x and y until V_t hits the decision threshold for choosing x and they then choose x at time point t^*. So, t^* is the response time that the agent needs to make this choice.

The drift diffusion model predicts that response times give information about preferences. The larger $U(x)-U(y)$, the quicker agents will hit the decision threshold and make their decision. So, response times give information about utility differences. We saw in Chapter 3 that for many economists utility differences had no meaning. Neuroeconomics may make utility differences measurable after all.

Carlos Alós Ferrer, Ernst Fehr, and Nick Netzer (2021) show that when choices are stochastic, the Fechner model can only recover underlying preferences by making assumptions about the error distribution. The conclusions can change by changing these assumptions. For example, David Buschena and David Zilberman (2000) found that expected utility is the best model for risk if errors depend on the size of the outcomes, but not if errors are independent of the size of the outcomes.

If we also take response times into account then we can measure preferences without making assumptions about the error distribution. Moreover, if we are willing to make assumptions about the distribution of the errors (e.g. that it is symmetric, like the normal distribution) then we can recover preferences from response times without needing actual choice data. This is another example of how behavioural economics uses new data to measure preferences.

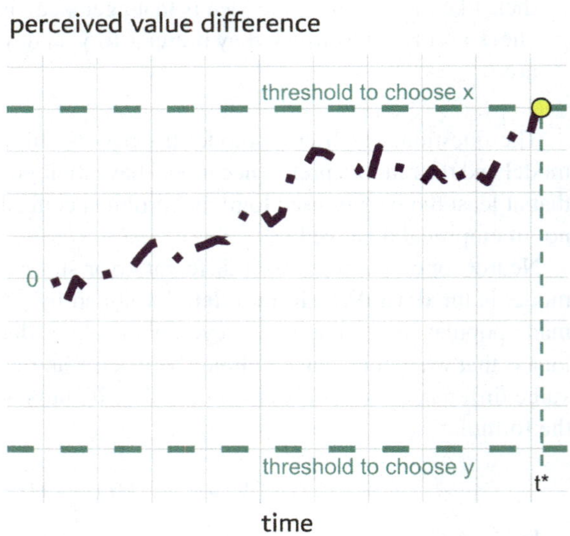

Fig. 6.1 The drift diffusion model

As another example, Paul Stillman et al. (2020) show how **measuring mouse movements** can give information about people's risk preferences. They first measured subjects' risk aversion and then looked at those subjects who preferred a risky option to a certain option. Risk averse people tend to be attracted to certainty (see Chapter 9). So among the subjects who choose the risky option, the more risk averse hesitate most. For them the utility difference between the risky and the certain option will be smaller and the drift diffusion model predicts that they need more time to decide. Subjects' mouse movements from one option to the other measure this conflict. More risk averse subjects moved their mouse more.

6.1.6 Gul and Pesendorfer's Criticism of Neuroeconomics

Faruk Gul and Wolfgang Pesendorfer (2008) criticized neuroeconomics and other approaches that use non-choice data like happiness or genes (see Sect. 6.2). They claim that neuroscientific, and more broadly psychological and physiological, evidence is irrelevant for economics. Economics makes no predictions about how the brain works and, conversely, neuroscience cannot address the questions that interest economists.

In many respects, Gul and Pesendorfer's argument is a return to the neoclassical notion of utility. The basic data of economics are revealed preferences, i.e. choices. From these data economists build models that predict equilibrium outcomes like prices. It echoes Pareto who writes "I am interested only in seeing whether I can discover which regularities are presented by prices". The distinction between what people choose and what they, perhaps, intended to choose is not relevant for economics because it cannot be distinguished from choices. This is like the point made above that economists are interested in the outcomes of choice, not in its processes.

Gul and Pesendorfer give the example of the model of David Kreps and Evan Porteus (1978). In this model, agents have preferences about when the uncertainty they face is resolved. For instance, in medical decisions people often prefer to wait before learning the outcome of a test. An example is Huntington's disease, an incurable neurodegenerative disease that is mostly inherited. It leads to increasing lack of coordination and in an advanced stage to unability to talk, depression, impulsivity, and, ultimately, dementia. A child of a parent with the disease has a 50% probability to develop it. Genetic tests are 100% reliable. In spite of this, around 80% of children with parents who have the disease, prefer not to test and wait for the uncertainty to resolve with time.

Standard economic models cannot explain such preference for the timing of resolution of uncertainty. Kreps and Porteus show how it can be modelled. For their model and its predictions it is irrelevant why people have this preference. It could be anxiety, hope, or any motivation about the planning of life events like having children, buying a house, or following an education. Distinguishing these motivations is important for psychology and neuroscience, but, as Gul and Pesendorfer write, not for economics. Economics is only interested in the result of this preference not why it occurs.

Extension 6.2: Kreps and Porteus

Kreps and Porteus' paper is complex, but the intuition underlying their model is easy. Consider Huntington's disease. Suppose there are two periods *now* and *future*. Children with a parent who carries the gene causing Huntington's disease can take a DNA test. If they do, they know now whether they will have the disease in the future. They can also decide not to take the test. Then they only know in the future whether they have the disease.

Children with a parent who has the disease have a 50% probability to develop the disease. The expected utility of not taking the test is $0.5 \times U(\text{no disease}) + 0.5 \times U(\text{disease})$. In the model of Kreps and Porteus, the expected utility of taking the test is equal to $\phi\Big(0.5 \times U(\text{no disease}) + 0.5 \times U(\text{disease})\Big)$, which we can also write as $0.5 \times U^0(\text{no disease}) + 0.5 \times U^0(\text{disease})$ for an appropriately chosen U^0. The function ϕ reflects the child's attitude to the timing of resolution of uncertainty. If ϕ is concave, and thus U^0 is more concave than U, the child prefers later resolution of uncertainty, and will not take the test. If ϕ is convex (U^0 is more convex than U) then the child prefers earlier resolution of uncertainty and will take the test.

Gul and Pesendorfer also argue against maximizing experienced utility instead of decision utility. According to Gul and Pesendorfer, economics is about explaining market data, not about making people happy. Economists are no therapists.

Gul and Pesendorfer's critique is a reminder of what economics is about and against the, perhaps, overenthusiastic early contributions in neuroeconomics. I believe they are right that describing neuroeconomics as a "radical challenge to economics" (as early proponents of neuroeconomics did) is only justified if it "yields great economic insights". Something neuroeconomics has thus far been unable to do.

Their critique is too extreme. Excluding all data but choices deprives economists of useful data. For example, knowing where risk aversion comes from can tell us about its rationality. Remember Sen's criticism of revealed preference. Somehow, we must decide whether preference conditions are normatively acceptable. Here neuroeconomics can help. Another example is the usefulness of the drift diffusion model in modelling stochastic choice and of response times in identifying economic preferences. Moreover, many economic constructs, particularly in applied work, are unobservable. This complicates econometric analyses. Here neuroeconomics and genoeconomics, to which I turn next, may have a useful role to play.

6.2 Genoeconomics

In his documentary "Three identical strangers" (2018), Tim Wardle tells the true story of Edward Galland, David Kellman, and Robert Shafran, identical triplet brothers[4] who were separated at birth in the 1960s and adopted by separate families. By chance, the brothers meet again at age 19 and the documentary, which won a Jury Award for storytelling at the 2018 Sundance Film Festival, tells the story of their lives from then on. Initially the brothers cherish their similarity and discover, among other things, that they like the same type of women, smoke the same brand of cigarettes, and all wrestled in high school. The brothers become a media hype, appear in talk shows, and open a restaurant (called Triplet's).

After this fairytale-like beginning, the story turns grim. The brothers and their adoptation families discover that they were part of a scientific experiment to test the effects of "nature and nurture". They and other twins were subjects in a study run by Yale psychology professor Peter Neubauer to explore what the effect is on genetically identical persons of growing up in different socio-economic circumstances and with different parenting styles.

Over time the brothers become more aware of their differences and Edward, who grew up in a wealthy but emotionally cold family, commits suicide in 1995 after a struggle with mental illness. Even though the results of Neubauer's experiments were never published (Yale University has sealed them until 2065), the conclusion of the documentary is clear: The impact of genetic factors is small compared to those of the circumstances in which the triplets grew up. Nurture trumps nature.

Genoeconomics tries to answer the same question as Neubauer: What is the impact of our genes on explaining economic behaviour? Fortunately, it does so by more humane methods. Genoeconomics became popular around 2010. The impetus for the field was the deciphering of the human genome in 2001 and the subsequent development of fast and cheap technologies for measuring and analysing it. This made it possible to easily gather information on genetic variation. In that sense genoeconomics differs from neuroeconomics, which measurements are longer and more expensive (especially fMRI scans).

However, like neuroeconomics, that has difficulty pinning down behaviours to specific brain zones, genoeconomics, has difficulty pinning down behaviours to specific genes. Usually many genes are active and each contributes only little. Evidence from medicine, which is more advanced, is not reassuring. Information on genetic variation is so far insufficient to set an accurate diagnosis. On the other hand, studies of twins suggest that economic outcomes and preferences are as heritable as traits like cognitive ability and personality. Hence, genoeconomics may offer benefits although, thus far, they have been limited. The main problem is that it is difficult to replicate earlier associations. But before I turn to these problems, let me first explain what genoeconomics is (for a more extensive overview see Benjamin et al. 2012a or Biroli et al. 2022).

[4] They were actually quadruplets, but the fourth brother died at birth.

6.2.1 Background

Human DNA consists of a sequence of approximately 3 billion pairs of nucleotide molecules. The human genome is divided into 23 pairs of chromosomes, where for each pair one chromosome is inherited from the father and one from the mother. Chromosomes in turn have subsequences called genes. Humans have around 25,000 genes. They give the order to build proteins, which determine the structure and functioning of the cells in the human body.

Human DNA is for 99.9% the same for each person. The segments where it differs are called **genetic polymorphisms** and their location in the body is known. The most common genetic polymorphisms are **single-nucleotide polymorphisms** (SNPs). These differ only for a single pair of nucleotides. The human genome has tens of millions of SNPs. Most genoeconomics studies focus on the SNPs. Nucleotides are usually of two types: the more common major allele and the less common minor allele. For a given SNP, one allele is transmitted from each parent. That means that each SNP can have 0, 1, or 2 minor alleles (and of course also 0, 1, or 2 major alleles). Geneticists count the number of minor alleles per SNP. This number is the individual's **genotype**.

The basic question of genoeconomics is to relate an economic variable of interest y (for example, income, unemployment, risk aversion, time preference or the degree of altruism) to individual genotypes:

$$y_i = \mu + \sum_{j=1}^{J} \beta_j x_{ij} + e_i. \tag{6.6}$$

In Eq. 6.6, μ is the mean of y, β_j denotes the causal impact of SNP j, and x_{ij} is agent i's genotype for SNP j. The sum $g_i = \sum_{j=1}^{J} \beta_j x_{ij}$ is the agent's **genetic endowment** and e_i captures the impact of other variables than genetic endowment on y. For example, in *Three identical strangers*, e_i includes socio-economic circumstances and parenting style while growing up. Berkeley economist Ulrike Malmendier and her co-authors found that earlier life experiences like economic depression and high inflation impact economic decisions (see Example 6.1). As these experiences are independent of genetic endowment, they are captured by e_i. Another way to write equation 6.6 is:

$$outcome = genetics + environment.$$

Example 6.1: The Impact of Life Experiences

Do experiences of economic fluctuations affect decisions? Standard economics says they should not: People's preferences are unaffected by economic experiences and they take all available information into account when forming their preferences. However, research suggests that the circumstances in which people grow up matter. For example, Ulrike Malmendier and Stefan Nagel (2011) found that people who grew up during a recession invest less in stocks than people who grew up during booms. The generation that grew up during the great depression of the 1920s and 1930s was particularly averse to investing in the stock market. Experience effects are long-lasting, but not immutable. They also affect experts. Ulrike Malmendier et al. (2011) show that CEOs who grew up during the great depression have less faith in external capital markets and make more use of internal funds to finance investments compared to CEOs who grew up during other periods.

Equation 6.6 makes two simplifying assumptions:

1. The effect of each SNP is independent, i.e. there is no interaction between SNPs.
2. There is no interaction between genotype and e_i.

These assumptions are strong. For example, let y_i be education and let e_i include quality of teaching. People who genetically benefit more from education probably also benefit more from high-quality teaching. In that case, we need to include an interaction term between quality of teaching and genotype in Eq. 6.6. In a large study involving nearly 15 million twin pairs, Tinca Polderman and co-authors (2015) found that an additive model often does well, particularly for physiological variables. It performs worse for psychological and behavioural variables.

6.2.2 Heritability: Twin Studies

There are two approaches to genoeconomics: **behavioural genetics** and **molecular genetics**. Behavioural genetics is the traditional approach. It seeks to determine which proportion of the variance in y, the economic variable of interest, is due to variation in genetic endowment: $\frac{var(g_i)}{var(y_i)}$. In other words, behavioural genetics is interested in **heritability**.

The classical way to perform heritability studies is to compare monozygotic (identical) and dizygotic (fraternal) twins. Monozygotic twins are genetically identical, while dizygotic twins are genetically as equal as normal siblings. If an economic variable is more correlated for monozygotic twins than for dizygotic twins then this is interpreted as evidence that genetics plays a role in explaining this variable.

Heritability research dates back to the late nineteenth century with the work of Francis Galton, the first who tried to separate the impacts of nature and nurture. Most human traits are heritable. Tinca Polderman and co-authors concluded that "there is compelling evidence that all human traits are heritable". Their estimates of heritability vary between 20% and 60%.

This also holds for economic outcomes. Income is for 20 – 40% heritable and economic preferences like risk attitude, patience, and trust for 20 – 30% (Beauchamp et al. 2011).

Whether these findings are interesting for economics is controversial. Is it relevant to know that income is largely determined by heritable factors? A first intuitive reaction may be to say "yes", as it seems to limit the scope for policy. The larger heritability, the lower policy effectiveness. But this is too simplistic. Whether a factor is important for economic policy depends whether policy can do something about it. Arthur Goldberger (1979) gives the example of eyesight. Eyesight is largely heritable, yet by funding glasses policy can do a lot about it. The role of heritability for economic policy is unclear (Manski 2011).

Perhaps the main role of information on heritability is as an input for the molecular genetics studies, discussed next. If we know that an outcome, like income, is for 40% heritable then this indicates what studies on individual SNPs could possibly explain. It is to those studies that I turn now.

6.2.3 Molecular Genetics

Molecular genetics explores the role of SNPs in explaining economic variables. A naive approach is to estimate Eq. 6.6 with all SNPs included. However, this does not work. To estimate Eq. 6.6, we must have more observations of y than there are independent variables. As there are millions of SNPs, this is impossible and estimations will be indeterminate. Genoeconomic studies therefore run separate regressions

$$y_i = \mu + \gamma_j \times x_{ij} + e_i \tag{6.7}$$

for each of K preselected SNPs. I use γ in Eq. 6.7 instead of the β of equation 6.6 to emphasize that this "solution" biases estimates of the effects of the genes. In Eq. 6.7, we omit many variables (all the other SNPs). This leads to **omitted variable bias,** because the effects of the omitted genotypes are attributed to the one that is included. Unless the genotypes of the SNPs are uncorrelated, this procedure gives biased and inconsistent estimates.[5] The estimated γs differ from the true βs.

There are two methods to choose the K SNPs in Eq. 6.7. **Candidate gene studies** are theory-based. Researchers specify ex ante hypotheses (based on biology) about the SNPs that most likely affect the outcome variable y and run regressions for each of them. Candidate gene studies were common in the early days of genoeconomics, but they have become less popular. One reason is that information on SNPs is now cheap. Another is that the results of candidate gene studies were disappointing. Their main problem is that their results could not be replicated.

Genome-wide association studies (GWAS), which are now common, have no basis in theory. Researchers estimate Eq. 6.7 for all of the K SNPs measured and then check which are significant. This means estimating Eq. 6.7 millions of times.

[5] Inconsistency means that even for large datasets, the estimator does not converge to the true value.

A problem with running so many estimations is **multiple significance testing**. If we use a significance level of 5%, then for each test that we run there is a 95% probability that we will not reject the null hypothesis of no effect if it is true. However, if we test two hypotheses, the probability that in both tests we do not reject the null when it is true drops to $0.95 \times 0.95 = 90.25\%$. There is an almost 10% chance that we wrongly reject the null.

Exercise 6.4: Multiple Significance Testing

Suppose that we run 100 tests, in all of which the null is true. Show that the probability that there is at least one in which we wrongly reject the null is 99.4%.

Exercise 6.4 shows that if we run 100 regressions we are almost certain to find one significant association even if the null is true. Imagine what happens if we run millions of regressions!

GWAS studies correct for multiple significance testing by using low significance levels (mostly $p < 5 \times 10^{-8}$). This low significance level combined with the common finding that each individual SNP contributes little makes that GWAS studies need large samples to be able to detect anything. Such large samples are often not possible. Researchers have used two strategies to solve this:

1. They combined their data into meta-studies.
2. They combined SNPs into **polygenetic indices** (PGIs).

PGIs are a weighted combination of the individual SNPs with the weights equal to the coefficients estimated in Eq. 6.7:

$$PGI_i = \sum_{j=1}^{J} \gamma_j x_{ij}. \tag{6.8}$$

The best PGI usually includes all SNPs. From its construction, we can immediately note some problems of PGIs:

1. They are a linear combination of individual genotypes and therefore exclude all interactions.
2. They use the weights γ_j, which may be biased due to omitted variables.
3. Their construction is circular. First, we use regressions of individual genotypes on y to find the weights γ_j to construct the PGI and then we use the PGI as a regressor on y. Technically, PGI is a "generated regressor". Adrian Pagan (1984) shows that using generated regressors leads to the wrong standard errors and overstates t-values. Thus associations are declared significant when they are not.

Genotypes predict poorly. This is a puzzle of genetics research. Take height, which is for 56% heritable. So, ideally, the relevant genotypes should predict 56% of the differences in human height. However, the genotypes known to be associated with height only explain 10% of the variation. Apparently, many genotypes contribute something. Identifying them all is a Herculean task that requires unrealistically large sample sizes.

Using PGIs improves matters somewhat, but still much is left to explain and it requires large datasets. For example, educational attainment is for 25% heritable (Rietveld et al. 2013). Constructed PGIs can explain half of that variation. To go from explaining one-quarter of the variation to explaining one-half of the variation the sample size had to increase from 400,000 to 3.3 million subjects. The benefits of increasing sample size seem subject to decreasing marginal returns.

6.2.4 The Possible Contributions of Genoeconomics

Even if genotypes could perfectly explain heritability, why would that interest economists? The benefits for economic theory seem limited for the same reason as for neuroeconomics: economists are interested in the outcomes of decisions and less in the processes that underly them. The possible contributions of genoeconomics mainly lie in data analysis. I list three:

1. **Better predictions**. I already discussed omitted variable bias. If economic outcomes are partly determined by genetic factors then including them in our models improves predictions and avoids biases.
2. **Better targeted policies**. If we know that particular groups are genetically disadvantaged then we can target policies to better help them. If a child's educational endowment is low, we can set up supporting teaching programmes from a young age on.
3. **Instrumental variables**. Economists are interested in finding causal relations, e.g. whether an increase in immigration affects the wages of native workers. To test for causality economists use **instrumental variables**. These are correlated with the independent variable (e.g. immigration), but not with the dependent variable (wages). Finding good instrumental variables is an art. Genes might help. See Extension 6.3.

Extension 6.3: Genes as Instrumental Variables

Causality is often hard to establish. For example, Sven Drefahl of the University of Stockholm looked at Danish men over 50 and found that those with a younger spouse survived longer than those with a spouse their age even after controlling for education and wealth. Can we conclude that marrying a younger woman is good for your health? Probably not. Healthy men may also be more attractive for younger women and causality goes the other way.

Ideally, we run an experiment in which subjects are randomly assigned to treatments. Unfortunately, this is often practically or ethically impossible. We cannot randomly assign spouses to men or, as another example, if we want to explore the effects of maternal prenatal alcohol consumption on children's school performance later in life, we cannot randomly assign pregnant women to different alcohol intake treatments.

Econometricians have tried to solve this by instrumental variables. These correlate with one variable but not with the other. Take the impact of education on earnings. Because students with more learning talent spend both more time in school and earn more, it is hard to establish the direct effect of education on earnings. Joshua Angrist and Alan Krueger (1991) circumvented this problem using a characteristic of the American educational system. In the US, children are allowed to drop out of school when they turn 16, but all children born in the same year enter school at the same date (the beginning of the academic year). As a consequence, among the children who drop out at age 16, those born in December have had nearly an extra year of schooling than those born in January. And they earned more later in life. Angrist and Krueger estimated that an extra year of schooling increased wages by 7.5%. As date of birth is unrelated to cognitive ability, it is safe to conclude that the added schooling led to the increase in wages.

Exercise 6.5: College Graduates

Angrist and Krueger also found that date of birth had no impact on earnings for college students (who voluntarily choose to receive more education). Argue that this supports their conclusion that the increased wages among dropouts were due to the extra schooling they received.

The study of Angrist and Krueger shows that a good instrumental variable (birth date in their study) influences the outcome variable (earnings) only through its effect on the treatment variable (years of schooling) and not through any other variable. Stephanie von Hinke and co-authors (2016) discuss whether genotype can be used as an instrumental variable. The main problem is that individual SNPs explain little. We could use many SNPs, but this leads to bias. Instrumental variables that are weakly correlated with the endogenous regressor are biased and this bias rises with the number of instrumental variables.

6.2.5 Wrapping Up

Like neuroeconomics, genoeconomics attempts to use new types of data to improve economics. It fits in the open-minded approach of behavioural economics to other disciplines (biology in this case). Like neuroeconomics, early contributions have overstated the importance of their new line of research for economics. To speak about a "genetics revolution" in economics means that genoeconomics should lead to fundamentally new insights. Thus far, it has not achieved this. Economists may have contributed more to genetics research than the other way around. In particular, the rich collection of methods from econometrics has improved genetics research. Whether genoeconomics will also improve economic theory is an open question.

6.3 Reproducibility

Reproducibility is not only a concern for genoeconomics. In 2005, Stanford professor John Ioannidis published an article with the provocative title "Why most published research findings are false". Ioannidis takes issue with the common claim that a research finding is convincing if it has a p-value less than 0.05. The probability that a research finding is indeed true depends on three variables:

1. the ratio R of "true relationships" to "no relationships". R depends on whether a field of science focuses on likely relationships or tests many relationships in the hope of finding one that is true (like genoeconomics). If R is $1/9$, it means that of the 10 hypotheses tested 1 is true and 9 are false.

Exercise 6.6: True Relationships

Show that the proportion of true relationships among all tested is 100% × $R/R+1$.

2. the **power** of the study, β, which is the probability of finding a relationship when it exists.
3. the probability of claiming a relationship when none exists. This is the Type I error α from statistics.

Exercise 6.7: Ioannidis

Let c be the number of relationships tested. Show that:
1. The number of true relationships is $c \times \frac{R}{R+1}$.
2. The probability that a study finds this is $c \times \beta \times \frac{R}{R+1}$.
3. The probability that a relationship is not true is $c \times (1 - \frac{R}{R+1}) = \frac{c}{R+1}$.
4. The probability that a study falsely concludes that a relationship exists is $\frac{c\alpha}{R+1}$.

From, Exercise 6.7 we see that a research finding is more likely true than false if:

$$\beta \times R > \alpha. \tag{6.9}$$

The ratio of true to false research findings is $\frac{\beta \times R}{\alpha}$. The probability that a research finding is true further decreases if results are reported with bias (e.g. including or excluding observations to reach statistical significance) or if different research teams are working independently on the same questions (which affects both the power and the Type I error (due to multiple significance testing)).

Equation 6.9 shows that research findings are less likely to be true if:

1. The study has a small sample size. Smaller sample sizes lower the power β.
2. The effect size is small. The smaller the effect size the lower β.
3. Many relationships are tested. This lowers R. Theory-based testing is preferred to ad hoc testing.
4. The more flexibility there is in the design and analysis of the study. This increases the opportunities for manipulation and misreporting and thus bias.
5. The greater the financial and other interests and prejudices in a scientific field.
6. The hotter a scientific field. The more popular a field, the more researchers work on it and this makes it less likely that a research finding is true.

Ioannidis' analysis shows the importance of the power of a study, of large-scale evidence, and of looking at the totality of the evidence instead of at one study. Unfortunately, in the popular press arguments are often defended by the phrase "this is backed up by scientific evidence". Ioannidis shows that such claims are vacuous unless we know more about the details of the study.

Extension 6.4: Bias in Research

Researchers have freedom in performing their studies. Examples are how to treat outliers, which dependent variables to include, how many data to collect, which covariates to include, and which treatments to report. These are not cases of clear scientific fraud, but fall in the gray area of acceptable scientific practice. Leslie John et al. (2012) surveyed 2000 psychologists using the Bayesian truth serum (see Extension 4.2). 94% admitted to have engaged in questionable research practices. Most common were not be clear about the dependent variables used and collecting more data after looking to see whether the results were significant.

Joseph Simmons et al. (2011) show that these small deviations from what is acceptable matter. Abusing researcher degrees of freedom increases the probability of accepting a false hypothesis to 61% under the common threshold of $p < .05$. Even for $p < .01$ the probability of accepting a false hypothesis exceeds 20%. They show (using real data!) how abusing researcher degrees of freedom can lead to accept the (absurd) hypothesis that people get younger after listening to the Beatles' song "When I am 64".

Simmons et al. (2011) recommend 6 rules to prevent false-positive publications:

1. Decide the rule for terminating data collection before data collection begins and report it.
2. Collect at least 20 data points per treatment.
3. List all variables collected.
4. Report all experimental conditions, including the ones that show no result.
5. If data are removed (e.g. outliers), also report the results with these included.
6. If covariates are used, also report the results without them.

They have developed the **p-curve** to distinguish true effects from selective reporting (Simonsohn et al. 2014). For a given result, it shows the distribution of significant p-values found in the literature. If the result is true then this distribution is right skewed. More p-values are low (e.g. 1% or lower) than high (close to 5%). Collecting more data will make the p-values go to 0 if an effect is real.

However, if an effect results from selective reporting (***p*-hacking**) then the distribution of observed p-values is left skewed: There are more high than low p-values. Under the null of no effect the distribution of p-values is uniform. P-hacking shifts probability mass from p-values just above 5% to p-values just below 5% (e.g. a researcher finds $p = 0.054$ and reports $p = 0.05$). This makes the distribution of observed significant p-values left skewed. You can use the app p-curve.com to test whether an effect is real or not.

6.3.1 Replication

Ioannidis' paper stimulated studies of the reproducibility of scientific findings. Ioannidis himself studied a small sample of highly cited medical papers. He could confirm half of them. For another 20%, the effects were smaller, but in the same direction (Ioannidis 2005). Later results were worse. Glenn Begley and Lee Ellis (2012) could replicate only 11% of the results from cancer studies. Prinz et al. (2011), who included studies on women's health and cardiovascular disease, could replicate 25% of the results.

These findings are worrying. First, because published results led to follow-up publications. Second, because these results led to a waste of resources in developing new drugs and submitting patients to experimental treatments that did not work. Reproducibility was higher for studies that were careful in avoiding bias, published their data, and were open about the strategy of analysis followed. In other words, for studies that followed the guidelines of Extension 6.4.

Behavioural science also got interested in reproducibility. In 2015, a large study explored whether the key findings from 100 published psychology papers could be reproduced. The authors contacted the original authors to check if they used the same methodology and were testing the key finding. They made sure their replication study had high power (92% on average). In spite of all the care, they could only replicate 36% of the findings. The average effect size was half the original. The p-value of the original study was the best predictor of reproducibility. The lower p, the higher the chance of reproducibility. Characteristics of the research team (like experience) had little impact.

The reproducibility of behavioural economics findings is better. Camerer and co-authors (2016) reran 18 experimental economics studies published in the *American Economic Review* and the *Quarterly Journal of Economics*, two leading journals in economics. They could replicate 61% of the results. The effect size was 66% of the original. The p-value (the smaller the better) and sample size (the larger the better) best predicted reproducibility. The better reproducibility of behavioural economics studies may be because they are more based on theory.

Camerer et al. (2018) reran 21 social science studies from *Nature* and *Science*. Two-thirds of the studies had a significant effect in the same direction as the original studies. In the studies that could be replicated, the average effect size was 75% of the original.

These studies imply that we should not accept all results from behavioural economics at face value. Fortunately, behavioural economics has become more open. Data and code are now available and there is more attention for the power of the study. Also new techniques for data analysis are available that reduce the focus on p-values. I conclude this chapter by discussing one of these.

6.4 Bayesian Statistics

The problems of focusing on p-values and statistical significance led to a move from classical frequentist statistics to Bayesian statistics. Classical hypothesis testing discriminates against the null hypothesis for two reasons (Rouder et al. 2009):

1. It does not give evidence for the null hypothesis. The best that can happen for the null is that it is not rejected.
2. It overstates the evidence against the null hypothesis. This leads to false-positive results.

Suppose that we want to test whether the sum of money agents are willing to pay (WTP) for an improvement in health is the same as the sum they are willing to accept (WTA) for an equal deterioration in health. Economic theory says that WTP and WTA should be (about) the same. Behavioural economics says they differ (see Chapter 7). Researchers often test this difference by a t-test. If behavioural economics is right this makes sense. Collecting more data increases t-values, p-values go to zero and the probability of correctly rejecting the null that WTA and WTP are equal goes to 1.

The situation is more ugly when economic theory is right. Then collecting more data does not make it more likely that the null is not rejected. The t-values do not converge to any limit and all p-values are equally likely. If the null is true, the p-values are uniformly distributed between 0 and 1 regardless of the sample size.

So collecting more data does give more evidence for the alternative, but not for the null. In other words, classical significance tests overstate the evidence against the null and false-positive results are more likely. In statistical terms, if the null is true classical significance tests are **inconsistent**: They do not always give the correct answer for large samples. If the null is true the analyst will keep rejecting the null with probability α (usually 5%).[6]

A solution is to use Bayesian statistics. This makes it possible to compute how likely a hypothesis is given the observed data. That is, we can compute the **posterior odds ratio**

$$\Omega = \frac{P(H_1|data)}{P(H_0|data)}, \tag{6.10}$$

which expresses how much more likely the alternative H_1 is than the null H_0 given the data. Odds are intuitive. For example, if $\Omega = 20$, then the alternative is twenty times as likely as the null given the data. A common rule of thumb is that odds larger than 3 show **some evidence** for the alternative, odds larger than 10 show **strong evidence** for the alternative and odds larger than 30 show **very strong evidence** for the alternative. Symmetrically, odds less than 1/3 show some evidence for the null, odds less than 1/10 show strong evidence for the null, and odds less than 1/30 show very strong evidence for the null. For odds between 1/3 and 3, the evidence is **inconclusive**.

Equation 6.10 shows that the choice of the alternative is important. The null may be plausible compared to one alternative, but not to another.

Exercise 6.8: Bayes Factor

Bayes' formula says that

$$P(A|B) = \frac{P(B|A) \times P(A)}{P(B)}.$$

Use Bayes' formula to show that we can write equation 6.10 as:

$$\Omega = \frac{P(data|H_1)}{P(data|H_0)} \times \frac{P(H_1)}{P(H_0)}. \tag{6.11}$$

In Eq. 6.11, $\frac{P(H_1)}{P(H_0)}$ is the **prior odds ratio**. It reflects the prior beliefs about the plausibility of the null and the alternative before data collection. It is often set to 1. Then $\frac{P(data|H_1)}{P(data|H_0)}$ reflects the evidence from the data. This term is the **Bayes factor**. It shows how much more likely the alternative is than the null given the data.

---

[6] As confidence intervals are closely related to significance tests, they also discriminate against the null.

Bayes factors can be easily computed using statistical packages. I have calculated the Bayes factors reported throughout the book using the Bayes factor package in R (Morey et al. 2022). I like to check the validity of statistical results using Bayes factors. They are intuitive and show how convincing the evidence is. As we will see throughout the book, several conclusions based on classical significance tests are inconclusive using Bayes factors. However, Bayes factors are not a panacea. For example, they are as sensitive to *p*-hacking as classical tests. Bayes factors cannot be used as a substitute for the rules for careful research of Extension 6.4.

Extension 6.5: The Role of Priors

The likelihood of the alternative given the data depends on the choice of alternatives. For example, if we test the difference between WTP and WTA then we must specify beforehand which difference we believe is possible. Usually we specify the alternative as a distribution. For example, if we assume that the difference is normally distributed around zero then we must specify beforehand the variance σ_μ^2 of the distribution. Choosing a large σ_μ^2 means that implausibly high differences between WTP and WTA are allowed under the alternative. As these are not observed, this leads to Bayes factors that favour the null.

Usually priors are placed on the effect size $\delta = \frac{\mu}{\sigma}$, the mean divided by the standard deviation. The null has effect size zero and the alternative is then specified as a normal distribution with mean zero and variance σ_δ^2. Researchers consider effect sizes of 1 large. Using effect sizes larger than 6 is unrealistic. A reasonable assumption is $\sigma_\delta^2 = 1$. This is called the **unit-information prior**.

An alternative is to also use a distribution for σ_δ^2. For example, the inverse χ^2 distribution, which implies that the effect size has a Cauchy distribution. This is called the **JZS prior**. The JZS prior puts more weight on larger effect sizes than the unit-information prior and the resulting Bayes factors, therefore, favour the null more. The Bayes factor package uses the JZS prior. In practice, the choice of the prior is not so important and has little effect on the conclusions.

6.4.1 Redefining Statistical Significance

Benjamin et al. (2018) suggest to use a significance level of $p = 0.5\%$ instead of $p = 5\%$. Their argument is based on Eq. 6.11.

They claim that in psychology around 10% of the relations tested are indeed true. The prior odds of the alternative being true compared to the null being true is around 1:10. Or, $P(H_1)/P(H_0) = 1/10$. A *p*-value of 5% corresponds (under what they call plausible assumptions) to a Bayes factor between 2.5 and 3.4.

Exercise 6.9: Benjamin Part 1

Show by putting the above information into Eq. 6.11 that the posterior odds are between 0.25 and 0.34.

Exercise 6.9 shows that using a significance level of 5% coincides with some support for the null! In other words, using a significance level of 5% leads to too many false-positive results.

A significance level of 0.5% corresponds to a Bayes factor between 14 and 26, which is strong evidence for the alternative.

Exercise 6.10: Benjamin Part 2

Show using Eq. 6.11 that a significance level of 0.5% coincides with posterior odds between 1.4 and 2.6.

Exercise 6.10 shows that even with a significance level of 0.5% the evidence is inconclusive. So using a significance level of 0.5% may still be too lenient.

Their argument depends on the 1:10 prior odds, which is arbitrary. In fields where hypotheses follow from well-defined theories, as behavioural economics should be and perhaps is given its better reproducibility, the odds are more favourable for the alternative.

Exercise 6.11: Prior Odds

A significance level of 1% corresponds with a Bayes factor between 10 and 15 according to Benjamin et al. Compute the posterior odds when the prior odds are 1:2.

The paper by Benjamin et al. (2018) draws attention to derive hypotheses from sound theories, to take account of the power of a study, and to warn against blind faith in a significance level of 5%. However, the proposal to use $p = 0.5\%$ instead of $p = 5\%$ is ad hoc and I would not use it as a new general rule.

References

Alós-Ferrer, C., E. Fehr, and N. Netzer. 2021. Time will tell: Recovering preferences when choices are noisy. *Journal of Political Economy* 129: 1828–1877.

Angrist, J.D., and A.B. Krueger. 1991. Does compulsory school attendance affect schooling and earnings? *Quarterly Journal of Economics* 106: 979–1014.

Badger, G.J., W.K. Bickel, L.A. Giordano, E.A. Jacobs, G. Loewenstein, and L. Marsch. 2007. Altered states: The impact of immediate craving on the valuation of current and future opioids. *Journal of Health Economics* 26: 865–876.

Ballinger, T.P., and N.T. Wilcox. 1997. Decisions, error and heterogeneity. *Economic Journal* 107: 1090–1105.

Beauchamp, J.P., D. Cesarini, M. Johannesson, M.J.M. van der Loos, P.D. Koellinger, P.J.F. Groenen, J.H. Fowler, J.N. Rosenquist, A.R. Thurik, and N.A. Christakis. 2011. Molecular genetics and economics. *Journal of Economic Perspectives* 25: 57–82.

Becker, G.S., and K.M. Murphy. 1988. A theory of rational addiction. *Journal of Political Economy* 96: 675–700.

Begley, C.G., and L.M. Ellis. 2012. Raise standards for preclinical cancer research. *Nature* 483: 531–533.

Benjamin, D.J., D. Cesarini, C.F. Chabris, E.L. Glaeser, D.I. Laibson, et al. 2012. The promises and pitfalls of genoeconomics. *Annual Review of Economics* 4: 627–662.

Benjamin, D.J., J.O. Berger, M. Johannesson, B.A. Nosek, E.-J. Wagenmakers, R. Berk, K.A. Bollen, B. Brembs, L. Brown, C. Camerer, et al. 2018. Redefine statistical significance. *Nature Human Behaviour* 2: 6–10.

Biroli, P., T.J. Galama, S. von Hinke, H. Van Kippersluis, C.A. Rietveld, and K. Thom. 2022. The economics and econometrics of gene-environment interplay. arXiv preprint arXiv:2203.00729.

Botvinik-Nezer, R., F. Holzmeister, C.F. Camerer, A. Dreber, J. Huber, M. Johannesson, M. Kirchler, R. Iwanir, J.A. Mumford, R.A. Adcock, et al. 2020. Variability in the analysis of a single neuroimaging dataset by many teams. *Nature* 582: 84–88.

Buschena, D., and D. Zilberman. 2000. Generalized expected utility, heteroscedastic error, and path dependence in risky choice. *Journal of Risk and Uncertainty* 20: 67–88.

Camerer, C.F., G. Loewenstein, and D. Prelec. 2004. Neuroeconomics: Why economics needs brains. *Scandinavian Journal of Economics* 106: 555–579.

Camerer, C.F., A. Dreber, E. Forsell, T.-H. Ho, J. Huber, M. Johannesson, M. Kirchler, J. Almenberg, A. Altmejd, T. Chan, et al. 2016. Evaluating replicability of laboratory experiments in economics. *Science* 351: 1433–1436.

Camerer, C.F., A. Dreber, F. Holzmeister, T.-H. Ho, J. Huber, M. Johannesson, M. Kirchler, G. Nave, B.A. Nosek, T. Pfeiffer, et al. 2018. Evaluating the replicability of social science experiments in Nature and Science between 2010 and 2015. *Nature Human Behaviour* 2: 637–644.

Camille, N., G. Coricelli, J. Sallet, P. Pradat-Diehl, J.-R. Duhamel, and A. Sirigu. 2004. The involvement of the orbitofrontal cortex in the experience of regret. *Science* 304: 1167–1170.

Carbone, E. 1995. Incorporating a stochastic element into decision theories. *European Economic Review* 39: 641–648.

Carbone, E. 1997. Investigation of stochastic preference theory using experimental data. *Economics Letters* 57: 305–311.

De Martino, B., C.F. Camerer, and R. Adolphs. 2010. Amygdala damage eliminates monetary loss aversion. *Proceedings of the National Academy of Sciences* 107: 3788–3792.

Frydman, C., and C. Camerer. 2016. Neural evidence of regret and its implications for investor behavior. *Review of Financial Studies* 29: 3108–3139.

Glimcher, P.W. 2022. Efficiently irrational: deciphering the riddle of human choice. *Trends in Cognitive Sciences* 26: 669–687.

Goldberger, A.S. 1979. Heritability. *Economica* 46: 327–347.

Grossman, M. 1972. On the concept of health capital and the demand for health. *Journal of Political Economy* 80: 223–255.

Gruber, J., and B. Köszegi. 2001. Is addiction "rational" Theory and evidence. *Quarterly Journal of Economics* 116: 1261–1303.

Gul, F., W. Pesendorfer. 2008. The case for mindless economics. In *The foundations of positive and normative economics: A handbook*. Edited by A. Caplin and A. Schotter, 3–42. Oxford: Oxford University Press.

Harless, D.W., and C.F. Camerer. 1994. The predictive utility of generalized expected utility theories. *Econometrica* 62: 1251–1289.

Hey, J.D., and C. Orme. 1994. Investigating generalizations of expected utility theory using experimental data. *Econometrica* 62: 1291–1326.

Ioannidis, J.P. 2005. Contradicted and initially stronger effects in highly cited clinical research. *JAMA* 294: 218–228.

John, L.K., G. Loewenstein, and D. Prelec. 2012. Measuring the prevalence of questionable research practices with incentives for truth telling. *Psychological Science* 23: 524–532.

Kable, J.W., and P.W. Glimcher. 2007. The neural correlates of subjective value during intertemporal choice. *Nature Neuroscience* 10: 1625–1633.

Krajbich, I., and M. Dean. 2015. How can neuroscience inform economics? *Current Opinion in Behavioral Sciences* 5: 51–57.

Kreps, D.M., and E.L. Porteus. 1978. Temporal resolution of uncertainty and dynamic choice theory. *Econometrica* 46: 185–200.

Loomes, G., and R. Sugden. 1998. Testing different stochastic specifications of risky choice. *Economica* 65: 581–598.

Luce, R.D. 1959. *Individual choice behavior: A theoretical analysis*. New York: Wiley.

Malmendier, U., and S. Nagel. 2011. Depression babies: Do macroeconomic experiences affect risk taking? *Quarterly Journal of Economics* 126: 373–416.

Malmendier, U., G. Tate, and J. Yan. 2011. Overconfidence and early-life experiences: The effect of managerial traits on corporate financial policies. *Journal of Finance* 66: 1687–1733.

Manski, C.F. 2011. Genes, eyeglasses, and social policy. *Journal of Economic Perspectives* 25: 83–94.

McClure, S.M., D.I. Laibson, G. Loewenstein, and J.D. Cohen. 2004. Separate neural systems value immediate and delayed monetary rewards. *Science* 306: 503–507.

Morey, R.D., J.N. Rouder, T. Jamil, S. Urbanek, K. Forner, and A. Ly. 2022. Package 'BayesFactor'. https://cran.r-project.org/web/packages/BayesFactor/

Noussair, C.N., S. Tucker, Y. Xu, and A. Breaban. 2024. The role of emotions in public goods games with and without punishment opportunities. *Journal of Economic Behavior and Organization* 217: 631–646.

Pagan, A. 1984. Econometric issues in the analysis of regressions with generated regressors. *International Economic Review* 221–247.

Polderman, T.J., B. Benyamin, C.A. De Leeuw, P.F. Sullivan, A. Van Bochoven, P.M. Visscher, and D. Posthuma. 2015. Meta-analysis of the heritability of human traits based on fifty years of twin studies. *Nature Genetics* 47: 702–709.

Prinz, F., T. Schlange, and K. Asadullah. 2011. Believe it or not: How much can we rely on published data on potential drug targets? *Nature Reviews Drug Discovery* 10: 712–712.

Rietveld, C.A., S.E. Medland, J. Derringer, J. Yang, T. Esko, N.W. Martin, H.-J. Westra, K. Shakhbazov, A. Abdellaoui, A. Agrawal, et al. 2013. GWAS of 126,559 individuals identifies genetic variants associated with educational attainment. *Science* 340: 1467–1471.

Rouder, J.N., P.L. Speckman, D. Sun, R.D. Morey, and G. Iverson. 2009. Bayesian t tests for accepting and rejecting the null hypothesis. *Psychonomic Bulletin and Review* 16: 225–237.

Simmons, J.P., L.D. Nelson, and U. Simonsohn. 2011. False-positive psychology: Undisclosed flexibility in data collection and analysis allows presenting anything as significant. *Psychological Science* 22: 1359–1366.

Simonsohn, U., L.D. Nelson, and J.P. Simmons. 2014. P-curve: a key to the file-drawer. *Journal of Experimental Psychology: General* 143: 534–547.

Stillman, P.E., I. Krajbich, and M.J. Ferguson. 2020. Using dynamic monitoring of choices to predict and understand risk preferences. *Proceedings of the National Academy of Sciences* 117: 31738–31747.

Stott, H.P. 2006. Cumulative prospect theory's functional menagerie. *Journal of Risk and Uncertainty* 32: 101–130.

Tom, S.M., C.R. Fox, C. Trepel, and R.A. Poldrack. 2007. The neural basis of loss aversion in decision-making under risk. *Science* 315: 515–518.

Von Hinke, S., G.D. Smith, D.A. Lawlor, C. Propper, and F. Windmeijer. 2016. Genetic markers as instrumental variables. *Journal of Health Economics* 45: 131–148.

7 Reference-Dependence, Loss Aversion, and Endowment Effect

7.1 Prospect Theory's Value Function

Behavioural economics has made many contributions to decision under uncertainty and to intertemporal choice. I will discuss these in the chapters to come. In this chapter I discuss contributions which are not particularly tied to risk and time. I start with prospect theory's utility function. Prospect theory explains decision under risk, but its utility function has also been applied to other decision contexts.

Prospect theory's utility function has three properties:

1. Reference-dependence.
2. Diminishing sensitivity.
3. Loss aversion.

Reference-dependence says that preferences are defined over gains and losses from a reference point and not over absolute amounts as in traditional economics. Figure 7.1 shows the idea. Outcomes are defined as gains and losses relative to a reference point (the red point) and not as absolute amounts.

Prospect theory does not say what the reference point is. According to Tversky and Kahneman (1991), it is often the agent's current position (their status quo), but it can also be influenced by aspirations, expectations, norms, and social comparisons. We already saw the influence of social comparisons as a reference point when we discussed happiness. People's relative position was twice as important for their happiness as their absolute position. I will say more about the choice of reference points in Chapter 9.

Diminishing sensitivity means that differences between outcomes become less important when we move away from the reference point. For gains this is similar to decreasing marginal utility. Decreasing marginal utility leads to concave utility. Similarly, diminishing sensitivity leads to concave utility for gains. So for gains prospect theory coincides with traditional economic theory, see Fig. 7.2.

H. Bleichrodt, *Behavioural Economics*,
https://doi.org/10.1007/978-3-031-69166-9_7

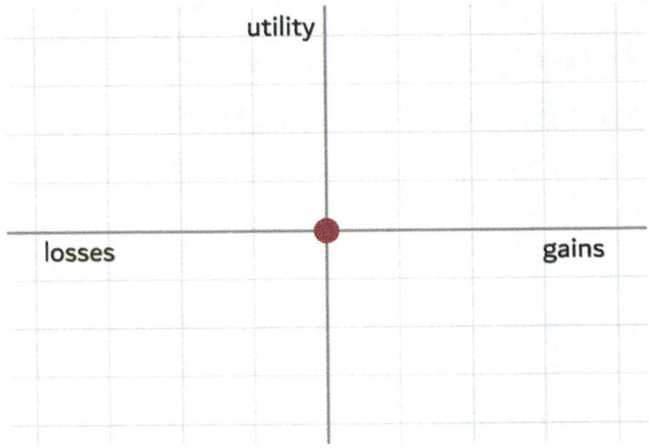

Fig. 7.1
Reference-dependence

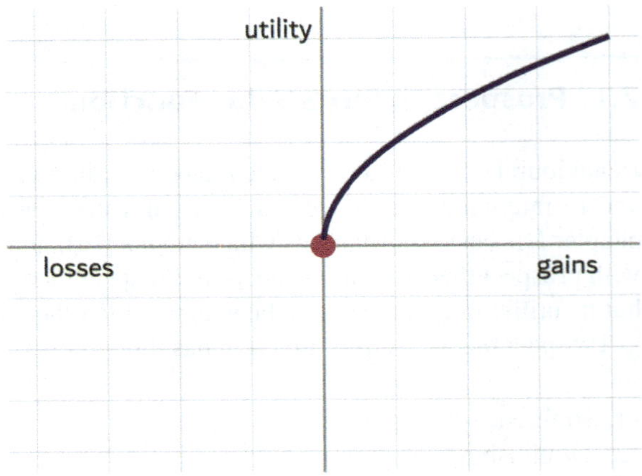

Fig. 7.2 Diminishing sensitivity for gains: concave utility

For losses the situation is different. Again, diminishing sensitivity says that differences between losses become smaller when we move away from the reference point. Thus the difference in utility between losing 5 and losing 10 is larger than that between losing 15 and losing 20. As Fig. 7.3 shows this leads to convex utility. So, for losses prospect theory and traditional economics differ. Prospect theory's utility function is **S-shaped**, convex for losses and concave for gains. The traditional economic utility function is everywhere concave.

The intuition underlying **loss aversion** is that losses loom larger than gains. People are more sensitive to losses than to equally sized gains. Even though its intuition is clear and loss aversion is one of the main ideas of behavioural economics, several definitions of it exist. The most common definition is that there is a kink at the reference point and the utility function at the reference point is steeper for losses than for gains. See Extension 7.1. Under this definition, the utility function is as in Fig. 7.4: concave for gains, convex for losses, and steeper for losses than for gains.

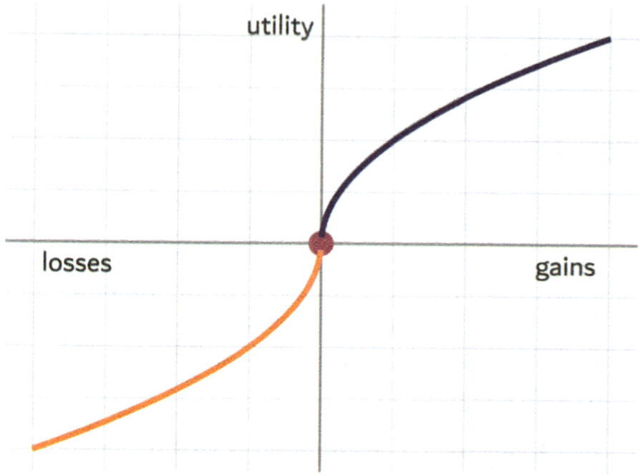

Fig. 7.3 Diminishing sensitivity for losses: convex utility

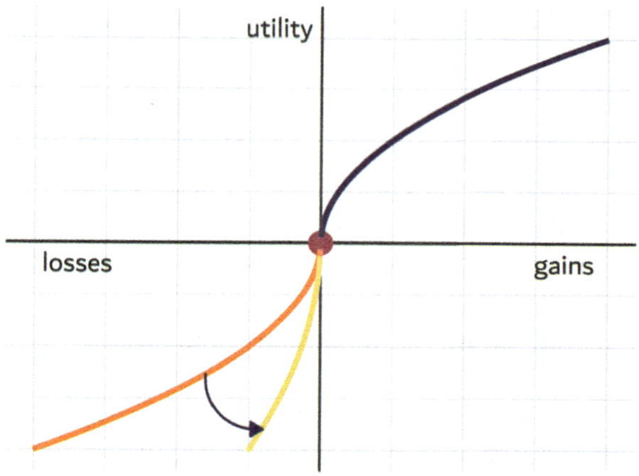

Fig. 7.4 Loss aversion

Extension 7.1: Defining Loss Aversion

Several definitions of loss aversion coexist. Kahneman and Tversky (1979) defined loss aversion as $-U(-x) > U(x)$ for all gains x. In words, the absolute value of utility at any loss exceeds that of its corresponding gain. Peter Wakker and Tversky (1993) defined loss aversion as $U'(-x) > U'(x)$ for all gains x. In words, utility is steeper at any loss than at its corresponding gain. Both definitions confound loss aversion and the curvature of utility (the degree of diminishing sensitivity). They also make it hard to define an index of loss aversion, which is useful in empirical work.

Veronika Köbberling and Wakker (2005) solved these problems. They defined loss aversion as the ratio of the left over the right derivative of utility at the reference point: $\frac{U'_{\uparrow}}{U'_{\downarrow}}$. This definition is independent of the degree of diminishing sensitivity and it is a single number so it can be used as an index of loss aversion.

Empirical studies often use a power specification for the prospect theory utility function:

$$U(x) = \begin{cases} x^{\alpha} & \text{if } x \text{ is a gain} \\ -\lambda(-x)^{\beta} & \text{if } x \text{ is a loss} \end{cases} \tag{7.1}$$

where the reference point is 0. The functions in Eq. 7.1 have extreme derivatives (0 or ∞) at 0 except when $\alpha = \beta = 1$ and utility is linear. If $\alpha = \beta$ the Köbberling-Wakker index can still be defined and is equal to λ. However, if $\alpha \neq \beta$ it is undefined.

Exercise 7.1: Exponential Utility

Show that the exponential specification

$$U(x) = \begin{cases} \frac{1-e^{-\mu x}}{\mu} & \text{if } x \text{ is a gain.} \\ \lambda\frac{e^{\eta x}-1}{\eta} & \text{if } x \text{ is a loss.} \end{cases} \tag{7.2}$$

does not have these problems at 0 (if μ or η is zero, utility is linear) and that the Köbberling Wakker coefficient of loss aversion is equal to λ.

Exercise 7.2: Definitions Compared

Show that if $\lambda \geq 1$ and $\mu > \eta > 0$, the definition of Köbberling and Wakker implies both Kahneman and Tversky's and Wakker and Tversky's definition of loss aversion.

In empirical studies, it is better to take the same curvature for gains and losses ($\alpha = \beta$ for the power function or $\mu = \eta$ for the exponential function). λ is underestimated when utility curvature can differ for gains and losses (Nilsson et al. 2011).

7.2 Empirical Evidence on Utility

7.2.1 Reference-Dependence

Taxi drivers. Colin Camerer et al. (1997) show how reference-dependence affects real-life decisions. They studied the labour supply of New York City cabdrivers. Unlike most professionals, whose wages and working hours are fixed, taxi drivers can decide how many hours to work and their income varies on a daily basis depending on the weather, special events, and public transport problems. In addition, their hours worked and income are measured by taxi meters.

Labour economics predicts that taxi drivers work more on busy days and less on quiet days. The number of hours worked depends on earnings, which are equal to the difference between the (fixed) price of a ride minus the effort to find a customer. On busy days, finding a customer is easier (effort is less) and neoclassical theory predicts that drivers will work more.

However, they do the opposite: on busy days taxi drivers work less and quit early. The explanation uses two ideas from behavioural economics: **narrow bracketing** and reference-dependence. Narrow bracketing is like isolation (see Chapter 5). It says that taxi drivers take each day at a time and do not see their work decision as part of a larger whole. In economic terms: Income effects dominate intertemporal substitution effects.

By reference-dependence, the taxi drivers have a daily target income. Once they reach their target, they quit. Extra income (gains) gives little extra utility. In other words, the marginal disutility of leisure is low until reaching the target income and then becomes high. Reference-dependence affects real-life decisions with high stakes and is not just an experimental artefact.

Extension 7.2: Is Camerer et al.'s Result Robust?

Labour economist Henry Farber criticized the findings of Camerer et al. on two grounds:

1. Camerer et al. assume that the wage rate is constant within days and only varies between days. Farber finds as much within-day variation as between-day variation.
2. Camerer et al.'s study suffers from **endogeneity bias**. They estimate the regression

$$lnH_{it} = \eta \times lnW_{it} + \beta_i \times X_{it} + \epsilon_{it},$$

where H_{it} stands for the hours worked by driver i on day t, W_{it} stands for the wage of driver i at day t, X_{it} are other factors affecting labour supply, and ϵ_{it} is the error term.

They compute W_{it} as Y_{it}, total income of driver i on day t divided by

H_{it}. The econometric problem is that H_{it} appears on both sides of the equation. Given measurement error (taxi receipts were hand-written) and imperfect model specification (Camerer et al exclude interaction effects), this will lead to a (negative) bias in the estimation of η.

Instead Farber uses a survival time model which estimates the probability that the driver will quit at different points in time. This probability depends on the number of hours already worked, but, in contrast with a target income model, not on the income already earned.

Farber (2008) estimates the reference point as the level of income where there is a kink in marginal utility (as suggested by Köbberling and Wakker). The reference income indeed affects the decision to stop, but it varies from day to day and is unlikely to be reached. Targets are too unstable to give a useful reference-dependent model of labour supply.

Vince Crawford and Juan Meng (2011) show that a model that combines a standard neoclassical part in which utility depends on absolute income and leisure and a reference-dependent part which has two targets, one for hours worked and one for income attained can explain Farber's data. The targets for hours worked and income are based on expectations, which they proxy by historical averages. They find that hours worked only impact the decision to stop when early-day incomes are high. Neoclassical theory cannot explain this, but reference-dependence can.

Because reference points are based on expectations, reference-dependence only shows up when wage changes are unexpected. Using a rich data set, Hai Long Duong et al. (2023) found evidence of this. They looked at cancellations and no-shows (CNS) for Singapore taxi drivers. Since CNS do not affect the wage rate, the neoclassical model predicts that CNS have no effect on decisions. Reference-dependence predicts that the drivers will work harder, because the CNS are unexpected losses. This is indeed what they found. The effects of CNS were strongest when income was close to the average income per shift. Again, this is in line with prospect theory, because utility is steepest near the reference point due to diminishing sensitivity. The unanticipated nature of the income loss was crucial: The reaction to an expected rise in fuel prices was as predicted by the neoclassical model. The effect of CNS is strongest in the first hour. Within 4 hours, their effects wane off and the reference point has adjusted.

The literature on the taxi drivers shows the beauty of scientific research. It starts with a hypothesis (taxi driver's behaviour is reference-dependent with a daily target income), which is challenged, nuanced, and reconsidered. Finally, a more subtle and detailed version remains: Reference-dependence affects behaviour but the reference point is updated dynamically and this occurs quickly.

Marathon Runners. In the analysis of the taxi drivers, expectations (about income and hours worked) were the reference point. Psychologists Chip Health et al. (1999) suggest that people take their **goals** as reference points. Prospect theory's utility function with a goal as the reference point can explain how goals affect effort, persistence, and performance.

Goals change the psychological value of outcomes. Setting a goal changes that outcome into a reference point and outcomes are seen as gains and losses relative to the goal. This can explain why people who set high goals feel worse about their performance than those who set no or low goals even though high-goal setters objectively perform better. Setting a high goal makes it more likely that you do not achieve it. This puts you into the loss domain and by loss aversion losses hurt more than gains relative to a lower reference point.

This does not mean that setting lower goals is better. If you set a low goal then diminishing sensitivity makes that you have little incentive to spend extra effort once the goal is reached. By contrast, if you set a higher goal you are on the steeper loss part of the utility function and extra effort to move towards the goal will lead to a larger increase in utility. The model of goal setting makes the following recommendations for daily life and for organizations who want to get the best out of their employees:

1. Set **high but realistic goals**. High goals mean that you are longer in the loss domain, which leads to more effort. However, unrealistic goals lead to sure losses and a refusal to do the task at all.
2. **Formulate subgoals**. People find it hard to start a task when the goal is difficult. The idea of writing a book of 300 pages is daunting. Splitting the goal into subgoals (write every day 2 pages) makes it more feasible. When I ran the Valencia marathon, 42 kilometres seemed overwhelming. Splitting the course into blocks of 3 kilometres made it manageable (although the last 10 kilometres hurt nevertheless).

Using goals as reference points predicts that the distribution of the data around the goal will be asymmetric: as people exert most effort when they are close to the goal we should see many observations just making the goal and fewer just failing to achieve the goal. Eric Allen and co-authors (2017) tested this for marathon runners. Marathon runners take round times (e.g. 4 hours) as their goal. Consistent with reference-dependence, the number of times just below a round number was indeed more frequent than the number just above. There were 30% more times between 3 hours 59 minutes and 4 hours than between 4 hours and 4 hours and 1 minute.

In addition:

1. Both predicted and experienced finishing times showed reference-dependence and loss aversion. Predicted and experienced utility may be closer than Chapter 4 suggested.
2. Marathon runners were too optimistic about reaching their goal: 75% thought they would beat their goal, but only 25% did. This is an example of overconfidence that I discuss in Chapter 8.
3. Both loss aversion and overconfidence were independent of experience.

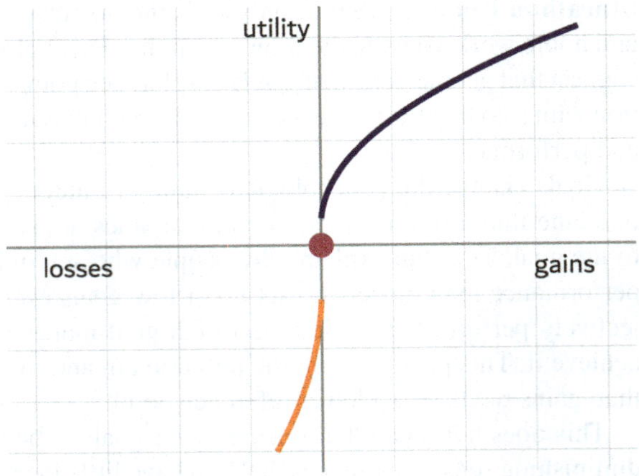

Fig. 7.5 A jump in utility at the reference point

4. There was a discontinuous jump at the reference point (see Fig. 7.5). This is in line with a model where the reference point is determined by people's aspirations (see Chapter 9).

7.2.2 Status Quo Bias

A consequence of loss aversion is that people stick to their status quo. Giving up the status quo is a loss and this loss weights heavily. William Samuelson and Richard Zeckhauser (1988) call this **status quo bias**. Status quo bias affects, for example, health insurance decisions. New employees choose new health insurance plans more often than existing employees. New employees do not yet have a health insurance plan and are unaffected by status quo bias. When people make changes to their plans they prefer small changes from the status quo over larger ones: they prefer a variant of their existing plan over a new alternative.

The Netherlands reformed its health care system in 2006. A mainstay of the reform was competition between private health insurers. People contract with a private health insurer, but can annually change their contract and insurer without cost. Health insurers make them a new offer each year, which is publicly announced. In spite of this transparency, few people switch. In the first years after the implementation only 3-4% did so. Since then, it has increased, but remains low at 6-7%. An explanation is status quo bias.

Chicago economist Steve Levitt (2021) shows how status quo bias can reduce well-being. His website (FreakonomicsExperiments.com) asks people about decisions they struggle with. These include trivial decisions like "should I dye my hair", but also important ones like "should I quit my job", "should I propose marriage", or "should I adopt a child". People can also create their own question. The website gives the option to let a coin toss decide. People who choose to let the coin decide are re-surveyed 2 and 6 months later. They could choose a third party to monitor their decision as an extra commitment device.

Over the one year study period, more than 20,000 coins were flipped. This also happened for important decisions. For example, more than 2000 coins were flipped for the job quitting decision. Those for whom the coin said "change" were happier than those who did not change, especially after 6 months. This is consistent with status quo bias, which makes people change too little and thereby decreases happiness. Subjects who were told to change by the coin toss were also more convinced that they had made the right decision and would stick to their decision if given the opportunity to choose again. It is in line with Kierkegaard's quote that "while change makes us temporarily lose our balance, not changing makes us permanently lose ourselves".

Bio 7.1: Søren Kierkegaard

Søren Kierkegaard (1813–1855) was a Danish philosopher. His work spans philosophy, religion, psychology, literary criticism, and social critique. Kierkegaard sees the human being as a goal to strive for, not as a metaphysical entity. The self must become what it is to become and humans play an active role in this process. Emotions and passions are an essential part of an authentic human life. We should not avoid, but explore them because they teach us about our vulnerabilities and mistakes.

Kierkegaard wrote the first book about anxiety. For him anxiety was inseparable of our life and our freedom. Anxiety arises when a human being becomes aware of their freedom, their responsibility, and their possibilities. This resembles Martin Heidegger and Jean-Paul Sartre's existentialism. A difference with Sartre is that Kierkegaard thought that self creation goes hand in hand with self acceptance: a recognition that the self is restricted by our limitations and biology and history. Kierkegaard impacted many later thinkers including Ludwig Wittgenstein who described him as "by far the most profound thinker of the 19th century".

The Copenhagen of Kierkegaard's time was a city full of religious movements. These criticized each other fiercely. In 1846, Kierkegaard, who was religious but critical of the Danish state church, got in conflict with Poul Martin Møller. Møller was the director of *El Corsario*, a satirical literary magazine, known for its caricatures of Danish public figures. Kierkegaard became the subject of a series of attacks. As a result the public perception of him changed from being an excentric but respected thinker to a ridicule. Kierkegaard's health deteriorated and in 1855, at the age of 42, he collapsed on the street and died. For more on Kierkegaard, see Garff (2013).

7.2.3 Default Bias

In the US more than 100,000 people are waiting to receive a donor organ and each day 17 people die waiting for an organ transplant. Many people support organ donation, but few are donors.

Eric Johnson and Daniel Goldstein (2003) showed how status quo bias can help increase donors. Countries differ in their donor registration system. While some use an opt-in system, in which people are no donor unless they choose to, others use an opt-out system in which people are a donor unless they state that they do not want to. Traditional theory says that this difference does not matter. To become a donor depends on preferences. The default is irrelevant. By contrast, status quo bias suggests that the default is important, because it affects what is a loss and what is a gain. Agents more likely choose an option when it is the default.

Figure 7.6 shows this **default bias**. In countries with an opt-in system, the percentage of donors varied between 4% and 27%. In countries with an opt-out system it was close to 100%. Since then Argentina (2005), Uruguay (2012), Chile (2013), Wales (2015), the Netherlands, England and France (all 2020), and Scotland (2021) have changed to an opt-out system. It shows that behavioural economics can have large effects. Many lives are saved thanks to a simple intervention based on behavioural economic insights.

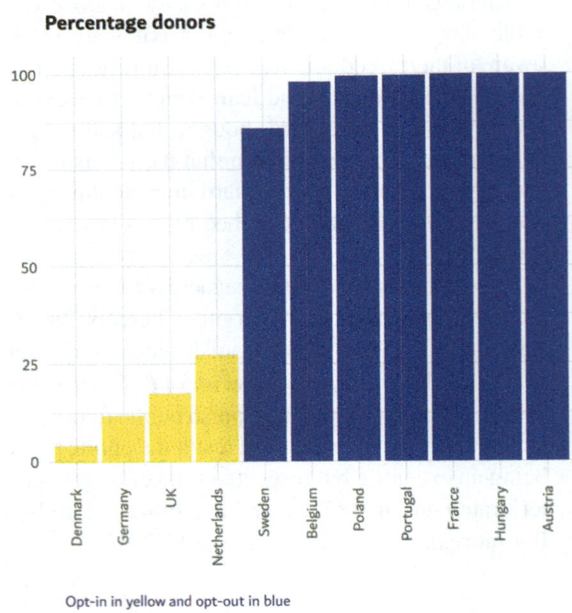

Fig. 7.6 The effect of defaults on organ donations

7.2.4 The Endowment Effect

Economics assumes that preferences do not depend on their endowments. Indifference curves are independent of current holdings and the Coase theorem says that initial entitlements do not affect trade. Loss aversion tells a different story. Giving up a good is a loss and this loss has more impact than obtaining the good. This means that sellers are reluctant to trade and demand a higher price than most buyers are willing to pay. Consequently, there will be less trade than the Coase theorem predicts. Loss aversion restricts trade.

Richard Thaler called this the **endowment effect**. The value of a good rises if it belongs to an agent's endowment. Joint with Kahneman and Jack Knetsch (Kahneman et al. 1990), Thaler showed that the endowment effect was robust against using incentives, market experience, and telling subjects the prices at which the goods were sold. Experiment 7.1 gives an example.

Experiment 7.1: Kahneman, Knetsch and Thaler

The experiment was run during 6 tutorials of a course in business statistics with 59 students. Half of these (the sellers) received a mug with a retail value of $6. They could sell it and indicated on a form with prices ranging from $0.50 to $9.50 in steps of $0.50 for which prices they were willing to sell the mug.

The other half (the buyers) could buy the mug. They indicated for each of the prices whether they were willing to buy the mug. Consistent with the endowment effect, the mean valuation of the mug differed: It was $2.21 for buyers and $5.78 for sellers.

As the allocation of the mugs was random, the distribution of valuations of the mug should be the same for buyers and sellers. The Coase theorem then predicts that half of the sellers trade. In reality only 20% of the sellers traded.

In the experiments of Kahneman, Knetsch, and Thaler, sellers and buyers both make a trade-off between the mug and money. But they do so from different points of reference. The sellers choose between giving up the mug and getting a sum of money. The buyers choose between giving up a sum of money and getting the mug.

The endowment effect is important for policy. As mentioned in Example 4.1, the time trade-off (TTO) is widely used to value health states. Health policy uses these valuations to decide which treatments to reimburse. To value back pain, for example, the TTO asks people to imagine living for, say, 40 years with back pain (followed by death) and to state how many of these 40 years they are willing to give up to live in full health instead.

Figure 7.7 shows the trade-off. People start in the point (40 years, back pain) and move along the indifference curve to the point (X years, full health). That is, they determine the loss $40 - X$ in life duration that is just sufficient to offset the gain in quality of life from living with back pain to living in full health. The utility of back

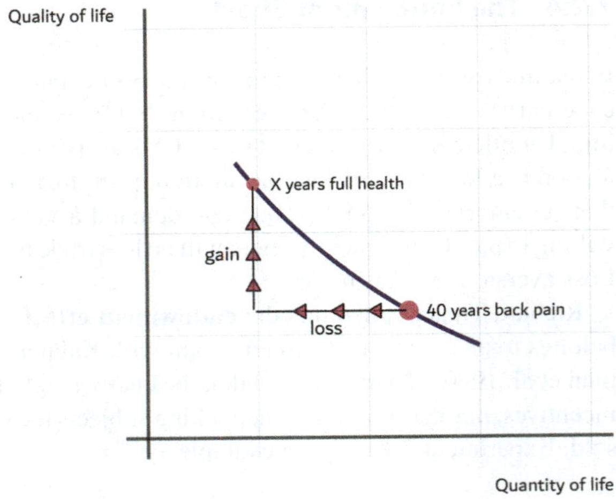

Fig. 7.7 The trade-off in the conventional TTO

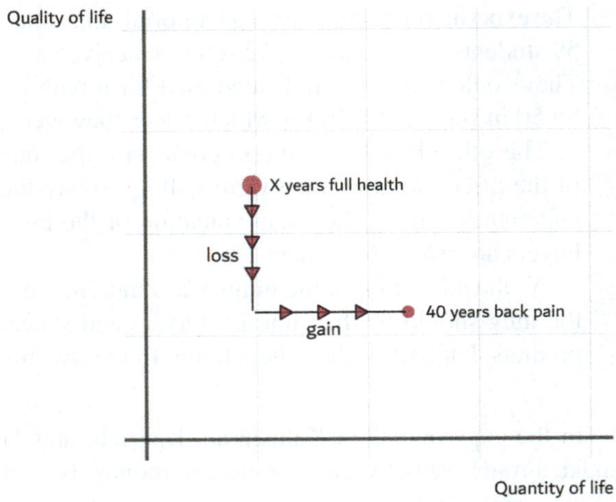

Fig. 7.8 The trade-off in the reverse TTO

pain is then set equal to $\frac{X}{40}$ and the burden of living a year with back pain (instead of full health) is $1 - \frac{X}{40}$.

Instead of asking the TTO in the above, conventional, way, we could also do it reversely. We start with asking people to imagine living for X years in full health (followed by death) and to state how many extra years of life they would want to compensate for living with back pain instead. Economic theory says that this change should not matter and that people reply 40 years. Loss aversion says it does matter. As shown in Fig. 7.8, the reference point shifts to (X years, full health) and the original gain in quality of life from back pain to full health is now a loss and weights

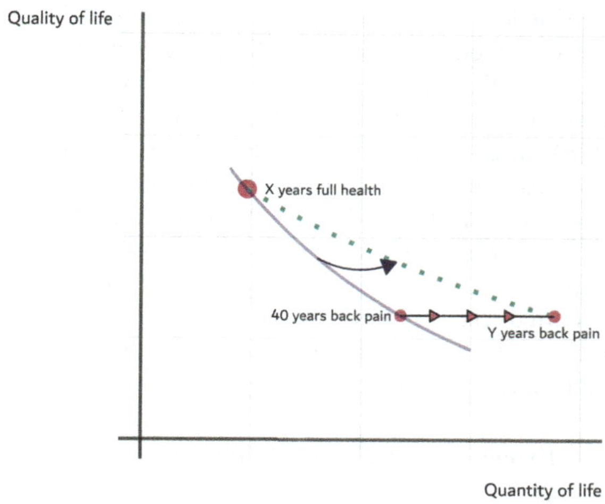

Fig. 7.9 The new reference point makes indifference curves flatter

more. Also, the original loss in life duration from 40 years to X years is now a gain and weights less. Combining these two effects implies that people will prefer (X years, full health) to (40 years, back pain).

Figure 7.9 shows that to restore indifference the number of years with back pain has to increase to $Y > 40$. Consequently, the new indifference curve shifts outwards and becomes flatter.

Exercise 7.3: Reverse TTO

Show that the reverse TTO leads to a lower utility of back pain than the conventional TTO.

In Bleichrodt et al. (2003) we found that the utility of back pain dropped from 0.67 to 0.50 when we used the reverse TTO. This is a problem for health policy: priority setting depends on the variant of the TTO used and there are no theoretical grounds to prefer one over the other.

Exercise 7.4: Health Policy

Explain that treating back pain will get more priority when the reverse TTO is used.

7.2.5 Is the Endowment Effect Real?

The endowment effect leads to a difference between willingness to accept (WTA) and willingness to pay (WTP) as we saw in the experiment of Kahneman, Knetsch, and Thaler. This creates a problem for policy. Policy requires taking into account the value of goods that are not traded on markets. Examples are environmental quality, the extinction of species, and the effects of health and safety measures. Not taking these into account means giving them value 0, which is undesirable. But if WTP and WTA differ, which of these is the correct measure?

Tuba Tunçel and Jim Hammitt (2014) found that the WTA-WTP gap was largest for environmental goods (with WTA more than 6 times as large as WTP) followed by health and safety (5 times as large). For ordinary goods (like mugs) and prospects it was about 1.5. So the gap is largest where it matters most. The WTA-WTP gap even occurred when subjects performed both a WTA and a WTP task (a within-subjects design). Apparently, they see the tasks as distinct. Incentives, the elicitation method, and experience had no effect on the gap.

Extension 7.3: The WTA-WTP Gap and Hicksian Theory

The WTA-WTP gap is not necessarily inconsistent with the neoclassical theory of consumer choice, as developed by Hicks (see Chapter 3). Take the study on road safety by Mike Jones-Lee and Graham Loomes. Their WTP question asks respondents how much they are willing to pay to reduce their annual risk of dying in a road accident from 6 (in 100,000) to 5 (in 100,000). That is they compare the options $(6, y)$ and $(5, y - wtp)$ where y is current monthly income. On the other hand, the WTA question asks respondents how much they are willing to accept for an increase in their risk of dying from 5 (in 100,000) to 6 (in 100,000). That is, they compare $(5, y)$ with $(6, y + wta)$. So, respondents are better off in the WTA question. If there is a strong income effect and the shape of the indifference curves changes when the agent is better off, then Hicksian demand theory predicts that WTA and WTP will be different. Usually the income effect is not so large that it can explain the WTA-WTP gap.

Michael Hanemann showed that the difference between WTA and WTP depends in Hicksian theory on the ratio between the income effect and the substitution effect. If a good has few substitutes then the theory predicts that the WTA-WTP gap can be large. But it is unclear how large the gap should be to refute Hicksian demand theory.

Ian Bateman and co-authors (1997) performed a test between Hicksian demand theory and reference-dependence. They asked the following four questions:

1. *willingness to pay*. Subjects are told they currently have $(6, y)$. They state the amount x_1 such that $(6, y) \sim (5, y - x_1)$. If $x_1 < 100$ then Hicksian demand theory implies that $(6, y) \succ (5, y-100)$ and reference-dependent theory implies that $(6, y) \succ_{(6,y)} (5, y - 100)$ where $\succ_{(6,y)}$ stands for "preferred from reference point $(6, y)$".
2. *willingness to accept*. Subjects are told they currently have $(5, y - 100)$. They state the amount x_2 such that $(6, y - 100 + x_2) \sim (5, y - 100)$. If

$x_2 < 100$ then Hicksian demand theory implies that $(6, y) \succ (5, y - 100)$ and reference-dependent theory implies that $(6, y) \succ_{(5,y-100)} (5, y-100)$.
3. *equivalent gain*. Subjects are told they currently have $(6, y - 100)$. They state the amount x_3 such that $(6, y) \sim (5, y - 100 + x_3)$. If $x_3 < 100$ then Hicksian demand theory implies that $(6, y) \succ (5, y - 100)$ and reference-dependent theory implies that $(6, y) \succ_{(6,y-100)} (5, y - 100)$.
4. *equivalent loss*. Subjects are told they currently have $(5, y)$. They state the amount x_4 such that $(6, y) \sim (5, y - x_4)$. If $x_4 < 100$ then Hicksian demand theory implies that $(6, y) \succ (5, y-100)$ and reference-dependent theory implies that $(6, y) \succ_{(5,y)} (5, y - 100)$.

In Hicksian demand theory the endowment is irrelevant and it predicts that the proportion of subjects preferring $(6, y)$ to $(5, y - 100)$ is the same in the four tasks. Because the comparison is always between $(6, y)$ and $(5, y - 100)$ income and substitution effects are controlled for.

Reference-dependence says that the proportions of subjects preferring $(6, y)$ to $(5, y - 100)$ will vary, because the reference point varies across tasks. In the WTP question, subjects compare a gain in road safety against a loss in money. On the other hand in the WTA question they compare a gain in money against a loss in road safety. Loss aversion predicts that more people will have the implied preference $(6, y) \succ_{(6,y)} (5, y - 100)$ than $(6, y) \succ_{(5,y-100)} (5, y - 100)$

Exercise 7.5: Equivalent Gain Equivalent Loss

Explain that loss aversion predicts that the proportion of people who have $(6, y) \succ_{(6,y-100)} (5, y - 100)$ (the equivalent gain question) and those who have $(6, y) \succ_{(5,y)} (5, y - 100)$ (the equivalent loss question) will be in between those who prefer $(6, y)$ in the WTP question and those who prefer $(6, y)$ in the WTA question.

The data supported reference-dependence and loss aversion. The proportion of people preferring $(6, y)$ to $(5, y - 100)$ indeed dropped from the WTP question through the EL and EG question to the WTA question.

Misunderstanding. Charles Plott and Kathryn Zeiler (2005) argued that the WTA-WTP gap was due to subjects' misunderstanding of the tasks. There was a WTA-WTP gap when they used the procedures of Kahneman, Knetsch, and Thaler, but it disappeared when they trained their subjects and gave them practice rounds. Their study is widely cited as evidence that the WTA-WTP gap does not exist. However, it has several problems.

1. The good they use is a mug. As we saw above, the WTA-WTP is smallest for such private goods. The results of Plott and Zeiler do not imply that there is no WTA-WTP gap for non-market goods.

2. Plott and Zeiler found a WTA-WTP gap for prospects even though they used the same procedures as for the mug. They argued that these prospects were meant as practice sessions, but they do not explain why. It makes it impossible to interpret their study as evidence that the WTA-WTP gap does not exist in general (Isoni et al. 2011).
3. Their data are inconclusive. They performed three studies, all with few subjects (31 in the first, 26 in the second, and 17 in the third). They reject the null of equal WTA-WTP in none of these. However, as we saw in Chapter 6, this does not mean that their data support the null. They probably had insufficient power to detect a difference given the low number of subjects. To say something about support for the null, I computed the Bayes factors. See Table 7.1. Remember that a Bayes factor smaller than 1/3 shows support for the null. None of the tests of Plott and Zeiler meet this, not even the pooled data. The data are inconclusive and do not show that there is no WTA-WTP gap.

Dietmar Fehr et al. (2015) tried to replicate the result of Plott and Zeiler using the same procedures, but with more subjects. They could not. The WTA-WTP gap was similar to the gap found by Tunçel and Hammitt for ordinary goods for both prospects, mugs, and USB sticks.

Simon Gächter et al. (2022) report the WTA and WTP for a large sample of customers of a car manufacturer. They valued a toy car model of the manufacturer. All subjects were interviewed at home by a professional as part of a market research interview. Although they used the incentive mechanism of Plott and Zeiler, the gap existed and was the same as in Tunçel and Hammitt for ordinary goods. This held both between subjects (subjects only performed the WTA or the WTP task) and within-subjects (subjects performed both tasks). The WTA-WTP gap is real and not due to subjects' misunderstanding.

Experience. John List (2003) claimed that the endowment effect disappears with market experience. He tested the endowment effect in a sportscard show and in a collector market of Walt Disney pins. List concludes that while inexperienced traders show the endowment effect, experienced traders do not. However, his sample sizes are small and a Bayesian reanalysis shows that his results for experienced traders are inconclusive. His data only support that the endowment effect exists for the whole sample and for inexperienced traders.

Later studies cast further doubt on List's conclusion. Santosh Anagol et al. (2018) studied the behaviour of 1.5 million Indian stock investors. In India, the shares of oversubscribed initial public offerings (IPO) (firms that for the first time go to

Table 7.1 Bayes factors for Plott and Zeiler's data

Experiment	Bayes factor
1	0.36
2	0.57
3	1.40
Pooled	0.43

the stock market) are randomly assigned. Because the assignments are random, the winners and losers of these lotteries have similar beliefs, preferences, and information about the stocks. Consequently, once the shares start trading, and winners and losers have equal opportunities to trade, economic theory predicts that their holdings of these shares are equal.

However, even 2 years after the lottery, winners were 35% more likely to hold the IPO stock than losers. This is in line with a robust endowment effect that hardly diminished over time. Experienced lottery winners were still about 30% more likely to hold the stock than experienced losers. Tunçel and Hammitt also found that market experience had little effect on the WTA-WTP gap. The study by Anagol et al. also is additional evidence against Plott and Zeiler. Their data satisfy all the conditions Plott and Zeiler propose to make the endowment effect go away, but it does not.

Exercise 7.6: Endowment Effect

1. Engelmann and Hollard (2010) suggest that the reluctance to trade implied by the endowment effect stems from **trade uncertainty**: unfamiliarity with the costs or risks associated with trading. Think of an experiment that could test this hypothesis. Check their paper for a solution.
2. McGranaghan and Otto (2022) suggest that the endowment effect is also due to **choice uncertainty**: uncertainty about the product and preferences. Think of an experiment that could test this hypothesis. You can check their paper.
3. Explain why these two hypotheses imply that the WTA-WTP gap for non-market goods is hard to resolve.

Loss aversion is important even in settings with high stakes and experienced players. We already saw this in the labour supply decisions of taxi drivers and the race strategy of marathon runners. Other evidence includes:

- House owners are reluctant to sell when the price of their house is below the purchase price (even correcting for mortgage restrictions). From a rational economic point of view the purchase price is irrelevant (it is a sunk cost). However, David Genesove and Christopher Mayer (2001) found that it impacted the decision to sell in the Boston housing market. Mikko Einiö et al. (2008) studied over 300,000 transactions in the housing market of Helsinki. The probability of selling was lower when the price was below the purchase price, this was not caused by mortgage restrictions, and there was "bunching" at the purchase price: many houses sold for exactly the purchase price. This is comparable to the bunching of marathon times. The reluctance to realize losses was the same for first time sellers and for more experienced sellers.
- Professional golf players are more likely to make a shot when they are slightly under par (the typical number of shots professionals need to complete a hole) than when they are above par (Pope and Schweitzer 2011). This holds even though

professional golf players are experienced in making these shots and the prize money in golf is high.

- Consumers react stronger to increases in prices than to decreases in prices. In other words, price elasticities are asymmetric (Hardie et al. 1993).
- Participants in high-stake game shows take more risks after experiencing unfavourable outcomes. Unfavourable outcomes move participants into the loss domain and they try to get back into the gain domain by taking more risks. This holds even when the prize money is millions of euros (Post et al. 2008).

The Causes of the Endowment Effect

Exercise 7.7: Loss Aversion and the Endowment Effect

Argue how loss aversion can explain the endowment effect.

Gächter et al. (2022) found that the gap between WTA and WTP was related to loss aversion. The correlation was substantial (0.68). Mark Dean and Pietro Ortoleva (2019) who compared the correlation between various deviations from traditional economics, found a similar correlation (0.62).

Dean and Ortoleva used undergraduate students. In a later study joint with Jonathan Chapman, Colin Camerer, and Erik Snowberg they used a representative sample from the US population (Chapman et al. 2023). They only found a correlation between loss aversion and the WTA-WTP gap (measured for prospects) for subjects with higher cognitive abilities. For the full sample there was no correlation. They do not explain why. Possible causes are:

1. **Error**. Perhaps the tasks were too confusing for people with less cognitive abilities and their responses reflect mainly noise.
2. The review of Tunçel and Hammitt found that the **WTA-WTP gap** was **low for prospects**. If there is not much of an endowment effect in the first place, it cannot be explained by loss aversion either.
3. **Constructed preference**. Economists tend to think that people have preferences and by asking the right questions they will reveal them. By contrast, psychologists believe that people do not have ready-made preferences, but that they are constructed during the experiment and depend on the response mode. As WTA and WTP are different response modes they lead to different cognitive processes in which loss aversion plays a different role.
4. **Imprecision** and **caution**. Suppose people's preference are imprecise and they are cautious (see Chapter 2). In the WTA, the cautious response is to state the highest price for which agents are unsure (they do not want to sell the prospect for too little). In the WTP the cautious response is to state the lowest price (they do not want to pay too much). Loss aversion plays no role in this argument and, consequently, it cannot explain the WTA-WTP gap for those with lower cognitive ability.

Even though the evidence is not unanimous, I believe the most likely explanation for the endowment effect is loss aversion. All the studies on the correlation between the endowment effect and loss aversion use a crude measure of loss aversion. Typically, they ask people to choose between 0 and a lottery giving a chance of 50% of a gain x and a 50% chance of a loss y, where the loss is varied until the subject is indifferent. The degree of loss aversion is then computed as $^x/_y$.

There are two problems with this procedure. First, people are averse to receiving 0 (Incekara-Hafalir et al. 2021). This **zero effect** biases their preferences towards accepting the prospect. Second, $^x/_y$ does not measure loss aversion under prospect theory. It confounds loss aversion with diminishing sensitivity and probability weighting. I will explain this in Chapter 9 and I will also show how to construct a correct measure of loss aversion under prospect theory.

Exercise 7.8: Zero Effect

Show that the zero effect implies that the measure $^x/_y$ will underestimate loss aversion.

Extension 7.4: Is There Loss Aversion for Money?

Are people loss averse for both goods and money or only for goods in WTP/WTA tasks? Tversky and Kahneman thought that giving up money in the WTP is seen as a foregone gain and not as a loss. So loss aversion plays no role. On the other hand, Ian Bateman and co-authors (see Extension 7.3) believe that there is also loss aversion for money.

To settle the issue, Kahneman and Bateman et al. performed an **adversarial collaboration**, a project carried out by research teams with conflicting hypotheses that seek to resolve their conflict (Bateman et al. 2005). Both parties agree on the experiment and each party proposes a test that supports its hypothesis, but that the other party expects to fail. The parties commit to publication to avoid publishing only successful experiments. An adversarial collaboration can avoid overreporting of results and **confirmation bias**, the tendency to look for tests that confirm prior hypotheses.

For consistency, let's use again the terminology of Jones-Lee and Loomes. So (x, y) stands for an annual risk of dying in a road accident of x in 100,000 and y stands for monthly income y. Kahneman et al. asked three questions:

1. **WTP**. Subjects are endowed with $(6, y)$ and say how much they are willing to pay to face a risk of 5 (in 100,000) instead: $(6, y) \sim (5, y - wtp)$
2. **WTA**. Subjects are endowed with $(5, y)$ and say how much they are willing to accept to face a risk of 6 (in 100,000) instead: $(6, y + wta) \sim (5, y)$

3. **EG**. Subjects are endowed with $(6, y)$ and say which money gain makes them indifferent between $(6, y + eg)$ and $(5, y)$

Utility over pairs of road safety and money is defined over changes from the current endowment and is **additively separable**: $U(\Delta x, \Delta y) = u_s(\Delta x) + u_m(\Delta y)$ where u_s stands for the utility over changes in road safety and u_m stands for the utility over changes in money. $u_s(-\Delta x) = a_s \times (-\Delta x)^\beta$ for decreases in the risk of dying (gains in safety) and $u_s(\Delta x) = -b_s \times (\Delta x)^\beta$ for increases in the risk of dying (losses in safety). Let $0 < \beta < 1$ to reflect diminishing sensitivity and $0 < a - S < b_s$ to reflect loss aversion for safety. $u_m(-\Delta y) = a_m \times (\Delta y)^\beta$ for gains in income and $u_m(\Delta y) = -b_m \times (\Delta y)^\beta$ for losses in income. Kahneman predicted that $a_m = b_m$ (no loss aversion for money), Bateman et al. thought that $b_m > a_m$. Both assume that $b_s > a_s$ (loss aversion for safety).

The evaluation of the WTP is then:

$$a_s = b_m \times (wtp)^\beta.$$

Exercise 7.9: WTA and EG

1. Show that the evaluation of the WTA is:

$$a_m \times (wta)^\beta = b_s.$$

2. Show that the evaluation of the EG is:

$$a_s = a_m \times (eg)^\beta.$$

Exercise 7.10:

Explain that Bateman et al. predict that $WTP < EG < WTA$ and Kahneman that $WTP = EG < WTA$.

The data supported $WTP < EG < WTA$. There was modest loss aversion for money: $\lambda_m = ({}^{b_m}/{}_{a_m})^{({}^1/{}_\beta)}$ varied between 1.25 and 1.67. Subjects were loss averse for both money and goods.

7.3 Criticism of Loss Aversion

Several studies challenge whether loss aversion exists or is robust. Most involve risk and I will discuss these in Chapter 9. Some arguments apply, however, to the ideas discussed in this chapter.

Psychologists Jon Baron and Ilona Ritov (1992; 1994; 1995) argued that status quo bias is confounded with **omission bias**: a preference for harm caused by inaction (omission) over harm caused by action (commission). An example of omission bias are vaccinations. Some people prefer not to vaccinate their child even when the risk of death from disease is less than the vaccination risk. Apparently, people feel more responsible for the bad outcomes of active decisions (vaccinate) than for those of inactive decisions (do nothing).

The status quo often involves inaction, and part of it may be due to omission bias. Early findings of Baron and Ritov indeed suggested this, but in later papers they downplayed omission bias (Ritov and Baron 1995; Baron and Ritov 1994). Status quo bias cannot be fully explained by omission bias.

David Gal and Derek Rucker (2018) claim that the endowment effect can also be explained by a difference between action and inaction. Take again the case of Jones-Lee and Loomes. If agents do nothing in the WTP question they end up with $(6, y)$, if they do nothing in the WTA question they end up with $(5, y)$. Because agents dislike action their WTP to move to $(5, y - wtp)$ will be low and their WTA to move to $(5, y + wta)$ will be high. This can explain the WTP-WTA gap.

If true, this explanation has implications for policy. To solve the difference between WTP and WTA, most economists argue in favour of WTP. They believe that people exaggerate the compensation required in WTA questions. An example is the NOAA (National Oceanic and Atmospheric Administration) panel, a group of economists presided by Nobel laureate Ken Arrow. It was installed in reaction to the Exxon Valdez environmental disaster. On March 24, 1989, the oil tanker Exxon Valdez struck a reef and spilled more than 40 million litres of crude oil in the Gulf of Alaska. At the time it was the largest oil spill in US waters (until the Deep Water Horizon oil spill in 2010) contaminating 1300 kilometres of coastline and killing 250,000 sea birds, 3000 otters, 300 seals, 250 bald eagles, and 22 killer whales.

US Congress passed in 1990 the Oil Pollution Act, one of which aims was to establish procedures for assessing the damage oil spills cause to the environment. While some of these damages can be measured through market transactions (for example, the reduction in the herring trade, which never recovered), others (**existence** or **non-use values**) like enjoying the mere existence of natural resources, are harder to value. The NOAA panel recommended to value these through a conservative estimate of WTP. WTP estimates include an element of "warm glow", the feeling of contributing something to a good cause, like the environment, which has little to do with the good in question. However, omission bias suggests that the WTP is too low and will underestimate existence values. This implies in turn that the benefits of public health and environmental measures will be underestimated.

The generality of omission bias is unclear. Anthony Patt and Richard Zeckhauser (2000) show that people prefer action over inaction in environmental decisions. This holds in particular when the benefits of action are clear and those of inaction are harder to bring to mind. People prefer to clean up a polluted river, the benefits of which are visible, over preventing reductions in air quality, which benefits are less visible. People like to take credit, whether they are acting for themselves or for others.[1]

The above **action bias** leads to a larger difference between WTA and WTP. It can explain why the WTA-WTP gap is largest for environmental goods. Patt and Zeckhauser do not deny the importance of loss aversion, but they conjecture that loss aversion particularly affects decisions that people believe are beyond their control.

The data of Bateman et al. (see Extension 7.3) contradict that the endowment effect is due to a preference for inaction. In the WTP and equivalent gain (EG) questions the result of inaction was the same, but the endowments differed. Similarly, in the WTA and equivalent loss (EL) questions the results of inaction were the same but the endowments differed. Hence, a preference for inaction cannot explain the observed differences between WTP and EG and between WTA and EL. Loss aversion can.

Decision by Sampling Psychologist Neil Stewart proposed an alternative explanation for loss aversion: **decision by sampling**. Decision by sampling is based on Allen Parducci's (1965) **range-frequency model**. Parducci's model is an example of **context-dependent preferences** and says that the valuation of an outcome depends on its rank compared to the other outcomes under evaluation. For example, €200 will have a larger subjective value when evaluated jointly with €0, €25, €50, €100, and €400 where it is the second highest outcome, than when evaluated jointly with €50, €250, €500, €1000, and €4000, where it is the second-lowest outcome.

Experiment 7.2: Context Effects in Medical Decisions

Angela Robinson et al. (2001) show the impact of context-effects on health valuation. They take three nonfatal road traffic injury descriptions, *R*, *S*, and *X* (the descriptions were similar to those in Table 2.4). In one experimental treatment they included these health states in a set of mild health states, in the other in a set of more severe health states. Subjects then valued these health states on a rating scale ranging from 0 ("worst") to 100 ("best"). Parducci's model predicts that subjects will use the full scale and so the rating scale value of the common health states *R*, *S*, and *X* will be lower when paired with the mild health states than when paired with the more severe health states. Figure 7.10 shows that this is indeed what they observed.

Range effects can also explain loss aversion. In real life people face more small losses than small gains (usually salary is a large monthly lump sum payment while we face many small expenses (losses)). Thus, a small loss will have a higher rank among losses than a gain of the same size has among gains.

[1] Patt and Zeckhauser quote Aristotle who wrote that "in the arena of human life the honours and rewards fall to those who show their good qualities in action".

Fig. 7.10 Evidence of range effects in health state valuation

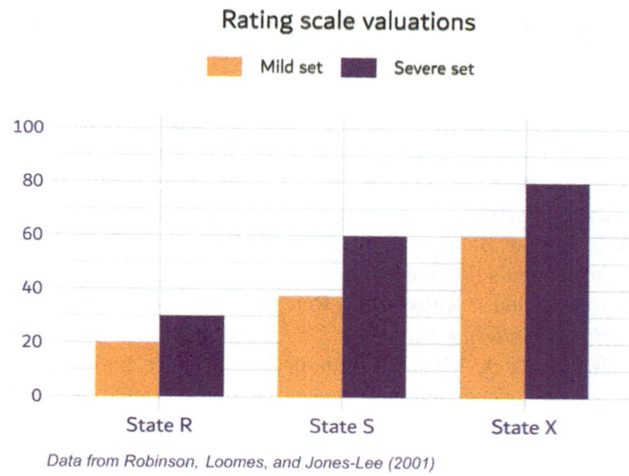

Exercise 7.11: Decision by Sampling

Explain how this can lead to a pattern that looks like loss aversion.

Walasek and Stewart (2015) argue that by choosing the stimuli appropriately they can make loss aversion disappear. For example, by choosing the range of losses larger than that of gains (e.g. from €0 to –€60 for losses and from €0 to €20 for gains) loss aversion disappears.

It is hard to explain all evidence on loss aversion by decision by sampling. In an adversarial collaboration, Despoina Alempaki and co-authors (2019) tested the predictions of decision by sampling in a series of 14 experiments. They could replicate earlier results, but in new experiments found violations of decision by sampling. Probably, earlier studies on decision by sampling misspecified the errors in people's choices. In summary, it is unlikely that decision by sampling explains the loss aversion observed in earlier studies. Loss aversion is robust and cannot simply be turned on and off by varying the range of outcomes.

7.4 Conclusion

In this chapter we have seen how reference-dependence and loss aversion affect decisions. They are among the main insights from behavioural economics. We saw that they have been challenged, but that these challenges did not stand scrutiny. Reference-dependence and loss aversion (and related concepts like status quo bias and endowment effects) are robust and help to better understand people's decisions and to design more effective policy measures.

References

Alempaki, D., E. Canic, T. L. Mullett, W. J. Skylark, C. Starmer, N. Stewart, and F. Tufano. 2019. Reexamining how utility and weighting functions get their shapes: A quasi-adversarial collaboration providing a new interpretation. *Management Science* 65: 4841–4862.

Allen, E. J., P. M. Dechow, D. G. Pope, and G. Wu. 2017. Reference-dependent preferences: Evidence from marathon runners. *Management Science* 63: 1657–1672.

Anagol, S., V. Balasubramaniam, and T. Ramadorai. 2018. Endowment effects in the field: Evidence from India's IPO lotteries. *Review of Economic Studies* 85: 1971–2004.

Baron, J., and I. Ritov. 1994. Reference points and omission bias. *Organizational Behavior and Human Decision Processes* 59: 475–498.

Bateman, I., A. Munro, B. Rhodes, C. Starmer, and R. Sugden. 1997. A test of the theory of reference-dependent preferences. *Quarterly Journal of Economics* 112: 479–505.

Bateman, I., D. Kahneman, A. Munro, C. Starmer, and R. Sugden. 2005. Testing competing models of loss aversion: An adversarial collaboration. *Journal of Public Economics* 89: 1561–1580.

Bleichrodt, H., J. L. Pinto, and J. M. Abellan-Perpiñan. 2003. A consistency test of the time trade-off. *Journal of Health Economics* 22: 1037–1052.

Camerer, C., L. Babcock, G. Loewenstein, and R. Thaler. 1997. Labor supply of New York City cabdrivers: One day at a time. *Quarterly Journal of Economics* 112: 407–441.

Chapman, J., M. Dean, P. Ortoleva, E. Snowberg, and C. Camerer. 2023. *Willingness to pay and willingness to accept are probably less correlated than you think.* Technical report. National Bureau of Economic Research.

Crawford, V. P., and J. Meng. 2011. New York City cab drivers' labor supply revisited: Reference-dependent preferences with rational-expectations targets for hours and income. *American Economic Review* 101: 1912–1932.

Dean, M., and P. Ortoleva. 2019. The empirical relationship between nonstandard economic behaviors. *Proceedings of the National Academy of Sciences* 116: 16262–16267.

Duong, H. L., J. Chu, and D. Yao. 2023. Taxi drivers' response to cancellations and no-shows: New evidence for reference-dependent preferences. *Management Science* 69: 179–199.

Einiö, M., M. Kaustia, and V. Puttonen. 2008. Price setting and the reluctance to realize losses in apartment markets. *Journal of Economic Psychology* 29: 19–34.

Engelmann, D., and G. Hollard. 2010. Reconsidering the effect of market experience on the "endowment effect". *Econometrica* 78: 2005–2019.

Farber, H. S. 2008. Reference-dependent preferences and labor supply: The case of New York City taxi drivers. *American Economic Review* 98: 1069–1082.

Fehr, D., R. Hakimov, and D. Kübler. 2015. The willingness to pay-willingness to accept gap: A failed replication of Plott and Zeiler. *European Economic Review* 78: 120–128.

Gächter, S., E. J. Johnson, and A. Herrmann. 2022. Individual-level loss aversion in riskless and risky choices. *Theory and Decision* 92: 599–624.

Gal, D., and D. D. Rucker. 2018. The loss of loss aversion: Will it loom larger than its gain? *Journal of Consumer Psychology* 28: 497–516.

Garff, J. 2013. *S⊘ren Kierkegaard: A Biography*. Princeton University Press.

Genesove, D., and C. Mayer. 2001. Loss aversion and seller behavior: Evidence from the housing market. *Quarterly Journal of Economics* 116: 1233–1260.

Hardie, B. G., E. J. Johnson, and P. S. Fader. 1993. Modeling loss aversion and reference dependence effects on brand choice. *Marketing Science* 12: 378–394.

Heath, C., R. P. Larrick, and G. Wu. 1999. Goals as reference points. *Cognitive Psychology* 38: 79–109.

Incekara-Hafalir, E., E. Kim, and J. D. Stecher. 2021. Is the Allais paradox due to appeal of certainty or aversion to zero? *Experimental Economics* 24: 751–771.

Isoni, A., G. Loomes, and R. Sugden. 2011. The willingness to pay-willingness to accept gap, the "endowment effect," subject misconceptions, and experimental procedures for eliciting valuations: Comment. *American Economic Review* 101: 991–1011.

Johnson, E. J., and D. Goldstein. 2003. Do defaults save lives? *Science* 302: 1338–1339.

Kahneman, D., J. L. Knetsch, and R. H. Thaler. 1990. Experimental tests of the endowment effect and the Coase theorem. *Journal of Political Economy* 98: 1325–1348.

Köbberling, V., and P. P. Wakker. 2005. An index of loss aversion. *Journal of Economic Theory* 122: 119–131.

Levitt, S. D. 2021. Heads or tails: The impact of a coin toss on major life decisions and subsequent happiness. *Review of Economic Studies* 88: 378–405.

List, J. A. 2003. Does market experience eliminate market anomalies? *Quarterly Journal of Economics* 118: 41–71.

McGranaghan, C., and S. G. Otto. 2022. Choice uncertainty and the endowment effect. *Journal of Risk and Uncertainty* 65: 83–104.

Nilsson, H., J. Rieskamp, and E.-J. Wagenmakers. 2011. Hierarchical Bayesian parameter estimation for cumulative prospect theory. *Journal of Mathematical Psychology* 55: 84–93.

Parducci, A. 1965. Category judgment: A range-frequency model. *Psychological Review* 72: 407–418.

Patt, A., and R. Zeckhauser. 2000. Action bias and environmental decisions. *Journal of Risk and Uncertainty* 21: 45–72.

Plott, C. R., and K. Zeiler. 2005. The willingness to pay-willingness to accept gap, the "endowment effect," subject misconceptions, and experimental procedures for eliciting valuations. *American Economic Review* 95: 530–545.

Pope, D. G., and M. E. Schweitzer. 2011. Is Tiger Woods loss averse? Persistent bias in the face of experience, competition, and high stakes. *American Economic Review* 101: 129–157.

Post, T., M. J. Van den Assem, G. Baltussen, and R. H. Thaler. 2008. Deal or no deal? Decision making under risk in a large-payoff game show. *American Economic Review* 98: 38–71.

Ritov, I., and J. Baron. 1992. Status-quo and omission biases. *Journal of Risk and Uncertainty* 5: 49–61.

Robinson, A., G. Loomes, and M. Jones-Lee. 2001. Visual analog scales, standard gambles, and relative risk aversion. *Medical Decision Making* 21: 17–27.

Samuelson, W., and R. Zeckhauser. 1988. Status quo bias in decision making. *Journal of Risk and Uncertainty* 1: 7–59.

Tunçel, T., and J. K. Hammitt. 2014. A new meta-analysis on the WTP/WTA disparity. *Journal of Environmental Economics and Management* 68: 175–187.

Tversky, A., and D. Kahneman. 1991. Loss aversion in riskless choice: A reference-dependent model. *Quarterly Journal of Economics* 106: 1039–1061.

Wakker, P., and A. Tversky. 1993. An axiomatization of cumulative prospect theory. *Journal of Risk and Uncertainty* 7: 147–175.

Walasek, L., and N. Stewart. 2015. How to make loss aversion disappear and reverse: Tests of the decision by sampling origin of loss aversion. *Journal of Experimental Psychology: General* 144: 7–11.

Weber, B. J., and G. B. Chapman. 1995. Outcome knowledge, regret, and omission bias. *Organizational Behavior and Human Decision Processes* 64: 119–127.

Probability Judgement

8

In his memoirs, Barack Obama explains that early in his presidency he realized that the problems that arrived on his desk had no solution. If they did, any of the clever persons that stood below him in the chain of command would have found it. We all face problems without an easy solution. Regardless of whether you are thinking about a career choice, a medical operation, or choosing a mortgage, we live in uncertainty and whether we like it or not, we have to deal with it. So how did Obama solve his problems? He learnt to think in probabilities and to choose. In fact, what Obama did was to solve problems of decision under uncertainty.

Decision under uncertainty is the area where behavioural economics has contributed most. In the next three chapters I describe the contributions of behavioural economics to decision under uncertainty. This chapter explores how we assign probabilities to events and the biases to which they are subject. I then turn to the question of how we evaluate uncertain situations once we have assigned probabilities. Chapter 9 looks at risk as the special case where probabilities are known. Chapter 10 treats ambiguity as the more realistic case where probabilities are unknown.

8.1 The Properties of Probability

The origins of **probability theory** date back to the seventeenth century. It first emerged in the correspondence between the French scientists Pierre de Fermat and Blaise Pascal. Three years later, the Dutch Christiaan Huygens gave the first scientific treatment of probability. He developed among others the concept of expected value.

H. Bleichrodt, *Behavioural Economics*,
https://doi.org/10.1007/978-3-031-69166-9_8

Bio 8.1: de Fermat, Pascal, and Huygens

Pierre de Fermat (1601–1655) was trained as a lawyer, mathematics was his hobby. He also spoke 6 languages fluently and was an expert on classical Greek texts. He is best known for his last theorem. In 1637 de Fermat wrote in the margin of a book that he had found a proof that the equation $a^n + b^n = c^n$ has no positive integer solutions if $n > 2$ (for $n = 1$ and $n = 2$ it was well-known that there are infinitely many positive integer solutions). The proof was too long to write down in the margin. Fermat usually omitted (large parts of) his proofs, but his other theorems had been shown to be true later. This claim, which was only discovered after his death and was referred to as Fermat's last theorem, proved resilient. It took mathematicians 357 years of unsuccessful attempts until the British mathematician Andrew Wiles finally proved it in 1994 (after 7 years of work).

Blaise Pascal (1623–1662) was a child prodigy who contributed to many fields. He did pioneering work on calculating machines and in his *Pensées* gives a probabilistic argument why it is rational to believe in God. Pascal is also known for the quote "all of humanity's problems stem from man's inability to sit quietly in a room alone", which got particular significance during the Covid pandemic.

Like Fermat and Pascal, Christiaan Huygens (1629–1695) had broad interests. He made significant contributions to mathematics and physics, discovered Saturnus' largest moon Titan, invented the pendulum clock, and improved the telescope. He also was an early science fiction writer and he speculated about life on other planets. For similar speculations, the Inquisition burned alive the Italian philosopher Giordano Bruno in 1600.

The Russian mathematician Andréi Kolmogorov developed modern probability theory. Kolmogorov gave three axioms for a **probability** from which other properties followed (see Extension 8.1). Consider a chance experiment, for example, rolling a fair dice. There are six possible outcomes (throwing one, throwing two, etc.). Collections of possible outcomes are called **events**. For example, the event "throwing less than four" consists of the outcomes $\{1, 2, 3\}$. Kolmogorov's axioms are:

1. The probability of each event E is a nonnegative real number: $P(E) \geq 0$.
2. The probability of the event consisting of all possible outcomes is equal to 1. In the example of the dice, the probability of throwing a six or less is equal to 1: $P(\{1, 2, 3, 4, 5, 6\}) = 1$.
3. If E_i and E_j are two events that have no outcomes in common (they are **disjoint**) then the probability that any of these events occurs is equal to the sum of their probabilities.

Extension 8.1: Kolmogorov's Axioms

Let Ω be the set of all possible outcomes of a chance experiment, one and only one of which occurs. Subsets of Ω are events. $\emptyset$ is the empty set which contains no outcomes. $\mathcal{F}$ is the set of all events. $\mathcal{F}$ is a σ-algebra meaning that it contains Ω, that if an event E belongs to $\mathcal{F}$ then its complement E^c (i.e. those outcomes in Ω that are not in E) also belongs to $\mathcal{F}$, and if a countable set of events $E_1, E_2, \ldots$ are all in $\mathcal{F}$ then their countable union $\bigcup_{i=1}^{\infty} E_i$ is also in $\mathcal{F}$. It is often easier to think of $\mathcal{F}$ as the set of all subsets of Ω.

A function P on the set of events $\mathcal{F}$ is a **probability measure** if it is nonnegative, $P(\Omega) = 1$ and it is additive: for any countable collection of disjoint events $\{E_i\}_{i=1}^{\infty}$ in $\mathcal{F}$: $P(\bigcup_{i=1}^{\infty} E_i) = \sum_{i=1}^{\infty} P(E_i)$. From these conditions, we can derive other well-known properties of probabilities.

Monotonicity: for all $E_1, E_2 \in \mathcal{F}$, if $E_1 \subseteq E_2$ then $P(E_1) \leq P(E_2)$.
Proof. Let E_2/E_1 denote those elements that are in E_2 but not in E_1. Then $E_1 \cap (E_2/E_1) = \emptyset$ and $E_1 \cup E_2/E_1 = E_2$. By additivity $P(E_1) + P(E_2/E_1) = P(E_2)$ and because $P(E_2/E_1) \geq 0$ it follows that $P(E_1) \leq P(E_2)$.

Exercise 8.1: Properties of Probability

Show that it is also true that

- $P(\emptyset) = 0$ (hint: use that for all $E \in \mathcal{F}$, $E \cup \emptyset = E$).
- For all $E \in \mathcal{F}$, $P(E^c) = 1 - P(E)$.
- For all $E \in \mathcal{F}, 0 \leq P(E) \leq 1$.

8.2 Biases in Probability Judgements

8.2.1 Belief in the Law of Small Numbers

The law of large numbers says that large samples look like the population from which they are drawn. If we toss a fair coin many times, head and tails both come up about half of the time. People believe that this law also holds for small samples. Tversky and Kahneman (1971) call this the **law of small numbers**. People believe that two small samples drawn from the same population must look similar and that sampling is a self-corrective process: if deviations are observed then a correction in the other direction will take place. In other words, people underestimate the degree of sampling variability. If we have thrown four consecutive heads with our fair coin then people expect that tails is more likely on the next toss. This is called the **gambler's fallacy**.

The law of small numbers leads to misinterpretation of data. Many countries publish rankings of hospitals based on survival rates. Typically, small hospitals score best. People conclude from this that small-scale hospitals are better. However, it may be a consequence of deducing too much from small samples. Because the sample of patients is smaller in small hospitals, a few "good" patients push their survival rates upwards. Larger hospitals have more patients and, thus, their survival rates are closer to the average. The hospitals with the worst survival rates are also the small ones. Something similar holds for schools. The best schools are often small, rural schools. The worst ones as well.

Economists Sigrid Suetens and co-authors (2016) and Tong Wang and co-authors (2016) tested the gambler's fallacy in lotto gambling. Lotto draws are random and skill plays no role. Lottery players rarely changed their selected numbers, but if so, they avoided winning numbers, as the gambler's fallacy predicts.

Daniel Chen, Tobias Moskowitz, and Kelly Shue (2016) found the gambler's fallacy in three real-world decisions of experienced agents. The first case were US judges in refugee asylum cases. They were 3.3% more likely to reject a case if they approved the previous one (correcting for case quality). While 3.3% may sound little, these judges make thousands of decisions. So the gambler's fallacy resulted in hundreds of wrongly rejected asylum requests. Given the large human cost, the judges' mistaken belief in the law of small numbers caused large human suffering.

The second were loan applications by Indian officers. Approval was 9% less likely after a previous application had been approved.

The final case were umpires in the Major League Baseball, the world's most important baseball competition. The umpire has to decide whether a pitch is a strike (which is bad for the batter) or ball. With three strikes the batter is out and four balls give a free run to the first base. The location of each pitch is measured so that the quality of each call can be determined.[1] Controlling for pitch quality, umpires were 1.5% less likely to call a pitch strike when the previous pitch was called a strike. This effect more than doubled if the pitch was close to the strike zone. Again, we are talking about thousands of decisions that are affected by the gambler's fallacy. In all three cases the stakes are high and the agents are experienced. The law of small numbers affects important decisions and has real-world consequences.

[1] Umpires do not receive feedback from the system so they have to make their own call.

8.2.2 The Hot Hand Fallacy

The flip side of the law of small numbers is that people question the randomness of a sequence after a series of "successes". This is called the **hot hand fallacy**. It is another manifestation of people's struggles with randomness. As so many biases, the hot hand fallacy comes from the research of Amos Tversky. He proposed it joint with psychologists Tom Gilovich and Robert Vallone (Gilovich et al. 1985).

The term hot hand comes from basketball where it is widely believed that a player is hot after making several shots and more likely to make the next shot. Likewise, a player who missed a series of shots is cold and more likely to also miss the next shot. Tversky, Gilovich, and Vallone challenge this belief. They show for a sample of players from the Philadelphia 76-ers, the New York Knicks, and the New Jersey Nets that the probability of a hit is no more likely after a series of hits than after a series of misses. Their paper had a large impact. In the words of Nobel laureates Richard Thaler and Daniel Kahneman, it convinced the research community that the hot hand is a "myth" and "a massive and widespread cognitive illusion".

The hot hand fallacy can explain why people have too much confidence in financial experts who beat the market a few years in a row. This might be due to chance. But as people expect that short random sequences look more random than they often do, they give too much credit to the abilities of these lucky "experts". Even in the lotto a minority bets on winning numbers. Most likely because they believe these are hot.

Recent evidence challenges the hot hand fallacy. Joshua Miller and Adam Sanjurjo (2018) showed that the analysis of Tversky, Gilovic, and Vallone suffered from a statistical bias, that I explain in Sect. 8.3. After correcting for this bias, the hot hand did exist and players shot around 13% better when on a 3 hit streak than when on a 3 miss streak.

Moreover, basketball is not the best sport to look for a hot hand. It is a contact sport and if a player is scoring several consecutive points the other team reacts by putting its best defender on this player or by even double teaming (putting two defenders on the player). Data from non-contact sports suggest that a hot hand does exist. German psychologist Gerd Gigerenzer, joint with Markus Raab and Bartosz Gula (2012), looked at volleyball, where players are separated by a net. They found data consistent with a hot hand for half of the players. Brett Green and Jeffrey Zwiebel found evidence of a hot hand in baseball.[2] They looked at 10 measures of success (5 for batters and 5 for pitchers) and found evidence of a hand for all 10 of these. They also found that the other team reacted to a hot batter by not pitching a good ball. So players are able to detect a hot hand and adjust their behaviour to it.

In summary, the hot hand fallacy in basketball may actually be a fallacy itself and not a "massive cognitive illusion". Perhaps it is comforting that even the gods of behavioural economics are only human. This does not mean that a hot hand fallacy never exists. People's struggles in understanding randomness explain why they see a pattern where none exists (see Example 8.1).

---

[2] On the other hand, Ötting et al. (2020) found only a small hot hand effect in darts.

Example 8.1: Paul the Octopus

An example of a hot hand fallacy is Paul the Octopus. He became world news during the 2010 World Cup football in South Africa when he correctly predicted the results of the seven matches of the German team and the final. Paul lived in the Sea Life Centre in Oberhausen Germany. Before each match Paul chose between two boxes containing food. The boxes bore the flags of the two competing countries. The flag he chose was predicted to be the winner. After correctly predicting Germany to win its first 5 matches, in the semifinal Paul chose Spain, which indeed won (goal Carlos Puyol). When angry German fans threatened to eat Paul, the Spanish prime minister Jose Luis Zapatero offered to send bodyguards in protection. Paul's pick for the final Spain-the Netherlands was broadcast live on Spanish television. Unfortunately, he also got that one right.

Paul's predictions could be explained by chance even if the probability of choosing any box is $1/2$. Paul also predicted the results of Euro 2008 where he got 4 out of 6 matches right (he predicted that Germany would win everything, but they lost their group match against Croatia and the final against, again, Spain). Moreover, as Paul almost always picked Germany as the winner, his keepers may have somehow biased him to select Germany. Further, the German team was strong and their chances of winning higher than one half in most matches.

Paul passed away 3 months after the World Cup final. He ended better than Rabio the octopus who correctly predicted the results of Japan's three group stage games at the 2018 World Cup. He was killed, sold to the market, and eaten.

8.2.3 Partition Dependence

Probabilities are additive: if we split an event into disjoint subevents, then the sum of the probabilities of these subevents is equal to the probability of the event itself. Unfortunately, probability judgements do not satisfy this. They show **partition dependence**: the probability of an event increases when it is split up into subevents.

Baruch Fischhoff, Paul Slovic, and Sarah Lichtenstein (1978) asked car mechanics to judge the probability of causes why a car did not start. The pruned treatment had four categories: battery, fuel system, engine, and *other*. In the nonpruned treatment the category other was subdivided into starting system, ignition system, mischief, and *other*. This subdivision impacted subjective probability. In the nonpruned treatment, the sum of the probabilities of starting system, ignition system, mischief, and *other* was 44.4%. In the pruned treatment, the probability of *other* was only 21.5%. Self-rated knowledge and experience did not improve this partition dependence.

Donald Redelmeier, Derek Koehler, Varda Liberman, and Amos Tversky (1995) gave 59 physicians at Stanford University the following case:

> A well-known 22 year-old Hollywood actress presents to the emergency department with pain in the right lower quadrant of her abdomen of 12 hours' duration. Her last normal menstrual period was four weeks ago.

Half of the physicians estimated the subjective probabilities for two diagnoses, gastroenteritis and ectopic pregnancy, and for the residual category *none of the above*. For the other half, the residual category was subdivided into appendicitis, pyelonephritis, pelvic inflammatory disease, and *none of the above*. Consistent with partition dependence, in the first group the estimated probability of the residual category was 50%, while in the second group the joint probability of appendicitis, pyelonephritis, pelvic inflammatory disease, and *none of the above* was 69%. The probability of gastroenteritis dropped from 31% in the first group to 16% in the second.

These examples show that experts also suffer from partition dependence. Other evidence that experience does not remove partition bias comes from options traders (Fox et al. 1996) and even decision theorists, who are trained in probability theory and know the biases in probability judgements (Fox and Clemen 2005). A theory that predicts partition dependence is support theory, described in Extension 8.2.

In the above studies, the sum of the probabilities had to be 100%. If we relax that restriction, partition dependence predicts that the sum of the probabilities will be larger if we distinguish more events. Craig Fox and Amos Tversky (1998) asked basketball fans, which of 8 remaining teams would win the 1995 NBA playoffs. The NBA is divided into the Eastern and the Western conferences, the winners of which play in the NBA finals against each other. The fans estimated that the probability that a team from the east would win the NBA was 50% and that a team from the west would win was 52%. These probabilities approximately sum to 100%. However, when asked to estimate for each team the probability that it would win the NBA, the sum of the eight probabilities was 218%.[3]

Extension 8.2: Support Theory, Tversky's Final Contribution

In the final years of his life Amos Tversky worked on a theory that could explain how people formed probability judgements. He called it **support theory** (Tversky and Koehler 1994; Rottenstreich and Tversky 1997). The key idea is that people give probability judgements to descriptions of events and not to the events themselves. So two different descriptions of the same event can

[3] The fans gave a 40% win probability to both the Chicago Bulls and the San Antonio Spurs. They gave the Houston Rockets, who won the NBA that year, a 19% win probability, the second lowest.

lead to different probability judgements. The data of Fischhoff et al. on the car mechanics and those of Redelmeier et al. on the Hollywood actress are examples.

Formally, let $\mathcal{F}$ be the set of events and $\mathcal{H}$ the set of hypotheses that describe the events in $\mathcal{F}$. Each hypothesis $A \in \mathcal{H}$ corresponds to a unique event $A' \in \mathcal{F}$. Different hypotheses A and B can correspond to the same event: $A' = B'$. Hypothesis A is null if $A' = \emptyset$. $\mathcal{H}$ is finite and contains at least one hypothesis for each event in $\mathcal{F}$.

Hypotheses A and B are **exclusive** if $A' \cap B' = \emptyset$. An example of exclusive hypotheses are gastroenteritis and ectopic pregnancy in the study of Redelmeier et al. For any two exclusive hypotheses $A, B \in \mathcal{H}$, their **explicit disjunction** $A \vee B$ is also in $\mathcal{H}$. Moreover, $(A \vee B)' = A' \cup B'$. Explicit disjunctions are hypotheses that list their individual components. In Redelmeier et al., the second group faced the hypotheses of appendicitis, pyelonephritis, pelvic inflammatory disease, and none of the above and these were taken together (an **implicit disjunction**) as none of the above in the first group. The assumption about explicit disjunctions ensures that the descriptions refer to the same event.

Support theory assumes that there is a ratio scale s, which gives the degree of support for each hypothesis. For any two exclusive hypotheses $A, B \in \mathcal{H}$, the probability $P(A, B)$ that A rather than B holds is equal to:

$$P(A, B) = \frac{s(A)}{s(A) + s(B)}.$$

The crucial assumption of support theory is that s is **subadditive**: if we have a partition A_1, A_2 of hypothesis A (so that $A' = (A_1 \vee A_2)'$) then

$$s(A) \leq s(A_1 \vee A_2) \leq s(A_1) + s(A_2).$$

In other words, unpacking a description into disjoint components increases its support. Unpacking reminds of overlooked possibilities and enhances their salience. The unpacking inequality holds only when the agent believes that $A' = (A_1 \vee A_2)'$. This assumption is hard to verify and complicates tests of support theory.

Exercise 8.2:

Show that under support theory the following hold:

- **Binary complementarity**: $P(A, B) + P(B, A) = 1$.
- The **product rule**: For B nonnull, let $R(A, B) = \frac{P(A,B)}{P(B,A)}$, i.e. R gives the odds for A against B. For mutually exclusive A, B, C, D:

$$\frac{R(A, B)}{R(B, D)} = \frac{R(A, C)}{R(C, D)} \text{ and}$$

$$R(A, B) \times R(B, D) = R(A, D).$$

- The **odds inequality**: For mutually exclusive A_1, A_2, B and $A' = (A_1 \vee A_2)'$,

$$R(A, B) \geq R(A_1 \vee A_2, B) \geq R(A_1, B) + R(A_2, B).$$

The properties in Exercise 8.2 give tests of support theory. They also characterize support theory. If we assume binary complementarity, the product rule, and the odds inequality then probability judgement can be represented by support theory. The support function can be derived from the subjective probability judgements. Because it is a ratio scale, we can choose a hypothesis A and set $s(A) = 1$. $s(B)$ then follows from asking for $P(A, B)$ or $R(A, B)$. Continuing this way we can measure s for as many hypotheses as we like.

8.3 Bayesian Updating

We frequently get new information. Examples are medical tests, election polls, or market research. To update subjective probabilities when receiving new information, rational theory tells us to apply a rule developed by Thomas Bayes in the eighteenth century.

Bio 8.2: Thomas Bayes

Bayes was not only a statistician and a philosopher, but also a Presbyterian minister. His interest in statistics may have come from a wish to counter David Hume who argued against the existence of miracles. Bayes never published anything on statistics during his life. Based on his notes, his friend Richard Price published Bayes' famous rule posthumously.

Suppose we have collected data D. We want to know how likely an event or hypothesis A is given D. In other words, we want to know $P(A \mid D)$, the posterior probability of A given the new data. Bayes' rule says that

$$P(A \mid D) = \frac{P(D \mid A) \times P(A)}{P(D)}. \tag{8.1}$$

In Eq. 8.1, $P(A)$ is the prior probability of A, the probability of A before the new data, $P(D)$ is the probability of the data, and $P(D \mid A)$ is the probability of observing the data given that A is true.

Exercise 8.3: Bayes' Theorem

Prove Bayes' theorem using the definition of conditional probability: $P(A \mid D) = \frac{P(A \cap D)}{P(D)}$ (Hint: use $P(D \mid A) = \frac{P(A \cap D)}{P(A)}$ and solve for $P(A \cap D)$).

From Bayes' theorem we can express how much more likely one hypothesis (or event) A is than another B given the data D. This is also called the odds of A over B. It equals:

$$\frac{P(A \mid D)}{P(B \mid D)} = \frac{P(D \mid A)}{P(D \mid B)} \times \frac{P(A)}{P(B)}. \tag{8.2}$$

In words, the posterior odds are equal to the Bayes factor (see Chapter 6) times the prior odds.

It is important to keep in mind that $P(A \mid D) \neq P(D \mid A)$. The belief that they are equal is called the **prosecutor's fallacy**. An example are the events A = "is an NBA player" and D = "is at least 1 meters 90 tall". $P(D \mid A)$, the probability that a man is at least 1.90 tall given that he plays in the NBA, is high. On the other hand $P(D \mid A)$, the probability that a man plays in the NBA given that he is at least 1.90 tall is very low (unfortunately, I am 1.90). As we will see below, a failure to understand the prosecutor's fallacy can lead to serious mistakes of justice.

8.3.1 Flaws in Bayesian Reasoning

People are bad at Bayesian reasoning. Consider the following example of the psychologist Ward Edwards. Think about it for a second and write down your answer.

Example 8.2: Bayesian Updating

Imagine two urns filled with millions of poker chips. The first urn has 70% red and 30% blue chips. The second has 30% red and 70% blue chips. An urn is randomly chosen and 12 chips are drawn from it: 8 are red and 4 blue. What is the probability that the first urn was chosen?

When I present Edwards' example in class, most students give a number between 50% and 70%. The actual probability is 96.7%.[4]

8.3.2 The Monty Hall Problem

Edwards' example shows that we are too conservative in updating our subjective probabilities. We underestimate the value of information. Another example of this **conservatism bias** is the **Monty Hall problem**. The problem is based on the American television show *Let's make a Deal*, which started in the 1960s and was presented for many years by Monty Hall, hence its name. It became famous when Marilyn vos Savant (who according to the Guinness Book of Records has the highest IQ in the world (228)) presented it in her column "Ask Marilyn" in the Sunday newspaper *Parade*. The problem was so counterintuitive that thousands of readers, including professors of mathematics, wrote to Parade claiming Savant must be wrong. She was right.

Example 8.3: The Monty Hall Problem

Suppose you are on a game show. You have the choice between three doors. Behind one door is a car, behind the other two are goats. You pick a door, say door 1. The host, who knows behind which door is the car and who, to increase the tension, will not open your door or a door behind which is the car, opens randomly another door, say door 3. The host then gives you the option to switch doors, from 1 to 2. Should you do so?

---

[4] By Eq. 8.2

$$\frac{P(\text{urn 1}|\text{data})}{P(\text{urn 2}|\text{data})} = \frac{P(\text{data}|\text{urn 1})}{P(\text{data}|\text{urn 2})} \times \frac{P(\text{urn 1})}{P(\text{urn 2})}.$$

Because the urn was randomly chosen $P(\text{urn 1}) = P(\text{urn 2})$. By the binomial distribution, $P(\text{data} \mid \text{urn 1})$, the probability of drawing 8 red and 4 blue chips from the first urn is $\binom{12}{8} \times 0.7^8 \times 0.3^4 = 0.231$. The probability of drawing 8 red and 4 blue from the second urn is $P(\text{data} \mid \text{urn 2}) = \binom{12}{8} \times 0.3^8 \times 0.7^4 = 0.008$. The posterior odds in favour of the first urn are $\frac{0.231}{0.008} = 28.875$. It is almost 30 times as likely that the chips were drawn from the first urn. The probability that the chips were drawn from the first urn is equal to $\frac{\text{odds}}{\text{odds+1}} = \frac{28.875}{29.875} = 96.7\%$.

Most people, including nearly all of my students, prefer not to switch. They reason that there is both a probability $\frac{1}{2}$ that the car is behind their door and that it is behind door 2. So, it does not make sense to switch (and they would feel regret if they switched and the car were behind their door).

However, this ignores information: The host will not open your door and a door behind which there is a car. This means that the host is more restricted if the car is behind door 2 than when it is behind your door. If it is behind door 2, the host can only open door 3. If the car is behind your door, the host can open both doors 2 and 3. The probability that the host opens door 3 given that the car is behind door 2, $P(\text{door 3}|\text{door 2})$, is equal to 1 while $P(\text{door 3}|\text{door 1})$ is equal to $\frac{1}{2}$. By Eq. 8.2, the posterior odds that the car is behind door 2 is twice as large as that the car is behind your door. Or, given that the host opened door 3, the probability that the car is behind door 2 is $^2/_3$, while the probability that it is behind your door is $^1/_3$. You better switch.

8.3.3 The Hot Hand Fallacy Revisited

The principle of restricted choice also explains why the hot hand fallacy is not a fallacy (at least in basketball). Take Steph Curry, probably the best shooter of all time. We look at his three point shots and we want to check whether at times he has a hot hand. We select 1000 of his shots and look whether the next shot after a series of 3 hits is a hit or a miss. That is, we compute $P(h \mid hhh)$ and $P(m \mid hhh)$ where h stands for hit and m for miss.

Suppose we look at shot number 421. This means that Steph must have made shots 418, 419, and 420. Curry's career three point percentage is 43% so we can look at all shots after a series of three hits. If the proportion of three point shots made were 43% then we might conclude that Curry has no hot hand. This is what Tversky and co-authors did.

Why is it wrong? It ignores information. That we select shot 421 gives information. If 421 would be a hit then we could have selected both shot 421 and shot 422 (because 419, 420, and 421 were all hits). However, if 421 was a miss we could only select shot 421. So $P(421 \mid \text{miss}) > P(421 \mid \text{hit})$. It follows from Eq. 8.2 that the posterior probability that Steph would make shot 421 is actually less than 43%. So if we observe that Steph makes 43% of his shots when he is on a streak of three hits means that he is actually shooting better than usual. The hot hand does exist. Miller and Sanjurjo (2018) give a proof of the above intuition.

8.3.4 The Winner's Curse

The winner's curse means that the winner of an auction usually pays too much and earns less than expected. The term was coined by three engineers Capen, Clapp, and Campbell who studied the bidding for oil and gas drilling rights in the Gulf of Mexico. The Gulf of Mexico is rich in oil and gas and oil prices rose tenfold in the 1970s as a result of the oil crises of 1973 (the Yom Kippur War) and 1979 (the

Iranian revolution). In spite of these favourable circumstances, companies earned little return on their investments. Only one fifth of the leases in the Gulf of Mexico turned out to be profitable.

Why? As before, bidders fail to take all information into account. The value of oil drilling rights is uncertain and firms rely on the estimates from their experts. These estimates diverge. The firm with the most optimistic experts wins the rights and probably pays too much. The winner is cursed.

The rule to "follow the expert" is irrational. It ignores information about what the other bidders do. If other firms bid less, their experts are less optimistic. The optimal bid must take this into account. According to Bayes' rule, this information must be used to update beliefs. One solution is to bid conservatively, especially if there are many bidders. The downside of this strategy is that a firm wins few auctions and may go out of business. A better strategy is to share the understanding of the winner's curse with competitors so that they reduce their bids as well.

8.3.5 Base Rate Fallacy

Equation 8.2 consists of two parts. The ratio $\frac{P(D|A)}{P(D|B)}$ on which I have focused so far, and the ratio $\frac{P(A)}{P(B)}$, which reflects how likely the hypotheses are a priori. People often fail to take this a priori likelihood into account. This negligence is called the **base rate fallacy**.

The base rate fallacy is common in medical tests. See Example 8.4. In this example, most people say that the probability that a woman who tests positive indeed has breast cancer is between 70% and 90%. They based their estimate on the high sensitivity and specificity of the test. What they forget is that the prior probability that a woman has breast cancer is (fortunately) low. Those who do realize this, adjust their estimate downwards, but not enough. They typically answer around 50%.

Example 8.4: Breast Cancer Screening

In most Western countries women above 50 are screened for breast cancer every 2–3 years. The number of new cases per 2 years among women above 50 is approximately 6 in 1000 (0.6%). The sensitivity of the screening test (the probability that a woman who has breast cancer tests positive) is 70%. The specificity (the probability that a woman who does not have breast cancer tests negative) is 96%. Suppose a woman tests positive. What is the probability that she indeed has breast cancer?

The true probability is 9.5%. By Eq. 8.2,

$$\frac{P(\text{breast cancer} \mid \text{test positive})}{P(\text{no breast cancer} \mid \text{test positive})} = \frac{P(\text{test positive} \mid \text{breast cancer})}{P(\text{test positive} \mid \text{no breast cancer})} \times \frac{P(\text{breast cancer})}{P(\text{no breast cancer})} = \frac{.7}{.04} \times \frac{.006}{.994} \approx .105. \quad (8.3)$$

So it is about ten times as likely that a woman who tests positive does not have breast cancer. The probability that a woman who tests positive has breast cancer is $100 \times \frac{.105}{1.105} = 9.5\%$.

Another way to see this is the following. For every 10,000 women who test, 60 have breast cancer (0.6% of 10,000). Of these 42 test positive (70% of 60). Of the 9940 who do not have breast cancer, 398 test positive (4% of 9940). So in total 440 women test positive and of those 42 have breast cancer. This is 9.5%. The lower the prior probability, the higher the probability of false positives. For this reason, public health authorities do not screen women under 50 and men.[5]

Experience does not help. The base rate fallacy has been found among psychologists, doctors, judges, and accountants. Edward Joyce and Gary Biddle (1981) asked 132 auditors of the top 8 US public accounting firms to estimate the probability that a manager had committed fraud when a test for fraud gave a positive result. They knew that:

- If a manager has been involved in fraud, the test procedure indicates "fraud" 8 times out of 10.
- If a manager has not been involved in fraud the test nonetheless indicates "fraud" 4 times out of 100.
- Evidence indicates that 1 manager in 100 involves in fraud.

Exercise 8.4: Auditors Suffer from the Base Rate Fallacy

Show that the probability of fraud given a positive test result is 16.8%.

The average guess of the auditors was 52.8%. So even experienced decision makers, whose job it is to detect fraud, suffer from the base rate fallacy.

[5] Male breast cancers account for less than 1% of all diagnosed breast cancers. If the prior probability drops to 0.006% then the probability that a man who tests positive has breast cancer is only 0.095%.

Example 8.5: The Case Lucia de B.

The case of Lucia de Berk shows that the base rate fallacy can have serious consequences. It is one of the worst mistakes of justice in the Netherlands. It highlights the cognitive and statistical biases that affect our decisions.[a]

Lucia de Berk was a paediatric nurse at Juliana Children's Hospital (JCH) in The Hague. In 2001, when she was on duty, a baby died unexpectedly. A colleague alerted superiors that there were more incidents during de Berk's shifts than during those of other nurses in her ward and they put Lucia on non-active. Criminal investigation found 7 more suspicious incidents during her shifts (and 0 when she was not on duty). They found 6 more suspicious cases when she was on duty in the Red Cross Hospital (RCH), where she had worked before on wards RCH 41 and RCH 42. Again, more than when other nurses were on duty. Table 8.1 summarizes the data.

Lucia was arrested in December 2001 and convicted to life imprisonment in 2003 for 4 murders and 3 attempted murders. The media jumped on the case and described de Berk as a "murder nurse" and an "angel of death". Her strong personality and colourful past only made her more suspicious in the public's eyes. An appeals court added 3 murders to her charge and convicted her again. The Dutch Supreme Court upheld her conviction 2 years later.

One number played a crucial role in her conviction: 1 in 342 million. According to a Dutch statistician and expert witness for the prosecution, this was the probability that the number of incidents on de Berk's shift were due to coincidence. He made 2 assumptions. First, that there was a fixed probability p of an incident during a shift. Second, that incidents occur independently of each other.

He computed for each of the three wards (JCH, RCH 41, and RCH 42) the probability that L incidents occur during Lucia's S shifts given T total incidents during N total shifts. So for JCH this was $\frac{\binom{S}{L}\times\binom{N-S}{T-L}}{\binom{N}{T}}$, which is approximately 1 in 9 million.

A problem with this analysis is that the same data that were used to formulate the hypothesis that Lucia was guilty, were also used to test it. The statistician corrected this by multiplying the 1 in 9 million chance by the number of nurses on Lucia's ward. This led to a chance of 3 in a million. He performed the same analysis for the other 2 wards and then multiplied the probabilities for the three hospitals (which gave 1 in 342 million). This was a mistake. It implies that

Table 8.1 Data on shifts and incidents

Hospital	JCH	RCH 41	RCH 42	Total
Total number of shifts	1029	366	339	1734
Lucia's number of shifts	142	1	58	201
Total number of incidents	8	5	14	27
Number of incidents during Lucia's shifts	8	1	5	14

a nurse working in several hospitals has a higher chance of being present at inexplicable incidences than a nurse working in just one hospital. Looking at the data from the three wards simultaneously gives a probability of 1 in 3.8 million, still low but 100 times higher than the one estimated by the statistician.

This was not the only mistake. Problems already began with the data collection. In statistics data collection must be uniform and definitions must be clear. On the other hand, criminal investigation starts with a suspicion and the data collection serves to corroborate this suspicion. Statisticians call this "painting the target around the arrow". In behavioural economics it is known as **confirmation bias**: we admit evidence that is in line with our beliefs and discard evidence that is not.

For example, Charles Lord, Lee Ross, and Mark Lepper (1979) selected two groups of subjects, one supporting the death penalty and the other opposing it. They gave them two studies. One showing that the death penalty reduced crime, the other that it did not. Subjects were presented with the strengths and weaknesses of both studies. Both proponents and opponents judged that the study that was in line with their beliefs was more convincing. The net effect was more polarization: both groups were more convinced of their point of view after seeing the evidence.

Related to confirmation bias is the **Baader Meinhof phenomenon** (named after the founders of the German terror group Red Army Fraction, which terrorized German society in the 1970s and early 1980s) or **frequency bias**: Just one occurrence of an unusual event makes people aware of its existence and they start seeing it everywhere.

In Lucia's case these biases were all over the place. Incidents outside of her shifts were discarded, some initially reported incidents were later relabeled without clear reasons, events during Lucia's shift that were initially not reported as an incident were redefined as incidents, staff was explicitly asked to make a list of events that happened during or shortly after Lucia's shifts, and data collection rested for a large part on memory. A surprising aspect of Table 8.1 is that there are 0 incidents outside of Lucia's shifts. People die in hospitals and this 0 suggests that the data collection was biased. Both the statistician and the prosecution ignored that in the three years before Lucia joined the JCH ward there were more deaths (7) than during the three years that she worked there (6).

Further, the assumption that the incident probability is constant across shifts is questionable. Incidents are higher during night and weekend shifts and nurses differ in how often they do these, terminally ill patients prefer to die on the shifts of nurses with whom they feel comfortable, nurses differ in quality and experience, and the policy of the hospital may vary. For example, the JCH changed its policy whether very ill children could die at home or that they should die in the hospital in the period when Lucia worked there.

Allowing for heterogeneity in the incident rate increased the probability that the incidents had happened by pure coincidence from 1 in 342 million to 1 in 49. In other words, from something that is almost impossible to something mildly unusual.

Mistakes were also made in the interpretation of the statistical analysis. In particular, we know from the prosecutor's fallacy that the probability that Lucia has the same incidence rate as other nurses given that she was present at so many incidents is not the same as the probability that she was present at so many incidents given that she has the same incidence rate as other nurses. The wording of the verdict suggests that the court made this mistake.

A correct Bayesian analysis should go as follows. Let G denote the event "Lucia is guilty", let I denote "Lucia is innocent", and L the number of incidents at which Lucia was present. The odds of Lucia being guilty versus her being innocent given the data is then:

$$\frac{P(G \mid L)}{P(I \mid L)} = \frac{P(L \mid G)}{P(L \mid I)} \times \frac{P(G)}{P(I)}.$$

As we saw, $P(L \mid I)$ is 1 in 49. $P(L \mid G)$ is probably high. However, because $P(G)$ is very low (unless you believe that there are many serial killers among the nurses in the Netherlands), $P(I)$ is close to 1. As a result, the posterior odds are strongly in favour of Lucia being innocent.

Fortunately for Lucia, Metta de Noo, a geriatrician whose sister-in-law was the head paediatrician at Juliana (their relation got destroyed as a result of de Noo's efforts to show Lucia's innocence) was not convinced of the medical evidence. She turned to her (other) brother Ton Derksen, a philosopher of science who wrote a book on the case. This book drew the attention of two statisticians, Peter Grünwald and Richard Gill. They showed that the statistical analysis was flawed. The voices for reopening the case increased and in 2008 the Supreme Court agreed. In 2010, the court in Arnhem exonerated Lucia de Berk.

Unfortunately, the case of Lucia de Berk is not the only one in which poor understanding of statistics led to mistakes of justice. In the UK Sally Clarke was convicted in 1999 of murdering her 2 infant sons and exonerated in 2003. She never fully recovered from this traumatic experience and died of alcohol poisoning in 2007.

Daniela Poggiali, an Italian nurse, described as the "terror nurse", was convicted of murdering 2 hospital patients in 2014 and pardoned in 2021, thanks partly to the efforts of Richard Gill. Kathleen Folbigg, an Australian woman spent 20 years in prison after being convicted for the murder of three of her children and for manslaughter in the death of the fourth. She was pardoned in 2023.

According to Richard Gill, the cases of Ben Geen, a UK nurse who serves life sentence for 2 murders and 15 cases of grievous bodily harm, and Lucy Letby, a UK nurse who serves 15 life sentences after being convicted for murdering 7 babies and attempting to murder 6 more, resemble the case of Lucia and have the potential for the same statistical mistakes and mistakes of justice. As Lucia de Berk and Daniela Poggiali, they were vilified by the media and on social media.

A problem is that people do not believe in chance. If something with a small probability happens, people think it cannot be a coincidence and something strange must be going on. Remember what we discussed in Chapter 6 about the brain's preference for sense-making. However, unlikely events happen all the time. One time I was hiking the Pennine Way in a remote area on the border between England and Scotland when I met a good friend from Barcelona with his wife waiting for the bus. Chances were small that I would meet them in this scarcely populated area far from both our homes, but it happened. Many things can happen so everything that happens has a small probability. But when a series of bad things happen we cannot accept that this can be due to chance. We believe someone must be responsible. This explains the witch hunt in the cases above. They show the importance of understanding statistical and cognitive biases. And to refrain from judging quickly, if at all.

[a] For more details see Cathleen O'Grady's (2023) article in Science. For statistical details about the case see Gill et al. (2018). There is also a movie about the case, called Lucia de B. (in the Netherlands, criminal suspects are for privacy reasons only known by the first letter of their surname).

8.4 Heuristics

Daniel Kahneman and Amos Tversky explain the biases in people's probability judgements through three heuristics: representativeness, availability, and anchoring and adjustment. These heuristics simplify probability judgements. They generally work well, but in some cases they go astray and lead to the errors described above.

8.4.1 Representativeness

Representativeness says that people judge the probability of an event by the extent to which it resembles the underlying population. For example, people believe that the exact birth sequence $GBGBBG$ is more likely than the exact birth sequence $BGBBBB$. They are equally likely as for each child there is a 50% probability of a girl (G) and a 50% probability of a boy (B). However, the first sequence is more representative of the general population.

Exercise 8.5: Representativeness

Argue that representativeness can explain both the gambler's fallacy and the base rate fallacy.

Representativeness predicts that people are insensitive to sample size. If probabilities of events are judged by how much they resemble the underlying population then sample size plays no role. People believe that the number of days on which more than 60% of the children born are boys is the same in a small and in a large hospital. Statistics says there will be more such days in the small hospital, because the number of children born per day is smaller.

Representativeness also implies that people have trouble understanding **regression to the mean**. If we take two samples from variables X and Y with equal distributions then those who score extreme on X will score less extreme on Y. For example, sons of tall fathers are usually shorter than their fathers (and sons of short fathers taller), students who score well on a test do worse on the next test (and students who score badly do better), and highly intelligent women are often married to less intelligent men. The reason is that the extreme scores were partly due to chance.

The Lucia de Berk case highlights that people do not understand chance and invent spurious causal relations. A popular myth for why highly intelligent women marry less intelligent men is that they are afraid of competition. Tversky and Kahneman give the example of the Israeli Air Force. Experienced instructors noted that praising pilots who had performed well on a landing led them to do worse on the next one, while criticizing those who had landed poorly led them to do better. The instructors concluded that punishment works better than reward. However, the results were probably caused by regression to the mean.

Regression to the mean also explains why sports teams after a string of bad results fire their coach. Usually the new coach starts better, giving support for the decision. However, it may be regression to the mean. The true test is what happens to teams who had a similar dip but did not fire their coach. Evidence suggests that they also improved. Firing a coach usually does not help.

Representativeness leads to an **illusion of validity**. Confidence in predictions depends on how much the predicted outcome resembles the input information, regardless of the reliability of the information or the predictability of the outcome. Psychological tests are poor predictors of job success and psychologists know this. Nevertheless they keep using them in job interviews. Likewise, we have faith in stock market and political experts even though the stock market and political events are hard to predict. High internal consistency does not mean high predictability. Correlated inputs are consistent, but less informative than independent inputs. A group of experts who share the same information are more consistent, but less informative than a group of experts who use independent sources of information. Unfortunately, people neglect correlations between information inputs (see Enke and Zimmermann 2019).

Representativeness can also explain Kahneman and Tversky's famous **Linda problem**. See Example 8.6.

Example 8.6: The Linda Problem

Lind is 31 years old, single, outspoken, and very bright. She majored in philosophy. As a student she was deeply concerned with issues of discrimination and social justice, and also participated in anti-nuclear demonstrations.

Kahneman and Tversky asked their subjects what was more probable,

1. Linda works in a bank.
2. Linda works in a bank and is active in the feminist movement.

Because event 2 is a subset of event 1, it can never be more likely. Nevertheless, 85% of their subjects thought it was. The reason is that the second statement is more representative of the description of Linda.

Gigerenzer (1996) criticized the Linda problem. The laws of probability, like the conjunction rule, only apply to well-defined problems and the Linda problem is not one. The description of Linda creates context that makes it reasonable to deviate from the conjunction rule. For example, up to half of the subjects believe that the statement "Linda is a bank teller" means that she is not active in the feminist movement. Subjects read different things in the Linda description. When I discuss the Linda problem with students, they often see it as a trap question.

8.4.2 Availability

Availability means that the judged probability of events depends on the ease with which they come to mind. An example is the study by Redelmeier et al. on the Hollywood actress with pain in her abdomen. By subdividing the category "none of the above" into appendicitis, pyelonephritis, pelvic inflammatory disease, and none of the above, the doctors were reminded of other possibilities. This increased its judged probability.

Another example is the impact of incidents. When low probability events, like floodings or plane crashes, occur, they lead to a surge in people's subjective probability of these events. Partly this is rational as Bayes' formula shows that we should update our beliefs when new information arrives. But people overreact.

Rachel Dalafave and Kip Viscusi (2023) looked at the effects of the May 2022 Buffalo and Uvalde mass shootings. These happened in a grocery store and an elementary school and were salient. Assessments of the risk of mass shootings went up after the shootings and exceeded the objective risks. The proportion of respondents who believed that the risk of dying in a mass shooting was larger than the risk of dying in a (less salient) firearm homicide went up from 15% to 45%. In reality, the annual risk of dying in a firearm homicide is 40 times larger. In the US less than 500 persons die each year in a mass shooting, while between 15,000 and 25,000 die in firearm homicides.

Exercise 8.6: Dread

Dread for mass shootings increased after the Buffalo and Uvalde mass shootings. A question is whether these exaggerated beliefs should be reflected in policy. It may lead (temporally) to a higher perception of safety, but at the cost of a suboptimal allocation of resources. What do you think?

8.4.3 Anchoring and Adjustment

Anchoring and (insufficient) adjustment affects many decisions. People make an estimation based on an initial value, which they then adjust. This adjustment is typically insufficient.

An example is the road safety valuation of Jones-Lee and Loomes. They used two versions. In one, subjects first said whether they would pay £25 for a device that reduced their risk of a road accident by 1 in 100,000. Then they stated their WTP. In the other, this initial amount was £75. The mean WTP was significantly higher in the second version. Subjects used the initial amount as an anchor and then adjusted. But they adjusted too little. Most thought £25 was too low and they adjusted upwards, but not enough, say to £40. Most thought £75 was too high and they adjusted downwards. But again not enough, say to £60. Anchoring and insufficient adjustment led to a disparity.

Exercise 8.7: Anchoring

Dan Ariely, Loewenstein, and Prelec (2003) asked their subjects to write down the last two digits of their social security number. They then asked their willingness to pay for a variety of goods. What does anchoring and adjustment predict for these valuations? Check their paper to see if you are right.

Anchoring and adjustment can explain partition dependence. Suppose people initially give the same probability to each category and then adjust. This explains why Redelmeier et al. found that the probability of gastroenteritis dropped from 31% in the first scenario (where there were three categories) to 16% in the second scenario (where there were six categories).

Anchoring and adjustment can also explain why people overestimate the probability of conjunctive events, e.g. drawing a red marble 7 times in succession from a bag containing 90% red marbles and 10% white marbles, and underestimate the probability of disjunctive events, e.g. drawing at least one white marble from this bag. For the conjunctive event, people anchor on the probability 90% and then adjust this downwards. The downward adjustment is not enough leading to an overestimation. For the disjunctive event, people anchor on the 10% probability and then adjust upwards. But, again, not enough.

Conjunctive events are relevant in planning decisions. A project's success depends on each of several steps being fulfilled. If there are many steps, even though each has a high probability of success, the probability that the plan succeeds may be low. Anchoring and adjustment explains why the planning of firms and individuals is too optimistic.[6]

The evaluation of risks is an example of disjunctive events. A system fails if any of its components fails. Even if the risk of failure is low for each component, the overall risk can be high if there are many components. The 2011 Fukushima nuclear plant accident was the result of a chain of low likelihood events.

8.4.4 A Critique on Heuristics and Biases

Gerd Gigerenzer criticized the heuristics and biases approach for being too vague. It is unclear when the heuristics work and how. As a result, they can basically explain any experimental result. For example, the base rate fallacy can be explained by representativeness, but the opposite result, conservatism, can be explained by anchoring. It is unclear when representativeness applies and when anchoring.

A similar objection can be raised against reference points. Leaving the reference point unspecified and adjusting it depending on the decision context gives too many degrees of freedom and makes it possible to explain almost anything.

Gigerenzer argues that what is needed are models that explain how probability judgements are formed and that make predictions. Gigerenzer is a psychologist and the models he has in mind are less interesting for economists (see the criticism of Gul and Pesendorfer in Chapter 6). A model of probability judgements that is interesting for behavioural economics is support theory (see Extension 8.2).

8.5 Motivated Beliefs

In *Funes el memorioso*, Jose Luis Borges tells the story of Ireneo Funes, a 19-year-old Uruguayan boy who after falling from a horse remains paralysed without the possibility of recovery, but with perfect memory. Funes loses the possibility to

[6] Joshua Lewis, Daniel Feiler, and Ron Adner (2023) show that managers are not always rational in eliminating these risks. They prefer to improve the success probability of the steps that are least likely to succeed even when this reduces the overall success probability of the project. They call this the **worst-first heuristic**.

forget. This makes his world almost intolerable, so rich and sharp. He remembers the forms of every cloud he has seen on an arbitrary morning years ago, every leaf on every tree he has seen, and the continuing advances of decay and death in his own face. He had learned without effort English, French, Portuguese, and Latin, but, as Borges writes, he was probably unable to think because thinking requires to forget differences, to abstract, and to generalize. In the overcrowded world of Funes' mind there were only details. He could not understand that one general term *dog* could encompass so many individual dogs of different sizes and shapes.

Borges' story shows that we need to forget. According to Nietzsche (who influenced Borges who describes Funes as a type of Zaratustra), we can live without memories and live happily, but it is impossible to live without forgetting.

But what do we forget and do we have influence over what we forget? Psychologists suggest that we think too positively of ourselves. An example is the **above-average effect**. On desirable traits, from kindness to trustworthiness to the ability to get along with others, people believe they score better than the average. 94% of university professors (including myself) believe they teach better than average and most drivers believe they drive better than average (here I am less sure about myself). Evidence also suggests that optimists do better on the labour market, work more, save more, retire later, and are more likely to remarry after divorce. Moreover, CEOs are more optimistic than average. Being optimistic pays off.

Behavioural economists have modelled these positive self views by **motivated beliefs**. There are three reasons for such overly optimistic beliefs:

1. **Consumption value**: People derive utility from positive beliefs about themselves and find a negative self-image painful. Psychologists call this the affective benefits of self esteem. Holding optimistic views of the future reduces anxiety and increases hope of good outcomes.
2. **Signalling value**: Thinking positively about yourself makes it easier to convince others of it.
3. **Motivation value**: Confidence in your abilities helps to undertake more ambitious goals and to go on in the face of adversity. This motive is related to the evidence cited above that optimistic people do better in life.

Behavioural economists have centered on the motivation value of optimistic beliefs. A model of motivated beliefs was suggested by the French economists, Roland Bénabou and Jean Tirole (Nobel laureate in 2014) (see Extension 8.3).

Extension 8.3: A Model of Motivated Beliefs

The model of Bénabou and Tirole (2002) has three periods $t = 0, 1, 2$. The agent has to decide at time point 1 whether to undertake a task, which has a cost of c. At time point 0 the agent only knows the distribution $F(c)$ of the cost, but not its actual value. The probability θ that the task succeeds depends on the agent's ability. If it succeeds it gives benefit V in period 2. If it fails, it gives no benefit. Utility is linear. Agents give too much weight to the present (see Chapter 11). They discount the next period by $\beta\delta$ (with $0 < \beta, \delta < 1$) and the period thereafter by $\beta\delta^2$. β denotes the extra weight given to the present. The lower β, the more the agent overweights the present.

Bénabou and Tirole model motivated beliefs as a game between agents' selves at time points 0 and 1. Self 0 receives a signal s about ability θ that is bad (b) with probability $1 - q$ and contains no news ($\emptyset$) with probability q. The belief about ability is lower if the signal is bad than when it contains no news:

$$\theta_b = E[\theta \mid s = b] < E[\theta \mid s = \emptyset] = \theta_\emptyset.$$

If selves 0 receive no news they report this truthfully to selves 1. However, if they receive a bad signal, they may suppress this to selves 1. Let $\hat{s}$ denote the recollection of self 1 of the signal s. This may differ from s either because self 0 does not give the bad news or because of memory decay.

Exercise 8.8: Reliability Signal

Let h_b^* be self 1's belief that there was indeed no bad signal if they remember not having received bad news. Use Bayes' rule to show that the reliability of a no signal message is:

$$r^* = P\left[s = \emptyset \mid \hat{s} = \emptyset\right] = \frac{q}{q + (1-q)(1-h_b^*)}.$$

Given the reliability r^* (see Exercise 8.8), selves 1's estimated ability is

$$\theta^* = r^*\theta_\emptyset + (1 - r^*)\theta_b.$$

If $\theta^* > \theta_b$, which happens if $h_b^* < 1$, selves 1 will be overconfident about their abilities.

Because self 1 gives excessive weight to the present there is a conflict between the interests of selves 0 and 1. Selves 1 will undertake the task if $\beta\delta\theta^* V > c$. Selves 0 would like them to undertake it if $\beta\delta^2\theta^* V > \beta\delta c$, i.e. if $\delta\theta^* V > c$. Because $\beta < 1$, it is possible that selves 1 do not undertake the task, but selves 0 would like them to.

If the signal contains no news, there is nothing selves 0 can do. However, if the signal is bad, they can withhold it to boost self 1's confidence. Ideally, self 0 would like to boost self 1's confidence so that $\theta^* = \theta_b/\beta$. This overcomes their present bias in case of a bad signal. Selves 1 are aware of this and are not so easily fooled.

The benefits for selves 0 of boosting selves 1's confidence are:

$$\beta\delta \int_{\beta\delta\theta_b V}^{\delta\theta_b V} (\delta\theta_b V - c)\,\mathrm{d}F(c), \tag{8.4}$$

which are the extra costs for which selves 1 will now undertake the task.[a] There is, however, a risk that withholding the bad signal boosts selves 1's confidence too much and they undertake the task even when self 0 prefers they do not. This cost of overconfidence is:

$$\beta\delta \int_{\delta\theta_b V}^{\beta\delta\theta^* V} (c - \delta\theta_b V)\,\mathrm{d}F(c). \tag{8.5}$$

Self 0 chooses h_b^* such as to maximize the difference between benefits (Eq. 8.4) and costs (Eq. 8.5). Self 1 knows self 0's optimizing problem and uses it in a Bayesian way to assess the reliability of their memory.

As we saw, the motive for self-deception depends on the value of β. If $\beta < 1$, the agent can be time inconsistent (self 0 and self 1 have different preferences). The model combines irrationality (time inconsistency) with rationality (Bayesian updating). As such, it is vulnerable to Rubinstein's critique (see Chapter 2). We can bring in imperfect updating by assuming that self 1 computes the reliability of no signal as $\frac{q}{q+\pi(1-q)(1-h_b^*)}$ with $0 < \pi < 1$. Most results still hold true if π is not too low.

[a] We could include the affective part of beliefs in this model by adding a term $a(\theta^* - \theta_b)$, where a reflects the importance of self-esteem.

8.5.1 Implications of Motivated Beliefs

The model of motivated beliefs implies the following:

1. **Information avoidance**. People avoid unwelcome information. Examples are investors who do not look at their stocks when the market is down (the **ostrich effect**), patients avoiding diagnostic tests, and managers who avoid feedback on their decisions. Information avoidance can lead to selfish or even immoral decisions. Examples are ignoring climate change or the harsh living conditions of animals in the farming industry. Not all information avoidance is bad, however. The ostrich effect may avoid financial markets to overreact to negative news.
2. **Asymmetric updating**. The motivated beliefs model predicts that people react stronger to positive than to negative news. This is called the **good news bad news effect**. David Eil and Justin Rao (2011) found that subjects used Bayes' rule to update their beliefs about their intelligence and beauty when feedback was positive, but ignored or conservatively updated negative feedback. The good

news bad news effect does not seem to be robust. Later studies found no evidence of asymmetric updating or even found a stronger reaction to negative feedback.

3. **Selective recall**. A consequence of motivated beliefs is that people forget past negative events and even fabricate nonexisting positive events. Chew Soo Hong, Wei Huang, and Xiaojian Zhao (2020) found evidence for this. Their subjects first took an IQ test. Several months later, they saw 6 questions and the correct answers. Four of these were from the IQ test and 2 were new. For each question, subjects said whether their answer in the IQ test was correct, incorrect, whether they did not see the question, or did not remember. Subjects who answered a question wrongly were more likely to forget whether they had seen the question than those who had answered it correctly. This may have nothing to do with motivated beliefs: you are more likely to remember topics you know than topics you do not know. For new questions, around 60% of the subjects said they had answered them correctly and only 5% said that their answer was wrong.
   David Huffman, Collin Raymond, and Julia Svets (2022) found selective recall among store managers competing for bonuses who receive regular feedback. Top performers recalled their performance well. Worse performers made recall errors and had overly optimistic memories.
4. **Stakes-dependent beliefs**. People weight and interpret evidence to support what they are motivated to believe. An example is Lord et al.'s study of the death penalty, discussed above. As another example, Linda Babcock and co-authors (1995) gave subjects a file from a lawsuit. One subject got the role of plaintiff, the other the role of defendant. They were asked to negotiate a settlement and to predict the ruling of the judge. When roles were assigned before the negotiations, their predictions about a fair settlement and the ruling of the judge differed and a settlement was unlikely. When the roles were assigned afterwards, differences were smaller and a settlement was more likely.
   Professional auditors from big US accounting firms were 30% more likely to say that financial statements complied with the generally accepted accounting practices when they were told that they had been hired by the firm they were auditing than when they were told that they had been hired by a competitor of the firm they were auditing.
   A final example of stakes-dependent beliefs is the study of Schwardmann et al. (2022) discussed in Chapter 5. Debaters were more likely to believe that a factual statement was true if it supported their position and they became more confident that their argument would win as the competition went on.

8.5.2 Overconfidence

The best known implication of motivated beliefs is **overconfidence**. It has been linked to societal ills like wars, business failures, stock market bubbles, and political polarization. Don Moore and Paul Healy (2008) distinguish three types of overconfidence:

1. **Overestimation** of one's actual ability or performance.
2. **Overplacement** of one's position relative to others. The above-average effect belongs to this category.
3. **Overprecision**: too much confidence in the accuracy of one's beliefs. When people estimate, for example, a 90% confidence interval around their answer, the correct answer lies in this interval less than 90% of the time. Typically, something like 50%.

Most research focused on overestimation. Ulrike Malmendier and Geoffrey Tate[7] studied the behaviour of overconfident CEOs.[8] They found that:

1. Overconfident CEOs rely too much on internal funds to finance investments. They believe that the market undervalues the price of equity in the firm.
2. Overconfident CEOs undertake too many mergers
3. Firms with overconfident CEOs also pay less dividend per share and use more aggressive accounting practices.

Not all overconfidence is bad though. Often firms and individuals are too risk averse (see Chapter 9). Mild overconfidence counters this.

Overestimation and overplacement are not universal. There is a **hard-easy effect**. For hard tasks people overestimate their performance, but underplace themselves compared with others. For easy tasks, they underestimate their performance, but overplace themselves compared with others.

Ido Erev, Thomas Wallsten, and David Budescu (1994) suggest that the explanation is regression to the mean. When we discussed regression to the mean, we saw that if two random variables X and Y are not perfectly related (like the length of fathers and sons), the prediction of each from the other is regressive to the mean. The same holds for judgements of own performance. When people have imperfect knowledge of their performance, the error in their judgements will make their estimates of their performance regressive. If performance is low, there is more room for error above than below it. If performance is high, the opposite holds: there is more room for error below than above it. As a result, people overestimate their performance when it is low and underestimate it when it is high. Figure 8.1 gives an example. Because people are more unsure about others' performance than about their own, their estimates of others' performance will be even more regressive.

Exercise 8.9: The Hard-Easy Effect

1. Explain how regressive judgements can explain the hard-easy effect.
2. Explain that motivated beliefs cannot explain the hard-easy effect.

[7] Malmendier and Tate (2015) gives an overview of their research.

[8] They defined overconfident CEOs as those who take longer to exercise the stock options in their firm than rational theory prescribes. The reason is that they overestimate the future prospects of their firm.

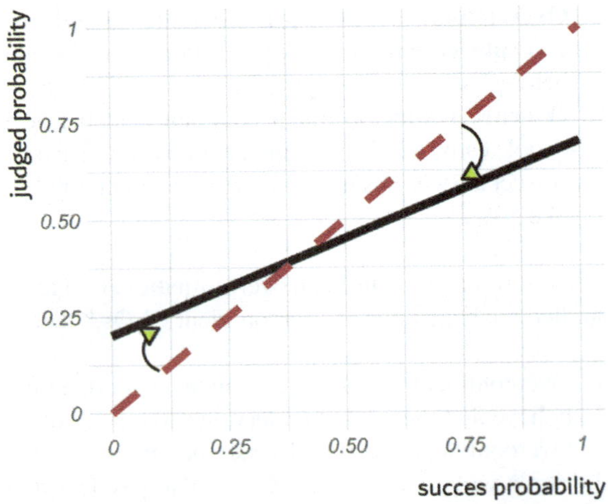

Fig. 8.1 Regressive beliefs

Pietro Ortoleva and Erik Snowberg (2015) show that overprecision can lead to political polarization. People learn about events through their experiences, but they forget that these experiences are correlated (correlation neglect, discussed above). If they only consult right-wing media and do not discount that the reporting of these media is correlated, they have more confidence in right-wing policies than when they would also consult left-wing outlets. Voters who show more overprecision, have more extreme views and turn out more for elections (they are more likely to believe that one party has the right policy for them). Overprecision occurs both on the right and on the left, but more so for conservatives. Communication worsens polarization. Overprecise voters are less inclined to attribute differences to their ideas being wrong.

8.5.3 Doubts About Motivated Beliefs

The model of motivated beliefs explains overconfidence by an (optimistic) bias in beliefs. This is the common explanation in the literature. I do have some doubts, however. First, as Exercise 8.9 shows, motivated beliefs cannot explain the hard-easy effect. Second, some of my own research casts doubt on the explanation that overconfidence is due to a bias in beliefs.

David van Ass, Olivier L'Haridon, and I (2018) measured the risk preferences of the players of the Dutch national field hockey team. At the time, they were the second best team in the world (after Australia) and had just become European champion beating Germany 6-1 in the final (which for a Dutch team is the zenith of achievement).

Because David van Ass' father was the coach of the team, we could interview all players individually in one hour sessions giving (unusually) rich data. The hockey professionals answered questions about lotteries with given probabilities. So, belief bias played no role. We compared their preferences with those of a group of recreational players matched in terms of age, social background, and education level.

Professional and recreational players differed in their weighting of probabilities. Professionals gave more weight to the probability of success than recreational players. That optimistic people are more successful, referred to above, may have more to do with risk attitudes (the weighting of beliefs) than with a distortion of beliefs as the motivated beliefs model suggests.

Mohammed Abdellaoui, Cédric Gutierrez, and I (2024) ran an experiment where people bet on their performance in an IQ test. We measured beliefs and the weighting of these beliefs. We found both evidence of overconfidence and the hard-easy effect. However, in contrast with a model of motivated beliefs, this was not caused by optimistic beliefs. Beliefs were underconfident. Observed overconfidence was, again, caused by the overweighting of these beliefs.

In both studies, our measurements corrected for the biases in decision under risk and ambiguity that I will discuss in Chapters 9 and 10. They suggest that overconfidence has more to do with risk and ambiguity preference than with optimistic beliefs. Let us therefore turn now to the discussion of these preferences.

References

Abdellaoui, M., H. Bleichrodt, and C. Gutierrez. 2024. Unpacking overconfident behavior when betting on oneself. *Management Science* 70: 7042–7061.

Ariely, D., G. Loewenstein, and D. Prelec. 2003. "Coherent arbitrariness": Stable demand curves without stable preferences. *Quarterly Journal of Economics* 118: 73–106.

Babcock, L., G. Loewenstein, S. Issacharoff, and C. Camerer. 1995. Biased judgments of fairness in bargaining. *American Economic Review* 85: 1337–1343.

Bénabou, R., and J. Tirole. 2002. Self-confidence and personal motivation. *Quarterly Journal of Economics* 117: 871–915.

Bleichrodt, H., O. L'Haridon, and D. Van Ass. 2018. The risk attitudes of professional athletes: Optimism and success are related. *Decision* 5: 95–118.

Chen, D.L., T.J. Moskowitz, and K. Shue. 2016. Decision making under the gambler's fallacy: Evidence from asylum judges, loan officers, and baseball umpires. *Quarterly Journal of Economics* 131: 1181–1242.

Chew, S.H., W. Huang, and X. Zhao. 2020. Motivated false memory. *Journal of Political Economy* 128: 3913–3939.

Dalafave, R.E., and W.K. Viscusi. 2023. The locus of dread for mass shooting risks: Distinguishing alarmist risk beliefs from risk preferences. *Journal of Risk and Uncertainty* 66: 109–139.

Eil, D., and J.M. Rao. 2011. The good news-bad news effect: Asymmetric processing of objective information about yourself. *American Economic Journal: Microeconomics* 3: 114–138.

Enke, B., and F. Zimmermann. 2019. Correlation neglect in belief formation. *Review of Economic Studies* 86: 313–332.

Erev, I., T.S. Wallsten, and D.V. Budescu. 1994. Simultaneous over-and underconfidence: The role of error in judgment processes. *Psychological Review* 101: 519–527.

Fischhoff, B., P. Slovic, and S. Lichtenstein. 1978. Fault trees: Sensitivity of estimated failure probabilities to problem representation. *Journal of Experimental Psychology: Human Perception and Performance* 4: 330–344.

Fox, C.R., and R.T. Clemen. 2005. Subjective probability assessment in decision analysis: Partition dependence and bias toward the ignorance prior. *Management Science* 51: 1417–1432.
Fox, C.R., and A. Tversky. 1998. A belief-based account of decision under uncertainty. *Management Science* 44: 879–895.
Fox, C.R., B.A. Rogers, and A. Tversky. 1996. Options traders exhibit subadditive decision weights. *Journal of Risk and Uncertainty* 13: 5–17.
Gigerenzer, G. 1996. On narrow norms and vague heuristics: A reply to Kahneman and Tversky. *Psychological Review* 193: 592–596.
Gill, R.D., P. Groeneboom, and P. De Jong. 2018. Elementary statistics on trial-the case of Lucia de Berk. *Chance* 31: 9–15.
Gilovich, T., R. Vallone, and A. Tversky. 1985. The hot hand in basketball: On the misperception of random sequences. *Cognitive Psychology* 17: 295–314.
Huffman, D., C. Raymond, and J. Shvets. 2022. Persistent overconfidence and biased memory: Evidence from managers. *American Economic Review* 112: 3141–3175.
Joyce, E. J. and G. C. Biddle. 1981. Anchoring and adjustment in probabilistic inference in auditing. *Journal of Accounting Research* 120–145.
Lewis, J., D. Feiler, and R. Adner. 2023. The worst-first heuristic: How decision makers manage conjunctive risk. *Management Science* 69: 1575–1596.
Lord, C.G., L. Ross, and M.R. Lepper. 1979. Biased assimilation and attitude polarization: The effects of prior theories on subsequently considered evidence. *Journal of Personality and Social Psychology* 37: 2098–2109.
Malmendier, U., and G. Tate. 2015. Behavioral CEOs: The role of managerial overconfidence. *Journal of Economic Perspectives* 29: 37–60.
Miller, J.B., and A. Sanjurjo. 2018. Surprised by the hot hand fallacy? A truth in the law of small numbers. *Econometrica* 86: 2019–2047.
Moore, D.A., and P.J. Healy. 2008. The trouble with overconfidence. *Psychological Review* 115: 502–517.
O'Grady, C. 2023. Unlucky numbers. *Science (New York, NY)* 379: 228–233.
Ortoleva, P., and E. Snowberg. 2015. Overconfidence in political behavior. *American Economic Review* 105: 504–535.
Ötting, M., R. Langrock, C. Deutscher, and V. Leos-Barajas. 2020. The hot hand in professional darts. *Journal of the Royal Statistical Society Series A: Statistics in Society* 183: 565–580.
Raab, M., B. Gula, and G. Gigerenzer. 2012. The hot hand exists in volleyball and is used for allocation decisions. *Journal of Experimental Psychology: Applied* 18: 81–94.
Redelmeier, D.A., D.J. Koehler, V. Liberman, and A. Tversky. 1995. Probability judgment in medicine: Discounting unspecified possibilities. *Medical Decision Making* 15: 227–230.
Rottenstreich, Y., and A. Tversky. 1997. Unpacking, repacking, and anchoring: Advances in support theory. *Psychological Review* 104: 406–415.
Schwardmann, P., E. Tripodi, and J.J. Van der Weele. 2022. Self-persuasion: Evidence from field experiments at international debating competitions. *American Economic Review* 112: 1118–1146.
Suetens, S., C.B. Galbo-Jørgensen, and J.-R. Tyran. 2016. Predicting lotto numbers: A natural experiment on the gambler's fallacy and the hot-hand fallacy. *Journal of the European Economic Association* 14: 584–607.
Tversky, A., and D. Kahneman. 1971. Belief in the law of small numbers. *Psychological Bulletin* 76: 105–110.
Tversky, A., and D.J. Koehler. 1994. Support theory: A nonextensional representation of subjective probability. *Psychological Review* 101: 547–567.
Wang, T.V., R.J.P. van Loon, M.J. Van den Assem, and D. Van Dolder. 2016. Number preferences in lotteries. *Judgment and Decision Making* 11: 243–259.

Decision Under Risk

9

9.1 The Basic Problem

An agent who makes a decision under uncertainty faces a set of possible **states of the world**. One of these states occurs, but the agent does not know which one. An example is Redelmeier's Hollywood actress who has symptoms which could be consistent with various diseases. In this example the states are the possible diseases. Other examples are the performance of the stock market, the result of an election, or the future rise in temperature.

A **prospect** defines which outcome occurs under each state of the world. In the medical example, the prospect is a treatment, which defines health for each of the possible diseases.

In this chapter I assume that the probabilities of the states of the world are known. We call this **decision under risk**. I discuss decision under ambiguity, where probabilities are unknown, in the next chapter.

Risky prospects are written as $(p_1 : x_1, \ldots, p_n : x_n)$. This stands for getting outcome x_1 with probability p_1, outcome x_2 with probability p_2, etc. If a risky prospect has only two possible outcomes, I will use the shorthand $x_p y$ for the prospect $(p : x, 1 - p : y)$.

9.2 Expected Value

How can we represent the agent's preferences over risky prospects? The first suggestion, dating back to Pascal and Huygens, was to use **expected value**.

H. Bleichrodt, *Behavioural Economics*,
https://doi.org/10.1007/978-3-031-69166-9_9

Definition 9.1: Expected Value

Let $V(p_1 : x_1, \ldots, p_n : x_n)$ denote the agent's utility of the risky prospect $(p_1 : x_1, \ldots, p_n : x_n)$. **Expected value** holds if

$$V(p_1 : x_1, \ldots, p_n : x_n) = \sum_{i=1}^{n} p_i \times x_i.$$

We multiply each outcome by its probability and then sum these products over probability outcome pairs. Expected value has been used a lot in applied work. For example, in medical decision making where interventions were compared based on their costs and their expected gain in life duration. Tammy Tengs and co-authors (1995) compared the costs per life-year gained for 500 US policy interventions. The costs varied from \$0 (compulsory seat belt use) to \$18 million (making buildings earthquake proof). In general, environmental measures were most expensive and medical interventions least.[1] The dispersion in the costs of saving lives implies wasting public money: By shifting money from more expensive to less expensive interventions more lives can be saved with the same budget.

Exercise 9.1: A Limitation of Expected Value

Explain that expected value can only be applied to quantitative outcomes (like life duration) and not, for example, to quality of life measurement. What does this mean for policy?

9.2.1 The St. Petersburg Paradox

In 1713 the Swiss mathematician Nicolas Bernoulli proposed a thought experiment that challenged expected value. It is called the **St. Petersburg paradox**, after the city in which his cousin Daniel resided when he gave a solution to the problem (see below).

Bio 9.1: The Bernoulli Family

The Bernoulli family contained several prominent mathematicians. Johann Bernoulli discovered the rule of L'Hôpital. They had signed a contract which gave l'Hôpital the right to publish Bernoulli's results under his own name. L'Hôpital recognized this in the preface to his book. Johann was a jealous

[1] But keep in mind that environmental measures often have more goals than saving lives.

character who envied both his brother Jakob and his son Daniel. He allegedly plagiarized results from Daniel on hydrodynamics. This led to a split between father and son that never healed.

Jakob Bernoulli was Nicolas' uncle and his PhD advisor (Nicolas' father was a painter). Jakob derived the first version of the law of large numbers and discovered the mathematical constant e.

Daniel Bernoulli was born in Groningen, the Netherlands. His family had fled from Antwerp to escape the Spanish prosecution of protestants in the southern Netherlands, which had remained under Spanish rule after the 80 year war. Later he moved to Basel, Switzerland. Apart from his work on economics and statistics, he is known for **Bernoulli's principle**, a key result in fluid dynamics, which relates pressure, speed, and height. It is used in aerodynamics. In 2002, Daniel Bernoulli was inducted in the International Air and Space Hall of Fame for his contributions to aerospace flight and technology.

Experiment 9.1: The St. Petersburg Paradox

Suppose that we toss a fair coin until it lands on heads. Then the game ends. You get €2^n where n is the toss on which the coin lands on heads. So if the coin lands heads on the first toss you get €2, if it lands heads on the second toss your get €$2^2 = 4$, et cetera. How much are you willing to pay to play this game?

Exercise 9.2: The St. Petersburg Paradox

Show that the expected value of the St. Petersburg game is infinite

Because the expected value of the St. Petersburg game is infinite, expected value maximizers will pay all they have to play it. In reality, people do not. My students typically say they would play the game for €5 or less. The expected value of the game is infinite, but people are only willing to pay a small amount to play it. Expected value does not describe their preferences.

The problem of expected value is that it assumes that people are neutral to risk. They are indifferent between a gamble and its expected value. Consider a choice between two medical treatments. One gives 20 years in good health for sure after which you die. The other gives 40 years in good health (after which you die) with probability 50% but also a probability of 50% that you die immediately. Expected value says you should be indifferent between these treatments (why?). However, almost everyone prefers the 20 years for sure. We are not neutral, but averse to risk.

9.3 Expected Utility

To solve the St. Petersburg paradox and allow for risk aversion, Daniel Bernoulli suggested to maximize **expected utility** instead of expected value.

Definition 9.2: Expected Utility

Expected utility holds if

$$V(p_1 : x_1, \ldots, p_n : x_n) = \sum_{i=1}^{n} p_i \times U(x_i).$$

where U is a utility function over outcomes. If U is concave, expected utility can explain that people are only willing to pay a modest amount to play the St. Petersburg gamble. Bernoulli proposed the logarithmic utility function $U(x) = ln(x)$.

Exercise 9.3: Logarithmic Utility

Show that expected utility with logarithmic utility predicts that people are willing to pay approximately €1.40 to play the St. Petersburg gamble.

9.3.1 von Neumann Morgenstern

Bernoulli's suggestion to use expected utility solved the St. Petersburg paradox, but it was ad hoc. He did not explain why people would or should behave according to expected utility. It took another two centuries to do so.

In 1944 during World War II, a mathematician, John von Neumann, and an economist, Oskar Morgenstern (who we already encountered in Chapter 3) wrote the *Theory of Games and Economic Behavior*. In this book, they laid the foundations of game theory. They used expected utility as the unit of exchange for their games. In an appendix, von Neumann and Morgenstern gave an axiomatization of expected utility. That is, they wrote down the conditions under which people's preferences over risky prospects can be represented by expected utility. These conditions were appealing, both normatively and, as people believed, descriptively. von Neumann and Morgenstern's result became the argument for using expected utility in evaluating decisions under risk.

Bio 9.2: John von Neumann

When I wrote "the mathematician John von Neumann", I did not do him justice as von Neumann made pathbreaking contributions in many fields. His colleagues at Princeton joked that he was the living proof that extraterrestrials existed and had learnt to perfectly imitate humans. Highly intelligent acquaintances (who also knew Einstein) remarked that it was as if von Neumann was the only person who was really awake.

von Neumann was born in 1903 as János Lajos Neumann (he changed his name to John when he fled Nazism for the US in 1933). He was a genius. He had a photographic memory and could recite full chapters from books he had read years back. Legend goes that a famous professor of Byzantine history only agreed to come to a party at Princeton if von Neumann promised not to talk about his discipline, afraid as he was of losing his prestige.

At age 17, von Neumann solved Bertrand Russell's paradox. Russell had shown in 1901 that mathematical set theory led to the contradiction that it was possible to construct sets that simultaneously contained and not contained themselves. Russell and others had for years unsuccessfully tried to solve this paradox. A Hungarian school kid solved it.

In physics von Neumann reconciled the two distinct formulations of quantum mechanics by Heisenberg's matrix formulation and Schrödinger's wave mechanics. These theories appeared different, but both worked well. Von Neumann showed they were equivalent.

Von Neumann was a driving force behind the Manhattan project in Los Alamos. It developed the atomic bombs that destroyed Hiroshima and Nagasaki (von Neumann was involved in selecting these cities) and ended World War II. He developed the first digital computer and together with Alan Turing is seen as the father of modern informatics.

After World War II, von Neumann was the leading US expert on nuclear weapons and the leading defence scientist at the Pentagon. At times he was in such demand that a US Air Force plane was kept on standby to move him from one meeting to another. Based on his game theoretic work, von Neumann was convinced that the only way for the US to avoid nuclear war was to strike preemptively against the Soviet Union. Yet, he was not a cold-hearted warmonger. He was a cheerful and cooperative person, an optimist who believed in the progress of humanity. As his second wife Klári Dán (herself an eminent scientist and Hungarian champion of figure skating) wrote: "von Neumann was an enigma of nature that will forever remain unresolved". John von Neumann died in 1957 of cancer, probably caused by exposure to radiation at Los Alamos.[a]

[a] For more on von Neumann see Ananyo Bhattacharya (2021) The man from the future: The visionary life of John von Neumann, Allen Lane.

Niels Erik Jensen (1967) gave the presentation of von Neumann and Morgenstern's result that I find most intuitive. He imposed three conditions. The first is the usual assumption that preferences $\succcurlyeq$ over prospects are complete (for any two prospects f and g either $f \succcurlyeq g$, $g \succcurlyeq f$ or both) and transitive (for any prospects f,g, and h, if $f \succcurlyeq g$ and $g \succcurlyeq h$ then also $f \succcurlyeq h$).

The second assumption is a continuity assumption. A sure outcome x is the **certainty equivalent** of a risky prospect f if the agent is indifferent between x and f: $x \sim f$. Jensen assumed that each prospect has a certainty equivalent. This is a technical requirement that is not restrictive.

Extension 9.1: Continuity

Jensen imposed a slightly different continuity condition. I use the certainty equivalent (CE) formulation, because I find it intuitive and certainty equivalents are often used to measure expected utility. The CE condition requires that outcomes are quantitative. To formulate continuity for qualitative outcomes we can replace the CE condition by a **probability equivalence** (PE) condition: For any outcomes x, y, z with $x \succ y \succ z$, there is a unique probability p such that $y \sim x_p z$. The PE condition uses the (natural) richness of the probabilities to find indifference and imposes no restrictions on the set of outcomes except that there are three nonindifferent outcomes.

The third condition, vNM independence, is the central condition. For any two prospects f and h and $\lambda \in [0, 1]$, let $\lambda f + (1 - \lambda)h$ denote the (mixing) prospect that gives f with probability λ and h with probability $(1 - \lambda)$. So if $f = 100_{1/2}0$, $h = 50$, and $\lambda = 1/4$, $\lambda f + (1 - \lambda)h$ is the prospect $(1/8 : 100, 3/4 : 50, 1/8 : 0)$.

Exercise 9.4: Mixing Prospects

What is $\lambda f + (1 - \lambda)h$ when $f = 75_{1/5}10$, $h = 35_{2/3}20$, and $\lambda = 2/3$?

vNM independence says that for any two prospects f and g such that f is preferred to g ($f \succcurlyeq g$), any mixture $\lambda f + (1 - \lambda)h$ of f with a third prospect h is also preferred to the same mixture $\lambda g + (1 - \lambda)h$ of g with h. Intuitively, vNM independence says that preferences do not depend on the common part of prospects. The mixtures have $(1 - \lambda)h$ in common and vNM independence says that this part does not matter. Preferences depend on where the prospects differ and that is in λf and λg. So preferences are governed by the preference between f and g. As agents prefer f to g they should also prefer $\lambda f + (1 - \lambda)h$ to $\lambda g + (1 - \lambda)h$

We can now state the following result:

Theorem 9.1: Expected Utility

The following two statements are equivalent:

1. Preferences over prospects are complete and transitive, each prospect has a certainty equivalent, and vNM independence holds.
2. Expected utility holds.

Moreover, the utility function is cardinal: We can freely choose the utility of two outcomes.

Theorem 9.1 shows the importance of von Neumann and Morgenstern's result. It gives intuitive conditions that ensure that people behave according to expected utility. Of these conditions completeness, transitivity, and the certainty equivalent assumption are standard. The central condition, vNM independence, is normatively plausible and easy to test. Finally, the cardinality of utility in Theorem 9.1 resurrected the debate about the nature of utility as we saw in Chapter 3 and it is useful for practical applications.

9.3.2 Risk Attitudes

In expected utility risk attitudes are modelled through the utility function.

Definition 9.3: Risk Attitudes

Agents are:

1. **Risk averse** if they always prefer the expected value of a prospect to the prospect itself.
2. **Risk loving** if they always prefer a prospect to its expected value.
3. **Risk neutral** if they are indifferent between a prospect and its expected value.

An expected value maximizer is risk neutral. Because an expected value maximizer has linear utility over outcomes, risk neutrality and linear utility are equivalent. Let us now see what happens if the agent has a concave utility function as in Fig. 9.1a. Consider a prospect that gives a 50% chance of β and a 50% chance of α. The expected value of this prospect is $\frac{(\alpha+\beta)}{2}$ and its expected utility is $\frac{U(\alpha)+U(\beta)}{2}$. Figure 9.1b shows that the utility of the expected value is higher than the expected utility. Agents with concave utility prefer the expected value of the prospect to the prospect itself and, by Definition 9.3, they are risk averse.

Figure 9.1c shows another way to express risk aversion. The certainty equivalent of the prospect (CE) is smaller than its expected value. The **risk premium** (π) is the difference between the expected value and the certainty equivalent of a prospect. The risk premium of a risk averse agent is positive. It shows how much the agent is willing to pay to avoid the risk of the prospect.

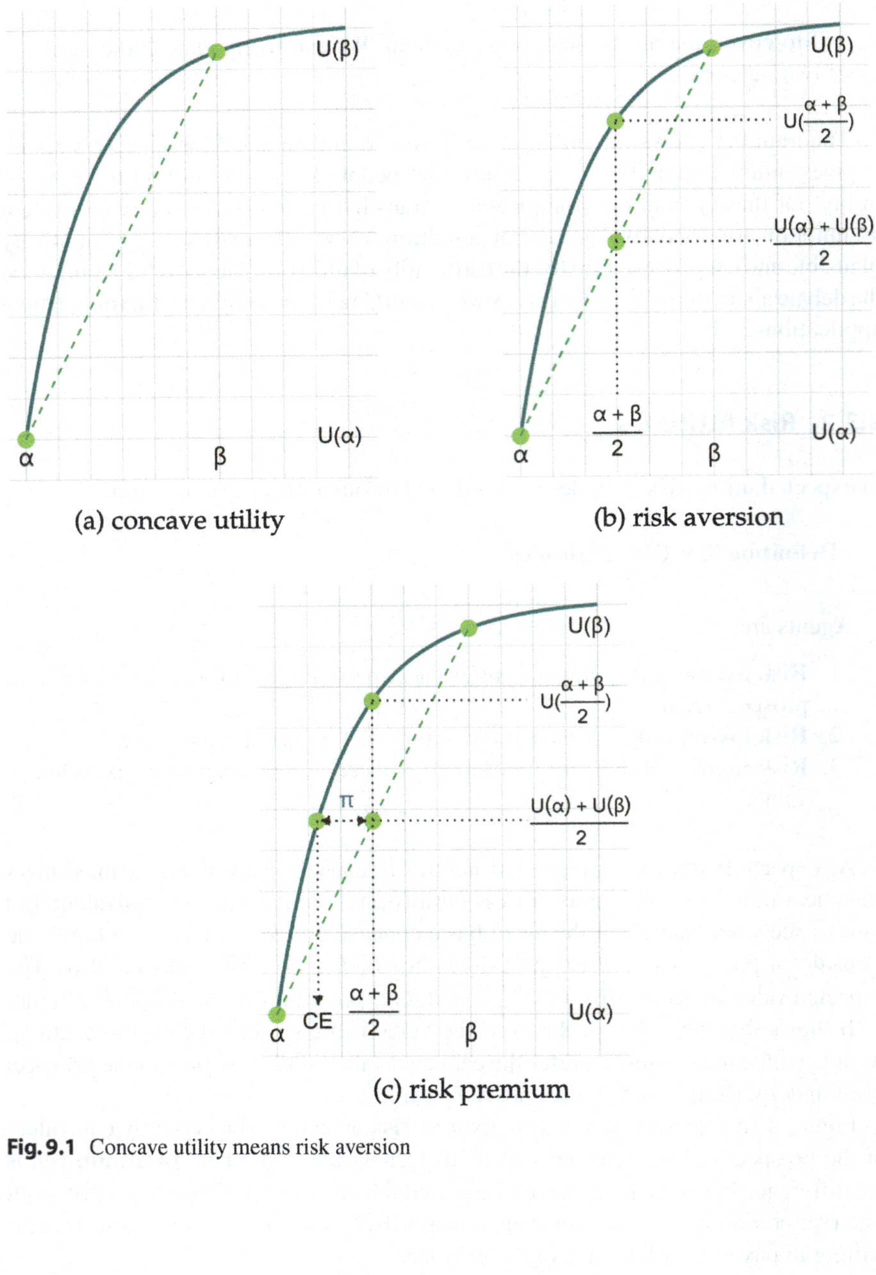

Fig. 9.1 Concave utility means risk aversion

So we have the following:

Theorem 9.2: Risk Aversion

Under expected utility the following are equivalent:

1. The agent is risk averse.
2. The agent has concave utility.
3. The agent's risk premium is positive.

Exercise 9.5: Risk Loving

Use a similar graphical analysis as in Fig. 9.1 to show that the following are equivalent:

1. The agent is risk loving.
2. The agent has convex utility.
3. The agent's risk premium is negative.

9.3.3 Measuring Utility

Expected utility can easily be measured, which makes it suitable for applications. There are two main measurement methods: the certainty equivalence method and the probability equivalence method.

The **certainty equivalence (CE) method** fixes a prospect M_pm with $M \succ m$ and asks subjects for the sure outcome α that is equivalent to this prospect: $\alpha \sim M_pm$ (hence the term certainty equivalent). Evaluating this indifference by expected utility gives:

$$U(\alpha) = pU(M) + (1 - p)U(m). \tag{9.1}$$

Equation 9.1 has three unknowns: $U(\alpha)$, $U(m)$, and $U(M)$. By Theorem 9.1 we can choose the utility of two outcomes. We set $U(M) = 1$ and $U(m) = 0$ and get:

$$U(\alpha) = p. \tag{9.2}$$

The probability p is usually set to an easy number, e.g. $1/2$. Then $U(\alpha) = 1/2$. To find the outcome that has utility $1/4$ we can do two things: either we set $p = 1/4$ and ask for the outcome $\alpha_{1/4}$ that is equivalent to the prospect $M_{1/4}m$ or we keep $p = 1/2$ and we ask for the outcome $\alpha'_{1/4}$ that is equivalent to the prospect $\alpha_{1/2}m$.

Exercise 9.6: CE Method

1. Show that under expected utility $\alpha_{1/4} = \alpha'_{1/4}$.
2. Which questions could we ask to find the outcome with utility $1/8$?
3. And that with utility $3/4$?

Because the CE method uses outcomes to give indifference, it only works for quantitative outcomes. To measure utility for any outcome we can use the **probability equivalence (PE) method**. Suppose, for example, that we want to know the utility of living with migraine. In medical research, health states are often described by the level of functioning on various dimensions. The description of mild migraine is:

- slight problems with mobility.
- no problems with self-care.
- moderate problems with usual activities.
- moderate pain or discomfort.
- not anxious or depressed.

To find the utility of migraine, the PE method (which in medical research is called the **standard gamble method**, see Example 4.1) asks people to compare the option of living with migraine (Mg) for the rest of their lives to a risky treatment that gives full health (FH) for the rest of their lives with probability p and death within a week (D) with probability $1 - p$. People are asked to state the probability p for which they see these two options as equivalent (hence the term probability equivalence method).

Applying expected utility gives:

$$U(Mg) = pU(FH) + (1 - p)U(D). \tag{9.3}$$

Again, we have one equation with three unknowns. Expected utility permits choosing the utility of two outcomes. We set $U(FH) = 1$ and $U(D) = 0$. Then:

$$U(Mg) = p. \tag{9.4}$$

Exercise 9.7: Chained PE

A concern with the PE method to value health is that the possibility of death makes people reluctant to accept much (if any) risk in the treatment option. To solve this, we could choose a health state Y close to death and use a chained measurement. First we ask the probability q such that the patient is indifferent between living with migraine and FH_qY. Then we ask the probability r such that $Y \sim FH_rD$. Show that $U(Mg) = q + (1 - q)r$.

Extension 9.2: Insurance

Expected utility is easy to apply to real-world problems. Consider the decision to take insurance. Expected utility predicts that risk averse agents will take more insurance.

Suppose agents with wealth W who face a loss $\mathcal{L}$ with probability p. The agents can choose insurance coverage $\mathcal{C}$ for which they pay premium $\pi\mathcal{C}$. So the premium is a fixed percentage of the chosen level of coverage. The agents' wealth in the case of loss is then $W_{\mathcal{L}} = W - \mathcal{L} + \mathcal{C}(1-\pi)$ and in the case of no loss it is $W_{N\mathcal{L}} = W - \pi\mathcal{C}$.

The agent's optimization problem is:

$$\max_{\mathcal{C}} pU(W_{\mathcal{L}}) + (1-p)U(W_{N\mathcal{L}}).$$

Exercise 9.8: Optimal Insurance

Show that the agent's first order condition (FOC) is:

$$p(1-\pi)U'(W_{\mathcal{L}}) - \pi(1-p)U'(W_{N\mathcal{L}}) = 0.$$

Let's look at two implications of Exercise 9.8. First, when will agents choose full insurance, $\mathcal{C} = \mathcal{L}$? A sufficient and necessary condition is that the first order condition (FOC) at $\mathcal{C} = \mathcal{L}$ is nonnegative. Substituting gives

$$U'(W - \pi L)\,[pL - \pi L]\,,$$

which is nonnegative if $pL \geq \pi L$, i.e. if the premium is actuarially fair. If the insurance company charges a premium higher than the expected value of the loss, agents will take less than full insurance.

A second implication of Exercise 9.8 is that a more risk averse agent will take more coverage. Let V be the utility function of a more risk averse agent. Under expected utility, V is a concave function of U: $V = k(U)$ with $k' > 0$ and $k'' < 0$. Substituting this in the FOC gives:

$$p(1-\pi)k'(U(W_{\mathcal{L}}))U'(W_{\mathcal{L}}) - \pi(1-p)k'(U(W_{N\mathcal{L}}))U'(W_{N\mathcal{L}}),$$

which is positive because $U(W_{\mathcal{L}}) < U(W_{N\mathcal{L}})$ and $k'(U(W_{\mathcal{L}})) > k'(U(W_{N\mathcal{L}}))$ by the concavity of k. Because the FOC is positive, $\mathcal{C}$ has to increase to make it zero again.

9.4 The Allais Paradoxes

While expected utility is elegant and the von Neumann Morgenstern axioms have normative appeal, it soon became clear that expected utility had descriptive shortcomings. In 1953 the French economist Maurice Allais, winner of the 1988 Nobel Prize in economics, suggested two paradoxes that challenged expected utility as a description of people's preferences.

9.4.1 The Common Ratio Effect

The **common ratio effect** consists of the two choices shown in Table 9.1. The second choice results from the first by multiplying the winning probabilities by a common ratio $1/4$. Hence, the name common ratio effect. The majority choices are in Table 2.1 green. What would you choose?

These choices violate expected utility. In terms of expected utility and setting $U(0) = 0$, the choice of A over B implies that

$$U(3000) > 0.8 \times U(4000), \tag{9.5}$$

while the choice of D over C implies that

$$0.25 \times U(3000) < 0.2 \times U(4000). \tag{9.6}$$

Multiplying both sides of equation 9.6 by 4 gives:

$$U(3000) < 0.8 \times U(4000). \tag{9.7}$$

Equations 9.5 and 9.7 cannot hold simultaneously so the common ratio effect violates expected utility.

9.4.2 The Common Consequence Effect

Table 9.2 shows the two choices in Allais' **common consequence effect**. Again, the commonly chosen options are in green. What you would choose?

Table 9.1 The common ratio effect

	Which do you prefer?	
Choice 1	Prospect A	100% chance of €3000
	Prospect B	80% chance of €4000
		20% chance of €0
Choice 2	Prospect C	25% chance of €3000
		75% chance of €0
	Prospect D	20% chance of €4000
		80% chance of €0

Table 9.2 The common consequence effect

	Which do you prefer?	
Choice 1	Prospect A	100% chance of €1 million
	Prospect B	10% chance of €5 million 89% chance of €1 million 1% chance of €0
Choice 2	Prospect C	11% chance of €1 million 89% chance of €0
	Prospect D	10% chance of €5 million 90% chance of €0

Table 9.3 The common consequence effect violates independence

		0.10	0.89	0.01
Choice 1	Prospect A	1M	1M	1M
	Prospect B	5M	1M	0
Choice 2	Prospect C	1M	0	1M
	Prospect D	5M	0	0

Exercise 9.9: Common Consequence Effect

Write down what these choices imply in terms of expected utility and show that they lead to a contradiction.

Exercise 9.9 shows that the choices in the common consequence effect violate expected utility. Another way of seeing this is to write the choices as in Table 9.3. It shows that prospect C is obtained from A and D from B by changing the common outcome 1 million into the common outcome 0. vNM independence says that preferences are independent of common outcomes and so if A is preferred to B then C should be preferred to D. The common consequence effect violates vNM independence. For a proof see Extension 9.3.

Extension 9.3: The Common Consequence Effect Violates Independence

Let f be the prospect that gives 1 million for sure and g the prospect $5M_{10/11}0$. Let $\lambda = {}^{11}/_{100}$. The first choice in the common consequence effect implies that $\lambda f + (1-\lambda) f \succcurlyeq \lambda g + (1-\lambda) f$. By independence, $f \succcurlyeq g$. Let h be the prospect that gives 0 for sure. By independence, $\lambda f + (1-\lambda)h \succcurlyeq \lambda g + (1-\lambda)h$. That is, prospect C in the common consequence effect should be preferred to prospect D. However, the majority preference is $D \succcurlyeq C$.

9.5 Are the Allais Paradoxes Normative?

If you want to satisfy vNM independence then Theorem 9.1 says that the Allais paradoxes are not normative. However, you may not be convinced about vNM independence. Peter Wakker has shown that if you choose *A* in the first choice of the common consequence effect and *D* in the second then you must give up at least one of four principles. Figure 9.2 explains. Squares indicate the moment of choice and circles denote chance.

Figure 9.2a shows the choice between *A* and *B* in the common consequence effect. In Fig. 9.2b you face the same choice, but you arrive at this choice because you were successful in an earlier (first stage) prospect. The dashed lines show that the risks were borne in the past. **Consequentialism** says that such risks do not matter. All that matters is the options you face now, not how you reached them. Consequently, your choice should be the same in Fig. 9.2a and b. Wakker calls this "don't believe in ghosts".

Figure 9.2c is the same as Fig. 9.2b except that you must commit before the resolution of the first stage prospect what you choose at the choice node (and you cannot change this commitment). **Dynamic consistency** says that what is best at the choice node does not depend on when you decide. So you should make the same choice in Fig. 9.2b and c.

Figure 9.2d obtains from Fig. 9.2c by moving the decision forward. Instead of committing you already choose. Because the commitment in Fig. 9.2c was binding, the two figures show the same situation. **Context independence** says that two equivalent descriptions of the same situation should lead to the same choice.

Finally, Fig. 9.2e obtains from Fig. 9.2d by reducing the two-stage prospects to one-stage prospects using the laws of probability. **Reduction** says that these choices are equivalent.

However, Fig. 9.2e shows the second choice in the common consequence effect, where most people choose the lower option. So if you choose *A* in the first choice and *D* in the second choice and you believe that these choices are rational then you must give up at least one of consequentialism, dynamic consistency, context independence, or reduction. Decide for yourself which one, if any, you want to give up.

Exercise 9.10: Dynamic Decision Principles and the Common Ratio Effect

Show by a similar figure as 9.2 how the common ratio effect can be dissected by consequentialism, dynamic consistency, context independence, and reduction.

Robin Cubitt, Chris Starmer, and Robert Sugden (1998) tested the dissection of the common ratio effect mentioned in Exercise 9.10. The most common violation was dynamic consistency. This shows where expected utility goes wrong descriptively. They did not test whether their subjects found the principles normatively appealing.

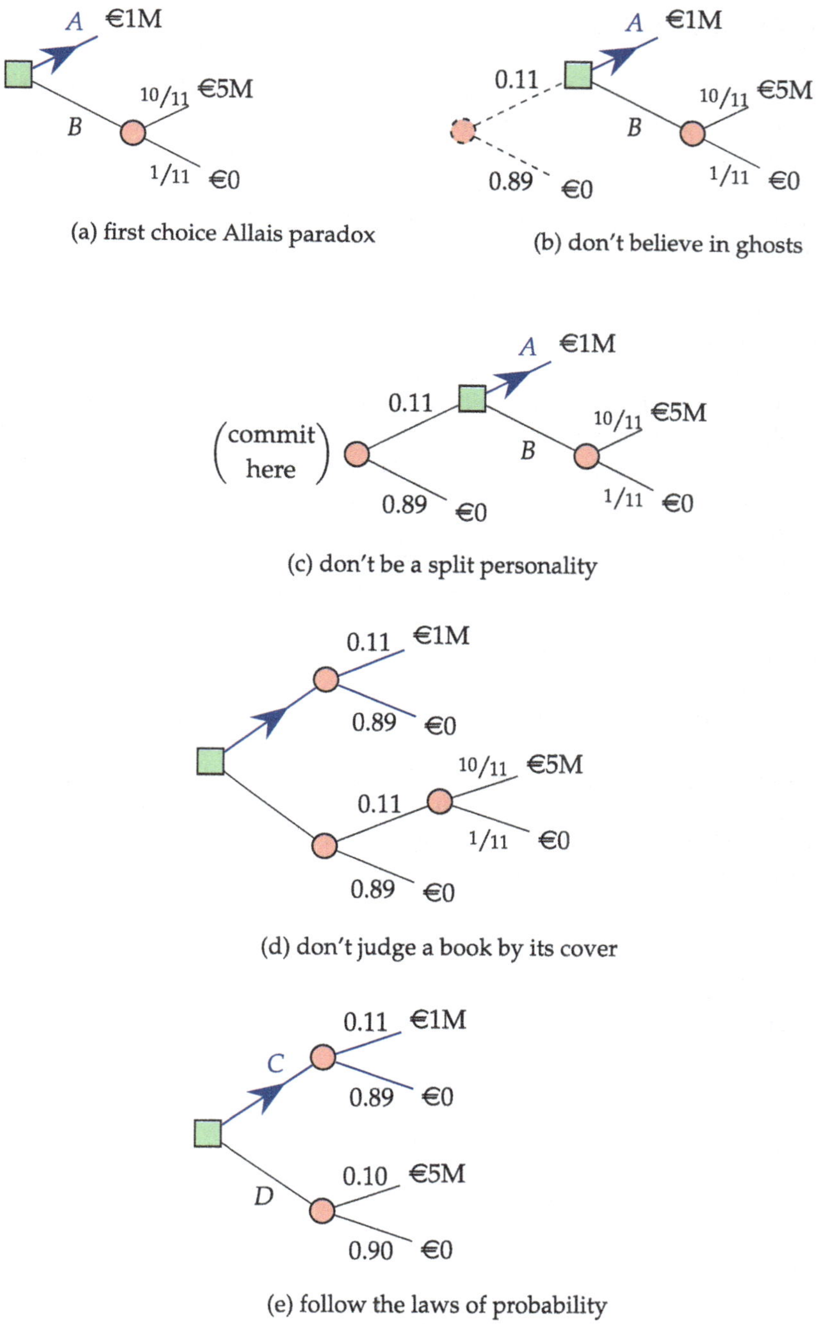

Fig. 9.2 Is the Allais paradox normative?

9.6 Probability Weighting

In both the common ratio and the common consequence effect the move from prospect A to prospect C involves a change from certainty to risk. There is no such move in going from B to D. Both are risky. The Allais paradoxes suggest that people are more sensitive to a change from certainty to probable than from probable to less probable. This overweighting of certainty is called the **certainty effect**.

Something similar happens on the other end of the probability scale when we change possible into impossible. For example, people are more sensitive to reduce the risk of a cancer from 2% to 0% than to reducing this risk from 10% to 8%. This is called the **impossibility effect**.

In expected utility, people evaluate probabilities linearly. Consequently, it cannot explain the certainty and impossibility effects. To explain these we must allow for **probability weighting**. The typical probability weighting function looks like Fig. 9.3. It is steeper near 0 and 1 than in the middle range to capture the impossibility and certainty effects. This function, which empirically is usually found, is called **inverse S**, because its shape looks like an inverse S.

Inverse S implies that small probabilities are overweighted and medium and large probabilities are underweighted. Empirical studies suggest that the probability at which the probability weighting function changes from overweighting to underweighting probabilities lies approximately at $p = 1/3$. At the individual level, however, it varies.

The overweighting of small probabilities can explain why people simultaneously gamble (which implies risk loving) and take insurance (which implies risk aversion). Expected utility cannot explain this. Arrow (1951, p. 407) called it a requirement for any theory of decision under risk. Probability weighting can explain it. As both the probability of winning in a lottery and the probabilities of most losses against which we insure are small, they are both overweighted. Consequently, both gambling and insurance look attractive.

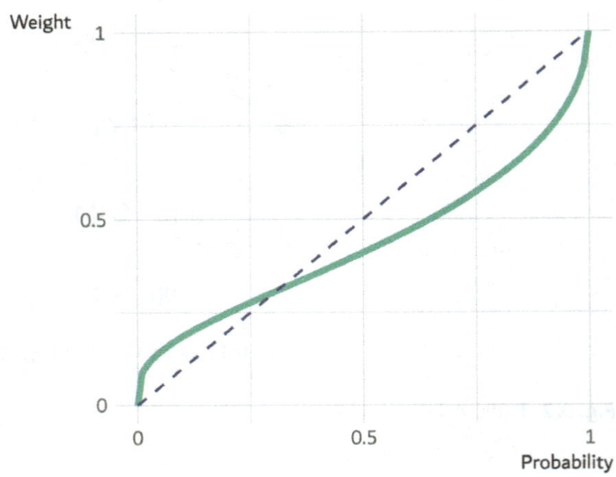

Fig. 9.3 Probability weighting

9.6.1 Modelling Probability Weighting

The obvious way to model probability weighting is to replace probabilities by probability weights in the expected utility function $\sum_{i=1}^{n} p_i \times U(x_i)$:

$$V(p_1 : x_1, \ldots, p_n : x_n) = \sum_{i=1}^{n} w(p_i) \times U(x_i). \tag{9.8}$$

This form was suggested by Ward Edwards. Kahneman and Tversky also used it in an early working paper version of prospect theory (called value theory). Jagdish Handa (1977), suggested it in an article in the *Journal of Political Economy*. In reaction, the journal received 10 comments of which it published Peter Fishburn's (1978). Exercise 9.11 shows what is wrong with Eq. 9.8.

Exercise 9.11: Violations of Monotonicity

Suppose $w(0.05) > 1/2 \times w(0.10)$. For example, let $w(0.05) = 0.10$ and $w(0.10) = 0.15$. Suppose utility is linear. Consider two prospects $(0.05 : 90, 0.05 : 70, 0.90 : 0)$ and $(0.10 : 100, 0.90 : 0)$. Compute the utility of these prospects according to Eq. 9.8.

Exercise 9.11 shows that Eq. 9.8 predicts that the prospect $(0.10 : 100, 0.90 : 0)$ is not chosen even though it gives for each state of the world at least as good an outcome as $(0.05 : 90, 0.05 : 70, 0.90 : 0)$. Empirically, we never observe this. For that reason, Eq. 9.8 is not a good model of probability weighting.

Exercise 9.12: Another Problem

Show that if people overweight small probabilities, for example, $w(0.10) > 0.10$ then Eq. 9.8 predicts that a prospect that gives 10 different outcomes each with probability 10% will be preferred to its expected value. Empirically, we do not find this.

Kahneman and Tversky (1979) solved this problem by including an **editing phase**. In this phase agents screen the prospects and realize that $(0.10 : 100, 0.90 : 0)$ dominates $(0.05 : 90, 0.05 : 70, 0.90 : 0)$. They then choose it without further evaluating the prospects. The editing phase is an ad hoc solution. Kahneman and Tversky dropped it in their 1992 version of prospect theory. They could do so because by then the problem of how to model probability weighting had been solved by an Australian economics student: John Quiggin.

9.6.2 Rank-Dependent Utility

John Quiggin was one of the people who wrote a comment on Handa's paper to the JPE. It went unpublished, but this did not stop him from trying to find the correct way to model probability weighting. He published it in his master's thesis, a remarkable achievement. It was later published in Quiggin (1982). It is an example of how economics, with its rich modelling tradition, can improve psychological models.

Quiggin realized that we should weight cumulative instead of individual probabilities. His model has three steps:

1. We rank-order the outcomes of a prospect from best to worst. Let $(p_1 : x_1, p_2 : x_2, \dots, p - n : x_n)$ be a rank-ordered prospect such that $x_1 \succcurlyeq x_2 \succcurlyeq \dots \succcurlyeq x_n$.[2]
2. We evaluate a rank-ordered prospect as:

$$V(p_1 : x_1, \dots, p_n : x_n) = \sum_{i=1}^{n} \pi_i \times U(x_i), \tag{9.9}$$

   where the π_i are **decision weights.**
3. The decision weights are equal to:

$$\pi_i = w(\sum_{j=1}^{i} p_j) - w(\sum_{j=1}^{i-1} p_j), \tag{9.10}$$

   where w is the probability weighting function.[3] So the decision weight of any outcome x_i in a rank-ordered prospect is equal to the weight of the probability of getting x_i or something better minus the weight of the probability of getting something better.

Because the evaluation of prospects depends on the rank ordering of the outcomes, Quiggin's model is called **rank-dependent utility** (RDU).[4]

Under RDU, violations of monotonicity cannot occur. Take the example of Exercise 9.11. Evaluating the two prospects by RDU gives:

$$RDU(0.10 : 100, 0.90 : 0) = w(0.10)U(100) + [1 - w(0.10)]\,U(0) \tag{9.11}$$

and

$$\begin{aligned} &RDU(0.05 : 90, 0.05 : 70, 0.90 : 0) = \\ &w(0.05)U(90) + [w(0.10) - w(0.05)]\,U(70) + [1 - w(0.10)]\,U(0). \end{aligned} \tag{9.12}$$

---

[2] For indifferent outcomes it does not matter how we rank them.

[3] $w(\sum_{j=1}^{0} p_j) = 0$ and $w(\sum_{j=1}^{n} p_j) = 1$.

[4] Quiggin called his model anticipated utility. Nowadays rank-dependent utility is used.

Because $w(0.10)U(100) = w(0.05)U(100) + [w(0.10) - w(0.05)]\,U(100)$, it follows that $RDU(0.10 : 100, 0.90 : 0) > RDU(0.05 : 90, 0.05 : 70, 0.90 : 0)$.

RDU evaluates binary prospects $x_p y$ with $x \succ y$ as $w(p)U(x)+(1-w(p))U(y)$ The probability weight is the weight of the best outcome. The higher this weight, the more agents focus on the best outcome and the more optimistic they are.

9.6.3 Measuring Probability Weighting

Exercise 9.13: Standard Gamble

The standard gamble asks for the probability p such that a patient is indifferent between living with, for example, migraine for the rest of their life and a risky treatment that gives full health with probability p and death within a week with probability $1 - p$. Show that under RDU the utility of migraine is equal to $w(p)$ (hint: under RDU the utility function is also cardinal so you can freely choose the utility of two outcomes).

Exercise 9.13 shows that to apply RDU, we must measure not only utility, but also probability weighting. Mohammed Abdellaoui (2000), Richard Gonzalez and George Wu (1999), and José Luis Pinto and I (Bleichrodt and Pinto 2000) proposed methods to do so without making assumptions about the shapes of the utility or the probability weighting function. In Extension 9.4, I explain Abdellaoui's method.

Extension 9.4: Measuring w

We first measure utility. Fix three outcomes $x_0 \succ R \succ r$ and a probability p. Then we ask for x_1 such that ${x_1}_p r \sim {x_0}_p R$. Because $R \succ r$, $x_1 \succ x_0$ and so the prospects are rank-ordered.

Exercise 9.14:

Show that

$$U(x_1) - U(x_0) = \frac{1 - w(p)}{w(p)}\,[U(R) - U(r)]\,.$$

Next we substitute x_1 for x_0 and ask for x_2 such that ${x_2}_p r \sim {x_1}_p R$.

Exercise 9.15:

Show that

$$U(x_2) - U(x_1) = \frac{1 - w(p)}{w(p)} [U(R) - U(r)] .$$

From Exercises 9.14 and 9.15, we see that $U(x_2) - U(x_1) = U(x_1) - U(x_0)$. We proceed this way. We substitute x_j for x_{j-1}, $j = 2, \ldots$ and ask for x_{j+1} such that $x_{j+1_p} r \sim x_{j_p} R$. We find that $U(x_{j+1}) - U(x_j) = U(x_1) - U(x_0)$.

By selecting 5 outcomes we can approximate the utility function well. So we have a **standard sequence** $x_0, x_1, \ldots x_5$ for which the utility difference between successive outcomes is constant.

Exercise 9.16: Utility

Set $U(x_0) = 0$ and $U(x_5) = 1$. Show that $U(x_j) = {}^j/_5$.

We now use the standard sequence to measure probability weighting. If we want to know the probability that has weight ${}^j/_5$, we ask for p such that $x_j \sim x_{5_p} x_0$.

Exercise 9.17:

Show that $w(p) = {}^j/_5$.

We can also use the standard sequence to test whether people behave according to RDU. For example, we can ask for the probability q such that $x_j \sim x_{j+1_q} x_{j-1}$ and for the probability r such that $x_j \sim x_{j+2_r} x_{j-2}$.

Exercise 9.18:

Show that RDU implies that $q = r$.

Extension 9.4 shows that we can measure w without making assumptions about utility or probability weighting. Empirical studies often simplify the measurement by assuming functional forms. Then fewer measurements are necessary. This has two limitations. First, the functional forms may not reflect people's preferences. For example, the most common parametric form for utility is the power function

Table 9.4 Parametric forms for the probability weighting function

Name	Functional form
Tversky Kahneman	$\frac{p^{\gamma}}{(p^{\gamma}+(1-p)^{\gamma})^{1/\gamma}}$
Goldstein Einhorn	$\frac{\alpha p^{\beta}}{\alpha p^{\beta}+(1-p)^{\beta}}$
Prelec	$\exp\left(-\alpha\,(-\ln p)^{\beta}\right)$
Neo-additive	$\begin{cases} 0 & \text{if } p=0 \\ \alpha+\beta p & \text{if } 0<p<1 \\ 1 & \text{if } p=1 \end{cases}$
HEU	$\frac{\alpha(1-\beta)p}{(1+\beta)(1-p)+(1-\beta)p}+\frac{(1-\alpha)(1+\beta)p}{(1-\beta)(1-p)+(1+\beta)p}$

$U(x) = x^{\rho}$. In Chapter 5 we saw that agents become more risk averse if the stake sizes are multiplied (increasing relative risk aversion). The power function implies constant relative risk aversion and, therefore, cannot explain this.

A second limitation of assuming functional forms is that utility and probability weighting are estimated simultaneously. This can lead to confounding. Utility may pick up some effects of probability weighting and vice versa. Different combinations of utility and probability weighting parameters can explain the same behaviour. For example, there are many different combinations of probability weighting and utility that can explain the common ratio effect. Parameter-free methods avoid such confounding.

For probability weighting several functional forms have been proposed, summarized in Table 9.4.

Tversky Kahneman's form is often used, but it performs worse than the others. It has only one parameter and probability weighting has two dimensions. One is the height of the curve, which shows attitude towards risk. A more elevated curve means more weight to the best outcome and more risk loving. Figure 9.4a shows this for Prelec's weighting function. In Prelec's function a higher value of α shifts the weighting function down (the dotted line). Thus in Prelec's function α is an index of risk aversion: higher values imply more risk aversion.

The other dimension of probability weighting is sensitivity to changes in probability. A steeper probability weighting function means more sensitivity to changes in probability. Figure 9.4b shows that in Prelec's weighting function a higher value of β means more sensitivity to changes in probability.

The parameters of risk aversion and sensitivity to probability may interact. A high α can lead to less risk aversion if it is accompanied by high sensitivity (high β). Figure 9.4c gives an example. The solid line has lower α than the dotted line, which suggests more risk loving, but, due to its lower sensitivity it only gives more weight to probabilities up to $1/2$.

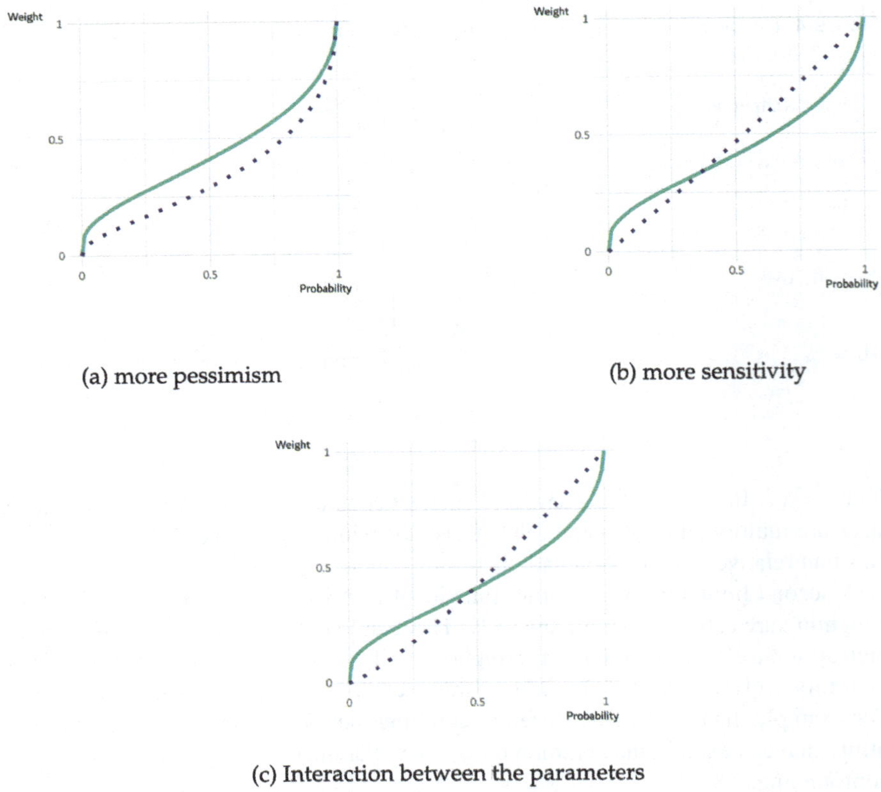

Fig. 9.4 The role of the two parameters in probability weighting

Exercise 9.19: Goldstein Einhorn

Drawing graphs as in Fig. 9.4 show that higher α in the Goldstein Einhorn weighting function (for constant β) leads to more risk loving, higher β (α constant) leads to more sensitivity, but α and β also interact. That is, the effect of higher α on risk loving may be offset by less sensitivity.

Exercise 9.20: HEU

Show by drawing graphs that in the HEU weighting function higher α (holding β constant) means more risk averse and higher β (holding α constant) leads to less sensitivity.

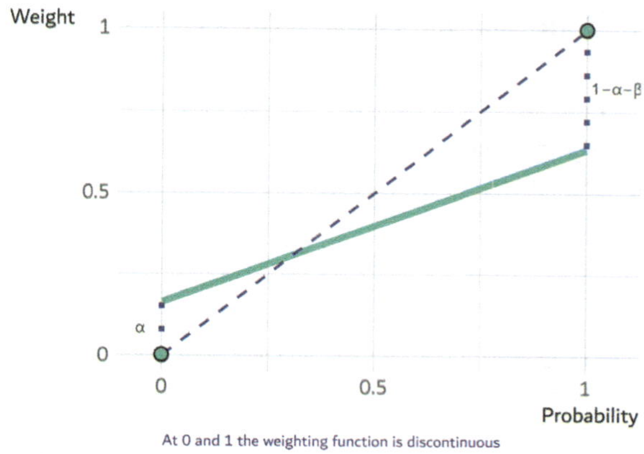

Fig. 9.5 Neo additive weighting

The neo-additive form assumes jumps at 0 and 1, to reflect the impossibility and the certainty effect, and is linear for all other probabilities (although with a slope less than 1 to reflect insensitivity). Figure 9.5 gives an example. There is a jump α at 0 which reflects the impossibility effect and a jump of $1 - \alpha - \beta$ at 1, which reflects the certainty effect. The difference between these two jumps $(1 - \beta - 2\alpha)$ is an index of risk aversion. The larger it is the more risk averse is an agent. The slope for intermediate probabilities is equal to β, which is less than 1 (the interrupted line).

Exercise 9.21: Neo-Additive Weighting

What would be an index of insensitivity for the neo-additive weighting function?

The neo-additive function can easily be applied empirically, but it fits less than the other three two-parameter forms. These fit equally well.

9.7 Reference-Dependence and Loss Aversion

Prospect theory adds to RDU the distinction between gains and losses from a reference point and loss aversion. As we saw in Chapter 7, this leads to an S-shaped utility function with a kink at the origin. The S-shape reflects diminishing sensitivity for both gains and losses. The kink reflects loss aversion. Reference-dependence also affects probability weighting: The weighting function w^+ for gains may differ from the weighting function w^- for losses. However, empirically they are close.

Extension 9.5: Prospect Theory

Let $(p_1 : x_1, \ldots, p_j : x_j, p_{j+1} : x_{j+1}, \ldots, p_n : x_n)$ be a rank-ordered prospect, i.e. $x_1 \succcurlyeq \cdots \succcurlyeq x_n$. All outcomes up til x_j are gains and all outcomes from x_{j+1} onwards are losses. The prospect theory formula is:

$$PT((p_1 : x_1, \ldots, p_j : x_j, p_{j+1} : x_{j+1}, \ldots, p_n : x_n)) = \sum_{i=1}^{j} \pi_i^+ U(x_i) + \sum_{i=j+1}^{n} \pi_i^- U(x_i), \tag{9.13}$$

where the decision weights π_i^+ and π_i^- are defined as:

$$\pi_i^+ = w^+\left(\sum_{k=1}^{i} p_k\right) - w^+\left(\sum_{k=1}^{i-1} p_k\right), \tag{9.14}$$

$$\pi_i^- = w^-\left(\sum_{k=i}^{n} p_k\right) - w^-\left(\sum_{k=i+1}^{n} p_k\right). \tag{9.15}$$

Two remarks:

1. The prospect theory functional is a sum of the gain part and the loss part. So the gain and the loss part are evaluated separately.
2. The decision weights for gains are as in RDU. They are defined as the weight of the probability of getting at least x_i minus the weight of getting something better than x_i. For losses, we take the dual. The decision weights are the weight of the probability of getting at most x_i minus the weight of the probability of getting something worse than x_i. The intuition is that prospect theory (with inverse S-shaped probability weighting) gives extra weight to extreme outcomes, i.e. to the best gain and to the worst loss. RDU does that for gains but if we would apply the RDU formula to losses it would give most weight to the "best" loss, i.e. the one closest to the reference point. This makes no intuitive sense and we therefore take the dual.

9.8 The Reflection Effect

Theorem 9.2 says that concave utility contributes to risk aversion and convex utility to risk loving. So the S-shaped utility function predicts that people are risk averse for gains and risk loving for losses. This is indeed what we often observe. Kahneman and Tversky (1979) gave their subjects the choices of Table 9.5. The majority choices are in green.

In the first choice 80% chose A and in the second choice 92% chose D. The prospects A and B and C and D have equal expected value (check!) and so, in the first choice the majority chose the expected value of the prospect over the prospect

Table 9.5 The reflection effect

	Which do you prefer?	
Choice 1	Prospect A	100% chance of €3000
	Prospect B	45% chance of €6000
		55% chance of €0
Choice 2	Prospect C	100% chance to lose €3000
	Prospect D	45% chance to lose €6000
		55% chance to lose €0

Table 9.6 Violation of monotonicity

	Which do you prefer?	
Choice 1	Prospect A	100% chance to win €240
	Prospect B	25% chance of to win €1000
		75% chance to win €0
Choice 2	Prospect C	100% chance to lose €750
	Prospect D	75% chance to lose €1000
		25% chance to lose €0

itself, while in the second choice they chose the prospect over its expected value. In other words, for gains they were risk averse, but for losses they were risk loving. This reversal of risk attitudes is called the **reflection effect**.

The reflection effect can lead to suboptimal choices. See Table 9.6, which comes from Tversky and Kahneman (1981). Check what you would choose.

The majority choices are in green. They agree with risk aversion for gains and risk loving for losses. The problem is that *A* and *D* jointly give a 25% chance to win €240 and a 75% chance to lose €760 (check), while *B* and *C* jointly give a 25% chance to win €250 and a 75% chance to lose €750. So under each state of the world you are better off by choosing B and C than by choosing A and D. Apparently, changing risk attitudes across domains is not a good strategy.

In companies, different departments often have different attitudes towards risk. For example, the marketing and product innovation departments are more risk loving than the legal department. Max Bazerman and Matthew Rabin (2019) argue, based on Table 9.6, that this can lead to inefficiencies. Companies benefit from having a consistent attitude towards risk across departments.

The reflection effect is also observed among professionals. Barbara McNeil and co-authors (1982) asked 238 patients with chronic medical problems and 424 radiologists to choose between two treatments for lung cancer: radiation and surgery. One group saw the options in survival terms, the other in mortality terms.

The survival framing was:

- *Surgery*: of 100 people having surgery 90 live through the post-operative period, 68 are alive at the end of the first year, and 34 are alive at the end of 5 years.
- *Radiation*: of 100 people having radiation all live through the treatment, 77 are alive at the end of the first year, and 22 are alive at the end of 5 years.

The mortality framing was:

- *Surgery*: of 100 people having surgery 10 die during surgery or the post-operative period, 32 die by the end of the first year, and 66 die by the end of 5 years.
- *Radiation*: of 100 people having radiation none die during treatment, 23 die by the end of the first year, and 78 die by the end of 5 years.

The two framings are equivalent in final outcomes, but they affected subjects' preferences. In the survival frame, 11% chose radiation against 28% in the mortality frame. Avoiding deaths during treatment made radiation more attractive. Professional experience did not help. Nine per cent of the radiologists chose radiation in the survival frame against 28% in the mortality frame.

Making the treatments anonymous (surgery was treatment A and radiation treatment B), led to more support for radiation: 42% chose it in the mortality frame and 31% in the survival frame. Again, this also held for the radiologists. The only difference was that for the anonymous treatments the survival versus mortality framing did not impact their choices.

9.9 The Fourfold Pattern of Risk Attitudes

S-shaped utility contributes to risk aversion for gains and risk loving for losses. However, probability weighting also affects risk attitudes. For gains, the probability weight is the weight given to the best outcome. Inverse S-shaped probability weighting means that small probabilities are overweighted. So if a prospect gives a small probability of a gain, people will overweight that gain and this contributes to risk loving. This effect is usually stronger than the risk aversion produced by concave utility. So, people are risk loving for unlikely gains. If gains are likely, however, their probability will be underweighted which adds to the risk aversion produced by concave utility for gains.

For losses this pattern is reflected. Unlikely losses are overweighted, which gives risk aversion and goes against the risk loving produced by convex utility. Likely losses are underweighted which gives extra risk loving on top of the risk loving produced by convex utility.

So prospect theory predicts a **fourfold pattern of risk attitudes**:

1. Risk loving for unlikely gains.
2. Risk aversion for likely gains.
3. Risk aversion for unlikely losses.
4. Risk loving for likely losses.

This pattern can explain empirical phenomena that are hard or impossible to explain under expected utility. It can explain the joint occurrence of gambling (risk loving for unlikely gains) and insurance (risk aversion for unlikely losses). It can also explain the disposition effect in finance, the finding that investors sell winning stocks too soon (risk aversion for gains) and hold on to losing stocks (risk loving for losses).[5]

Exercise 9.22: House Owners

Show that the fourfold pattern can also explain the low trading of houses when prices are below the purchase price.

9.10 Rabin's Paradox

Matthew Rabin (2000) derived another challenge of expected utility. Rabin conjectured that most people reject a prospect that gives a gain of €11 with probability $^1\!/_2$ and a loss of €10 with probability $^1\!/_2$ (check for yourself what you would do). He then showed that under expected utility this means that if we increase the loss to €100, there is no gain that would make the agent accept the prospect. So even if the gain would be €10 million, the agent would reject the prospect $10M_{^1\!/_2} - 100$. In other words, **Rabin's paradox** shows that under expected utility a plausible preference (rejection of $11_{^1\!/_2} - 10$) has implausible implications. This does not mean that people's preferences are wrong. It means that expected utility is wrong.

Extension 9.6: Rabin's Paradox

The intuition underlying Rabin's result is as follows. Under expected utility risk aversion is modelled through the utility function. The rejection of $11_{^1\!/_2} - 10$ means that marginal utility must fall sufficiently between -10 and 11. However, if we extrapolate this decrease, utility in the loss domain falls quickly while in the gain domain it rises slowly. In fact, so slowly that the drop in utility when we move to -100 cannot be compensated by any gain.

Rabin's paradox also holds under rank-dependent utility. Rabin suggested that the explanation for his paradox was loss aversion. The possible loss of €10 makes the

[5] Alex Imas (2016) shows that the impact of losses depends on whether the loss has been realized or not. If it has not been realized and only exists on paper, people are risk loving. Once it has been realized people become risk averse.

prospect $11_{1/2} - 10$ unattractive and not a decrease in marginal utility. This implies that under prospect theory, Rabin's paradox will not occur.

In Bleichrodt et al. (2019), we found that most subjects indeed rejected $11_{1/2} - 10$, that rank-dependent utility could not explain it, but loss aversion could. Rabin's paradox shows the importance of loss aversion for risk attitudes.

9.11 What Is the Reference Point?

Prospect theory does not explain what the reference point is. As mentioned in Chapter 7, Kahneman and Tversky hypothesized that it is often the status quo, but it can also be formed by expectations, aspirations, norms, and social comparisons. Extension 9.7 describes the effect of aspirations on utility.

Extension 9.7: A Model of Aspiration Levels

Enrico Diecidue and Jeroen van de Ven (2008) present a model of **aspiration levels**. It is motivated by research on managers who see risk as the probability of not reaching their target and on psychological research showing sensitivity to the overall probabilities of success and failure.

Let $(p_1 : x_1, \ldots p_j : x_j, p_{j+1} : x_{j+1}, \ldots p_n : x_n)$ be a prospect with outcomes ordered from best to worst ($x_1 \succcurlyeq \cdots \succcurlyeq x_n$). x_j is above the aspiration level and x_{j+1} below. Let $P^+ = \sum_{i=1}^{j} p_j$ be the probability of meeting the aspiration level and $P^- = \sum_{i=j+1}^{n} p_j$ the probability of not meeting the aspiration level.

Diecidue and van de Ven's model is equal to:

$$V(p_1 : x_1, \ldots p_j : x_j, p_{j+1} : x_{j+1}, \ldots p_n : x_n) = \sum_{i=1}^{n} p_i \times u(x_i) + \mu \times P^+ - \lambda \times P^-. \quad (9.16)$$

Exercise 9.23: Aspiration

1. Show that Eq. 9.16 is equivalent to:

$$V = \sum_{i=1}^{j} p_i \times u(x_i + \mu) + \sum_{i=j+1}^{n} p_i \times u(x_i - \lambda).$$

2. Use the above equation to draw the utility function and show that it looks like the one in Fig. 7.5.

Exercise 9.23 shows that Diecidue and van de Ven's model of aspiration levels is equivalent to expected utility with a discontinuity in utility at the aspiration level.

Botond Köszegi and Matthew Rabin (2006) proposed a theory in which reference points are formed by people's rational expectations about outcomes. In their model, utility depends on both absolute and relative outcomes.[6] Their utility function is:

$$U(c, r) = u(c) + \phi(c|r). \tag{9.17}$$

In Eq. 9.17 u is a utility function over absolute amounts, ϕ reflects the attitude towards gains and losses, and r is the rational expectations reference point. Köszegi and Rabin call u **consumption utility** and ϕ **gain-loss utility**. Sugden (2003) used the same distinction and called u a satisfaction function and ϕ a gain/loss evaluation function.

Köszegi and Rabin's model has several problems, both conceptual, theoretical, and empirical:

1. A conceptual problem is that they model a cognitive bias (reference-dependence) using a high level of rationality (rational expectations). Thus their model is subject to Rubinstein's criticism, discussed in Chapter 2.
2. A theoretical problem is that they use utility as an input. This makes their model cyclical. We need utility to derive choices, but choices to define utility. It is a theoretical analogue of the endogeneity bias discussed in Chapter 7. The model cannot be derived from conditions on people's choices.
3. Another theoretical problem is that a common specification of Köszegi and Rabin's model is equivalent to the disappointment aversion model of Philippe Delquié and Alessandra Cillo (2006) that includes no reference-dependence. So we get the contradictory result that Köszegi and Rabin's model of reference-dependence is actually reference-independent (See Masatlioglu and Raymond (2016) for a proof).
4. An empirical problem is that the model does not seem to describe the available evidence well. Some papers (e.g. Abeler et al. (2011)) claim to find evidence for Köszegi and Rabin's model, but their data are also consistent with other reference points and so their interpretation is unclear.

Aurélien Baillon, Vitalie, Spinu, and I (2020) tested several reference points in an experiment run in Moldova. Moldova is the poorest country in Europe and the stakes that we could offer were up to monthly salaries. Two reference points stood out: the status quo and **maxmin**. Maxmin says that subjects select for each prospect in their

[6] Kahneman and Tversky (1979, p. 277) already pointed out that focusing on changes in money only is too restrictive. They compared people's attitudes to money with a book where each page described preferences over changes from a particular wealth level.

choice set the minimum outcome and then take the maximum of these minima as their reference point. It is a security level. It is the outcome that subjects can be sure to obtain. Status quo and maxmin jointly explained 70% of our data. Expectations-based reference points explained less than 20% of our data.

Exercise 9.24: Maxmin

What is the maxmin reference point in the following situations:

1. 100 for sure versus $200_{1/2}50$.
2. $400_{1/3}150$ versus $300_{1/2}200$.
3. A standard gamble question in which the subject chooses between living with migraine for sure and a treatment option that gives probability p of full health and probability $1 - p$ of death within a week.

Extension 9.8: Third Generation Prospect Theory

In prospect theory the reference point is certain. Ulrich Schmidt, Chris Starmer, and Robert Sugden (2008) take the reference point as risky. It is, however, still exogenous and not endogenous (determined by the choice set or chosen by the agent). They describe their theory as **third generation prospect theory**.[a]

In third generation prospect theory, the rank-ordering of the states of the world is determined by the difference in utility between what a prospect f gives and what the risky reference prospect r gives. This has the same drawback as Köszegi and Rabin's model: utility becomes a primitive as we need it to rank-order the states of the world.[b] We could solve it by assuming that the agent can also rank utility differences and impose Alt's (1936) axioms (see Chapter 3).

Let $u(f(s), r(s))$ be a function that specifies how attractive is $f(s)$, the outcome in state s under prospect f, relative to $r(s)$, the outcome the agent gets under the reference prospect r. Suppose that states of the world are ordered by $u(f(s), r(s))$ such that state 1 gives the largest utility difference and state n the lowest. Let states up to j give a positive value, i.e. f gives a gain. From $j+1$ onwards $u(f(s), r(s))$ is negative and f gives a loss. The third generation prospect functional is then

$$PT^3((f, r)) = \sum_{i=1}^{j} \pi_i^+ u(f_i, r_i) + \sum_{i=j+1}^{n} \pi_i^- u(f_i, r_i), \tag{9.18}$$

where the decision weights π_i^+ and π_i^- are defined as in Eqs. 9.14 and 9.15.

Unlike earlier versions of prospect theory, third generation prospect theory can explain the preference reversal phenomenon discussed in Chapter 2.

[a] First generation prospect theory is the 1979 version and second generation the 1992 version that includes rank-dependence. Models with an endogenous reference point as Köszegi and Rabin's might be called fourth generation prospect theory.
[b] Sugden (2003) also proposed a model with a risky reference point, but avoided this problem by assuming no probability weighting.

9.12 Evidence Against Prospect Theory

It is common in science that a dominant model gets challenged. This also happened to prospect theory. As it became more popular, it came under more intense scrutiny and deviations were found.

9.12.1 Violations of Rank-Dependence

Expected utility assumes independence: preferences between prospects do not depend on the value of common outcomes. Prospect theory (and rank-dependent utility) assume a weaker form of independence. Because the decision weights depend on the rank-ordering of the outcomes, prospect theory only assumes independence when a change in the common outcome does not affect the rank-ordering of the outcomes. This is called **comonotonic independence**.

Table 9.7 gives an example. Prospect theory predicts that agents who choose A in the first choice should choose C in the second (and if they choose B in the first, they should choose D in the second). The change in the common outcome does not change the rank-ordering.

However, in the third choice the rank-ordering changes (agents now get the best outcome with probability $1/2$). So, patterns ACF and BDE are allowed by prospect theory. Prospect theory says that changing the common outcome will have no effect when comparing choices 1 and 2, but it may when comparing choices 1 and 3 and choices 2 and 3.

Exercise 9.25: Comonotonic Independence

Show that expected utility excludes choice patterns ACF and BDE.

Many studies find rank-dependence. But not all. Peter Wakker, Elke Weber, and Ido Erev (1994) asked questions like those in Table 9.7. As we saw, prospect theory

Table 9.7 Comonotonic independence

		Probability		
		1/3	1/2	1/6
Choice 1	Prospect A	€100	€40	€0
	Prospect B	€80	€40	€20
Choice 2	Prospect C	€100	€60	€0
	Prospect D	€80	€60	€20
Choice 3	Prospect E	€100	€140	€0
	Prospect F	€80	€140	€20

predicts that changes of preferences are more common in choices 1 and 3 (and 2 and 3) than in choices 1 and 2. They did not find this.

Elke Weber and Britt Kirsner (1997) suggested that people simplify choices by cancelling common outcomes (an editing principle). Then all three choices in Table 9.7 are the same: a choice between a prospect that gives €100 with probability 1/3 and €0 with probability 1/6 and a prospect that gives €80 with probability 1/3 and €20 with probability 1/6. Their results indicate that the lack of support in Wakker et al. for comonotonic independence was due to a heuristic.

The psychologist Michael Birnbaum (2008) found that 66% of his subjects preferred the prospect $(0.43 : 92, 0.07 : 68, 0.50 : 0)$ to $(0.48 : 92, 0.52 : 0)$, but 62% preferred $(0.43 : 97, 0.05 : 92, 0.52 : 0)$ to $(0.43 : 97, 0.07 : 68, 0.50 : 0)$.

Exercise 9.26: Birnbaum

Show that these preferences violate prospect theory.

The reason is partition dependence (see Chapter 8). If we split an event into two (like we do when going from $(0.48 : 92, 0.52 : 0)$ to $(0.43 : 97, 0.05 : 92, 0.52 : 0)$) it becomes more attractive. Birnbaum calls it violations of **coalescing**. Economists have paid little attention to these violations, because it is hard to model them.

Tversky and Kahneman (1992, p. 317) realized that heuristics might lead to violations of prospect theory, but did not believe these could be modelled:

> "... the cumulative functional is unlikely to be accurate in detail. We suspect that decision weights may be sensitive to the formulation of the prospects, as well as to the number, the spacing and the level of outcomes. ... The present theory can be generalized to accommodate such effects but it is questionable whether the gain in descriptive validity, achieved by giving up the separability of values and weights, would justify the loss of predictive power and the cost of increased complexity... The heuristics of choice do not readily lend themselves to formal analysis because their application depends on the formulation of the problem, the method of elicitation, and the context of choice."

9.12.2 Violations of Gain-Loss Separability

Prospect theory evaluates the gain and the loss part of a prospect separately (see remark 1 in Extension 9.5). It then sums these two evaluations. This is called **gain-loss separability**. It implies that if both the gain and the loss parts of prospect f are preferred to those of prospect g then f should be preferred to g.

George Wu and Alex Markle (2008) found violations of gain-loss separability. While 52% of their subjects preferred $H = (0.50 : 4200, 0.50 : -3000)$ to $L = (0.75 : 3000, 0.25 : -4500)$, 85% preferred $(0.75 : 3000, 0.25 : 0)$ to $(0.50 : 4200, 0.50 : 0)$ and 63% preferred $(0.75 : 0, 0.25 : -4500)$ to $(0.50 : 0, 0.50 : -3000)$.

Exercise 9.27: Gain-Loss Separability

Show that these preferences violate gain-loss separability.

Wu and Markle suggested that their subjects were less sensitive to probabilities in mixed prospects. Subjects note that H gives both a higher gain and a lower loss than L, but they do not take sufficient account of the difference in probabilities. Again, this violation of prospect theory seems due to a heuristic that is hard to model.

9.12.3 Violations of Loss Aversion

Several papers argue that loss aversion is not robust. Eyal Ert and Ido Erev (2013) claim that it disappears for small stakes. Table 9.8 gives the data from their Study 2:

A Bayesian test supports that the proportions choosing prospect R differ for high and small stakes. Ert and Erev interpret this as no loss aversion for low stakes given that the proportions of subjects choosing prospects R and S in the low stakes condition are similar. Other studies confirmed their finding.

It is unclear what this evidence says about loss aversion. First, it defines loss aversion as aversion to symmetric gambles $x_p(-x)$. Under the 1979 version of prospect theory this implies that for $x > 0$, $U(x) < -U(-x)$. However, under the 1992 version, this no longer holds because probability weighting can be different for gains and losses. This definition also confounds loss aversion with a difference in utility curvature between gains and losses.

Table 9.8 Data from Erev and Ert's study 2

High stakes		$P(R)$	Low stakes		$P(R)$
Prospect S	0 for sure	22%	S	0 for sure	48%
Prospect R	100 with probability 0.5 –100 with probability 0.5		R	10 with probability 0.5 –10 with probability 0.5	

The preferred definition of loss aversion is by the kink at the reference point. Measuring this kink is not easy (but see Extension 9.9). Many empirical studies measure the kink by eliciting the gain x or the loss y such that subjects are indifferent between 0 and $x_{1/2}y$. They then measure loss aversion as $-x/y$.

Exercise 9.28: Measuring Loss Aversion

Show by evaluating the indifference $0 \sim x_{1/2}y$ by prospect theory that defining loss aversion as $-x/y$ confounds loss aversion with probability weighting and utility curvature.

Because of the confounding problem, derived in Exercise 9.28, evidence against loss aversion is inconclusive. Olivier L'Haridon and I (Bleichrodt and L'Haridon 2023) found that loss aversion no longer depends on stake size, once loss aversion is correctly measured.

Extension 9.9: Measuring Loss Aversion

Abdellaoui et al. (2016) show how loss aversion can be measured controlling for utility curvature and probability weighting. Their method consists of three steps:

1. Ask for the loss L such that $0 \sim G_pL$ where G and p can be chosen freely.

Exercise 9.29: Step 1

Show that step 1 implies that $w^+(p)U(G) = -w^-(1-p)U(L)$.

2. Ask for the gain x^+ such that $x^+ \sim G_p0$.

Exercise 9.30: Step 2

Show that step 2 implies that $U(x^+) = w^+(p)U(G)$.

3. Ask for the loss x^- such that $x^- \sim L_{1-p}0$.

Exercise 9.31: Step 3

Show that step 3 implies that $U(x^-) = -w^-(1-p)U(L)$.

$x^+/-x^-$ is a measure of loss aversion based on the kink at the reference point that is unaffected by utility curvature and probability weighting.

9.12.4 Lack of Predictive Power

The evidence discussed in this chapter shows that prospect theory can explain deviations from expected utility. It is less clear whether prospect theory predicts decisions under risk. Ido Erev and co-authors (2017) organized a prediction competition. They gathered three sets of data. The first was a replication set, which included many of the phenomena discussed in this chapter (common ratio effect, reflection effect, the loss aversion questions of Ert and Erev, St. Petersburg paradox, and Birnbaum's violations of coalescing). They could replicate all the deviations from expected utility.

They then collected another data set and asked researchers to estimate their preferred model on these data and send them the parameter estimates (Erev et al. 2017). These parameter estimates were used to predict the choices from a third experiment. Prospect theory did not predict choices well. Perhaps this was no surprise given that the estimation set included data that violated prospect theory (like Birnbaum's). The model that predicted best was a combination of expected value with five heuristics: *equal weighting* (pick the option with the highest expected value assuming all outcomes are equally likely), *payoff sensitivity* (select the prospect that maximizes the probability of a gain), *pessimism* (assume the worst), *minimization of regret* (select the option that minimizes the probability of regret), and *complexity aversion* (prefer prospects with fewer outcomes). They call this model BEAST, a name that adequately reflects its lack of beauty.

9.12.5 Violation for Health

In Exercise 9.7, we discussed the standard (direct) PE and the chained PE. The reason to use a chained measurement was to avoid that subjects would accept little or no probability of death in the direct question. This would give high health state utilities and little room for improvements in quality of life to affect health policy decisions.

Hillary Llewellyn-Thomas and co-authors (Llewellyn-Thomas et al. 1982) tested whether the direct and chained PE gave similar results. To their surprise, the chained PE gave higher utilities. Correcting for probability weighting only worsened this difference (Bleichrodt 2001). Loss aversion helps to reduce it, but as probability weighting is a central element of prospect theory, the discrepancy between direct and chained PE is evidence against prospect theory.

Peep Stalmeier (2002) explained the difference between direct and chained PE by anchoring and adjustment. In answering the chained PE, people take their direct PE answer as an anchor. They should lower it in the two chained questions, but do so insufficiently. This leads to a higher utility in the chained PE. Similarly, if they first answer the chained PE, they take their first answer as their anchor and adjust it insufficiently upwards in the direct PE. So, this violation of prospect theory is also caused by a heuristic that is hard to model.

9.13 Conclusion

In the chapter we have discussed expected utility, the main normative model of decision under risk. It is theoretically elegant, but people systematically deviate from it. These deviations are best described by prospect theory. Prospect theory cannot explain everything, but it is the best descriptive model available and deviations from it follow heuristics that are hard to model.

References

Abdellaoui, M. 2000. Parameter-free elicitation of utility and probability weighting functions. *Management Science* 46: 1497–1512.

Abdellaoui, M., H. Bleichrodt, O. l'Haridon, and D. Van Dolder. 2016. Measuring loss aversion under ambiguity: A method to make prospect theory completely observable. *Journal of Risk and Uncertainty* 52: 1–20.

Abeler, J., A. Falk, L. Goette, and D. Huffman. 2011. Reference points and effort provision. *American Economic Review* 101: 470–492.

Alt, F. 1936. Über die messbarkeit des nutzens. *Zeitschrift für Nationalökonomie/Journal of Economics* 161–169.

Arrow, K.J. 1951. Alternative approaches to the theory of choice in risk-taking situations. *Econometrica* 19: 404–437.

Baillon, A., H. Bleichrodt, and V. Spinu. 2020. Searching for the reference point. *Management Science* 66: 93–112.

Birnbaum, M.H. 2008. New paradoxes of risky decision making. *Psychological Review* 115: 463–501.

Bleichrodt, H. 2001. Probability weighting in choice under risk: An empirical test. *Journal of Risk and Uncertainty* 23: 185–198.

Bleichrodt, H., and O. L'Haridon. 2023. Prospect theory's loss aversion is robust to stake size. *Judgment and Decision Making* 18: e14.

Bleichrodt, H., and J.L. Pinto. 2000. A parameter-free elicitation of the probability weighting function in medical decision analysis. *Management Science* 46: 1485–1496.

Bleichrodt, H., J.N. Doctor, Y. Gao, C. Li, D. Meeker, and P.P. Wakker. 2019. Resolving Rabin's paradox. *Journal of Risk and Uncertainty* 59: 239–260.

Cubitt, R., C. Starmer, and R. Sugden. 1998. Dynamic choice and the common ratio effect: An experimental investigation. *Economic Journal* 108: 1362–1380.

Delquié, P., and A. Cillo. 2006. Disappointment without prior expectation: a unifying perspective on decision under risk. *Journal of Risk and Uncertainty* 33: 197–215.

Diecidue, E., and J. Van De Ven. 2008. Aspiration level, probability of success and failure, and expected utility. *International Economic Review* 49: 683–700.

Erev, I., E. Ert, O. Plonsky, D. Cohen, and O. Cohen. 2017. From anomalies to forecasts: Toward a descriptive model of decisions under risk, under ambiguity, and from experience. *Psychological Review* 124: 369–409.

Ert, E., and I. Erev. 2013. On the descriptive value of loss aversion in decisions under risk: Six clarifications. *Judgment and Decision making* 8: 214–235.

Fishburn, P.C. 1978. On Handa's "New theory of cardinal utility" and the maximization of expected return. *Journal of Political Economy* 86: 321–324.

Gonzalez, R., and G. Wu. 1999. On the shape of the probability weighting function. *Cognitive Psychology* 38: 129–166.

Handa, J. 1977. Risk, probabilities, and a new theory of cardinal utility. *Journal of Political Economy* 85: 97–122.

Imas, A. 2016. The realization effect: Risk-taking after realized versus paper losses. *American Economic Review* 106: 2086–2109.

Jensen, N.E. 1967. An introduction to Bernoullian utility theory: I. Utility functions. *Swedish Journal of Economics* 163–183.

Kahneman, D., and A. Tversky. 1979. Prospect theory: An analysis of decision under risk. *Econometrica* 47: 263–291.

Kőszegi, B., and M. Rabin. 2006. A model of reference-dependent preferences. *Quarterly Journal of Economics* 121: 1133–1165.

Llewellyn-Thomas, H., H.J. Sutherland, R. Tibshirani, A. Ciampi, J. Till, and N. Boyd. 1982. The measurement of patients' values in medicine. *Medical Decision Making* 2: 449–462.

Masatlioglu, Y., and C. Raymond. 2016. A behavioral analysis of stochastic reference dependence. *American Economic Review* 106: 2760–2782.

McNeil, B.J., S.G. Pauker, H.C. Sox Jr., and A. Tversky. 1982. On the elicitation of preferences for alternative therapies. *New England Journal of Medicine* 306: 1259–1262.

Quiggin, J. 1982. A theory of anticipated utility. *Journal of Economic Behavior and Organization* 3: 323–343.

Rabin, M. 2000. Risk aversion and expected utility theory: A calibration theorem. *Econometrica* 68: 1281–1292.

Rabin, M., and M. Bazerman. 2019. Fretting about modest risks is a mistake. *California Management Review* 61: 34–48.

Schmidt, U., C. Starmer, and R. Sugden. 2008. Third-generation prospect theory. *Journal of Risk and Uncertainty* 36: 203–223.

Stalmeier, P.F. 2002. Discrepancies between chained and classic utilities induced by anchoring with occasional adjustments. *Medical Decision Making* 22: 53–64.

Sugden, R. 2003. Reference-dependent subjective expected utility. *Journal of Economic Theory* 111: 172–191.

Tengs, T.O., M.E. Adams, J.S. Pliskin, D.G. Safran, J.E. Siegel, M.C. Weinstein, and J.D. Graham. 1995. Five-hundred life-saving interventions and their cost-effectiveness. *Risk Analysis* 15: 369–390.

Tversky, A., and D. Kahneman. 1981. The framing of decisions and the psychology of choice. *Science* 211: 453–458.

Wakker, P., I. Erev, and E.U. Weber. 1994. Comonotonic independence: The critical test between classical and rank-dependent utility theories. *Journal of Risk and Uncertainty* 9: 195–230.

Weber, E., and B. Kirsner. 1997. Reasons for rank-dependent utility evaluation. *Journal of Risk and Uncertainty* 14: 41–61.

Wu, G., and A.B. Markle. 2008. An empirical test of gain-loss separability in prospect theory. *Management Science* 54: 1322–1335.

Ambiguity

10

10.1 Subjective Expected Utility

In Chapter 9 probabilities were known. Utility was the subjective element. Let us now move to **decision under ambiguity** where probabilities are unknown. Unknown probabilities are more common in real life than known probabilities. Examples are the probability that the earth will warm up by more than 2 degrees in the coming 20 years, the probability of disease when a patient displays given symptoms, the outcome of an upcoming election or the probability that inflation will fall below 2% in the coming year. We may have some idea of the probability of these events, but we are unsure. Moreover, our probability is subjective and will differ from those of other agents.

Because probabilities are unknown, I will write prospects as $(E_1 : x_1, \ldots, E_n : x_n)$ where $E_i : x_i$ stands for the outcome x_i that the prospect gives if event E_i occurs.[1] Prospects specify for each event which outcome obtains. So a prospect can, for example, be a medical treatment which specifies for each of the possible diseases what health will be.

The normative model of decision under ambiguity is **subjective expected utility** (SEU). According to SEU, preferences over prospects $(E_1 : x_1, \ldots, E_n : x_n)$ are represented by:

$$V(E_1 : x_1, \ldots, E_n : x_n) = \sum_{i=1}^{n} P(E_i) \times U(x_i), \tag{10.1}$$

[1] The notation assumes that events are disjoint: for all i, j, $E_i \cap E_j = \emptyset$.

H. Bleichrodt, *Behavioural Economics*,
https://doi.org/10.1007/978-3-031-69166-9_10

where $P(E_i)$ is a unique subjective probability that satisfies the probability axioms of Chapter 8. U is a cardinal utility function, i.e. we can freely choose the utility of two outcomes.

In the early twentieth century, John Maynard Keynes and Frank Knight already studied decision under ambiguity. Keynes did not believe in subjective probability. For him, probability was a logical relation between a premiss in which we fully believe and a conclusion. The probability α reflects the extent to which our conclusion can be derived from our premiss. For Keynes, probability was objective. Any rational person would derive the same probability α according to Keynes.

Frank Ramsey, Keynes' student (see Bio 10.1), disagreed and convinced Keynes. In his *Truth and Probability*, Ramsey showed that subjective probabilities can be derived from people's choices between prospects. Around the same time, the Italian statistician Bruno de Finetti showed how SEU could be derived from a set of axioms. They did not derive SEU fully. Ramsey's approach was incomplete.[2] de Finetti assumed that utility was known (like von Neumann and Morgenstern assumed that probabilities were known).

Bio 10.1: Frank Ramsey

Frank Ramsey only became 26 years old, but made important contributions to mathematics, philosophy, and economics. There are about 50 techniques, models, theorems, and phenomena that carry his name. The funniest of these is the "**Ramsey effect**", coined by the American philosopher Donald Davidson. It describes the feeling, shared by many scientists, that your discovery that you thought to be original had already been discovered and more elegantly described by Ramsey.

Ramsey entered Cambridge at age 17 and was described by Keynes as "by far the most brilliant student that has appeared during many years in the fields of mathematics and philosophy".

He also managed to impress three of the greatest philosophers of his time, G.E. Moore, Bertrand Russell, and Ludwig Wittgenstein. Wittgenstein had written his Tractatus Logico-Philosophicus in German during World War I. In it he argued that all philosophical problems were the result of poor understanding of the logic of language. It was widely recognized as a masterpiece and gave him an almost divine status. Wittgenstein was so convinced that he was right and that he had solved all philosophical problems that he left philosophy and became a school teacher.

Translating the Tractatus in English turned out to be problematic. It is very complex and used a logic few were familiar with. Wittgenstein believed Moore

[2] Ramsey assumed that there was an "ethically neutral event" with known probability 0.50 from which he derived utility and the subjective probability of all other events. Ramsey also assumed expected utility maximization from the outset.

and Russell did not understand it. So the task fell on the 18-year-old Ramsey. Wittgenstein approved Ramsey's translation and thought that it was better than his own original.

What is more, Ramsey convinced Wittgenstein that the Tractatus did not solve all philosophical questions and it made him return to philosophy in Cambridge where he eventually got a PhD in philosophy under Ramsey's supervision.

Ramsey published only four works in economics: a note criticizing Douglas' social credit theory (published when he was 19 years old), two articles in the Economic Journal on optimal taxation and saving, which became classics, and his critical review of Keynes' A treatise on probability, which showed that subjective probabilities exist and how they can be derived.

Ramsey probably died from Weil's disease (spread to humans through rats' urine and faeces), which he contracted while swimming in the River Cam, one of his favourite pastimes. Weil's disease leads to kidney failure and bleeding from the lungs. As there were no antibiotics for it in Ramsey's time, he died a few days before turning 27.[a]

[a] For more on Ramsey see Cheryl Misak's biography "Frank Ramsey: A sheer excess of powers", published by Oxford University Press in 2020.

10.1.1 Savage

In 1954 Leonard (Jimmy) Savage gave a complete derivation of SEU based on 7 axioms (postulates). It is a beautiful result. David Kreps (1988) calls it the "crowning glory of decision theory".

The behaviourally most interesting postulates are P2 and P4 (the others are in Extension 10.1. To explain these, I need one more notation. Let $\alpha_E f$ stand for the prospect f with all outcomes of f for event E replaced by α. So for $f = (E_1 : f_1, \ldots, E_n : f_n)$, $\alpha_{E_i} f = (E_1 : f_1, \ldots, E_{i-1} : f_{i-1}, E_i : \alpha, E_{i+1} : f_{i+1}, \ldots, E_n : f_n)$.

Exercise 10.1: Notation

Suppose $f = (E_1 : f_1, \ldots, E_8 : f_8)$ and let E be the union of E_2, E_4, and E_6. What is, $\alpha_E f$?

Definition 10.1: Savage's P4 Independence of Beliefs from Tastes

Let $\gamma \succ \beta$ and $\gamma' \succ \beta'$. Then $\gamma_E\beta \succ \gamma_B\beta \iff \gamma'_E\beta' \succ \gamma'_B\beta'$.

The intuition behind P4 is as follows. If I rather receive the better outcome γ when event E occurs than when event B occurs, this suggests that I find E more likely than B. To make sense, this intuition must hold for any pair of outcomes. So, for another pair of outcomes $\gamma' \succ \beta'$, I should still prefer to get the better outcome γ' when E rather than B occurs. P4 ensures that we can define a "more likely than" relation over events, independent of utility.

Savage's crucial condition is P2, the **sure-thing principle** (see also Chapter 2).

Definition 10.2: P2 the Sure-Thing Principle

For all prospects $\alpha_E f, \alpha_E g, \beta_E f, \beta_E g : \alpha_E f \succ \alpha_E g \iff \beta_E f \succ \beta_E g$.

The sure-thing principle says that preferences do not depend on common outcomes. It is similar to von Neumann and Morgenstern's independence condition. The two prospects $\alpha_E f$, and $\alpha_E g$ have the same outcome (α) under event E. The sure-thing principle says that preferences stay the same if we change that common outcome into another common outcome β.

Savage's result is:

Theorem 10.1: Subjective Expected Utility

The following statements are equivalent:

1. P1-P7 hold.
2. SEU holds with P unique and U cardinal.

Extension 10.1: Savage's Postulates

Savage's other postulates are of two types. Three are (more or less) innocent. They are:

- P1 (weak order): The preference relation $\succcurlyeq$ over prospects is a weak order (transitive and complete).
- P3 (monotonicity): For nonnull events $E : \gamma \succcurlyeq \beta \iff \gamma_E f \succcurlyeq \beta_E f$ (an event is nonnull if an agent believes that it can occur. Formally, event E is nonnull if $\gamma_E\beta \succ \beta$ for some outcomes $\gamma \succ \beta$).[a]

- P5 (nontriviality): $\gamma \succ \beta$ for some outcomes γ, β.

Most decision models assume P1. We discussed it in Chapter 2. P3 says that agents prefer better outcomes to worse for events that they believe are possible. P5 says that there are at least two nonindifferent outcomes. As we will see in P6, Savage imposed richness on the set of events. He left the set of outcomes almost unconstrained.

The other two postulates are technical. P7 extends the theory to acts with infinitely many outcomes. P6 imposes richness on the set of events:

- P6 (richness of events): If $f \succ g$ then for all outcomes γ, β we can find an event E_i such that $\beta_{E_i} f \succ g$ and $f \succ \gamma_{E_i} g$.

In words, the event E_i is so small (unlikely) that regardless of how bad is β, $\beta_{E_i} f$ is still preferred to g and regardless of how good is γ, f is still preferred to $\gamma_{E_i} g$. Savage imposed P6, because his proof followed von Neumann and Morgenstern's derivation of expected utility for risk. Because they had known probabilities (and thus all probabilities available), Savage needed to assume something similar. Within SEU, P6 ensures that for each number λ between 0 and 1, there is an event E_i that has subjective probability λ. Mohammed Abdellaoui and Peter Wakker (2020) showed how Savage's richness of events can be relaxed.

[a] Lorenz Hartmann (2020) showed that P3 can be dropped when we assume Savage's other 6 postulates.

10.2 Ellsberg

Because Savage's postulates are plausible, many consider SEU the normative theory of decision under ambiguity. However, descriptively it has problems. In 1961 Daniel Ellsberg suggested two paradoxes that challenge SEU.

Bio 10.2: The Most Dangerous Man in America

Although economists know Ellsberg for his two paradoxes, he is more famous for leaking the Pentagon papers in 1971. Ellsberg had assessed the Vietnam war for the Department of Defense. He found out that the US government believed Vietnam probably could not be won and that multiple US presidents had lied about it to the American public and to Congress. Ellsberg decided to copy the secret Pentagon papers and hand them to the press. He was aware of the consequences. In an email just before his death in 2023, Ellsberg wrote that he "had every reason to think that he would be spending the rest of his life behind bars", but "it was a fate, I would gladly accept if it meant hastening the end of the Vietnam War, unlikely as that seemed".

Henry Kissinger, Nixon's national security advisor, who by a twist of fate died shortly after Ellsberg, dubbed Ellsberg "the most dangerous man in America". The Nixon administration tried to discredit Ellsberg and he was charged with espionage, theft, conspiracy, and other counts, carrying a maximum sentence of 115 years. But before the jury could reach a verdict, the judge, William Byrne Jr., dismissed the case against Ellsberg citing serious government misconduct. This included illegal wiretapping and breaking into the office of Ellsberg's psychiatrist. The burglars were the so-called "White House Plumbers", supervised by John Ehrlichman, one of Nixon's top aides. They would later carry out the Watergate burglaries, which led to Nixon's downfall.

10.2.1 Ellsberg's Two Urn Example

In Ellsberg's two urn example people face a known and an unknown urn. The known urn has 50 red and 50 black balls. The unknown urn also has 100 balls, which are either red or black, but people do not know how many balls are red or black. They receive €100 if a red ball is drawn and choose from which urn to draw a ball. Ellsberg conjectured that most people prefer to draw a ball from the known urn. Later empirical studies confirmed this.

In terms of SEU, this means that:

$$\tfrac{1}{2} \times U(100) > P(R) \times U(100). \tag{10.2}$$

Or, the subjective probability of drawing a red ball from the unknown urn is less than $\tfrac{1}{2}$. Because probabilities sum to one, this implies that if black is the winning colour people should prefer to draw from the unknown urn. However, they also prefer the known urn if black is the winning colour.

Exercise 10.2: Ellsberg Two Urn

Show that this means by SEU that:

$$P(B) < \tfrac{1}{2}. \tag{10.3}$$

Equations 10.2 and 10.3 imply that $P(R) + P(B) < 1$. This violates the laws of probability. Ellsberg's two urn paradox challenges the existence of subjective probabilities or, as Mark Machina and David Schmeidler (1992) call it, **probabilistic sophistication**. It means that agents have a subjective probability and always prefer to bet on events with higher subjective probability.

Extension 10.2: Ellsberg's Two Urn Paradox Also Violates RDU

Suppose that agents transform probabilities by a nondecreasing weighting function w. Preferring to draw from the known urn if red is the winning colour implies that:

$$w\,(P(R)) < w(1/2).$$

Preferring to draw from the known urn if black is the winning colour implies that:

$$w\,(P(B)) < w(1/2).$$

Again, $P(R) < 1/2$ and $P(B) < 1/2$, violating probabilistic sophistication.

10.2.2 Ellsberg's Single Urn Example

Table 10.1 shows Ellsberg's single urn problem. There is one urn containing 90 balls. Thirty are red, the remaining 60 are blue or yellow. The distribution of blue and yellow balls is unknown. One ball is drawn from the urn. As indicated in green, most people prefer the prospect that pays €100 when a red ball is drawn over the prospect that pays €100 when a blue ball is drawn.

Exercise 10.3: First Choice Ellsberg Single Urn

Show that this means by SEU that:

$$1/3 = P(R) > P(B). \tag{10.4}$$

Most people also prefer the prospect that pays €100 when a blue or a yellow ball is drawn to the prospect that pays €100 when a red or a yellow ball is drawn.

Table 10.1 Ellsberg's single urn paradox

		Color		
		Red	Blue	Yellow
Choice 1	Bet R	€100	€0	€0
	Bet B	€0	€100	€0
Choice 2	Bet RY	€100	€0	€100
	Bet BY	€0	€100	€100

Exercise 10.4: Second Choice Ellsberg Single Urn

Show that this means in terms of SEU that:

$$1/3 < P(B). \quad (10.5)$$

$P(B)$ cannot be both greater and smaller than ⅓ so we again have a violation of SEU. Ellsberg's single urn example also violates probabilistic sophistication (see Extension 10.3). Ellsberg's paradoxes are more fundamental than the Allais paradoxes. The Allais paradoxes challenge expected utility, but can be accommodated by non-expected utility models. Ellsberg's paradoxes challenge that uncertainty can be captured by subjective probabilities.

Extension 10.3: Ellsberg's Paradox Violates Probabilistic Sophistication

Machina and Schmeidler propose a model in which people's choices are based on their subjective probabilities even though they may deviate from expected utility. This means giving up Savage's P2 (which gives expected utility) and strengthening P4 to:

Definition 10.3: *P4 Strong Independence of Beliefs from Tastes**

Let $\gamma \succ \beta$ and $\gamma' \succ \beta'$. Let $\gamma_A\beta_B g$ denote the prospect g with the outcomes of g on event A replaced by γ and those on event B replaced by β. Then $\gamma_A\beta_B g \succ \beta_A\gamma_B g \iff \gamma'_A\beta'_B g' \succ \beta'_A\gamma'_B g'$.

Exercise 10.5: Strong Independence

1. Show that $P4^*$ implies Savage's P4. But P4 does not imply $P4^*$. In other words, $P4^*$ is a stronger condition than P4.
2. Show that Ellsberg's single urn example violates $P4^*$.

The second part of Exercise 10.5 shows that Ellsberg's paradox challenges any model in which people act on their subjective probabilities.

10.3 Ambiguity Aversion

Ellsberg conjectured that people's preferences over ambiguous prospects depend not only on their utility and beliefs, but also on the confidence they have in those beliefs. The less information they have, the more ambiguity they face about their subjective probabilities. People generally do not like this ambiguity and are **ambiguity averse**. However, Ellsberg noted that people may be **ambiguity loving** if the events are unlikely. If red is the winning colour and the known urn contains only 1 red ball, people choose the unknown urn.

Ambiguity aversion can explain empirical puzzles that expected utility cannot explain (Dimmock et al. 2016). Examples are:

1. The **nonparticipation puzzle**: Many people do not participate in the stock market, although finance models based on SEU predict that they will all do. The returns of stocks are ambiguous and ambiguity averse agents do not like this.
2. **Underinvestment in shares**: Those who participate in the stock market invest less in equity than theory predicts.
3. **Home bias**: People invest too much in stocks from companies based in their own country.
4. **Own company stock puzzle**: People hold too much equity in their own company.
5. **Portfolio underdiversification**: People invest in a limited number of familiar stocks.

Exercise 10.6: Financial Puzzles

Explain how ambiguity aversion can explain the underinvestment in shares, home bias, the own company stock puzzle, and underdiversification.

10.4 Is Ellsberg's Paradox Normative?

Ellsberg thought that the preferences of his paradox could be rational. He writes that "it would seem incautious to rule peremptorily that the people in question should not allow their perception of ambiguity, their unease with their best estimate of probability, to influence their decision....it seems out of the question summarily to judge their behavior as irrational". Decision theorists like Itzhak Gilboa, David Schmeidler, and Massimo Marinacci agree. SEU requires that people always can assign probabilities to events. This may be unrealistic, because in some situations people simply do not know their subjective probabilities. SEU does not allow expressing this ignorance.

Take the decision about school closures during Covid (Berger et al. 2021). There was no information about the role of school contact in Covid transmission, nor about the effect of school closures on the cognitive development of children. Nevertheless, SEU requires giving probabilities. This might be possible. Decision makers can form their best guess based on earlier experiences with influenza outbreaks. An alternative approach is to acknowledge the ignorance and assign a range of possible probabilities. Policy could then be based, for example, on the worst-case scenario.

Table 10.2 Raiffa's challenge to Ellsberg's single urn example

	Heads	Tails
Option A	R	$B \cup Y$
Option B	B	$R \cup Y$

Whether you believe in the rationality of the Ellsberg preferences depends on how appealing you find the sure-thing principle. In Chapter 2, we saw that Slovic and Tversky's subjects were not easily convinced by the sure-thing principle. In reaction to Ellsberg, Howard Raiffa (1961) gave a defence of the sure-thing principle, which convinced most of his subjects.

In the two urn example Raiffa first presented the usual choice by saying "first we toss a coin to determine the winning color and then we draw a ball". Raiffa found that people were willing to pay more to participate in this game for the known urn than for the unknown urn. Then Raiffa said "suppose we change the order. First we draw a ball without looking at its color and then we toss the coin. Red is the winning color if the coin comes up heads and black if it comes up tails. If the color of the ball matches the coin toss you win". The probability of winning is now $1/2$ for both urns.[3] Most of Raiffa's subjects agreed that it should not matter whether the coin was tossed first or that the ball was drawn first and they adjusted their willingness to pay for the unknown urn such that it was equal to that for the known urn.

Table 10.2 shows Raiffa's challenge to Ellsberg's single urn example. Suppose you have the usual Ellsberg preferences and prefer to bet on red (R) over blue (B) and to bet on blue or yellow ($B \cup Y$) over red or yellow ($R \cup Y$). Again, we toss a coin to determine which bet you play. Regardless of the coin toss, Option A gives you the option you prefer. Consequently, it makes sense that you choose Option A over Option B. If so, your payoff depends both on which ball is drawn and on the coin toss. Suppose a red ball is drawn. Then you win €100 with probability $1/2$ (if the coin comes up heads) and nothing with probability $1/2$ (if the coin comes up tails).

Exercise 10.7: Raiffa's Challenge of Ellsberg

Show that under Option B you also win €100 with probability $1/2$ and nothing with probability $1/2$ if a red ball is drawn. Next show that under both A and B you win €100 with probability $1/2$ and nothing with probability $1/2$ if a blue ball is drawn. Finally show that this also holds if a yellow ball is drawn.

Exercise 10.7 shows that A and B always give the same outcomes and are identical. Hence, your preference of A over B does not make sense and, according to Raiffa, you should reconsider your choices in Ellsberg's single urn example. For Raiffa, the

[3] Suppose the fraction of red balls is x. Then the fraction of black balls is $1 - x$. The probability that you draw a red ball and the coin comes up heads is $1/2 \times x$ and the probability that you draw a black ball and the coin comes up tails is $1/2 \times (1 - x)$. Summing gives a winning probability of $1/2$.

Ellsberg paradoxes show that people find it hard to deal with unknown probabilities. His subjects treated objective probabilities in a reflective manner, but for unknown probabilities there was a "shifting of gears" and people resorted to "seat of the pants" judgments. We have to teach people how to think about uncertainty in a purposeful and reflective manner. This shows how SEU aids decision making. If people behaved in line with SEU then this would increase its descriptive status, but decreases its normative status. After all, "we do not have to teach people what comes naturally".

Exercise 10.8: Raiffa on Normative Theories

Do you agree with Raiffa's arguments about normative theories?

10.5 Source Preference

In the Ellsberg examples, ambiguity aversion means that we prefer betting on the risky urn over betting on the ambiguous urn. However, Ellsberg's idea of ambiguity aversion as aversion to vagueness in subjective probabilities, means that we prefer in general sources of uncertainty for which we know more over sources for which we know less. An example is home bias. The underlying probabilities of success and failure of domestic stocks are ambiguous, but less so than the ambiguity about foreign stocks. Ambiguity is richer than the difference between risk and ambiguity alone. Ambiguity attitudes depend on the **sources of uncertainty**.

The idea that ambiguity attitudes are source-dependent comes from Tversky. He suggested that ambiguity attitudes depend on how competent people feel about a source. Chip Heath and Tversky (1991) divided their subjects into two subgroups: those who claimed to know a lot about football and little about politics and those who claimed to know a lot about politics and little about football. Both groups were ambiguity loving in the domain in which they felt competent (football experts for betting on football matches and political experts for betting on the outcome of the 1988 US presidential election), but ambiguity averse in the domain in which they felt incompetent.

An explanation for this **competence effect** is the attribution of success and failure by others. For risky prospects both winning and losing are due to luck. On the other hand, for uncertain prospects where the agent is competent, they receive credit for winning while losing is attributed to bad luck. For uncertain prospects where the agent is incompetent, this is reversed: Winning is attributed to luck and losing to ignorance.

Experiment 10.1: DVD Choices

Stefan Trautmann, Ferdinand Vieider, and Peter Wakker (2008) showed that ambiguity aversion was due to a fear of negative evaluation by others. Subjects could win one of two DVDs either with known or unknown probability. In one treatment subjects told the experimenter which of the two DVDs they preferred. In the other treatment, they did not tell this. Ambiguity aversion disappeared when fear of negative evaluation disappeared: Subjects were ambiguity averse when the preferred DVD was known, but not when it was unknown.

Craig Fox and Tversky (1995) show that feelings of competence (and thus ambiguity aversion) were mainly driven by comparisons. Their subjects were ambiguity averse when they compared an uncertain prospect with another prospect about which they know more or when they compared themselves with others who know more. However, there was no ambiguity aversion when subjects evaluated uncertain prospects in isolation.

They called this the **comparative ignorance hypothesis**. In one of their studies subjects priced bets depending on the temperature in San Francisco (their hometown) or Istanbul (which has a comparable climate). Subjects who saw both bets valued betting on San Francisco temperature 60% higher than betting on Istanbul temperature. However, subjects who only bet on San Francisco temperature or on Istanbul temperature valued the bets equally.

Later work by Craig Fox made a further nuance. The comparative ignorance hypothesis mainly holds for **epistemic uncertainty**: uncertainty that can be known. For **aleatory uncertainty**, uncertainty that is (more) random there is less ambiguity aversion.

Fox and his co-authors asked their subjects to make two choices prior to a German football match between Köln and Augsburg. First they chose between:

f: win €100 if the bookmakers favour Köln to win.
g: win €100 if Köln wins.

Then they chose between:

f': win €100 if the bookmakers favour Augsburg to win or draw.
g': win €100 if Augsburg wins or draws.

The bookmakers' favourite is knowable (epistemic uncertainty) and depends on what you know about football. On the other hand, the outcome of the match is more aleatory.

Exercise 10.9: Epistemic Versus Aleatory Uncertainty

Explain that the hypothesis that people are more averse to epistemic uncertainty predicts that subjects who rated their knowledge of football as "low" are more likely to choose g and g' while subjects who rate their knowledge as "high" are more likely to choose f and g' or g and f'. This was indeed what they found.

10.6 Modelling Ambiguity Aversion

Modelling ambiguity aversion turned out to be hard. It took more than 20 years after Ellsberg introduced his paradoxes before David Schmeidler developed two ways to do so: one by replacing additive probabilities by nonadditive decision weights and the other by replacing unique subjective probabilities by a set of possible probabilities.

10.6.1 Choquet Expected Utility

In Chapter 9, we saw that rank-dependent utility (RDU) explains the Allais paradoxes by replacing probabilities by probability weights. We can do something similar for decision under uncertainty: We replace the probabilities $P(E)$ in SEU by **event weights** $W(E)$. However, as for risk, we cannot simply replace subjective probabilities by event weights as we (again) would get violations of dominance that are empirically not observed (see Exercise 10.10).

Exercise 10.10: Violations of Dominance

Show that the model $V(E_1 : x_1, \ldots, E_n : x_n) = \sum_{i=1}^{n} W(E_i) \times U(x_i)$ with W nonadditive leads to violations of dominance (i.e. prospect f gives for all events at least as good an outcome as prospect g, but the model predicts that g is preferred). (Hint: Suppose that there are two events E_i and E_j with $E_i \cap E_j = \emptyset$ such that $W(E_i) + W(E_j) < W(E_i \cup E_j)$ and consider the prospects $f = (90 + \epsilon)_{E_i} 90_{E_j} h$ and $g = 90_{E_i \cup E_j} h$. For $\epsilon > 0$ small enough the model predicts that g will be preferred to f.)

To avoid violations of dominance, we weight cumulative events, not the events themselves. We first rank-order the outcomes of a prospect from best to worst. So for a rank-ordered prospect $(E_1 : x_1, \ldots, E_n : x_n)$ we have $x_1 \succcurlyeq x_2 \succcurlyeq \ldots \succcurlyeq x_n$. We then get the following model:

Definition 10.4: Choquet Expected Utility

According to Choquet expected utility (CEU), preferences over rank-ordered prospects $(E_1 : x_1, \ldots, E_n : x_n)$ are represented by:

$$V(E_1 : x_1, \ldots, E_n : x_n) = \sum_{i=1}^{n} \pi_i \times U(x_i), \tag{10.6}$$

where the π_i are decision weights that are defined as:

$$\pi_i = W\Big(\bigcup_{j=1}^{i} E_j\Big) - W\Big(\bigcup_{j=1}^{i-1} E_j\Big). \tag{10.7}$$

W is an event weighting function (also called capacity) that takes values between 0 and 1, is monotonic (if $E_i \subseteq E_j$ then $W(E_i) \leq W(E_j)$), but can be nonadditive. U is a cardinal utility function.

Extension 10.4: Choquet Integration

The derivation of CEU is mathematically complex, because it requires a non-additive theory of integration. Schmeidler (1989) developed this theory. He later learnt that the mathematician Gustave Choquet had developed a similar theory in the early 1950s. Hence, the name Choquet expected utility.

CEU can explain Ellsberg's two urn example. Suppose that expected utility holds for the known urn. Let R and B stand for the events that a red and a black ball are drawn from the unknown urn. Suppose $W(R) = W(B) = 0.4$. We then have

$$W(R) \times U(100) < {}^1\!/_2 \times U(100) \text{ and } W(B) \times U(100) < {}^1\!/_2 \times U(100).$$

The agent prefers drawing from the known urn when both red and black are the winning colours. The assumption of expected utility for the known urn is not necessary. If we assume instead that the agent evaluates the known urn by RDU then the argument remains true as long as $W(R) = W(B) < w({}^1\!/_2)$.

Exercise 10.11: CEU Can Explain Ellsberg's Single Urn Paradox

Give a numerical example to show that CEU can also explain Ellsberg's single urn paradox.

CEU can also explain ambiguity loving for unlikely events. Suppose that the known urn contains 5 red balls and 95 black balls. Then a CEU agent will prefer to bet on the unknown urn if $W(R) > .05$ (or $W(R) > w(.05)$ if we assume RDU for risk).

Extension 10.5: Bounded Subadditivity

In Chapter 9 we saw that the probability weighting function is inverse S-shaped. To capture ambiguity loving for unlikely events something similar must hold for the event weighting function W. Because we have no numerical probabilities available, characterizing this intuition is more complex (Tversky and Wakker 1995).

To capture ambiguity loving for unlikely events we impose **lower subadditivity**: for disjoint nonempty events A and B, $W(A) \geq W(A \cup B) - W(B)$. Adding event A to the empty set has more impact than adding A to a nonempty event B (provided $W(A \cup B)$ is sufficiently far from 1 to avoid the certainty effect). $W(A)$ is the weight of an outcome when it is the best outcome, while $W(A \cup B) - W(A)$ is its weight when it is not the best outcome. Lower subadditivity captures the intuition that people focus more on the best outcome than on intermediate outcomes.

Similarly, people focus more on the worst outcome. Tversky and Wakker characterize this by **upper subadditivity**: for disjoint A and B, $1 - W(S - A) \geq W(A \cup B) - W(B)$ where S is the set of all states of the world and $S - A$ means we remove A from S. In words, subtracting A from the universal set has more impact than subtracting A from an intermediate event $A \cup B$ (provided $W(B)$ is sufficiently far from 0 to avoid the impossibility effect). $1 - W(S - A)$ is the weight of an outcome when it is the worst outcome, while $W(A \cup B) - W(B)$ is its weight when it is an intermediate outcome.

Bounded subadditivity is the combination of lower and upper subadditivity.

10.6.2 Prospect Theory

CEU makes no distinction between gains and losses and, consequently, it cannot explain that people have different ambiguity attitudes for gains and losses. Like for risk, there is a **fourfold pattern of ambiguity attitudes**: ambiguity aversion for likely gains and for unlikely losses and ambiguity loving for likely losses and unlikely gains (Kocher et al. 2018).

Prospect theory extends CEU to include reference-dependence. That way it can explain the difference in ambiguity attitudes between gains and losses. It takes two CEU forms, one for gains and one for losses, and adds these. For losses, we take the dual form so that most weight goes to the extreme outcomes.

Definition 10.5: Prospect Theory for Ambiguity

Let $(E_1 : x_1, \ldots, E_j : x_j.E_{j+1} : x_{j+1}, \ldots, E_n : x_n)$ be a rank-ordered prospect such that all outcomes up to x_j are gains and all outcomes from x_{j+1} onwards are losses. Prospect theory evaluates this prospect as:

$$PT(E_1 : x_1, \ldots, E_j : x_j, E_{j+1} : x_{j+1}, \ldots, E_n : x_n) = \sum_{i=1}^{j} \pi_i^+ U(x_i) + \sum_{i=j+1}^{n} \pi_i^- U(x_i), \tag{10.8}$$

where the decision weights π_i^+ and π_i^- are defined as:

$$\pi_i^+ = W^+\left(\bigcup_{k=1}^{i} E_k\right) - W^+\left(\bigcup_{k=1}^{i-1} E_k\right). \tag{10.9}$$

$$\pi_i^- = W^-\left(\bigcup_{k=i}^{n} E_k\right) - W^-\left(\bigcup_{k=i+1}^{n} E_k\right). \tag{10.10}$$

Exercise 10.12: Bounded Subadditivity

Show that bounded subadditivity implies that prospect theory gives most weight to the extreme outcomes (the biggest gain and the largest loss).

An advantage of CEU and prospect theory is that methods exist to measure them (see Abdellaoui et al. 2016). This is not the case for other ambiguity theories.

10.6.3 Maxmin EU

The multiple priors models capture ambiguity by a set of possible probabilities. This is called the set of **multiple priors**. Itzhak Gilboa and David Schmeidler (1989) derived such a model, **maxmin expected utility**.

Let $\mathcal{P}$ denote the set of probabilities that an agent considers possible. In the school closure example, the analyst may believe, for instance, that there is between a 20% and a 50% probability that school closure leads to cognitive impairment. For any prospect f, agents compute its expected utility according to all probability distributions in the set of multiple priors $\mathcal{P}$. Then they compute the utility of a prospect as the minimum of these expected utilities:

$$V(E_1 : x_1, \ldots, E_n : x_n) = \min_{p \in \mathcal{P}} \sum_{i=1}^{n} p(E_i) \times U(x_i). \tag{10.11}$$

Consider Ellsberg's single urn example. Suppose the agent believes the urn can have between 10 and 50 blue balls and, therefore, may also have between 10 and 50 yellow balls. This is the set of priors. For risk the agent is sure about the probability, so the prior is unique, and the agent chooses according to EU. So the utility of betting on red is $1/3 \times U(€100)$. The minimum expected utility of betting on blue occurs when there are only 10 blue balls and is equal to $1/9 \times U(€100)$. Consequently, the utility of betting on red is higher than the utility of betting on blue and the agent bets on red.

For betting on blue or yellow, the agent knows the probability ($2/3$) and so its utility is $2/3 \times U(€100)$. For betting on red or yellow the probability is unknown and its minimum occurs when there are only 10 yellow balls in the urn. Then the probability of winning is $4/9$ and thus maxmin EU gives a utility of $4/9 \times U(€100)$ to $R \cup Y$. As this is less than the utility of $B \cup Y$, the agent prefers betting on blue or yellow, which is what we observe empirically.

Exercise 10.13: Maxmin and Ellsberg's Two Urn Paradox

Show that maxmin EU can also explain Ellsberg's two urn paradox.

Maxmin EU has descriptive problems:

1. It assumes expected utility for risk, which as we saw in Chapter 9 does not hold.
2. It is hard to measure, because it does not explain how we can find the set of priors.
3. It is (too) pessimistic. Agents base their decisions on the worst-case scenario (the minimum of the expected utilities), which is often too cautious. Because the model is so pessimistic it cannot explain ambiguity loving (like for losses and for unlikely events).

10.6.4 α-Maxmin EU

A more optimistic multiple priors model is **α-maxmin** EU. It was first proposed by Leonid Hurwicz (1951). Paolo Ghirardato, Fabio Maccheroni, and Massimo Marinacci (2004) gave a theoretical foundation for it.

α-maxmin EU evaluates prospects as a weighted average of the minimum and the maximum expected utility given the set of multiple priors $\mathcal{P}$. Formally, according to α-maxmin EU the utility of a prospect f equals:

$$V(E_1 : x_1, \ldots, E_n : x_n) =$$
$$\alpha \times \min_{p \in \mathcal{P}} \sum_{i=1}^{n} p(E_i) \times U(x_i) + (1-\alpha) \times \max_{p \in \mathcal{P}} \sum_{i=1}^{n} p(E_i) \times U(x_i). \tag{10.12}$$

The parameter α shows ambiguity aversion. The higher α, the more weight agents give to the worst-case scenario and the more ambiguity averse they are.

α-maxmin can explain that agents are simultaneously ambiguity averse for likely events and ambiguity loving for unlikely events. Let's return to Ellsberg's single urn paradox and the agent who believes that the number of blue (and yellow) balls can be any number between 10 and 50. Suppose this agent's α equals $^2/_3$. α-maxmin also assumes expected utility for risk so $V(R)$, the utility of betting on red is $^1/_3 \times U(€100)$. The utility of betting on blue is two-thirds the minimum EU, which is $^2/_3 \times {}^1/_9 \times U(€100)$ plus one-third the maximum EU, which is $^1/_3 \times {}^5/_9 \times U(€100)$. Summing gives a total utility of betting on blue of $^7/_{27} \times U(€100)$. This is less than $V(R)$ so the agent bets on red. Exercise 10.14 shows that the agent also bets on blue or yellow instead of on red or yellow.

Exercise 10.14: α-Maxmin

Show that the utility of betting on red or yellow for this agent is $^{16}/_{27} \times U(€100)$, which is less than $^2/_3 \times U(€100)$, the utility of betting on blue or yellow.

Consider now an unlikely event. For example, we have Ellsberg's two urn example and the known urn contains only 5 red balls. Suppose that the agent believes that the unknown urn may consist between 0 and 20 red balls. The utility of drawing from the unknown urn is then two-third times 0, the EU of the worst-case scenario in which there are no red balls in the urn, and one-third times $^1/_5 \times U(€100)$, the best-case scenario in which the urn contains 20 red balls. Summing gives $^1/_{15} \times U(€100)$, which exceeds $0.05 \times U(€100)$, the utility of drawing from the known urn.

The example shows that in α-maxmin ambiguity attitudes depend on both the parameter α and the set of priors. Ambiguity loving follows because the set of priors is asymmetric. This often occurs for unlikely events (with probability close to zero), because probabilities cannot be less than zero. In other words, there is little room below our best guess, but more above it as we could in principle include all probabilities up to 1 in the set of priors. This leads to asymmetric sets of priors.

So α-maxmin is more flexible than maxmin EU and can explain a richer variety of ambiguity attitudes. The price is the extra parameter α. α-maxmin shares with maxmin EU the limitations of assuming expected utility for risk and the difficulty of determining the set of priors.

Both maxmin EU and α-maxmin are crude as they only consider the worst- and the best-case scenarios. Extension 10.6 shows that this can lead to unlikely and undesirable predictions.

Extension 10.6: Maxmin and α-Maxmin Violate Dominance

Consider the Hollywood actress with pain in her abdomen discussed in Chapter 8. Her doctor believes she can have three possible diseases: gastroenteritis, pyelonephritis, and appendicitis. Treatment 1 treats gastroenteritis and pyelonephritis, but not appendicitis. Treatment 2 treats appendicitis, but not the other two diseases. The utility of treating a disease is 1 and the utility of not treating a disease is 0. Suppose the doctor's set of priors contains all probability distributions over the three diseases, i.e. all probability distributions are possible.

Exercise 10.15: Dominance

Show that both maxmin EU and α-maxmin predict that the doctor considers treatments 1 and 2 equally good, even though treatment 1 treats two possible diseases and treatment 2 only one.

10.6.5 The Smooth Ambiguity Model

A finer model of ambiguity preferences is Peter Klibanoff, Massimo Marinacci, and Sujoy Mukerji's (2005) **smooth ambiguity model**. Agents, again, have a set of possible subjective probability distributions $\mathcal{P}$. They also have a probability distribution μ about how likely each of these distributions in $\mathcal{P}$ are. Agents may have a best guess, but also consider other distributions that they weight according to their likelihood. This is a difference with maxmin EU and α-maxmin where agents do not consider the likelihood of the various distributions and only centre on the worst and (in the case of α-maxmin) best distribution.

Definition 10.6: The Smooth Ambiguity Model

The smooth ambiguity model values a prospect $(E_1 : x_1, \ldots, E_n : x_n)$ as:

$$V(E_1 : x_1, \ldots, E_n : x_n) = \sum_{j=1}^{m} \mu(P_j)\phi\Big(\sum_{i=1}^{n} P_j(E_i)U(x_i)\Big). \qquad (10.13)$$

The smooth model has two stages. Agents apply expected utility in both. For each of the probability distributions P_j in $\mathcal{P}$ that agents consider possible, they compute the expected utility of prospect $(E_1 : x_1, \ldots, E_n : x_n)$. They then take the utility $\phi(EU)$ over each of these expected utilities and multiply them with $\mu(P_j)$ the likelihood of the probability distributions. The shape of ϕ determines agents' ambiguity attitude. If it is concave the agent is ambiguity averse, if it is convex the agent is ambiguity loving and if it is linear the agent is ambiguity neutral.

Consider Ellsberg's single urn example. Suppose the agent believes that only three distributions of blue and yellow balls are possible: (30, 30), the urn contains 30 blue and 30 yellow balls, (60, 0), the urn contains 60 blue and no yellow balls, and (0, 60), the urn contains no blue balls and 60 yellow balls. Suppose the agent gives probability $1/2$ to distribution (30, 30) (so $\mu(30, 30) = 1/2$) and probability $1/4$ to both distributions (60, 0) and (0, 60) ($\mu(60, 0) = \mu(0.60) = 1/4$). Let $\phi(EU) = \sqrt{EU}$ and let U be linear.

For risk, the agent is sure about the probability and so the utility of betting on red is $\sqrt{1/3 \times 100} = 5.77$. For distribution (30, 30) the EU of betting on blue is $1/3 \times 100$. For distribution (60, 0) it is $2/3 \times 100$ and for distribution (0, 60) it is 0. So the total utility of betting on blue is $1/2 \times \sqrt{33^1/_3} + 1/4 \times \sqrt{66^2/_3} + 0 = 4.93$. The agent bets on red.

Exercise 10.16: The Smooth Model and Ellsberg's Single Urn

Show in the above example that the agent bets on blue or yellow instead of red or yellow.

Exercise 10.17: The Smooth Model and Ellsberg's Two Urns

Show by an example that the smooth model also predicts the preferences in Ellsberg's two urn paradox if ϕ is concave (e.g. take $\sqrt{EU}$).

The smooth model applies expected utility twice. In Chapter 9, we saw that expected utility efficiently analyses risk attitudes. The smooth model extends this efficiency to ambiguity. Because it is based on expected utility, we can use all the elegant methods based on expected utility.

The smooth model can explain why ambiguity attitudes differ for gains and losses. This follows if we take the function ϕ concave for gain prospects and convex for loss prospects.

The smooth model has several limitations:

1. It assumes expected utility for risk.
2. Because it models ambiguity attitudes by a utility function ϕ, it cannot explain why there is simultaneous ambiguity aversion for likely events and ambiguity loving for unlikely events.
3. It is hard to apply and test because it is unclear how to measure the set of possible probability distributions $\mathcal{P}$ and their likelihood as measured by μ.

10.7 Empirical Tests of Ambiguity Models

Testing ambiguity models is complex, because they use unobservable concepts like the set of multiple priors or the second-order probability distributions. Empirical tests have generally focused on qualitative predictions. For example, Robin Cubitt, Gijs van de Kuilen, and Sujoy Mukerji (2020) test whether α-maxmin's focus on only the best and the worst-case scenario is too crude compared with the smooth model's finer focus on all possible expected utilities. Their data support the smooth model over α-maxmin.

Chew Soo Hong, Bin Miao, and Songfa Zhong (2017) use variations on Ellsberg's two urn examples to test ambiguity models. In one of their questions they ask their subjects to value an urn that contains either 0 or 100 winning balls and one that contains either 25 or 75 winning balls.

Exercise 10.18: Test of Maxmin

Show that maxmin EU predicts that the urn containing 25 or 75 winning balls should be preferred to the urn containing either 0 or 100 winning balls.

In contrast with maxmin EU, subjects valued the $\{0, 100\}$ urn higher than the $\{25, 75\}$ urn. If subjects' second-order distributions μ over $\{y, x\}, y < x$ are the same for the $\{0, 100\}$ and the $\{25, 75\}$ urns then their preference for the $\{0, 100\}$ urn also violates the smooth model with ambiguity aversion.

Subjects also preferred the $\{0, 100\}$ urn to an urn where the number of winning balls could be any number between 0 and 100 (the $\{n, 100 - n\}$ urn). Exercise 10.19 shows that this violates α-maxmin. It is also hard to reconcile with the smooth model.

Exercise 10.19: Test of α-Maxmin

Show that the preference for the $\{0, 100\}$ urn over the $\{n, 100 - n\}$ urn violates α-maxmin.

The data of Chew et al. are most consistent with a model of source preference that uses RDU to evaluate risk.

Aurélien Baillon and I (2015) tested the ambiguity models by measuring matching probabilities for events. Consider the prospect $x_E 0$ that pays €x if event E occurs and nothing otherwise. We next find the risky prospect $x_p 0$ (€x with probability p and nothing otherwise) that the agent finds equally good as $x_E 0$: $x_E 0 \sim x_p 0$. This probability p is the **matching probability** of event E. So if $x_E 0 \sim x_{0.25} 0$, the matching probability of E is 0.25.

Matching probabilities can test the ambiguity models. For example, we elicited the matching probability of event E and its complement E^c both when x was a gain of €10 and when it was a loss of €10. Under maxmin EU, agents will base their decisions on the worst-case scenario. So for gains they focus on the minimum probabilities of events E and E^c that they see possible, but for losses they focus on the maximum probabilities of events E and E^c that they see possible. Hence, maxmin EU predicts that the sum of the matching probabilities of E and E^c will be lower for gains than for losses. Similarly, we could derive predictions for the other ambiguity models using matching probabilities.

Around 85% of our subjects behaved in line with prospect theory. One-third behaved according to Choquet expected utility, and around 25% according to α-maxmin and the smooth model. Hardly any subject behaved according to maxmin EU.

10.8 Source Theory

Ellsberg's paradoxes challenge the existence of subjective probabilities. We also saw that ambiguity attitudes can differ between sources. Because economists are reluctant to give up subjective probabilities, they started to explore whether these could be defined within, although not between, sources. Chew Soo Hong and Jacob Sagi (2006; 2008) defined conditions that ensured this. Empirical evidence suggests that these conditions indeed hold (Abdellaoui et al. 2011; Bleichrodt et al. 2023).

If subjective probabilities exist within sources, we can model source preference by taking prospect theory with a source-dependent probability weighting function. This is the idea of **source theory**. Abdellaoui et al. (2011) first suggested it. Preference conditions are in Baillon et al. (2025). Let us formally define it:

Definition 10.7: Source Theory

Let $(E_1 : x_1, \ldots, E_j : x_j, E_{j+1} : x_{j+1}, \ldots, E_n : x_n)$ be a rank-ordered prospect with all events coming from the same source of uncertainty. Source theory evaluates such prospects as Eq. 10.8 with $W(E_i)$ replaced by a source-dependent probability weighting function $w^s(P(E_i))$.

Because subjective probabilities exist within sources we can replace the event weighting function by a (source-dependent) probability weighting function. The shapes of these weighting functions define ambiguity attitudes.

In Chapter 9, we discussed that probability weighting functions have two parameters: one defining elevation, the other sensitivity to changes in probabilities. The source-dependent probability weighting functions are characterized by the same two parameters.

The elevation parameter shows how attractive an agent finds a source. This is called **source preference**. Figure 10.1 shows source preference. The weights in prospect theory show the weight of the best outcome. So, a more elevated weighting function means more weight to the best outcome. Consequently, the source corresponding to the solid weighting function in Fig. 10.1 is preferred to the source corresponding to the dotted weighting function as it gives more weight to the best outcome.

Fig. 10.1 Source preference

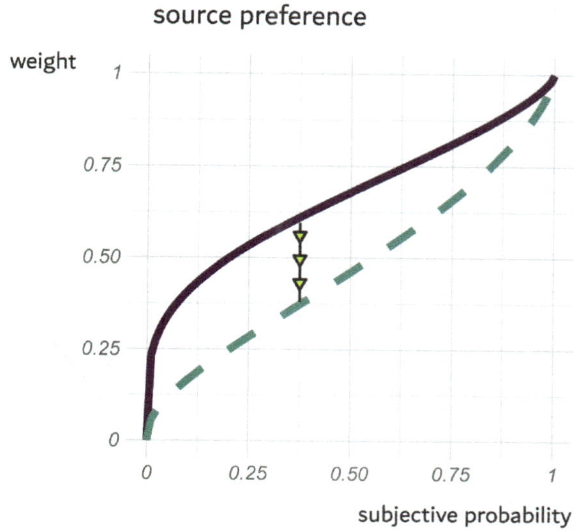

In the two urn Ellsberg example, the solid line could be the weighting function for the source "draw from the known urn" and the dotted line the weighting function for the source "draw from the unknown urn".

It is plausible that for both the known and the unknown urn $P(Red) = P(Black) = 1/2$. However, because the weight of probability $1/2$ is higher for the known urn, people bet on the known urn both when red is the winning colour and when black is the winning colour. Source theory can explain the two urn Ellsberg paradox by taking the known and the unknown urn as distinct sources of uncertainty. Another example of source preference are Heath and Tversky's football fans with the solid line corresponding to betting on the results of football matches and the dotted line corresponding to betting on the results of presidential elections.

Exercise 10.20: Home Bias

Home bias means that people prefer buying stocks from their own country over stocks from other countries. If we take "stock from own country" and "stock from a foreign country" as two sources of uncertainty, argue that source theory can explain home bias.

The other component of the source-dependent weighting functions is sensitivity to likelihood information. Figure 10.2 shows an example where an agent is more sensitive to information from the source with the solid weighting function. Empirical evidence suggests that people are more sensitive to information for risk than for ambiguity. Then the solid line shows weighting for risk and the dotted one weighting for uncertainty.

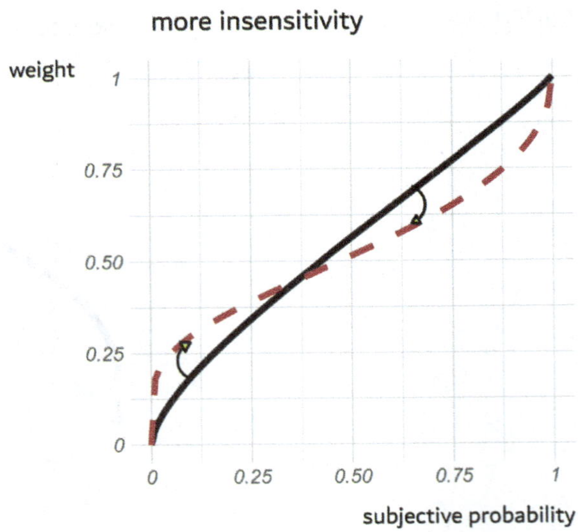

Fig. 10.2 Source sensitivity

Source theory has several advantages:

1. It can explain the fourfold pattern of ambiguity attitudes.
2. It can explain source preference.
3. It explains deviations from EU for risk.
4. It can be measured and thus applied in practice and empirically tested.

For these reasons, I believe source theory is currently the preferred descriptive theory of ambiguity.

Exercise 10.21: Ellsberg's Single Urn Paradox

Show that if we take drawing a ball from Ellsberg's single urn as one source of uncertainty, source theory cannot explain the single urn paradox. To explain it we must take drawing a ball with known probability and drawing a ball with unknown probability as distinct sources of uncertainty.

10.9 Machina's Paradoxes

I end this chapter with two paradoxes suggested by Mark Machina (2009) that challenge all of the above theories. Table 10.3 shows **Machina's 50:51 example**. An urn contains 101 balls, 50 with either number 1 (event E_1) or number 2 (E_2) on them

Table 10.3 Machina's 50:51 example

		50 balls		51 balls	
		E_1	E_2	E_3	E_4
Choice 1	f_1	€8,000	€8,000	€4,000	€4,000
	f_2	€8,000	€4,000	€8,000	€4,000
Choice 2	f_3	€12,000	€8,000	€4,000	€0
	f_4	€12,000	€4,000	€8,000	€0

and 51 with either number 3 (E_3) or number 4 (E_4) on them. Prospects f_1 and f_2 differ in how they place €4000 and €8000 across events E_2 and E_3. f_2 offers a slight advantage as there are 51 balls with a 3 or a 4 and only 50 with a 1 or a 2. On the other hand, f_2 is more ambiguous than f_1: in f_1 we know the probabilities of getting €4000 and €8000, but in f_2 not. For that reason, people may prefer f_1 over f_2. Which prospect would you prefer?

Prospects f_3 and f_4 are obtained from f_1 and f_2 by changing the common best outcomes from €8000 to €12,000 and the common worst outcomes from €4000 to €0. In Ellsberg's single urn example, changing the common outcome reversed the ambiguity of the prospects: the initially unambiguous prospect (betting on red) became ambiguous (red or yellow), and the initially ambiguous prospect (blue) became unambiguous (blue or yellow). Something similar happens here, but the reversal is less drastic. Changing the best and worst common outcomes makes that both f_3 and f_4 are ambiguous. Consequently, the advantage f_4 has over f_3, there are more balls with a 3 or a 4 than with a 1 or a 2, might become decisive and the agent chooses f_4 over f_3.

The combination $f_1 \succ f_2$ and $f_3 \prec f_4$ violates CEU (and thus prospect theory which is equivalent to CEU for gains). The changes in the common outcomes do not affect the rank-ordering of the events (remember that in CEU we can rank events with the same outcomes as we like). Therefore CEU predicts that these changes do not affect preferences. See also Exercise 10.22.

Exercise 10.22: Machina's 50:51 Example

Write out the choices in Machina's 50:51 example using Eq. 10.6, to show that they violate CEU.

As we only change the worst and the best outcomes, the choices also violate maxmin EU and α-maxmin. Aurélien Baillon, Olivier L'Haridon, and Laetitia Placido (2011) show that they also violate the smooth model. They could be consistent with source theory if we take drawing with known probability and drawing with unknown probability as distinct sources. This requires an extension of source theory that is currently unavailable.

Table 10.4 shows **Machina's reflection example**. There are 50 balls with either 1 or 2 and 50 balls with either 3 or 4. Consider the choice between f_5 and f_6. It is not obvious. On the one hand, f_6 is less ambiguous as it gives a known 50% probability

Table 10.4 Machina's reflection example

		50 balls		50 balls	
		E_1	E_2	E_3	E_4
Choice 1	f_5	€4,000	€8,000	€4,000	€0
	f_6	€4,000	€4,000	€8,000	€0
Choice 2	f_7	€0	€8,000	€4,000	€4,000
	f_8	€0	€4,000	€8,000	€4,000

of €4000, but f_5 has less spread in outcomes for E_3 and E_4. The crucial feature is that f_7 is similar to f_6 and f_8 to f_5. The only difference is that what was first obtained under E_1 is now obtained under E_4 and vice versa and the same role reversal holds for E_2 and E_3. Since E_1 and E_2 and E_3 and E_4 are equivalent except for the number on the ball, it is hard to see how this could matter. So, if agents prefer f_5 to f_6 they should also prefer f_8 to f_7 and if they prefer f_6 to f_5 they should also prefer f_7 to f_8.

However, such preferences violate CEU (and prospect theory). f_7 and f_8 are obtained from f_5 and f_6 by changing the common outcomes for the worst-ranked events E_1 and E_4 into other common outcomes. However, they remain the worst-ranked events and CEU says that these changes should not affect preferences. If you prefer f_5 to f_6 you should prefer f_7 to f_8 and if you prefer f_6 to f_5 you should prefer f_8 to f_7 (see also Exercise 10.23).

Exercise 10.23: Machina's Reflection Example

Write out the choices in Machina's reflection example using Eq. 10.6 to show that they violate CEU (Hint: assume, for example, $f_5 \succ f_6$. Write this out in terms of CEU and show that it implies $f_7 \succ f_8$).

The only way in which Machina's reflection example could be consistent with CEU is if agents were indifferent between f_5 and f_6 and between f_7 and f_8. However, Olivier L'Haridon and Laetitia Placido (2010) found that 70% of their subjects had a strict preference between these acts. Most preferred f_6 to f_5 and f_7 to f_8. Apparently, they preferred to have some ambiguity resolved.

These preferences (in combination with the usual Ellsberg preferences) also violate maxmin EU, α-maxmin, and the smooth model (Baillon et al. 2011). They could be consistent with source theory if drawing from an urn with at least some ambiguity resolved is seen as a distinct source. Again, this requires extensions of source theory currently unavailable.

Machina's examples emphasize what we have seen throughout this book: No model perfectly describes preferences. To explain his examples, we must allow for interactions between events. Such a model is complex and hard (if not impossible) to measure and apply to real-world problems. I prefer to have models that I can apply to help people and policy makers make better decisions even though they may sometimes fail. Machina's examples help to be aware of those failures.

References

Abdellaoui, M., and P. P. Wakker. 2020. Savage for dummies and experts. *Journal of Economic Theory* 186: 104991.

Abdellaoui, M., A. Baillon, L. Placido, and P. P. Wakker. 2011. The rich domain of uncertainty: Source functions and their experimental implementation. *American Economic Review* 101: 695–723.

Abdellaoui, M., H. Bleichrodt, and O. Haridon, and D. Van Dolder. 2016. Measuring loss aversion under ambiguity: A method to make prospect theory completely observable. *Journal of Risk and Uncertainty* 52: 1–20.

Baillon, A., and H. Bleichrodt. 2015. Testing ambiguity models through the measurement of probabilities for gains and losses. *American Economic Journal: Microeconomics* 7: 77–100.

Baillon, A., O. L'Haridon, and L. Placido. 2011. Ambiguity models and the Machina paradoxes. *American Economic Review* 101: 1547–1560.

Baillon, A., H. Bleichrodt, C. Li, and P.P. Wakker. 2025. Source theory: A tractable and positive ambiguity theory. *Management Science*.

Berger, L., N. Berger, V. Bosetti, I. Gilboa, L. P. Hansen, C. Jarvis, M. Marinacci, and R. D. Smith. 2021. Rational policymaking during a pandemic. *Proceedings of the National Academy of Sciences* 118: e2012704118.

Bleichrodt, H., S. Grant, and J. Yang. 2023. Testing Hurwicz expected utility. *Econometrica* 91: 1393–1416.

Chew, S.H., and J.S. Sagi. 2006. Event exchangeability: Probabilistic sophistication without continuity or monotonicity. *Econometrica* 74: 771–786.

Chew, S. H., and J. S. Sagi. 2008. Small worlds: Modeling attitudes toward sources of uncertainty. *Journal of Economic Theory* 139: 1–24.

Chew, S. H., B. Miao, and S. Zhong. 2017. Partial ambiguity. *Econometrica* 85: 1239–1260.

Cubitt, R., G. Van De Kuilen, and S. Mukerji. 2020. Discriminating between models of ambiguity attitude: A qualitative test. *Journal of the European Economic Association* 18: 708–749.

Dimmock, S. G., R. Kouwenberg, O. S. Mitchell, and K. Peijnenburg. 2016. Ambiguity aversion and household portfolio choice puzzles: Empirical evidence. *Journal of Financial Economics* 119: 559–577.

Fox, C. R., and A. Tversky. 1995. Ambiguity aversion and comparative ignorance. *Quarterly Journal of Economics* 110: 585–603.

Ghirardato, P., F. Maccheroni, and M. Marinacci. 2004. Differentiating ambiguity and ambiguity attitude. *Journal of Economic Theory* 118: 133–173.

Gilboa, I., and D. Schmeidler. 1989. Maxmin expected utility with non-unique prior. *Journal of Mathematical Economics* 18: 141–153.

Hartmann, L. 2020. Savage's P3 is redundant. *Econometrica* 88: 203–205.

Heath, C., and A. Tversky. 1991. Preference and belief: Ambiguity and competence in choice under uncertainty. *Journal of Risk and Uncertainty* 4: 5–28.

Hurwicz, L. 1951. Some specification problems and applications to econometric models. *Econometrica* 19: 343–344.

Klibanoff, P., M. Marinacci, and S. Mukerji. 2005. A smooth model of decision making under ambiguity. *Econometrica* 73: 1849–1892.

Kocher, M. G., A. M. Lahno, and S. T. Trautmann. 2018. Ambiguity aversion is not universal. *European Economic Review* 101: 268–283.

Kreps, D. 1988. *Notes on the Theory of Choice*. Boulder, Colorado: Westview Press.

L'Haridon, O., and L. Placido. 2010. Betting on Machina's reflection example: An experiment on ambiguity. *Theory and Decision* 69: 375–393.

Machina, M. J. 2009. Risk, ambiguity, and the rank-dependence axioms. *American Economic Review* 99: 385–392.

Machina, M.J., and D. Schmeidler. 1992. A more robust definition of subjective probability. *Econometrica* 60: 745–780.

Raiffa, H. 1961. Risk, ambiguity, and the Savage axioms: comment. *Quarterly Journal of Economics* 75: 690–694.

Schmeidler, D. 1989. Subjective probability and expected utility without additivity. *Econometrica* 57: 571–587.

Trautmann, S. T., F. M. Vieider, and P. P. Wakker. 2008. Causes of ambiguity aversion: Known versus unknown preferences. *Journal of Risk and Uncertainty* 36: 225–243.

Tversky, A., and P. Wakker. 1995. Risk attitudes and decision weights. *Econometrica* 63: 1255–1280.

Time Preference

11

The consequences of many decisions are spread over time. Examples are improvements in climate change or health care prevention programmes like breast cancer screening and the promotion of healthier lifestyles. The costs of such programmes often take place earlier than the benefits. How to account for such differences in timing is the topic of this chapter.

11.1 Why Time Preference?

There are several reasons why people prefer outcomes sooner than later:

1. **Impatience** also called pure time preference. We care less for future benefits because they occur in the future.
2. **Economic growth**. This applies mainly to money. Because we become richer over time, decreasing marginal utility implies that €x now is worth more than €x in the future.
3. **Inflation**. Inflation makes money now more valuable than money in the future.
4. **Uncertainty**. The future is uncertain. We may die before we receive a benefit. To reflect this uncertainty we give less weight to the future.

The above reasons for time preference differ between goods. This creates a dilemma for policy. For example, health policy trades off the costs of health care, measured in money, against its benefits measured in quality and quantity of life. While inflation and economic growth are reasons to discount the costs of health care for time preference, they are less relevant for quality and quantity of life. Several

H. Bleichrodt, *Behavioural Economics*,
https://doi.org/10.1007/978-3-031-69166-9_11

governments therefore use different adjustments for the costs and effects of health care programmes (e.g. the Netherlands, Belgium, Poland, and the UK for public health interventions).

11.2 Constant Discounting

The traditional model of time preferences is **constant discounting**, also called **exponential discounting**. Let $(x_0, \ldots x_n)$ be a **temporal prospect**, which gives outcome x_t at time point t. Time point 0 is the present.

Definition 11.1: Constant Discounting

According to constant discounting, temporal prospects $(x_0, \ldots, x_n)$ are evaluated as:

$$V(x_0, \ldots x_n) = \sum_{t=0}^{n} \delta^t \times U(x_n). \tag{11.1}$$

where U is a cardinal utility function and δ a constant discount factor.

Exercise 11.1: Discount Factor

Show that if people have positive time preference, i.e. they prefer to receive good outcomes sooner rather than later, then $0 < \delta < 1$.

The discount factor shows the weight we give to different periods. We can derive the **discount rate** from it. The discount rate shows by how much the weight of a period decreases per period.

Definition 11.2: Discount Rate

The discount rate ρ is equal to

$$\rho = \frac{1-\delta}{\delta}. \tag{11.2}$$

Cost-benefit analysis uses the discount rate to translate costs and benefits that occur at distinct points in time to their **net present value**. That way, they can be compared. For example, if a project costs €5 million now to give a benefit of €100 million in 30 years then we check whether it is worth the effort by computing the value now of these €100 million using the formula:

$$\text{net present value} = 100 \text{ million} \times \frac{1}{(1+\rho)^{30}}. \quad (11.3)$$

Exercise 11.2: Net Present Value

What is the net present value of 100 million in 30 years when

1. $\rho = 0.01$ (1%)?
2. $\rho = 0.03$ (3%)?
3. $\rho = 0.05$ (5%)?

Figure 11.1 shows that the weights of time points in the future fall rapidly under constant discounting. Even for a modest discount rate of 1.5%, benefits in 50 years receive less than half the weight of benefits now. At a discount rate of 5% these benefits count for only 10% of the benefits now.

The choice of discount rate is important in public policy, especially when benefits occur in the far future. Too high a discount rate implies that governments invest little in the benefits of future generations. Most governments use a discount rate between 2% and 5%. As Fig. 11.1 shows, this means that current benefits get substantially more weight than future benefits.

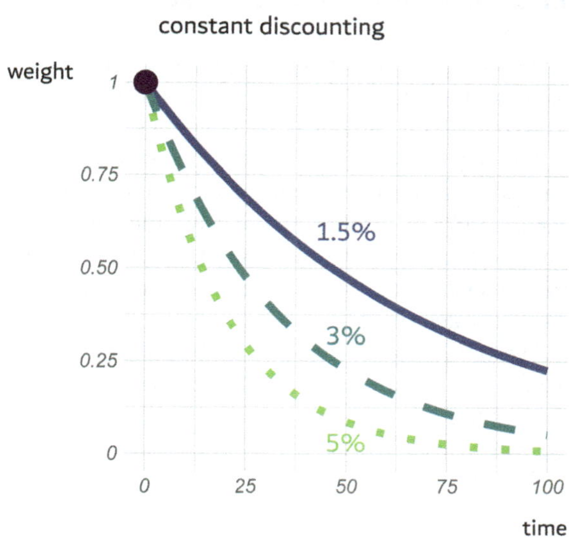

Fig. 11.1 The weights of benefits at different time points for discount rates 1.5%, 3%, and 5%

The Netherlands and France adjust the discount rate for the riskiness of the project. The Dutch discount rate for riskless projects is 1.6%, the standard rate is 2.25% and the rate for high-risk projects is 2.9%. France uses a risk-free rate of 1.2% and adds a term $\beta \times \pi$ to it, where β is a measure of the riskiness of the project (it is zero if the project has no risk) and $\pi = 2\%$ is a risk premium.

Extension 11.1: Ramsey Equation

If a project is riskless, economic theory says that the social discount rate should be based on an equation derived by Frank Ramsey (see Bio 10.1). Ramsey's equation is $\rho_s = \tau + \gamma \times \mu$, where ρ_s is the social discount rate, τ is the pure rate of time preference (impatience), γ reflects aversion to intergenerational inequality and μ is the growth rate of per capita consumption. In a growing economy, future generations will be better off and investing in the future will make them even better off. Depending on how undesirable we find inequality (the value of γ), we must discount these future benefits. If there is uncertainty about the growth of per capita consumption we should reduce ρ_s by $0.5 \times \sigma^2 \times \gamma^2$, where σ^2 is the variance of the distribution of μ. Ramsey's equation gives an argument why money and health may be discounted differently: both attitudes to inequality and the growth rate differ between health and consumption per capita.

11.3 Measuring Discount Rates

The social discount rate is usually based on some aggregate of individual discount rates. In the Ramsey equation (see Extension 11.1), we must know δ. A way to do so is to measure individual discount rates.

We can measure individual discount rates by market choices. Economists estimated discount rates from the extra amount people are willing to pay for more energy-efficient durables, more fuel-efficient and safer cars, from their food consumption, and from the choices of US military leaving the army between an annuity paying an amount every year and an immediate lump sum payment. The estimated discount rates are at least 10%.

For many goods (especially public goods), market data are unavailable. For these, we can use experiments to measure discount rates. Many of these experiments ask choices like:

€100 now or €x in one year.

They then vary x until the subject is indifferent. If we write this indifference in terms of constant discounting we get:

$$U(100) = \delta \times U(x). \tag{11.4}$$

To find δ (and thus ρ) from Eq. 11.4 we need to know U. Many studies assume that U is linear. Then $\delta = {}^{100}/_{x}$. This linear approach gives a wide array of discount rates varying from negative (suggesting that people prefer good outcomes later or bad outcomes earlier) to 1500%. Discount rates are usually high. A meta-analysis of 56 studies found a mean discount rate of 33% (Matousek et al. 2022). Such discount rates mean that the weight of benefits 20 years in the future is 0.3% of the weight of current benefits. They ignore the interests of future generations.

Linear utility may not hold and there is no normative reason why it should. If utility is concave, reflecting decreasing marginal utility, the linear approach will overestimate discount rates.

Exercise 11.3: Concave Utility Lowers the Discount Rate

Suppose that an agent is indifferent between €100 now and €120 in one year. Compute the discount rate

1. when utility is linear ($U(x) = x$).
2. when utility is concave (e.g. take $U(x) = \sqrt{x}$).

To correct the discount rate for utility, we must first compute the utilities of 100 and x and then compute the discount rate as ${}^{U(100)}/_{U(x)}$. There are several ways to do so:

1. Several studies **measure utility for risk** and then assume that this utility function can also be applied in Eq. 11.4. Steffen Andersen and co-authors (2008) measure utility by considering choices over risky prospects assuming expected utility. They then use this utility function to analyse intertemporal choices. This correction for utility curvature reduces the discount rate from 25% to 10%. Kan Takeuchi (2011) estimates ${}^{U(100)}/_{U(x)}$ by asking subjects for which probability p they are indifferent between €100 for sure and the risky prospect x_p0.

Exercise 11.4: Takeuchi

Show that the indifference $100 \sim x_p0$ implies under expected utility that

$$p = \frac{U(100)}{U(x)}.$$

A limitation of this approach is the assumption that utility for risk and time are the same. We saw in Chapter 3 that there is little support for this. An additional limitation is the assumption of expected utility. We saw in Chapter 9 that this is problematic.

2. James Andreoni and Charles Sprenger (2012) use allocations of tokens at two different dates to estimate time preferences. They call this the **convex time budget method**. Subjects are free to choose any allocation between the two dates. Tokens at the earlier date are worth less. For example, in one of their questions subjects had to allocate the 100 tokens when they were worth \$0.18 now or \$0.20 70 days later. From these choices, they derive the implied discount rate, which is around 30%. Their method has several limitations:

   - They assume a parametric form for utility. They use power utility, but show that their method also works for exponential utility.
   - It is complex for subjects to determine the exact allocation. If preferences are imprecise or they use corner solutions (all tokens to either the present or the future), then the method cannot measure discounting precisely.
   - They estimate utility curvature and the discount rate simultaneously and the two parameters may interact. Several pairs of discounting may describe the data. There is no clean separation between utility and discounting.

3. Mohammed Abdellaoui, Arthur Attema, and I (2010) designed a method that measured utility for time without making parametric assumptions and that achieved a clean separation between utility and discounting. Our method also works under more general discounting models (see Eq. 11.10). It assumes that intertemporal utility is additive. The method is explained in Extension 11.2. We found discount rates of 10% for gains and of 5% for losses.

Extension 11.2: A Clean Separation Between Utility and Discounting

Our method consists of two steps. G_0g_t denotes the temporal prospect that gives G now and g at time point t. We fix three outcomes G, G^*, g^0 and a time point t. We then ask a series of indifferences $G_0g_t^j \sim G_0^*g_t^{j-1}$, $j = 1, \ldots, k$.

Exercise 11.5: Standard Sequence of Outcomes

Show by substituting Eq. 11.1 that these indifferences imply that $U(g^j) - U(g^{j-1}) = U(g^1) - U(g^0)$ for $j = 1, \ldots, k$.

The sequence $g^0, g^1, \ldots, g^k$ is a **standard sequence of outcomes**. Because U is cardinal, we can set $U(g^k) = 1$ and $U(g^0) = 0$.

Exercise 11.6: Utility

Show that $U(g^j) = {}^j/_k$.

We next ask for indifferences $z \sim g_t^k 0$.

Exercise 11.7: Discounting

Show that under constant discounting this indifference implies that $U(z) = \frac{1}{(1+\rho)^t}$.

$U(z)$ can be determined using the elements of the standard sequence. Exercise 11.7 shows how we can measure the discount rate ρ. By repeating these indifferences for different time points t, we can get several estimates of the discount rate.

11.4 Is Constant Discounting Normative?

Many economists see constant discounting as normative, because it leads to **time consistent** behaviour. It means that people do not change their preferences over time. They make the same trade-off between two periods regardless of when they choose.[1]

Suppose, that agents prefer €120 in 12 weeks to €100 in 10 weeks. So they prefer to wait 2 more weeks to receive an extra €20. Then time consistency means that they stick to their plan and that after the ten weeks they are still willing to wait 2 more weeks for the extra €20.

Exercise 11.8: Time Consistency

Use Eq. 11.1 to show that constant discounting implies time consistency in the above example.

Exercise 11.8 shows that constant discounting implies time consistency. Robert Strotz (1955) showed that the implication also runs the other way: a time consistent agent must be a constant rate discounter. If we deviate from constant discounting, we must give up time consistency.

[1] Paul Samuelson, who first proposed constant discounting, did not argue that it was normative. He wrote that the assumption of constant discounting was a simplification that should be tested empirically.

Extension 11.3: Time Consistency, Stationarity, and Time Invariance

Time consistency and constant discounting are not the same. The central axiom of constant discounting is stationarity, proposed by Tjalling Koopmans in 1960. Let (x, t) stand for "receiving x at time point t".

Definition 11.3: Stationarity

Preferences $\succcurlyeq$ satisfy **stationarity** if for all outcomes x, y, time points s, t and positive constants $\epsilon > 0$:

$$(x, s) \succcurlyeq (y, t) \iff (x, s+\epsilon) \succcurlyeq (y, t+\epsilon).$$

Stationarity says that preferences over timed outcomes depend only on their difference in timing. Stationarity is a property of preferences at a given point in time. By contrast, time consistency is a condition about how preferences evolve over time. If at time point 0, the agent prefers (120, 12) to (100, 10) then this should also be true at any time point between 0 and 10. Formally,

Definition 11.4: Time Consistency

Let $\{\succcurlyeq_t\}_{t=0}^n$ be a set of timed preference relations. The set satisfies **time consistency** if for all outcomes $x < y$ and for all time points $r \leq s < t$:

$$(x, s) \succcurlyeq_0 (y, t) \iff (x, s) \succcurlyeq_r (y, t).$$

To relate stationarity and time consistency, we need to assume that preferences do not change over time.

Definition 11.5: Time Invariance

The set $\{\succcurlyeq_t\}_{t=0}^n$ satisfies **time invariance** if for all outcomes $x < y$, for all time points $s < t$, and for all $\epsilon > 0$:

$$(x, s) \succcurlyeq_0 (y, t) \iff (x, s+\epsilon) \succcurlyeq_\epsilon (y, t+\epsilon).$$

Time invariance says that only the time relative to the moment of evaluation matters. If we shift everything by the same time period ϵ then this does not affect preferences.

Yoram Halevy (2015) showed that under time invariance, stationarity and time consistency are the same. In his experiment, time inconsistent subjects satisfied stationarity (and thus constant discounting) half of the time. They violated time invariance. The link between constant discounting and time consistency, and thus the normative defence of constant discounting, is less strong than often thought.

11.5 Violations of Constant Discounting

Even though constant discounting is widely used, people deviate from it. Richard Thaler (1981) was the first to show this and his findings have been confirmed in many later studies. What is more, the violations of constant discounting are simple. They do not require clever arrangements of choices.

The violations of constant discounting can be summarized by five patterns.

1. The **common difference effect**. The central axiom of constant discounting is stationarity (see Extension 11.3). By stationarity, preferences between timed outcomes (x, t) depend only on the difference in timing between the outcomes. If agents are indifferent between €100 now and €120 in 2 months then they should also be indifferent between €100 in 10 months and €120 in 12 months, because the difference in the time of receipt stays the same.
   However, differences in the time of receipt become less important with the passage of time. If agents are indifferent between €100 now and €120 in 2 months then they will prefer €120 in 12 months to €100 in 10 months. People become more patient as time goes by.
   George Loewenstein and Drazen Prelec (1992) call this the common difference effect. It is similar to the common ratio effect in decision under risk. The common ratio effect implies that the difference between probabilities becomes less important if we multiply them by a common constant. Consequently, preferences shift in the direction of the prospect with the larger payoff. The common difference effect says that the ratio between discount factors becomes less important if we add a common delay to all outcomes. Again, this favours the prospect giving the larger payoff.

Exercise 11.9: Decreasing Discount Rates

The common difference effect says that if $(100, 0) \sim (120, 2)$ then agents will be indifferent between 100 in 10 months and x in 12 months for $x < 120$. Show that this implies that the discount rate decreases and, thus, agents give more weight to the future. In other words, the common difference effect implies **decreasing impatience**.

2. The **magnitude effect**. The magnitude effect says that people are more patient for larger outcomes. For example, Thaler's subjects were indifferent between \$15 now and \$60 in a year, between \$250 now and \$350 in a year, and between \$3000 now and \$4000 in a year. Multiplying the outcomes by a common constant (> 1) led to more patience.

Exercise 11.10: The Magnitude Effect

Show in the above example that discount rates fall for larger outcomes if utility is linear.

The magnitude effect leads to two problems for constant discounting. First, it is found for people with different wealth levels. This suggests that preferences are defined over changes with respect to a reference point (reference-dependence) instead of over absolute amounts, which is what constant discounting assumes. Second, the magnitude effect is inconsistent with concave utility, which is commonly assumed. This point is technical. I explain it in Extension 11.4.

The magnitude effect is similar to an outcome effect for risk preferences discussed by Harry Markowitz (1952). Markowitz suggested that people are risk loving for small gains and large losses and risk averse for large gains and small losses. This differs from the fourfold pattern of risk attitudes discussed in Chapter 9. The fourfold pattern says what happens to risk attitudes when the size of the probabilities changes. Markowitz's pattern says what happens when the size of the outcomes changes. It has largely been ignored in behavioural economics. Marc Scholten and Daniel Read (2014) found support for Markowitz's pattern for gains.

Extension 11.4: The Magnitude Effect Excludes Concave Utility

Let w be the agent's current wealth. Suppose that q is the willingness to pay now for a gain of x at time point t. In terms of constant discounted utility this means:

$$U(w-q)+\delta^t \times U(w+x)=U(w)+\delta^t \times U(w). \tag{11.5}$$

Solving for δ^t gives:

$$\delta^t=\frac{U(w)-U(w-q)}{U(w+x)-U(w)}. \tag{11.6}$$

If we multiply both q and x by a positive constant $\alpha > 1$ Eq. 11.5 becomes:

$$U(w-\alpha q)+\delta^t \times U(w+\alpha x)-U(w)-\delta^t \times U(w). \tag{11.7}$$

Differentiating equation 11.7 by α and letting α go to 1 gives:

$$-qU'(w-q) + x\delta^t U'(w+x), \quad (11.8)$$

which must be positive by the magnitude effect. Substituting Eq. 11.6 for δ^t and rearranging gives:

$$qU'(w-q)\big[U(w+x)-U(w)\big] < xU'(w+x)\big[U(w)-U(w-q)\big]. \quad (11.9)$$

Because U is concave, $\frac{U(w+x)-U(w)}{x} > U'(w+x)$ and $U'(w-q) > \frac{U(w)-U(w-q)}{q}$. However, this violates Eq. 11.9, so U cannot be concave.

3. The **gain-loss asymmetry**. Losses are typically discounted less than gains. This is what Mohammed Abdellaoui, Arthur Attema, and I found. It also appeared in the meta-analysis of Matousek et al. (2022). Many subjects even prefer a loss now to a loss in the future. Marjon van der Pol and John Cairns (2000) found that such negative discounting is common for health. Many people prefer to have spells of ill-health (including visits to the dentist) over sooner rather than later. Perhaps they feel dread.
   The gain-loss asymmetry violates constant discounting just like the reflection effect violates expected utility. Both constant discounting and expected utility assume that preferences are defined over final wealth levels and gains and losses are integrated into wealth. By contrast, the gain-loss asymmetry suggests that people segregate gains and losses from their wealth.
4. The **delay-speedup asymmetry**. People require a larger compensation to delay the delivery of a good from time s to time $t > s$ than they are willing to pay to speed up the delivery of the good from t to s. This is similar to the WTP-WTA disparity, which, as we saw in Chapter 7, can be explained by loss aversion. Delay and paying money are losses and these weight more than the gains speedup and getting compensation.
5. **Preferences for increasing sequences and variation**. In the above violations temporal prospects only had one outcome. Two types of violations have been found for sequences of outcomes. The first is a preference for improving over declining sequences (holding the total constant). For example, people prefer increasing income profiles over constant or decreasing ones.

Exercise 11.11: Increasing Sequences

Show that a preference for increasing sequences violates positive discounting.

The other sequence effect is a more serious challenge for constant discounting. People prefer to spread outcomes over time and have a preference for variation. I definitely prefer arroz a banda[2] over pasta, but if given the choice between eating arroz every day of the week or varying it with pasta on Tuesday and Friday, I prefer the latter.

Exercise 11.12: Preference for Variation

Show that the constant discounting model cannot explain such preference for variation.

11.6 Alternative Models

Alternatives to constant discounting generally assume the following functional form:

Definition 11.6: General Discounting

According to **general discounting**, temporal prospects $(x_0, \ldots, x_n)$ are evaluated as:

$$V(x_0, \ldots, x_n) = \sum_{t=0}^{n} \phi(t) \times U(x_n), \tag{11.10}$$

where $\phi(t)$ is a discount function.

The alternatives differ in their specification of the discount function $\phi(t)$. Before I discuss them, let me say a few words about the utility function.

11.6.1 Utility

To explain the gain-loss asymmetry and the delay-speedup asymmetry, the utility function must be reference-dependent and satisfy loss aversion.

[2] Arroz a banda is a specialty from the Alicante region made of rice with fresh seafood. Foreigners often confuse it with paella, which is a mistake.

Exercise 11.13: Loss Aversion Explains Preference for Increasing Sequences

Explain that reference-dependence and loss aversion can also explain the preference for increasing sequences of outcomes if we assume that people's reference point adapts to the most recently experienced outcome.

To explain the magnitude effect we need to add a condition to the reference-dependent utility function. The magnitude effect says that if agents are indifferent between q now and x at period t then they will prefer αx at time t to αq now when $\alpha > 1$. In terms of Eq. 11.10 this implies that:

$$\frac{U(q)}{U(x)} > \frac{U(\alpha q)}{U(\alpha x)}. \tag{11.11}$$

Equation 11.11 says that the same proportional change in payoffs leads to a larger increase in utility at higher payoff levels. The utility function is more linear for higher payoffs or, what is the same, it is more elastic for larger payoffs. To explain the Markowitz pattern of risk attitudes (risk loving for small gains but risk averse for large gains), the utility function must be less elastic for larger payoffs. This suggests, once again, that utility for time differs from utility for risk. Mohammed Abdellaoui, Olivier L'Haridon, and I (2013) found no support for increasing elasticity of the intertemporal utility function.

General discounting (Eq. 11.10) cannot explain a preference for variation, because it is additive. To explain it we need interactions between periods. Itzhak Gilboa (1989) proposed a model that can explain preference for variation, but, as far as I know, it has not been used in applications and the topic of modelling interactions between time periods remains unexplored.

11.6.2 Discounting

All alternatives to constant discounting explain that discount rates decrease over time. Two early proposals were **proportional discounting**, which has $\phi(t) = {}^{1}/_{(1+\alpha t)}$, and **power discounting**, which has $\phi(t) = {}^{1}/_{(1+t)^{\beta}}$. Exercise 11.14 shows that proportional and power discounting both imply that discount rates fall over time.

Exercise 11.14: Proportional and Power Discounting

The discount rate ρ_t at time point t is approximately equal to:

$$\rho_t = 1 - \frac{\phi(t+1)}{\phi(t)}.$$

Show that proportional and power discounting imply that discount rates decline with t.

The β - δ model

The most widely used alternative for constant discounting is the β - δ model, also known as **quasi-hyperbolic discounting**.

Definition 11.7: The β-δ Model

According to the β - δ model, temporal prospects $(x_0, \ldots, x_n)$ are evaluated as:

$$V(x_0, \ldots, x_n) = U(x_0) + \beta \sum_{t=0}^{n} \delta^{t-1} \times U(x_n), \tag{11.12}$$

where U is a cardinal utility function, $0 < \beta < 1$, and δ a constant discount factor

The β - δ model differs from constant discounting by multiplying the discount factors for all future periods by a constant β. β shows the extra weight given to the present. The β - δ model deviates from constant discounting by this **immediacy effect**, the different treatment of the present compared with the future. The immediacy effect is similar to the certainty effect in decision under risk, where people treat options that are certain different from options that are risky. If $\beta = 1$, the β - δ model is equal to constant discounting. Figure 11.2 shows that (for given δ), smaller values of β means more overweighting of the present relative to the future. β indicates the degree of **present bias**, the gap between the present and the future.

The β - δ model deviates minimally from constant discounting. It only violates stationarity when one of the outcomes is received immediately. When all outcomes are delayed, the model satisfies stationarity. Hence, β - δ discounting satisfies what we may call **quasi-stationarity** (Montiel Olea and Strzalecki 2014)

Exercise 11.15: β - δ

Show that the β - δ model explains that discount rates fall over time.

We saw that constant discounting is the only model in which agents are time consistent. Because the β - δ model differs from constant discounting by the parameter β, you might think that β determines an agent's propensity to be time inconsistent. The lower β the more likely is time inconsistent behaviour.

This is only true if δ is held constant. In general, time inconsistency is determined jointly by β and δ. If δ is low, agents will always prefer the sooner outcome regardless of β. Consequently, they will never be time inconsistent.

Rogier Potter van Loon, Drazen Prelec, and I (2022) showed that a measure of time inconsistency in the β - δ model is ${}^{\ln \beta}/_{\ln \delta}$. It measures the number of periods in which an agent is vulnerable to time inconsistency. The larger it is, the more likely the agent is time inconsistent.

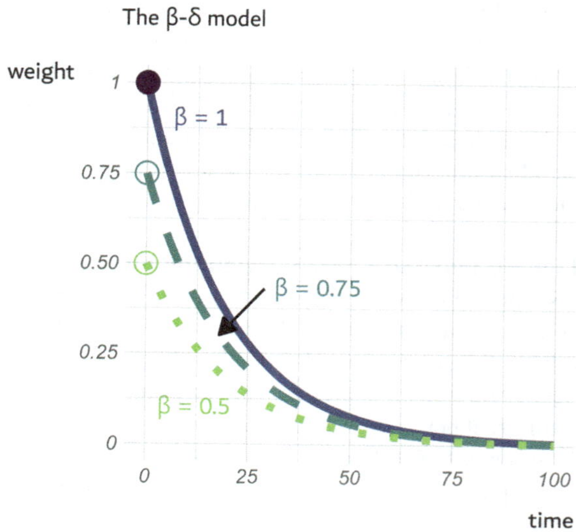

Fig. 11.2 The β - δ model for different values of β and $\delta = 0.5$

Exercise 11.16: A Measure of Time Inconsistency

Consider two agents who behave according to the β - δ model. Agent A has $\beta = 0.5$ and $\delta = 0.5$. Agent B has $\beta = 0.8$ and $\delta = 0.9$. Both have linear utility. Let there be two options: €100 in 5 years and €120 in 6 years.

1. Show that agent A is time consistent and will prefer the sooner option both now and after 5 years have passed.
2. Show that agent B will be time inconsistent and will switch options after 5 years have passed.
3. Show that $\ln \beta / \ln \delta$ is higher for agent B than for agent A.

The β - δ model can be seen as a conflict between two selves, one impatient, impulsive, and short-term oriented, the other patient, rational, and more long-term oriented. The impulsive self is characterized by β, the short-term discount rate, the rational self by δ, the long-term discount rate.

George Loewenstein calls this the **hot-cold empathy gap**. In hot states, the impatient impulsive self takes control. In cold states, the patient and rational self takes over.

Because β - δ discounting deviates minimally from constant discounting, it is useful in economic applications. It has been used to analyse people's undersaving (Laibson 1997) and smoking behaviour (Gruber and Köszegi 2001). The question whether smoking is rational or the result of time inconsistent preferences affects health policy. If it is rational, economic theory says that a tax on smoking should only compensate its external effects (the damage caused to other people's health). If smoking reflects time inconsistency then the tax should also include the internal effects (the harm caused by the impulsive self on the rational self). If the costs of smoking (which increase because of the higher tax) outweigh the benefits, people will quit or not even start smoking. Something the long-term self appreciates. The tax works as a commitment device that reduces the (short-term) smoker's self-control problems.

Even though the β - δ model is popular in economic analysis, it does not describe people's time preferences as good as other models. Let us therefore turn to two models that do better empirically.

Loewenstein and Prelec's Weighting Function β - δ only assumes a difference in discounting between the present and the future. Different future time points are discounted by a constant rate. Loewenstein and Prelec propose a discount function that relaxes this assumption. Remember that constant discounting says that preferences between timed outcomes depend only on their difference in timing. So, if agents are indifferent between €100 now and €120 in 2 months, they should also be indifferent between, say, €100 in 10 months and €120 in 12 months.

Empirical evidence suggests that people become more patient with time. Loewenstein and Prelec therefore replace stationarity, the assumption of constant discounting that

$$(x, 0) \sim (y, s) \iff (x, t) \sim (y, t + s) \tag{11.13}$$

by

$$(x, 0) \sim (y, s) \iff (x, t) \sim (y, kt + s), \tag{11.14}$$

where k is a constant that depends on x and y.

Exercise 11.17: Loewenstein and Prelec

Show that the common difference effect implies that $k > 1$.

Equation 11.14 implies that the discount function has the form:

$$\phi(t) = (1 + \alpha t)^{-\beta/\alpha}, \alpha, \beta > 0. \tag{11.15}$$

In Eq. 11.15, α determines the deviation from constant discounting. The larger α, the larger the deviation. If α goes to zero, Eq. 11.15 is equivalent to constant discounting. β can be seen as the discount rate of constant discounting. The degree of time inconsistency in Loewenstein Prelec (LP) discounting is determined only by α (see Extension 11.5). This unlike β - δ discounting where, as we saw in Exercise 11.16, it is determined by β and δ jointly.

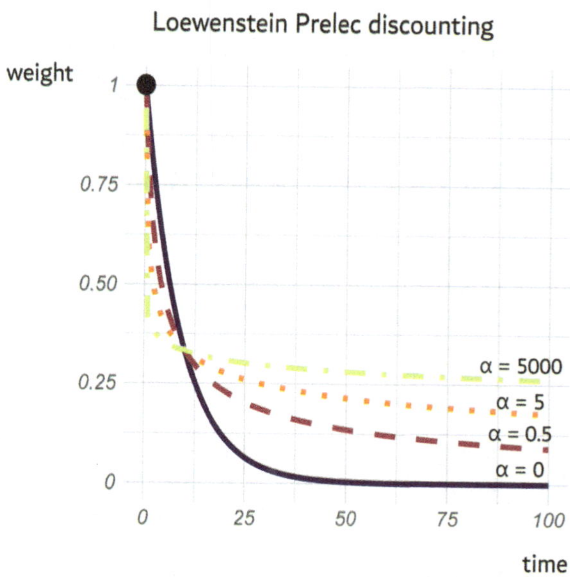

Fig. 11.3 Loewenstein and Prelec discounting for various values of α and β such that the curves cross at time = 10

Exercise 11.18: Special Cases

1. Show that proportional discounting is the special case of equation 11.15 where $\alpha = \beta$.
2. Show that power discounting is the special case of equation 11.15 where $\alpha = 1$.

Figure 11.3 shows the generalized hyperbolic discounting function for various values of α. I have adjusted β so that all graphs have weight $1/3$ for $t = 10$. The figure shows that LP discounting gives more weight to the farther future than constant discounting (the case $\alpha = 0$). This makes it more suitable to analyse long-term projects. As α becomes large (the case $\alpha = 5000$ in the figure), the discount function looks like a step function that gives weight 1 to the present and the same weight to all future time points. In other words, the agent distinguishes the present and the future but treats future time periods as one.

Extension 11.5: A Measure of Time Inconsistency

Kirsten Rohde (2010) developed the **hyperbolic factor** to measure time inconsistency without making assumptions about utility. Suppose we find two indifferences:

$$(x, s) \sim (y, t) \text{ and } (x, s + \sigma) \sim (y, t + \tau),$$

where $y \succ x$ The hyperbolic factor (HF) is defined as:

$$HF = \frac{\tau - \sigma}{t\sigma - s\tau}. \tag{11.16}$$

Exercise 11.19: Hyperbolic Factor

Suppose $t\sigma > s\tau$.

1. Show that decreasing impatience implies that $HF > 0$.
2. Show that under constant discounting $HF = 0$.
3. Show that under β - δ discounting $HF > 0$ if $s = 0$ and $HF = 0$ if $s > 0$.

Exercise 11.19 shows that we can test constant and β - δ discounting by computing the hyperbolic factor. We can also test other discount models. Under LP discounting the hyperbolic factor is equal to α (which shows that time inconsistency under LP discounting is determined by α only). Under power and proportional discounting the hyperbolic factor is equal to 1 and $\beta = \alpha$, respectively.

Empirical studies using the hyperbolic factor show that LP discounting and proportional discounting perform best.

Constant Sensitivity

The above discount functions have two limitations. First, they cannot explain increasing impatience $(x, s) \sim (y, t)$ and $(x, s + \sigma) \succ (y, t + \sigma)$. Up to one-third of the subjects in experiments are increasingly impatient. For these subjects we cannot estimate their discount functions. Some studies even found increasing impatience at the aggregate level, which means that we cannot estimate discount functions for aggregate data.

A second limitation is that they exclude strongly decreasing impatience. For example, indifferences between €100 now and €125 in 1 week and €100 in 4 weeks and €125 in 9 weeks cannot hold under LP discounting, because impatience decreases too quickly. However, these indifferences seem reasonable and we find them empirically.

The **constant sensitivity** discount function solves these problems. It can model any kind of impatience: decreasing, strongly decreasing, or increasing. A property of the function is that it can make a distinction between the near future, which is only discounted mildly, and the far future, which is discounted more heavily. This makes sense. When thinking of the present, people may include tomorrow or next week. The constant sensitivity function can take this into account.

To define the constant sensitivity function, we distinguish three cases:[3]

1. $b < 0$ (strong decreasing impatience): $\phi(t) = \exp^{(at)^b}$.
2. $b = 0$: $\phi(t) = \frac{1}{at}$.
3. $b > 0$: $\phi(t) = \exp^{-(at)^b}$.

Constant discounting is the special case $b = 1$. Figure 11.4 shows several cases. Figure 11.4a shows the constant sensitivity function for negative values of b, the case of strongly decreasing impatience. The functions drop fast initially and then level off.

Figure 11.4b shows constant sensitivity discounting for positive values of b. For values lower than 1, the constant sensitivity function looks like LP discounting and gives more weight to the far future than constant discounting. As b becomes larger, the constant sensitivity function looks more like a "step" function, where all time periods up to some threshold get weight 1 (the "extended present") and all time periods past that threshold get zero weight.

Figure 11.4 shows that the constant sensitivity function gives more flexibility to model time preferences. This flexibility is useful: the constant sensitivity function generally fits better than the other functions discussed in this chapter.

11.7 Naive Versus Sophisticated Time Inconsistency

The alternatives to constant discounting imply that agents can be time inconsistent. To what extent are they aware of this? The literature distinguishes between **naive** and **sophisticated** agents. Naive agents believe that they will stick to their plans and be time consistent. Sophisticated agents know that they are time inconsistent and adjust their plans accordingly.

Table 11.1 shows a patient who has to decide when to take a treatment giving temporary pain relief. The patient can only receive it once due to negative side effects. The table shows the increase in quality of life depending on when the patient gets the treatment.

Suppose the patient (or their doctor who decides for them) behaves according to β - δ discounting with $\beta = 0.7$ and $\delta = 1$. Suppose utility is linear in quality of life (or that the outcomes in the table are utilities).

[3] In the first two cases, $b \leq 0$, we must exclude $t = 0$, because the function is not defined there.

Fig. 11.4 The constant sensitivity discount function

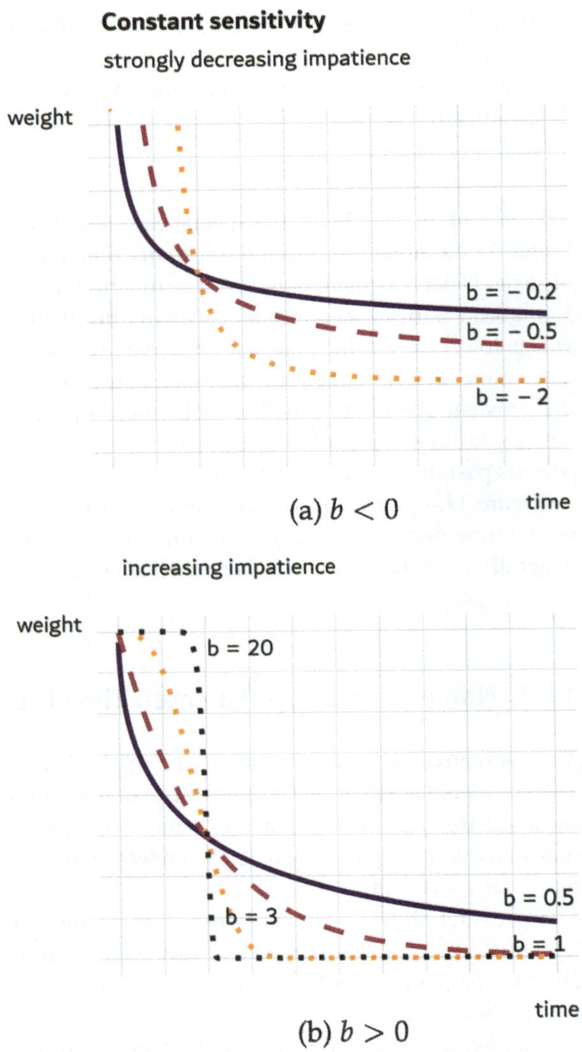

Table 11.1 Example naive versus sophisticated

1 week	2 weeks	3 weeks	4 weeks
4	5	7	9

Exercise 11.20: Constant Discounting

Show that a constant discounter ($\beta = 1$) would choose to take the treatment in week 4 (assuming $\delta = 1$ and utility linear).

Constant discounters are time consistent and stick to their plan. Naive agents do not. Exercise 11.21 shows that they will be time inconsistent and take the treatment in week 3 even though initially they prefer to take it in week 4.

Exercise 11.21: A Naive Patient

Suppose that patients are naive and unaware of their time inconsistency.

1. Show that in week 1 the patient concludes that it is best to take the treatment in week 4.
2. Show that in week 2 the patient still prefers the treatment in week 4.
3. Show that in week 3 the patient prefers to take the treatment now (i.e. in week 3).

Sophisticated patients know that they are time inconsistent and that they will never take the treatment in week 4. They know that when they arrive at week 3 they will take the treatment then. Given that it will not be chosen, they remove treatment in week 4 from their choice set.

Exercise 11.22: A Sophisticated Patient

Show that the patient also never will take the treatment in week 3 (Hint: show that in week 2 they prefer the treatment then instead of waiting one more week).

Exercise 11.22 shows that the patients will also remove treatment in week 3 from their choice set. So, the choice is between treatment in week 1 or week 2 and the patient will choose to take it in week 1.

The above model is too simple. First, it is unlikely that agents are fully naive. It is even more unlikely that they are fully sophisticated and can perfectly predict their time inconsistency. The idea of sophisticated agents is subject to Rubinstein's criticism, discussed in Chapter 2. It explains an irrationality (time consistency) by assuming a high degree of rationality (perfect foresight of this irrationality). Why would sophisticated agents fall prey to time inconsistency in the first place? Instead of removing the options they never choose from their choice set, it makes more sense to remove the options that produce time inconsistencies. For example, the patient could agree with the doctor to make the treatment unavailable in week 3. This would remove any time inconsistency.

A solution is to assume that agents are partly aware of their time inconsistency. In the example, naive agents think that their β is 1, while sophisticated agents know that their β is 0.7. In an intermediate case, partial sophistication, agents know that their β is less than 1, but they think it is higher than 0.7. However, this case is unsustainable in the long run. Exercise 11.23 shows that such agents believe they will stick to their optimal plan, but come to realize that they do not. The question then is how they react to this. Repeated time inconsistency may make them update their estimated β in the direction of their true β and we end up with fully sophisticated agents.

Exercise 11.23: A Partially Sophisticated Agent

Show that partially sophisticated agents with $\beta = 0.85$ believe that in week 3 they choose to take the treatment in week 4.

Extension 11.6: Commitment and Self-Control

Commitment means that agents restrict their options so as not to be tempted. A classic example is Homer's story of Odysseus and the temptation of the Sirens. Odysseus had been warned about the Sirens by Circe, a sorcerer, who had turned his men into pigs, but later fell in love with him.

The Sirens lived on an island surrounded by sharp rocks. With their singing, the sweetness of which no man could resist, they lured sailors to their island where they crashed on the rocks and died. Odysseus was determined to hear the singing of the Sirens without succumbing to their temptation. Circe told him how to do it. He should order his men to tie him to the mast. Then they should plug their ears with beeswax so they could not hear the singing. If he would ask them to untie him, they should tie him even tighter. And so it went. As soon as Odysseus heard the singing, he became enchanted and ordered his men to free him and steer towards the island. They ignored him, tied him even tighter, and only when the Sirens' singing could no longer be heard, did they remove the wax and free their grateful leader.

The literature often identifies commitment with self-control. However, they are different. I will explain this using a model developed by Faruk Gul and Wolfgang Pesendorfer (2001). Their model has two periods. In the first period, agents choose the set of alternatives among which they choose in the second period. Suppose agents prefer in period 1 to consume x instead of y in period 2. In Odysseus' case, period 2 is the moment his ship passes the island of the Sirens, x is being tied to the mast and y is not being tied to the mast and be free to steer to the island. Let $\{x\}$ describe the situation where the agent can only choose x in period 2 (i.e. y is not an option) and $\{x, y\}$ is the situation where both x and y are available.

Standard economic theory says that agents can never be made better off by removing options from their choice set. However, in period 2 agents are tempted to choose y (think of Odysseus). That is agents prefer to choose x in period 2 when only x is available than to choose x when both x and y are available. The reason is that if both x and y are available the agent must exert self-control, which is unpleasant. For Odysseus self-control was even impossible.

If y is tempting then the agents prefer $\{x\}$ to $\{x, y\}$. This is called preference for **commitment**. If the agents choose x at period 2 even though y is also available they exert **self-control**. That is, they prefer $\{x, y\}$ to $\{y\}$.

Commitment and self-control are distinct. Commitment is a period 1 decision to have smaller choice sets in period 2. Self-control is a period 2 decision to choose x even though y is tempting.

Gul and Pesendorfer characterize a preference for commitment by the following condition:

Definition 11.8: Set Betweenness

The preference $\succcurlyeq$ over choice sets (sets of available options) satisfies **set betweenness** if

$$A \succcurlyeq B \text{ implies } A \succcurlyeq A \cup B \succcurlyeq B.$$

Exercise 11.24: Preference for Commitment

Explain that set betweenness implies a preference for commitment.

Preferences over choice sets are represented by:

$$U(A) = \max_{x \in A} u(x) + v(x) - \max_{y \in A} v(y). \tag{11.17}$$

The function u ranks outcomes when the agent can avoid temptation through commitment. That is, it ranks the attractiveness of the outcomes as seen from the first period. The function v reflects the attractiveness of the outcomes in the second period.

Exercise 11.25: Cost of Self-Control

Explain that in Eq. 11.17 the term $\max_{y \in A} v(y) - v(x)$ measures the agent's cost of self-control.

By maximizing the sum of u and v, agents strike a balance between the utility under commitment and the cost of self-control.

11.8 Time and Risk

One reason why agents have time preference is that the future is uncertain. We also saw that various deviations from expected utility and constant discounting have similar structure. Several findings suggest that risk and time preferences are driven by the same psychological mechanisms:

1. The immediacy effect disappears when payoffs received now are risky (Keren and Roelofsma 1995). The certainty effect disappears when sure outcomes are delayed (Weber and Chapman 2005).
2. Probability weighting and decreasing impatience are related: the discount rates of subjects with more inverse S-shaped probability weighting decline faster (Epper et al. 2011).
3. Risk loving increases for outcomes in the future. The probability weighting function for future risk is more optimistic than the one for present risk (Abdellaoui et al. 2011).
4. The discount rate increases if we divide a period into subperiods. Theoretically, it should not matter whether we determine the discount rate for, say, a delay of 3 years directly (for example, by asking which payoff now is equivalent to €2000 in 3 years) or indirectly by determining the discount rate from year 0 to year 1, from year 1 to year 2, and from year 2 to year 3 separately and then multiplying these. However, Daniel Read (2001) showed that the indirect method led to higher discount rates. This is similar to partition dependence for probability judgments.

We can model the link between risk and time preference by taking into account that each future outcome is subject to survival risk[4] and to model this risk by prospect theory (Chakraborty et al. 2020; Epper and Fehr-Duda 2024). Suppose that an agent has each period a (constant) probability s to survive to the next period. The probability of surviving until period t is then s^t and a timed outcome (x, t) becomes a risky prospect $(s^t : (x, t))$. This prospect is evaluated as:

$$w(s^t) \times U(x) \times \delta^t, \tag{11.18}$$

where w is the probability weighting function and δ is the constant discount factor. The time weight in this model is

$$\phi(t) = w(s^t) \times \delta^t. \tag{11.19}$$

The discount rate ρ_t at point t is approximately:

$$\rho_t = 1 - \frac{\phi(t+1)}{\phi(t)}, \tag{11.20}$$

which is equal to

$$\rho_t = 1 - \frac{\delta \times w(s^{t+1})}{w(s^t)}. \tag{11.21}$$

[4] Sozou (1998) was a first to show that non-constant discounting can be the result of an unknown survival probability.

Equation 11.21 shows that if the ratio $\frac{w(s^{t+1})}{w(s^t)}$ decreases then discount rates fall as well. Over time, the survival probabilities become smaller. So, for discount rates to fall over time, the probability weighting function must satisfy for all $p < q$ and $0 < \lambda < 1$:

$$\frac{w(\lambda p)}{w(\lambda q)} \geq \frac{w(p)}{w(q)}. \tag{11.22}$$

In other words, the ratio of the probability weights must increase if probabilities are scaled down. This is called **subproportionality**.

Exercise 11.26: Subproportionality

Show that the common ratio effect (see Chapter 9) predicts subproportionality.

Subproportionality and inverse S are roughly the same. An example of a probability weighting function that always satisfies subproportionality is Prelec's function with $\gamma < 1$. The above analysis shows that decreasing impatience can be explained by probability weighting, i.e. attitudes towards risk.

The Probability and Time Trade-Off Model

Equation 11.18 treats risk and time separately. This cannot explain why the immediacy effect disappears when outcomes are risky. Manel Baucells and Franz Heukamp (2012) found that a majority of their subjects preferred a sure €100 now to a sure €110 in 4 weeks and a sure €110 in 30 weeks to a sure €100 in 26 weeks. This immediacy effect disappeared when the outcomes were risky: The same majority that preferred a sure €110 in 30 weeks to a sure €100 in 26 weeks preferred a 50% chance of €110 in 4 weeks to a 50% chance of €100 now.

Exercise 11.27: Risk and Time Interact

Show that a model that represents preferences over risky time prospects (x, p, t) (obtaining outcome x at time point t with probability p) as

$$V(x, p, t) = w(p) \times \delta^t \times u(x)$$

cannot explain that most people prefer a sure €100 now to a sure €110 in 4 weeks, but a 50% chance of €110 in 4 weeks to a 50% chance of €100 now.

Risk and time act as substitutes. To capture this, the **probability and time trade-off (PTT) model** of Baucella and Heukamp assumes a **probability discount rate** r_x that captures the trade-off between probability and time. It is decreasing in outcomes to capture the magnitude effect.

Definition 11.9: The PTT Model

The probability and time trade-off (PTT) model holds if preferences over risky time prospects (x, p, t) are represented as:

$$V(x, p, t) = w(pe^{-r_x t}) \times u(x). \quad (11.23)$$

Exercise 11.28: PTT

Show that the PTT model can explain that most people prefer a sure €100 now to a sure €110 in 4 weeks, but a 50% chance of €110 in 4 weeks to a 50% chance of €now.

Heuristic Models

Jane Ebert and Drazen Prelec (2007) suggest that time preferences are unstable and can easily be manipulated. For that reason, the models of this chapter may be too sophisticated. People may rely instead on a set of heuristics. One of these is **similarity** (Rubinstein 2003). Similarity says that in making a choice between options with two dimensions, like time prospects (x, t), people look first whether the options are similar on a dimension. If so, they decide on the basis of the other dimension. If not, they use another criterion. So if people choose between €100 now and €110 in 4 weeks, they may conclude that the options are sufficiently different on both dimensions and choose the option that is received earlier. However, when comparing €100 in 26 weeks and €110 in 30 weeks, they may conclude that waiting for 26 weeks and waiting for 30 weeks is similar and choose the larger money amount. So, similarity can explain the immediacy effect. Similarity leads to the lexicographic ordering that we discussed in Chapter 2.

References

Abdellaoui, M., A.E. Attema, and H. Bleichrodt. 2010. Intertemporal tradeoffs for gains and losses: An experimental measurement of discounted utility. *Economic Journal* 120: 845–866.

Abdellaoui, M., E. Diecidue, and A. Öncüler. 2011. Risk preferences at different time periods: An experimental investigation. *Management Science* 57: 975–987.

Abdellaoui, M., H. Bleichrodt, and O. L'Haridon. 2013. Sign-dependence in intertemporal choice. *Journal of Risk and Uncertainty* 47: 225–253.

Andersen, S., G.W. Harrison, M.I. Lau, and E.E. Rutström. 2008. Eliciting risk and time preferences. *Econometrica* 76: 583–618.

Andreoni, J., and C. Sprenger. 2012. Estimating time preferences from convex budgets. *American Economic Review* 102: 3333–3356.

Baucells, M., and F.H. Heukamp. 2012. Probability and time trade-off. *Management Science* 58: 831–842.

Bleichrodt, H., R.J. Potter van Loon, and D. Prelec. 2022. Beta-Delta or Delta-Tau? A reformulation of quasi-hyperbolic discounting. *Management Science* 68: 6326–6335.

Chakraborty, A., Y. Halevy, and K. Saito. 2020. The relation between behavior under risk and over time. *American Economic Review: Insights* 2: 1–16.

Ebert, J.E., and D. Prelec. 2007. The fragility of time: Time-insensitivity and valuation of the near and far future. *Management Science* 53: 1423–1438.

Epper, T.F., and H. Fehr-Duda. 2024. Risk in time: The intertwined nature of risk taking and time discounting. *Journal of the European Economic Association* 22: 310–354.

Epper, T., H. Fehr-Duda, and A. Bruhin. 2011. Viewing the future through a warped lens: Why uncertainty generates hyperbolic discounting. *Journal of Risk and Uncertainty* 43: 169–203.

Gilboa, I. 1989. Expectation and variation in multi-period decisions. *Econometrica* 57: 1153–1169.

Gruber, J., and B. Köszegi. 2001. Is addiction "rational"? Theory and evidence. *Quarterly Journal of Economics* 116: 1261–1303.

Gul, F., and W. Pesendorfer. 2001. Temptation and self-control. *Econometrica* 69: 1403–1435.

Halevy, Y. 2015. Time consistency: Stationarity and time invariance. *Econometrica* 83: 335–352.

Keren, G., and P. Roelofsma. 1995. Immediacy and certainty in intertemporal choice. *Organizational Behavior and Human Decision Processes* 63: 287–297.

Laibson, D. 1997. Golden eggs and hyperbolic discounting. *Quarterly Journal of Economics* 112: 443–478.

Loewenstein, G., and D. Prelec. 1992. Anomalies in intertemporal choice: Evidence and an interpretation. *Quarterly Journal of Economics* 107: 573–597.

Markowitz, H. 1952. The utility of wealth. *Journal of Political Economy* 60: 151–158.

Matousek, J., T. Havranek, and Z. Irsova. 2022. Individual discount rates: A meta-analysis of experimental evidence. *Experimental Economics* 25: 318–358.

Montiel Olea, J.L., and T. Strzalecki. 2014. Axiomatization and measurement of quasi-hyperbolic discounting. *Quarterly Journal of Economics* 129: 1449–1499.

Read, D. 2001. Is time-discounting hyperbolic or subadditive? *Journal of Risk and Uncertainty* 23: 5–32.

Rohde, K.I. 2010. The hyperbolic factor: A measure of time inconsistency. *Journal of Risk and Uncertainty* 41: 125–140.

Rubinstein, A. 2003. Economics and psychology? The case of hyperbolic discounting. *International Economic Review* 44: 1207–1216.

Scholten, M., and D. Read. 2014. Prospect theory and the "forgotten" fourfold pattern of risk preferences. *Journal of Risk and Uncertainty* 48: 67–83.

Sozou, P.D. 1998. On hyperbolic discounting and uncertain hazard rates. *Proceedings of the Royal Society of London. Series B: Biological Sciences* 265, 2015–2020.

Strotz, R.H. 1955. Myopia and inconsistency in dynamic utility maximization. *Review of Economic Studies* 23: 165–180.

Takeuchi, K. 2011. Non-parametric test of time consistency: Present bias and future bias. *Games and Economic Behavior* 71: 456–478.

Thaler, R. 1981. Some empirical evidence on dynamic inconsistency. *Economics Letters* 8: 201–207.

Van der Pol, M.M., and J.A. Cairns. 2000. Negative and zero time preference for health. *Health Economics* 9: 171–175.

Weber, B.J., and G.B. Chapman. 2005. The combined effects of risk and time on choice: Does uncertainty eliminate the immediacy effect? Does delay eliminate the certainty effect? *Organizational Behavior and Human Decision Processes* 96: 104–118.

Behavioural Economics and Policy 12

Welfare economics says that public decisions should be based on people's preferences. For that reason we put so much effort in measuring these preferences. They are assumed stable and independent of the context in which they are measured. Behavioural economics shows that these assumptions do not hold. People deviate from rational models and preferences are context-dependent. For example, we saw that their valuations of safety improvements depend on the starting value and whether we use willingness to pay or willingness to accept. Can valuations that are so unstable be used in public policy?

Behavioural economists made several proposals for how to use their insights in policy. The most influential are **nudges**.

12.1 Nudges

12.1.1 Libertarian Paternalism

Nudges were proposed by Richard Thaler and legal scholar Cass Sunstein (e.g. Thaler and Sunstein 2003, 2008, 2021). People often make choices that are not in their best interests. They save too little for their pension or choose inferior health care insurance. We have seen many reasons for this: present bias, status quo bias, default effects, and loss aversion, for example.

Thaler and Sunstein claim that these findings make paternalism unavoidable. Their classic example is a cafeteria owner who decides in which order to display food items. The order affects customers' choices, but is unrelated to their well-being. The owner can display the food such that customers choose the items that (according to the owner) are in their long-term interests or such that customers choose what they want. Even though the first choice is paternalistic, the second does not make sense, because

H. Bleichrodt, *Behavioural Economics*,
https://doi.org/10.1007/978-3-031-69166-9_12

customers lack well-defined preferences. If they can be affected by the order in which food is displayed then preferences do not exist. Paternalism is unavoidable.

However, paternalism need not be coercive. In the cafeteria example, customers do not have to choose the most prominently displayed food items. They are free to choose whatever they want. They are only nudged in a desirable direction. Thaler and Sunstein call this noncoercive paternalism **libertarian paternalism**. It is libertarian because people keep their freedom to choose and paternalistic because it aims to make people's lives better. It is also called **asymmetric paternalism**, because it helps those who make errors, while imposing little or no harm on those who choose rationally.

12.1.2 Nudge

Because paternalism is unavoidable and should be noncoercive, Thaler and Sunstein propose nudges.

Definition 12.1: Nudges

Nudges are interventions inspired by behavioural science that change people's behaviour towards what they would have chosen had they not been subject to specific limits of rationality without forbidding any options or significantly changing their economic incentives.

Nudges should be cheap and easy to avoid. They are not bans or mandates. Instead they alter the underlying **choice architecture**, the context in which people make their choices. An example are default effects of Chapter 7. Making donorship the default option, increased the proportion of blood donors. Changing the default leaves people's choice set intact: they can still choose not to be a donor. Nor do we change their incentives. Moreover, as one option has to be the default, paternalism is unavoidable. You may argue that we could make neither option the default and force people to choose. Thaler and Sunstein would reply that forcing people to choose is also paternalistic.

Nudges quickly became popular. Governments used them in policy and even created "nudge units": teams of behavioural experts who designed, tested, and implemented nudges. The Netherlands annually organizes the "Dag van het gedrag" (literally, day of behaviour, in Dutch it sounds better) where hundreds of policy makers and scientists meet to discuss the implementation of behavioural science in policy.

Nudges are based on the insights from behavioural science. The literature sometimes calls common sense interventions like writing a clear letter or sending an email reminder a nudge. As I want to show how behavioural economics can improve policy, I will instead discuss three examples, which use insights from behavioural economics.

12.1.3 Examples

Save More Tomorrow. One of the first examples of nudges was Thaler and Shlomo Benartzi's (2004) Save More Tomorrow (SMarT) programme. In many countries people save too little for retirement. In the US, more than half of employees cannot maintain their lifestyle when they retire. The aim of SMarT is to increase retirement saving. It consists of 4 elements, each inspired by behavioural economics.

1. People commit now to increase their saving rate in a few months. This counters the present bias that we discussed in Chapter 11.
2. The saving rate only increases when salary increases. Savings do not decrease income as they are paid out of income rises. This counters loss aversion.
3. People who sign up for the plan stay in it until their contributions reach a limit.

> **Exercise 12.1: SMarT**
>
> Explain that this part of the plan uses status quo bias (see Chapter 7) to make sure that people stay in the plan and keep saving until they have saved enough.

4. At any time people are free to opt out of the plan. This is to make it compatible with libertarian paternalism.

Participants in SMarT increased their savings from 3.5% to 13.6% of their income in 4 years. Benartzi and Thaler (2013) estimate that the programme led to a $7.4 billion increase in savings by the end of 2011.

Promoting Healthy Behaviours. George Loewenstein and Kevin Volpp show how insights from behavioural economics can promote healthy behaviours. They use two incentive schemes.

1. Participants put their own money in a deposit that they can only retrieve if they meet their health goals, like weight loss or smoking cessation. The contribution is usually matched by the researchers to give extra incentives. Because of loss aversion, losing the deposit hurts and people will be more motivated to reach their goals.
2. Each day they reach their goal participants take part in a lottery with a small (1 in 100) chance to win $100. Participants who do not reach their goal cannot take part in the lottery, but they know whether they would have won. Prospect theory with isolation says that by overweighting the small probability of winning, participants find the lottery attractive. Regret aversion says that people find being told that they would have won without taking part unattractive.

While around half of the subjects in the deposit and lottery schemes reached their weight goal, 10% in the control group (who only received dietary advice) did. However, the results did not last. Follow-up research showed that participants in the deposit treatment regained their weight after the study ended. For smoking, relapse was similar in the incentive and control treatments, although the overall proportion who stopped was slightly higher in the incentive treatment. Maybe the study periods were too short to change people's habits. There is some evidence that longer commitment contracts change habits. The effects are small, however, and healthy habits disappear over time.

Inappropriate Antibiotic Prescribing. Antibiotics are effective in treating and preventing bacterial infections. However, doctors overprescribe and use them in cases where they do no good. In the US, about half of the antibiotics are prescribed for diagnoses for which they have no benefit. This exposes patients' health to unnecessary risks and it increases health care costs and the prevalence of antibiotics-resistant bacteria. Changing the overuse of antibiotics is complex.

Daniella Meeker and co-authors (2016) tested the effect of behavioural interventions on inappropriate antibiotic prescribing. The intervention that worked best was peer comparison. The 10% of doctors who prescribed most appropriately received a message that they were "top performers". The remaining 90% received a message that they were "not a top performer". They were also told how their inappropriate prescription rate compared with that of the top performers.

Exercise 12.2: Peer Comparison

Explain that the peer comparison treatment is based on reference dependence where the performance of top performers acts as the reference point.

Over 18 months, the peer comparison reduced inappropriate antibiotic prescribing from around 20% to 3.7%. By comparison, in the control group (who only received education about inappropriate prescribing) it decreased from 24% to 13%. Peer comparisons reduce the overuse of antibiotics. However, again the effects fall over time. In the 12 months after the end of the interventions, the difference between the control and the peer comparison groups decreased, although it remained significant.

Moreover, Joseph Reiff and others (2022) showed that peer comparisons can have negative effects. They studied preventive care (like routine screenings) and found that peer comparisons did not improve physicians' performance. However, it reduced their job satisfaction and increased burnout. The physicians saw the comparison as a lack of support from leadership. It highlights the importance of looking at all effects of behavioural interventions.

12.1.4 The Effectiveness of Nudges

Nudges can be more effective than traditional policy instruments. Shlomo Benartzi and co-authors (2017) studied the benefits per dollar spent on nudges and other policy instruments. Nudges generally did well. Forcing new employees to choose their contribution to a retirement plan costs only $2 per worker and led to $100 extra savings per dollar spent. By comparison, the benefits of tax breaks and matching contributions (the employer or the government partly matches the contribution made by the employee), the traditional policy instruments to foster retirement savings, were between $1 and $5.50 per dollar spent.

Sending letters comparing people's energy use with that of their neighbours was more effective in saving energy than the traditional policy of discounts and education. The nudge saved 27.3 kilowatt per hour per dollar spent. Incentives and education half of that.

Nudges do not always work better. A nudge that made people aware of the loss of money implied by higher electricity bills (which supposedly invoked loss aversion) led to no saving in electricity. Also, automatically making an appointment to receive a flu shot (which could be canceled) led to 3.65 additional people vaccinated per $100 spent, while an educational campaign about the benefits of taking a flu shot led to 8.85 additional people vaccinated per $100 spent.

Exercise 12.3: Flu Shots

Which insight from behavioural economics is used by the nudge that automatically schedules people for a flu shot appointment that could be canceled?

Stephanie Mertens and co-authors (2022) studied over 400 nudges. They found that nudges had a small to medium effect. Nudges that changed the structure of the decision (like defaults, active choices, and the three examples discussed above) worked particularly well. However, Maximilian Maier and co-authors (2022) showed that their results were due to **publication bias**: a tendency to publish results where nudges worked. After correcting for publication bias, they found no evidence that nudges worked.

Nudges can decrease welfare. A problem in health insurance is **adverse selection**. People have different risks of falling ill and of medical costs. Typically the insured know more about their health risks than the insurer. The insurer bases premiums on average risk characteristics. As a result, health insurance will be too expensive for the low-risk agents, who take no insurance, and the insurer ends up with the high risks. This leads to further rises in premiums and people taking less insurance than they optimally would like.

Status quo bias counteracts adverse selection. Benjamin Handel (2013) studied the effects of forcing employees to give up their current health plan and requiring them to choose a new plan without a default option. From then on, employees stayed in their chosen plan if they took no action. There was clear status quo bias. Even though, the prices of the plans changed over time and the chosen plan was dominated by other plans, most employees stayed with their plan. There was also adverse selection: High-risk agents chose more comprehensive coverage. Nudges to reduce the status quo bias doubled the welfare loss from adverse selection. The nudges made low-risk agents change plans, which led to a rise in the price of insurance for high-risk agents.

The overall effects were negative. Since the high-risk agents suffer most, the nudges also had undesirable distributional consequences.

Nudges cannot always replace more traditional policy tools. In containing health care costs, a central concern in many countries, the role of nudges seems limited. It requires the hard choices implied by cost-effectiveness analysis. Nudges have little use here.

Nudges can crowd out other policy measures. A Japanese study (Werfel 2017) found that making people aware of what they did to save energy reduced their support for government environmental policies. This effect was strongest among those who saved most energy and was independent of political preference.

Exercise 12.4: Crowding Out

How can the diagnostic utility model discussed in Chapter 4 explain this crowding out effect? (Hint: both energy saving measures and support for government measures give a signal that an agent cares about the environment).

Finally, whether nudges work in the long run is an open question. We already saw that changes in health behaviour wear off with time and sometimes disappear. This is a general finding. Some studies suggest that some effect remains, while others suggest that the effect of nudges disappears altogether.

Nudges and Covid. The Covid pandemic proved fertile grounds to test whether nudges could change people's behaviour. A large study at the University of California Los Angeles (UCLA) (Dai et al. 2021) found that sending people text reminders increased vaccination rates by 4%. The message that worked best was one that emphasized ownership of the vaccine ("there is a vaccine waiting for you"). Research on flu shots also shows the power of this ownership wording.

Exercise 12.5: Ownership Framing

Explain how the endowment effect can explain the effect of the ownership framing in text messages.

Automatically making an appointment for a Covid vaccination instead of letting people make an appointment by themselves increased the vaccination rate by more than 10% in a sample of Swedish 16–17 year olds (Bonander et al. 2022). Again, changing the default is a powerful nudge.

By contrast, Campos-Mercade et al. (2021) found that nudges had no effect on vaccination rates. They could increase vaccination intentions (particularly a social nudge which asked subjects to write down the names of four people who would benefit from them taking the vaccine), but they did not increase actual rates. What worked was paying subjects $24 for being vaccinated (see Chapter 5). This increased vaccination rates by 4%.

In the US, several states introduced vaccine lotteries. These are lotteries in which only the vaccinated could participate or had a higher chance to win. These lotteries use the same idea as the lottery scheme of Loewenstein and Volpp. Prospect theory predicts that people will overestimate the small probability of winning and this makes the lotteries attractive. In Ohio the lotteries increased vaccination rate by 1.5% (Barber and West 2022). In Philadelphia they had no effect (Milkman et al. 2022).

12.2 Preference Purification

Nudges are an example of what Robert Sugden calls **preference purification.** When an agent's choices are inconsistent with defensible assumptions about rational choice, they are errors. The task for behavioural welfare economics is to correct these errors. We purify the rational preferences from their psychological biases. These purified preferences are then used in normative policy and welfare analyses.

This dual model of economic agents, an inner rational agent trapped inside a psychological shell which makes them deviate from rationality, is widely used in behavioural economics (see Extension 12.1). Many behavioural models take a standard utility function and then add a parameter to it to reflect deviations from rationality (e.g. Rabin 2013). An example is the β - δ model, discussed in Chapter 11. It deviates from constant discounting, the rational model, by adding a parameter β that reflects the overweighting of the present observed in empirical studies. The parameter β reflects the psychological shell.

Besides nudging, other approaches to preference purification have been proposed. I will present one of these, frame-dependent choice, and then explain Sugden's criticism of preference purification.

Extension 12.1: Dual Self Models

The idea that an agent consists of different selves with conflicting motives dates back to Adam Smith, who discusses it in his *Theory of Moral Sentiments*. Thomas Schelling (1978) gives the example of a movie about Admiral Byrd's Antarctic expedition that he saw as a boy. He was impressed that as a boy the admiral had gone outdoors in a t-shirt to toughen himself against the cold. Schelling decided to go to bed with one blanket less. That decision was made by a warm boy. Another boy woke up at night freezing cold, too cold to get the blanket, cursing the boy who had made the decision to remove the blanket, and determined to restore it the next day. But the next day the warm boy was in charge again, dreaming of Antarctica, and decided not to put the extra blanket, and so on it went.

Several behavioural economic models use dual selves. Thaler and Hersh Shefrin (1981) explain the demand for self-control (constraints on future behaviour) by modelling agents as being at the same time a farsighted planner and many myopic doers. The agent has an income stream $y = (y_1, \ldots, y_T)$ and a consumption plan $c = (c_1, \ldots, c_T)$. The planner cares about lifetime utility while the doers live only for one period and only care about that period. Period t doer controls consumption in period t and has utility function V_t, which depends only on c_t.

The planner cares about the doers and would like to maximize $U(V_1, \ldots, V_T)$ subject to $\sum_{t=1}^{T} c_t \le \sum_{t=1}^{T} y_t$, but this is impossible because the doers act purely selfish. This is similar to the conflict in firms between owners and managers. To solve it planners can either use incentives (in firms managers share in profits or owners use accounting methods to control managers) or rules (bans on borrowing or dissaving).

The model of Gul and Pesendorfer that we discussed in Chapter 11 also has conflicting selves. In their model v is the doer's utility and $u + v$ the planner's utility.

Other models with dual selves are those by Drew Fudenberg and David Levine (2006) which also consists of a long-run planner and a series of short-run doers who only care about the current period; by Douglas Bernheim and Antonio Rangel (2004), who analyse addiction decisions where agents operate either in a cold mode (where they follow their preferences) or in a hot mode (where they succumb to the temptation); by Isabelle Brocas and Juan Carrillo (2008), where the agent consists of an impulsive and a cognitive part and the impulsive part has more information about the marginal value of consumption than the cognitive part, and by Chandrasekher et al. (2022) who model ambiguity preferences as the outcome of a game played by a pessimistic and an optimistic self.

The diagnostic utility models that we discussed in Chapter 4 is another example where different selves have conflicting aims. Similarly, George Loewenstein's hold-cold empathy gap uses the idea of multiple selves.

12.2.1 Frame-Dependent Choice

Frame-dependent choice was proposed by Douglas Bernheim and Antonio Rangel (2009) and by Yuval Salant and Ariel Rubinstein (2008). Their approaches are similar. Both follow the revealed preference tradition and take choice as the input for policy. Salant and Rubinstein raise doubts, however, whether choice is the most appropriate input for welfare analysis. I discuss their doubts after Example 12.2. Bernheim and Rangel assume a first step of preference purification in which all choices that are errors are excluded. Errors may be that people ignore relevant information or do not understand the tasks well. In experiments, these are controlled by asking comprehension questions or repeating choices. The remaining choices are the welfare-relevant domain.

Choices are made from sets (X, f), called **extended choice problems**. X is the set of objects from which agents choose and f is a frame. A frame is the environment in which choices are made. It affects agents' choices, but according to the policy maker it should not. A frame reflects procedural and psychological factors that act on choice. Examples are default options or the status quo, using an anchor or expressing outcomes as gains and losses from a reference point.

Example 12.1: Status Quo Bias

Let (A, x) be a choice problem in which the agents choose from a set of options A and x is the status quo. They choose x if x is in A and $u(x)+\beta(x) \geq u(a)$ for all $a \in A$. Otherwise they choose the element in A with the highest utility u.

Exercise 12.6: Status Quo Bias

What is the sign of $\beta(x)$ if agents display status quo bias?

Example 12.2: Satisficing

One of the forerunners of behavioural economics is Herbert Simon's (1955) model of **bounded rationality**. Simon argued that agents do not choose the option that maximizes their utility, but **satisfice**: They choose the first option that meets a threshold or aspiration level v^*. If none of the options satisfies the threshold then agents choose the last option presented. Simon did not assume this, but I impose it to make sure that the agent always chooses an option. Let O denote the order in which agents consider the options and let v denote the value they give to each option. The frame is (A, O) and we can represent the agent's preferences as "choose the first option a for which $v(a) > v^*$. If none of the options satisfies this, choose the last option".

Example 12.2 shows why choice may not be useful for welfare economics. A **choice correspondence** $C(A)$ defines for each set of options A which ones the agent chooses. If x and y both have a value larger than the threshold then they are both elements of $C(A)$. x will be chosen for the frame in which x is presented first and y will be chosen for the frame in which y is presented first.

Welfare economics asks whether there is a preference relation that represents a choice correspondence. In Example 12.2 there is indeed a complete and transitive preference relation $\succcurlyeq$ that represents this rule. Because x and y are both chosen for some frame, we have $x \succcurlyeq y$ and $y \succcurlyeq x$ and so this relation says that x and y are indifferent. However, a policy maker may not be indifferent between the frames. If $v(x) > v(y)$, the policy maker prefers the frame in which x is presented first. We cannot derive this preference from an agent's choices. Choices do not tell the full story for policy making.

Example 12.3: Limited Attention

Theories of limited attention assume that agents cannot process all options, but they can choose which options they attend to. An example is Paolo Manzini and Marco Mariotti's (2007) **rational shortlist method** in which agents use one relation to determine the options they pay attention to and then another relation to choose between these. Another example is Tversky's (1972) **elimination by aspects** where an agent compares options according to an aspect and only selects those options that have that aspect. It is close to the lexicographic rule discussed in Chapter 2.

Let O be the ordering in which agents consider the options and let P denote their preference between these options. A choice frame (A, n) denotes that the agent considers the first n options in A according to the ordering O and chooses the best of these according to the ordering P.

Example 12.4: Scale Compatibility

In Chapter 2, we saw that scale compatibility explains the preference reversal phenomenon. Scale compatibility says that the dimension that is used to elicit responses is overweighted. So the probability dimension gets more weight if we vary probabilities to find indifference (like in the standard gamble) and the outcome dimension gets more weight if we vary the outcomes to find indifference (like in the certainty equivalence task). Frames are sets (A, r) where A is a set of prospects and r is the response scale. We can represent preferences by prospect theory with the probability weighting function more elevated when probability is the response scale.

In traditional welfare economics, choices are frame-independent. By the weak axiom of revealed preference (see Chapter 3), x is a welfare improvement over y if there is at least one situation in which x is chosen and y is not. When we allow for choice inconsistencies, this requirement must be strengthened. Now, x is a welfare improvement over y if y is never chosen when x is available. As this holds regardless of the frame, another way of saying this is that the relation between x and y is frame-independent. This is Bernheim and Rangel's solution: centre on those choices that are frame-independent and accept that for the remaining choices we cannot make welfare comparisons.

Extension 12.2: Acyclicity

Denote by $x \succ^* y$ the relation that y is never chosen when x is available. The relation $\succ^*$ is acyclic. That means that if for any finite set $x_1, \ldots, x_n$ we have $x_1 \succ^* \cdots \succ^* x_n$ we cannot have $x_n \succ^* x_1$. To show this, assume that agents always choose an option. Any option x_i with $1 < i < n$ cannot be chosen, because $x_{i-1} \succ^* x_i$. x_n cannot be chosen either because $x_{n-1} \succ^* x_n$. The only element that can be chosen is x_1. But if x_1 is chosen while x_n is available, we cannot have $x_n \succ^* x_1$. So $\succ^*$ is acyclic.

Acyclicity of $\succ^*$ plays a central role in welfare analysis because it makes it possible to find maximal elements in finite sets.

Bernheim and Ranger's approach is incomplete. For example, Jane Beattie and co-authors (1998) asked people their willingness to pay for road safety programmes. In one treatment they stated their WTP for a programme saving 5 lives per year and for a more extensive programme saving 15 lives per year. In the other treatment these numbers were 25 lives saved per 5 years and 75 lives saved per 5 years. We expect that people are willing to pay about 3 times as much for the more extensive programmes in both treatments and the same for a programme saving 5 (15) lives per year and 25 (75) lives saved per 5 years. However, WTP in the more extensive programmes was only 33% higher. Moreover, WTP was lower for lives saved per 5 years. As a result, the value of life varied between £2.5 million and £11 million. The researchers trained subjects and alerted them to the difference in the number of lives saved. Hence, these responses are probably no errors and, if so, which ones are wrong?

Bernheim and Rangel's response is that we should live with this ambiguity. We cannot make decisions for projects that save lives at a cost between £2.5 million and £11 million. For policy, where decisions have to be made, this does not help. As a practical tool, this approach is not useful.

Extension 12.3: Salant and Rubinstein

Salant and Rubinstein study when there exists a transitive or a transitive and complete relation $\succcurlyeq$ such that an option x is chosen in an extended choice problem (A, f) when $x \succcurlyeq y$ for all $y \in A$. They are less interested in welfare implications. They argue that focusing on choice ignores information for economic modelling and policy. First, choice may be uninformative (see the example above about the study of Beattie et al.). Second, there are plausible choice rules that cannot be described as the maximization of a transitive relation, and, third, policy may want to take other information than only choice into account (see the example about satisficing).

Let $C_c(A)$ be the set of options chosen from A in some frame f:

$$C_c(A) = \{x \in A \mid C(A, f) = x \text{ for some } f \in F\},$$

where C is a function that specifies the unique option chosen from (A, f) and F is the set of all possible frames.

There exists a transitive relation $\succ$ such that C_c consists of all options x in A for which there is no $y \in A$ such that $y \succ x$ under the following condition:

Definition 12.2: γ-Extended

Condition **γ-extended** says that if x is chosen from (A, f) and also from (B, g) then there is a frame h such that x is chosen from $(A \cup B, h)$.

In Examples 12.1–12.4 condition γ-extended holds. In Example 12.1, if the agent chooses x from (A, f) then (at least) $u(x) + \beta(x) > u(y)$ for all $y \in A$. This is true if x is the status quo. If x is chosen and not the status quo we have $u(x) > u(y)$ for all $y \in A$. Likewise, choosing x from (B, g) implies that (at least) $u(x) + \beta(x) > u(y)$ for all $y \in B$. By taking $h = x$, we have $u(x) + \beta(x) > u(y)$ for all $y \in A \cup B$ and thus x is chosen from $(A \cup B, h)$.

Exercise 12.7: Other Examples

Show that condition γ-extended also holds in Examples 12.2, 12.3, and 12.4.

The relation $\succ$ is defined as $x \succ y$ if $C(\{x, y\}, f) = x$ for every frame f. That is, when choosing between x and y, the agent always chooses x. This definition only considers binary choice and so it is finer than the condition of Bernheim and Rangel. There are pairs x, y that we can order by Salant and Rubinstein's relation, but not by Bernheim and Rangel's.

The relation $\succ$ need not be complete. We can make it complete by strengthening condition γ-extended to condition γ^+-extended:

Definition 12.3: γ^+-Extended

Condition **γ^+-extended** says that if x is chosen from (A, f) and $y \in A$ from (B, g) then there is a frame h such that x is chosen from $(A \cup B, h)$.

Exercise 12.8 shows that condition γ^+-extended is stronger than condition γ-extended. There are cases in which condition γ-extended holds, but condition γ^+-extended not. The opposite cannot be true (by taking $y = x$ condition γ^+-extended implies condition γ-extended).

Exercise 12.8: Examples

Show that condition γ^+-extended holds in Examples 12.2 and 12.4, but not in Examples 12.1 and 12.3.

12.3 Criticisms of Nudges and Preference Purification

The philosopher Daniel Hausman (2012) argues that nudges limit autonomy, by exploiting people's "psychological foibles" and by pushing them in a direction. Actions reflect the tactics of the choice architect rather than people's own evaluation of alternatives. Hausman prefers rational persuasion, which respects an agent's liberty.

Gerd Gigerenzer (2015) argues that libertarian paternalism views human beings too negatively. It assumes that people make errors and that they are unable to correct these. Psychological research does not justify this gloominess. Instead of accepting that cognitive biases are widespread and that people by themselves will not be able to correct them, he argues that we should teach people to be rational. In other words, we should "boost" instead of "nudge".

For example, people can learn to avoid the statistical biases of Chapter 8. While they have difficulty thinking in terms of probabilities, they are much better at processing frequencies (like 5 out of 100 people have a given characteristic). This makes them behave more in line with Bayes' rule.

An example is the base rate fallacy. People overestimate the probability that a woman has breast cancer after a positive mammography because they ignore the low incidence of breast cancer. This also held for gynaecologists: when the information was presented in terms of probabilities only 21% correctly computed the chance that a woman has breast cancer after a positive mammography. However, after they were trained to translate probabilities into natural frequencies, this proportion rose to 87%. Similar positive results were found with judges and attorneys assessing DNA samples. School children can also learn to reason by Bayes' rule and do not forget it. We can teach people to be rational. Rational persuasion can work and is preferable as it respects autonomy.

12.3.1 Sugden's Critique of Preference Purification

Sugden (2016, 2018, 2022) criticizes preference purification. According to Sugden, the idea of a rational self locked up in a psychological shell, which underlies behavioural welfare economics, is psychologically unrealistic. Thaler and Sunstein emphasize that the aim of nudging is to make people better off as judged by themselves. This assumes that people have access to a mode of latent reasoning which produces preferences that satisfy rational principles.

But rational preferences also need psychological justification. Kahneman (1996, pp. 251–252) sees the idea of a rational inner self as "deeply problematic": Behaviour consistent with rational choice theory cannot be free of psychology. It equally needs psychological explanation as deviations from that theory. The idea of an inner rational agent free from psychology resembles the behaviouralist revolution at the early twentieth century (see Chapter 3), which tried to free economics of all psychology. This revolution proved too limited. According to Sugden, any model using a rational inner agent free from psychology is equally doomed.

Sugden also argues against the assumption of dual process models that an impulsive and a rational self are simultaneously and independently at work. Dual self models often refer to neuroeconomics as evidence that different regions of the brain guide decisions. However, neuroeconomics also suggests that the rational part of our brain (the prefrontal cortex) was added later in our evolution to the more primitive part of our brain that we share with other mammals. But if the rational part is an add-on to the impulsive part it seems plausible that the two parts work in tandem. In Chapter 6, we saw that attempts to locate rational and impulsive behaviour in different parts of the brain were unsuccessful.

Finally, we may question the usefulness of preference purification. Preference purification suggests that some choices are errors. But which? In the mug experiments of Kahneman et al. (1990) subjects gave different buying and selling prices. But which of these reflects their true preferences? Preferences in the Ellsberg paradox are at odds with subjective expected utility, but which of these, if any, is wrong? And in Thaler and Sunstein's cafeteria example, how do we uncover if the agent's rational self really prefers a healthy to an unhealthy snack? If we do not know which preference is right how can we correct errors and nudge people in the right direction?

12.4 From Preference Purification to Preference Regularization

In 2001, Jose Luis Pinto Prades, Peter Wakker, and I wrote a paper (Bleichrodt et al. 2001), which, according to Sugden (2022, p. 766), advocated a form of behavioural welfare economics. Our aim was practical, to solve a problem in (health) utility measurement first discovered by John Hershey and Paul Schoemaker (1985). They found that **probability equivalence** (PE) and **certainty equivalence** (CE), two methods to measure utility that are equivalent under expected utility (see Chapter 9), gave different results. In particular, utility under PE was higher than utility under CE.

The CE finds indifference between a sure outcome and a prospect by varying the sure outcome. Take the risky treatment $40_{1/2}0$, which gives 40 years in good health with probability $1/2$ and death (living for 0 more years) with probability $1/2$. The CE asks for the number x of years in good health for sure that the agent sees as equivalent to the risky treatment.

Exercise 12.9: Certainty Equivalence

Show that under EU, this indifference implies that

$$U(x) = {}^1\!/\!_2.$$

(Hint: set $U(40) = 1$ and $U(0) = 0$, which we can do because EU's utility function is cardinal.)

The PE finds indifference between a sure outcome and a risky treatment by varying probabilities. Let the sure outcome be to live for 10 years in good health and then die. The PE finds the probability p such that the agent is indifferent between 10 years for sure and the risky treatment 40_p0.

Exercise 12.10: Probability Equivalence

Show that under EU, this indifference implies that

$$U(10) = p.$$

Hershey and Schoemaker first asked their subjects to do a CE task. For example, they found the x that was indifferent to $40_{1/2}0$. Suppose this x was 10 years. Then, after some filler tasks, they used the response from the CE in the PE task. They asked for the value of p that gave indifference between the risky treatment 40_p0 and 10 years for sure. Under EU, the response in the PE should be $p = {}^1\!/\!_2$. However, the subjects in Hershey Schoemaker gave a higher p, like $p = 0.70$.

This creates a problem for health policy. $U(10)$ is equal to 0.50 by the CE, but to 0.70 by the PE. The outcome of cost effectiveness analyses depends on which utility we use. Bernheim and Rangel say that we should live with this ambiguity. Health policy makers are unwilling to do so. They want answers.

Our solution was to assume that people analyse the CE and the PE by prospect theory. That is, their responses deviate from EU by probability weighting and loss aversion. Because we believe EU is the right normative (rational) model to use, by correcting PE and CE for loss aversion and probability weighting we get the corrected utilities that should be used in health policy. Extension 12.4 explains our corrections.

Extension 12.4: Correcting PE and CE for Prospect Theory

The crucial assumption is the location of the reference point. We assume that in the PE, where the sure outcome is held fixed and the probabilities vary, subjects use maxmin (see Chapter 9) and take the sure outcome as their reference point.

Then the PE indifference becomes:

$$0 = w^{+}(p)(U(40) - U(10)) + \lambda w^{-}(1-p)(U(0) - U(10)). \tag{12.1}$$

From which it follows that (setting $U(40) = 1$ and $U(0) = 0$):

$$U(10) = \frac{w^{+}(p)}{w^{+}(p) + \lambda w^{-}(1-p)}. \tag{12.2}$$

In the CE, the sure outcome is varied and it is therefore not the reference point. The most plausible assumption is that subjects take all life durations as positive numbers and thus gains. Then the CE indifference becomes:

$$U(10) = w^{+}(1/2). \tag{12.3}$$

Equations 12.2 and 12.3 show that prospect theory predicts that $U(10)$ differs between PE and CE. The equations also show that we need information on probability weighting for gains (w^{+}), probability weighting for losses (w^{-}), and loss aversion to compute the utilities. In practical applications, we often lack this information. Then we can use the parametric estimations found in the literature. We used the parametric weighting functions of Tversky and Kahneman (1992) and the values they found: $\gamma^{+} = 0.61$, $\gamma^{-} = 0.69$, and $\lambda = 2.25$.

Figure 12.1 shows that our corrections worked. The red points in Fig. 12.1a shows the differences between PE and CE under EU. PE is clearly higher than CE. The absence of a difference in test 5 is due to a ceiling effect: As the utilities were scaled between 0 and 1 and the CE already gave a utility close to 1, there was no room for the PE to exceed the CE in this test.

The purple diamonds in Fig. 12.1b show that the difference between PE and CE disappears after correcting for prospect theory. The points are scattered around the zero line.

Our paper gave a quantitative formula for preference purification. We saw the paper as correcting our subject's preferences for the biases modelled by prospect theory and to elicit what we called their basic values. These are what others later called true preferences. As such, our paper is subject to Sugden's criticisms.

However, we do not assume that people choose against their own interests and that we must help them to make better decisions. Our problem was to extract information from inconsistent responses so that policy makers can use this. Our approach is what Sugden calls **preference regularization**. This means constructing indices of individual welfare from survey responses that are consistent with the model of rational decision making that the policy maker wants to use. For Sugden this is a defensible basis for behavioural welfare economics, because it does not make the distinction between true preferences and bias for which he sees no psychological evidence. Raj Chetty (2015) proposes a similar approach to correct responses for behavioural biases

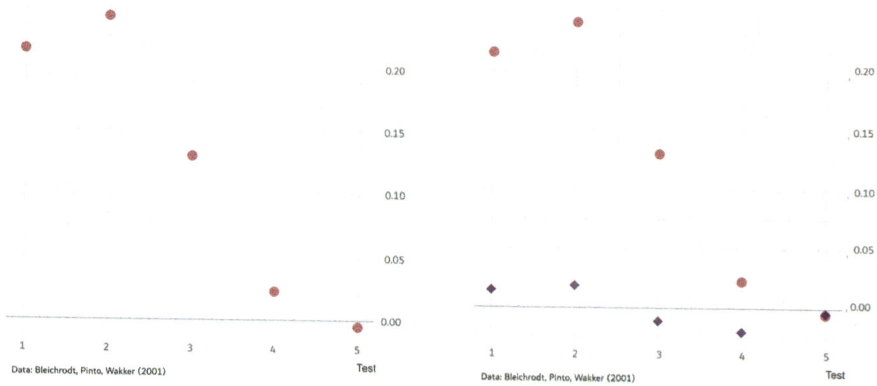

(a) Differences under EU (b) Improvement under prospect theory

Fig. 12.1 The difference between PE and CE. Data from Bleichrodt et al. (2001)

and estimate the utilities that the policy maker wants to use. A difference is that he sees experienced utility as the ideal.

In our corrections, policy makers believe subjects behave according to prospect theory with Tversky and Kahneman's parameters, but they prefer them to behave according to expected utility because they see this as the normative model. That means utility curvature is a behavioural parameter that can affect preferences, but probability weighting and loss aversion should be corrected for by a regulation procedure. Our corrections give such a regulation procedure. It does not assume that patients have latent or true preferences that satisfy expected utility. The desire to adhere to expected utility is a choice of the policy maker. True preferences are only true in the eye of the policy maker, not in that of the respondents.

References

Barber, A., and J. West. 2022. Conditional cash lotteries increase COVID-19 vaccination rates. *Journal of Health Economics* 81: 102578.

Beattie, J., J. Covey, P. Dolan, L. Hopkins, M. Jones-Lee, G. Loomes, N. Pidgeon, A. Robinson, and A. Spencer. 1998. On the contingent valuation of safety and the safety of contingent valuation: Part 1-caveat investigator. *Journal of Risk and Uncertainty* 17: 5–26.

Benartzi, S., and R.H. Thaler. 2013. Behavioral economics and the retirement savings crisis. *Science* 339: 1152–1153.

Benartzi, S., J. Beshears, K.L. Milkman, C.R. Sunstein, R.H. Thaler, M. Shankar, W. Tucker-Ray, W.J. Congdon, and S. Galing. 2017. Should governments invest more in nudging? *Psychological Science* 28: 1041–1055.

Bernheim, B.D., and A. Rangel. 2004. Addiction and cue-triggered decision processes. *American Economic Review* 94: 1558–1590.

Bernheim, B.D., and A. Rangel. 2009. Beyond revealed preference: Choice-theoretic foundations for behavioral welfare economics. *Quarterly Journal of Economics* 124: 51–104.

Bleichrodt, H., J.L. Pinto, and P.P. Wakker. 2001. Making descriptive use of prospect theory to improve the prescriptive use of expected utility. *Management Science* 47: 1498–1514.

Bonander, C., M. Ekman, and N. Jakobsson. 2022. Vaccination nudges: A study of pre-booked COVID-19 vaccinations in Sweden. *Social Science and Medicine* 309: 115248.

Brocas, I., and J.D. Carrillo. 2008. The brain as a hierarchical organization. *American Economic Review* 98: 1312–1346.

Campos-Mercade, P., A.N. Meier, F.H. Schneider, S. Meier, D. Pope, and E. Wengström. 2021. Monetary incentives increase COVID-19 vaccinations. *Science* 374: 879–882.

Chandrasekher, M., M. Frick, R. Iijima, and Y. Le Yaouanq. 2022. Dual-self representations of ambiguity preferences. *Econometrica* 90: 1029–1061.

Chetty, R. 2015. Behavioral economics and public policy: A pragmatic perspective. *American Economic Review* 105: 1–33.

Dai, H., S. Saccardo, M.A. Han, L. Roh, N. Raja, S. Vangala, H. Modi, S. Pandya, M. Sloyan, and D.M. Croymans. 2021. Behavioural nudges increase COVID-19 vaccinations. *Nature* 597: 404–409.

Fudenberg, D., and D.K. Levine. 2006. A dual-self model of impulse control. *American Economic Review* 96: 1449–1476.

Gigerenzer, G. 2015. On the supposed evidence for libertarian paternalism. *Review of Philosophy and Psychology* 6: 361–383.

Handel, B.R. 2013. Adverse selection and inertia in health insurance markets: When nudging hurts. *American Economic Review* 103: 2643–2682.

Hausman, D.M. 2012. *Preference, value, choice, and welfare*. Cambridge University Press.

Hershey, J.C., and P.J. Schoemaker. 1985. Probability versus certainty equivalence methods in utility measurement: Are they equivalent? *Management Science* 31: 1213–1231.

Infante, G., G. Lecouteux, and R. Sugden. 2016. Preference purification and the inner rational agent: A critique of the conventional wisdom of behavioural welfare economics. *Journal of Economic Methodology* 23: 1–25.

Kahneman, D. 1996. Rational Individual Behaviour in Markets and Social Choice Processes: Comment. In *The rational foundations of economic behaviour*, ed. K. Arrow, E. Colombatto, M. Perlman, and C. Schmidt, 251–254. The Macmillan Press LTD.

Kahneman, D., J.L. Knetsch, and R.H. Thaler. 1990. Experimental tests of the endowment effect and the Coase theorem. *Journal of Political Economy* 98: 1325–1348.

Maier, M., F. Bartoš, T. Stanley, D.R. Shanks, A.J. Harris, and E.-J. Wagenmakers. 2022. No evidence for nudging after adjusting for publication bias. *Proceedings of the National Academy of Sciences* 119: e2200300119.

Manzini, P., and M. Mariotti. 2007. Sequentially rationalizable choice. *American Economic Review* 97: 1824–1839.

Meeker, D., J.A. Linder, C.R. Fox, M.W. Friedberg, S.D. Persell, N.J. Goldstein, T.K. Knight, J.W. Hay, and J.N. Doctor. 2016. Effect of behavioral interventions on inappropriate antibiotic prescribing among primary care practices: A randomized clinical trial. *JAMA* 315: 562–570.

Mertens, S., M. Herberz, U.J. Hahnel, and T. Brosch. 2022. The effectiveness of nudging: A meta-analysis of choice architecture interventions across behavioral domains. *Proceedings of the National Academy of Sciences* 119: e2107346118.

Milkman, K.L., L. Gandhi, S.F. Ellis, H.N. Graci, D.M. Gromet, R.S. Mobarak, A.M. Buttenheim, A.L. Duckworth, D. Pope, A. Stanford, et al. 2022. A citywide experiment testing the impact of geographically targeted, high-pay-off vaccine lotteries. *Nature Human Behaviour* 6: 1–10.

Rabin, M. 2013. Incorporating limited rationality into economics. *Journal of Economic Literature* 51: 528–543.

Reiff, J.S., J.C. Zhang, J. Gallus, H. Dai, N.M. Pedley, S. Vangala, R.K. Leuchter, G. Goshgarian, C.R. Fox, M. Han, et al. 2022. When peer comparison information harms physician well-being. *Proceedings of the National Academy of Sciences* 119: e2121730119.

Salant, Y., and A. Rubinstein. 2008. (A, f): Choice with frames. *Review of Economic Studies* 75: 1287–1296.

Schelling, T.C. 1978. Egonomics, or the art of self-management. *American Economic Review* 68: 290–294.

Simon, H.A. 1955. A behavioral model of rational choice. *Quarterly Journal of Economics* 69: 99–118.

Sugden, R. 2018. *The community of advantage: A behavioural economist's defence of the market*. Oxford University Press.

Sugden, R. 2022. Debiasing or regularisation? Two interpretations of the concept of 'true preference' in behavioural economics. *Theory and Decision* 92: 765–784.

Thaler, R.H., and S. Benartzi. 2004. Save more tomorrow™: Using behavioral economics to increase employee saving. *Journal of Political Economy* 112: S164–S187.

Thaler, R.H., and H.M. Shefrin. 1981. An economic theory of self-control. *Journal of Political Economy* 89: 392–406.

Thaler, R.H., and C.R. Sunstein. 2003. Libertarian paternalism. *American Economic Review* 93: 175–179.

Thaler, R.H., and C.R. Sunstein. 2008. *Nudge: Improving decisions about health, wealth, and happiness*. Yale University Press.

Thaler, R.H., and C.R. Sunstein. 2021. *Nudge: The final*. Yale University Press.

Tversky, A. 1972. Elimination by aspects: A theory of choice. *Psychological Review* 79: 281–299.

Werfel, S.H. 2017. Household behaviour crowds out support for climate change policy when sufficient progress is perceived. *Nature Climate Change* 7: 512–515.

Index

H. Bleichrodt, *Behavioural Economics*,
https://doi.org/10.1007/978-3-031-69166-9

The manufacturer's authorised representative in the EU is Springer Nature Customer Service Centre GmbH, Europaplatz 3, 69115 Heidelberg, Germany. If you have any concerns regarding our products, please contact ProductSafety@springernature.com

Printed and bound by CPI Group (UK) Ltd, Croydon, CR0 4YY
28/09/2026
02224073-0010